Street Meeting

Street Meeting

*Multiethnic Neighborhoods
in Early Twentieth-Century Los Angeles*

Mark Wild

UNIVERSITY OF CALIFORNIA PRESS
Berkeley · Los Angeles · London

University of California Press
Berkeley and Los Angeles, California

University of California Press, Ltd.
London, England

Library of Congress Cataloging-in-Publication Data

Wild, H. Mark, 1970–.
    Street meeting : multiethnic neighborhoods in early
twentieth-century Los Angeles / H. Mark Wild.
        p.   cm.
    Includes bibliographical references and index.
    ISBN 0–520–24083–9 (cloth : alk. paper)
    1. Los Angeles (Calif.)—Ethnic relations—History—
20th century.   2. Ethnic neighborhoods—California—
Los Angeles—History—20th century.   I. Title.

F869.L89A1   2005
305.8'009794'9409041—dc22

                                          2004013432

Manufactured in the United States of America
13   12   11   10   09   08   07   06   05
10   9   8   7   6   5   4   3   2   1

Printed on Ecobook 50 containing a minimum 50%
post-consumer waste, processed chlorine free. The
balance contains virgin pulp, including 25% Forest
Stewardship Council Certified for no old growth tree
cutting, processed either TCF or ECF. The sheet is acid-
free and meets the minimum requirements of ANSI/NISO
Z39.48–1992 (R 1997) (Permanence of Paper).♾

Contents

Illustrations and Tables

TABLES

Acknowledgments

To steal a pet phrase from an old friend, I "fell uphill" when I entered the history profession a decade ago. It has been my great fortune to work among those whose support—intellectual, emotional, spiritual, and otherwise—has kept me on balance. I continue to draw momentum from my halcyon days at the University of California, San Diego (UCSD), and am especially grateful to Mary Lillis Allen, Eric Boime, Krista Camenzind, Rene Hayden, Christina Jimenez, Phoebe Kropp, John Lee, David Luft, Ken Maffitt, Tanalis Padilla, Natalie Ring, Sarah Schrank, and Gabriela Soto Laveaga for creating a warm and invigorating community. Michael Bernstein and Susan Davis provided helpful suggestions for transforming my dissertation into this book. Michael Parrish was especially helpful in getting me to frame my work in broader contexts. David Gutierrez opened my eyes to the political relevance of historical scholarship, helped me to develop a mission for my career, and continues to be generous with his advice and encouragement.

Archivists who aided this project include Dacey Taube at the University of Southern California's Regional History Center, Ruth Britton at the University of Southern California's California Social Welfare Archives, Linda Jordan at the Bancroft Library, Jay Jones at the Los Angeles City Archives, Robert Marshall at the Urban Archives Center at California State University Northridge, Kristi French and Irene Still-Meyer at the Department of Special Collections at California State University Long Beach, and Sarah Cooper at the Southern California Library for Social

Research. Lil Carlson, Archie Green, Dorothy Healey, Morris Kadish, Michio Kunitani, Miriam Johnson, and Larue McCormick generously agreed to share their recollections of prewar Los Angeles. Gordon and Lynn Bailey, Lars Florio, Joe Gawronski, Rene Hayden, and Nicole Kresge sheltered me during several important research trips out East.

For financial support, I would like to thank the History Department and the Center for the Humanities at UCSD, the Historical Society of Southern California, the Haynes Foundation/Huntington Library Fellowship Program, the Social Science Research Council, and the University of California's Kevin Starr Fellowship Program. Portions of chapters 4 and 5 appeared in different forms in the following articles, respectively: "Red Light Kaleidoscope: Prostitution and the Politics of Cross-Cultural Sex in Los Angeles, 1880–1940," *Journal of Urban History* 28 (September 2002): 720–42; "'So Many Children at Once and So Many Kinds': Schools and Ethno-racial Boundaries in Early Twentieth Century Los Angeles," *Western Historical Quarterly* 33 (Winter 2002): 453–76. This material is adapted with permission.

In Los Angeles I took part in two enormously valuable reading groups, whose members included Eric Avila, Shana Beth Bernstein, Clark Davis, Daniel Hurwitz, Ben Johnson, Anthony Macias, Natalia Molina, Michelle Nickerson, R. J. Smith, Roberto Lint Sagarena, Sarah Shrank, and Mike Willard. A gifted cohort of post-docs at the Humanities Research Institute, Peter Cahn, Jerry Miller, Mimi Saunders, and Chiou-Ling Yeh, worked out an untold number of kinks in the study and provided good company as well. Carl Abbott, Chris Endy, Mike Engh, Greg Hise, Donna Gabaccia, Marixa Lasso, Ken Marcus, Becky Nicolaides, and Josh Sides at various times addressed key parts of the manuscript that needed rethinking. I am grateful to Monica McCormick and Randy Heymann at University of California Press for shepherding this project to publication.

I owe my greatest professional debts to my mentor, Bill Deverell, who continues to inspire me with his enthusiasm, thoughtfulness, and commitment. Over time he has shown me not only how to become a better historian, but a better person. I am proud to consider him a friend.

Like so many others I suffered an enormous blow with the death of Clark Davis, a man of extraordinary insight and warmth. His considerable influence on the ideas presented in this study was the least of the benefits I derived from our friendship. Clark left his friends a silver lining in the community he wove that has sustained us in the aftermath. I will resist the temptation to go on at length about all the wonderful people who have come together for his family, his incomparable wife, Cheryl Koos, and their son, Jackson Patrick Koos Davis. I value especially my friendships with Cheryl, Natalie Fousekis, Charles Romney, Sarah Schrank, and Josh Sides. Finally, I want to thank Craig Snellings and Rich Wolf, my chief advisers, gurus, and guardians since time out of mind. I would not have made it anywhere close to this point without them.

Over the years I have come to appreciate the enormous blessing that is my family. My brother's blunt honesty and his quest for a deeper level of experience amaze me. My father remains the standard by which I judge personal dignity and manhood. I am grateful for his patience and love. My mother was my first history teacher and showed me the good that is possible in this world. I miss her every day.

Introduction

In August 1944 authorities at the Manzanar Relocation Center in the high desert of eastern California, where several thousand Japanese had been confined during World War II, made a strange discovery. Two years earlier a high school student named Ralph Lozo had registered for internment despite the fact that both his parents were of Mexican ancestry.[1] He had been living at Manzanar ever since. "My Japanese-American friends . . . were ordered to evacuate the West Coast, so I decided to go with them," the unapologetic Lozo explained. "Who can say I haven't got Japanese blood in me? Who knows what kind of blood runs in their veins?"[2]

Lozo was not the only non-Japanese confined at the internment camps. Elaine Black Yoneda, the daughter of Russian Jewish immigrants, voluntarily accompanied her husband, Karl Yoneda, to Manzanar. The Yonedas were regional leaders in the Communist Party and had met at a demonstration in downtown Los Angeles ten years earlier. Elaine was a principal officer of International Labor Defense, the legal arm of the party. Karl had organized longshoremen, cannery workers, and other laborers up and down the West Coast. According to Yoneda, he was the only Asian longshoreman on the western seaboard at the time of his internment. A reluctant International Longshoreman's Association admitted him only after his African American friend, Len Greer, "adopted" him in front of the membership committee to take advantage of a union tradition that permitted the automatic induction of the children of union members. The Yonedas brought along their three-year-old son, Thomas Culbert, named after union activist Tom Mooney and California Governor Culbert Olsen. At Manzanar Elaine identified seven other whites who had incarcerated themselves by choice. Most had Japanese spouses, but one was a prostitute who had followed her clientele to the camp.[3]

Other observers counted many more non-Japanese at the camps. Touring the assembly centers (temporary holding areas maintained while the permanent camps were completed) in 1942, California Commission of Immigration and Housing Director Carey McWilliams marveled at the number of Korean, Chinese, Mexican, and African American spouses, as well as the mixed-ethnicity internees who qualified under the government's "one drop" policy. According to historian Paul Spickard, relocation centers around the country may have held as many as twelve hundred persons of mixed or non-Japanese ancestry.[4] While at the camps, some residents maintained contact with friends or neighbors they had left behind. Observers noted that a steady stream of African American, Jewish, Chinese, Mexican, and Anglo visitors traveled to the Santa Anita and Pomona assembly centers in Southern California. Some internees relied on non-Japanese friends to hold and look after property while they were away. Others simply continued friendships they had developed before removal.[5]

The multiethnic social networks that developed in cities like Los Angeles in the decades before World War II illustrate a point few historians would deny: workers and immigrants of the early twentieth century encountered and frequently cultivated relationships outside their ethnic community. Many of these relationships developed in the diverse working-class districts that proliferated in step with the country's industrialization and urbanization of the late nineteenth and early twentieth century. These kinds of neighborhoods were not as evident in the northeastern cities that have received the most scholarly attention, though they did exist. They were more common, however, in the fast-growing metropolises of the West, where eclectic mixtures of newcomers settled neighborhoods with no dominant ethnic population. In places such as West Fresno, San Francisco's Tenderloin and South of Market neighborhoods, Seattle's Central District, Denver's Curtis Park, and parts of Los Angeles east and west of the Los Angeles River one could find by the early twentieth century cosmopolitan areas where residents of all races mingled in the streets and public establishments.[6]

In one sense, the relationships that emerged out of these environments marked the newest chapter in a long-standing American tradition. As a number of recent studies document, ethnoracial interaction and amalgamation have constituted defining elements of American history since the arrival of Europeans and Africans on North American soil. In the "motley crews" of sailors and passengers that traversed the Atlantic, on the "middle ground" where Indians, settlers, and slaves encountered each other, and in the cosmopolitan ports of North America during the first centuries of colonization and nationhood emerged an American cultural tradition centered not just on the diverse experiences of different ethnoracial groups but on the common experience of ethnoracial diversity. Even as different groups sought to enforce hierarchies, bar cross-cultural contact, or (later) dictate the social, cultural, and political parameters of American identity, some interaction and amalgamation continued.[7] This tradition suggests that the cultural genealogy of the United States involved less a partial or wholesale assimilation into an Anglo-American norm than a continuous process of cultural interaction and conflict, violence and accommodation, which gradually wove the American social fabric.

In this light, Lozo and the Yonedas stand as the figurative descendants of the motley crews and middle ground dwellers. Yet the multiethnic American populations of the early twentieth century differed substantially from those of earlier periods. For one thing, this latter generation lived firmly within the geopolitical boundaries of the United States. The various colonial and Native American governments and divided territories of North America before Anglo conquest, which provided recourse to different residents of that era, no longer existed. Just as important, these new neighborhoods appeared during a period when modern industrialization and urbanization were transforming the working and living spaces of the United States, generating new migrant streams from different parts of the world (Asia, Latin America, eastern and southern Europe) to fuel the country's economy. Anglos who clung to a vision of the United States as a "white republic" found their fantasy dissipating under a swell of ethnoracially diverse Americans whose lives bore little resemblance to the agrarian ideal championed by the founding fathers.[8] The neighborhoods that materialized to accommodate these newcomers were in some sense novel to everyone—to older residents who did not recognize such crowded, multiethnic, industrial regions in their own experiences and to those newer residents from less diverse parts of the world who were encountering these communities for the first time.

This new kind of urban environment complicated long-standing questions about the relationship among race, ethnicity, and American identity. Who should be included in this new, modern industrial American community, and on what terms? What sorts of relations should residents of different backgrounds develop with each other? On what basis, if any, could such an eclectic population unite under a common identity? One might view the middle-class and elite Anglo confrontation with the growing diversity of the United States as part of a broader effort to reconcile early-twentieth-century urban America with traditional concepts of social relations. The "search for order," as the historian Robert Weibe termed it, took many forms and encapsulated topics as diverse as corporate business practices, consumer culture, and gender roles.[9] Middle-class and elite Anglo Angelenos extended the search for order to racial and ethnic communities in their city, variously attempting to assimilate, exclude, or incorporate them at a subordinate level and thus neutralize their perceived threats to American social structures. Such efforts paralleled the emergence of large corporations in American economic life and their heightened demand for low-cost wage labor. This "corporate reconstruction" of ethnoracial communities entailed a two-part process—recognizing the existence of non-Anglo populations and their potential as political actors and isolating them from Anglos (and each other) as discrete entities with specific symbiotic roles to fill in the social and economic life of the city, thereby diluting their collective strength.[10] Accomplishing this task would contain, or perhaps absorb, these populations within the city's social and physical landscape and eliminate any challenge they might present to existing power structures.

But just as Americans contested the advent of corporate liberal politics in other arenas, so the corporate reconstruction of ethnoracial communities came under challenge. Scholars of immigration, ethnicity, and urbanization have produced hundreds of studies and several schools of thought on the ways in which individual ethnic communities have variously or selectively assimilated into, resisted, or transformed themselves vis-à-vis mainstream Anglo parameters of American identity.[11] But far fewer have grappled with the ways in which immigrants, African Americans, and working-class Anglos confronted one another in the urban districts they shared. Recent studies on industrial labor unions have begun to shed light on the promise and problems of coalition building in the workplace.[12] But early-twentieth-century unionization efforts reached only a small percentage of immigrants and nonwhites, many of whom labored in ethnic-specific occupations. What about the more numerous residents of integrated residential districts? Did they prefer to maintain the ethnic community as the primary unit of social structure, or did they seek to bridge the cultural distances between their neighbors of different backgrounds? What consequences did making such choices have for their lives in their new homes? Addressing these issues involves more than simply rounding out our picture of early-twentieth-century urban America. The question of ethnoracial interaction constituted one of the most vexing dilemmas for urban residents seeking to render the modern American city coherent and knowable. The ways in which urban residents sorted out the meanings and boundaries of racial and ethnic communities would have crucial implications for their lives in twentieth-century America.

This book delves into the question of ethnoracial interaction by examining a city that perhaps epitomized the explosive changes reverberating through the United States between the 1880s and World War II. At the beginning of this era, Los Angeles was little more than an outsized village. By the end, it had become one of the largest metropolitan regions in the country, a vast urban behemoth engulfing an ever-larger territory. As Robert Fogelson argued in *The Fragmented Metropolis,* the city's convulsive growth spurts during this period undermined many efforts to construct the settled communities that middle-class Anglo settlers desired.[13] Working-class, immigrant, and African American newcomers found the environment even less stable. Confined to districts either built from scratch or abandoned by wealthier Anglos, these Angelenos entered a new kind of cosmopolitan social space conditioned by the exigencies of modern urban life.

Born out of the specific confluence of economic development and immigration patterns, these areas generated new patterns of inter-ethnoracial contact and reactions against them. In the street meetings that dominated working-class politics and in the less formal practices of street meeting that were so important to working-class social relations, Angelenos of different backgrounds transgressed ethnic and racial boundaries. At the same time, however, many residents chose to confine their social and political activities to their own ethnic communities. Moreover, middle-class and elite Anglos labored to reconstruct these neighborhoods and their populations in ways that would eliminate what they perceived as the threat of inter-ethnoracial alliances and amalgamation. By the time Lozo and the Yonedas journeyed to Manzanar, changes were already under way that would ultimately redraw these neighborhoods as the segregated, impoverished "inner cities" of postwar America.

The social landscapes of Los Angeles and other American cities look very different today, but the questions raised by the changing population of urban America during the early twentieth century have yet to fade. When I began this project in the mid-1990s, they echoed in contemporary debates over free trade agreements, border policy, noncitizens' access to welfare, English-only initiatives, and affirmative action. The modern dilemma of American identity—how to find a basis for unity amid persistent cultural diversity and inequality—continues to captivate mainstream political discourse and to confound conventional parameters for establishing community membership. By avoiding abstract political issues in favor of everyday interaction at the fraying edges of ethnoracial groups, this study will do little to clarify or simplify such definitions. Though it may or may not have been their primary motivation, individuals who crossed ethnoracial lines challenged established and, from their point of view, restrictive notions of national, ethnic, or racial identities. In doing so, they carved out a space where they could expand their social and cultural opportunities, a space where more inclusive notions of community, however inchoate, might compete with narrower definitions.

But the ramifications of these actions extended beyond the fulfillment of particular personal desires. They also transpired within environments riven by political, social, and economic inequality, and therefore threatened other strategies of seizing or maintaining power. The multivalent and contested expressions of "imagined community"—on the levels of race, ethnicity, neighborhood, and nationality—that resulted speak to the process of confronting diversity not simply as an existential dilemma but as a constant series of social choices fraught with possibility and peril.[14]

Given the continued salience of these issues, at the level of both informal interaction and government policy, it is time to take another look at the diverse working-class residents of early-twentieth-century Los Angeles. In making new homes and confronting new neighbors, they experienced on a smaller scale what more and more Americans must face as immigration patterns and demographic changes continue to diversify the country's population. The 2000 census confirms that the white population of California has dropped below 50 percent of the total, that other regions are diversifying more rapidly than anyone predicted, and that these patterns of ethnoracial interaction and segregation, accommodation and conflict, are percolating throughout much of the country. Americans as a whole need to have a better historical sense of these patterns, and of the specific ways that economic forces, cultural values, and demographic changes have affected them over time. For, as historians of this country's prenational period have pointed out, these patterns form the basis of that messy, complicated, and contradictory concept, the American character. If we hope to reconcile the diverse genealogy of this country's population with the possibilities for civic or national unity, we need to speak not simply of Anglo-centric notions of formal citizenship, English skills, patriotism, and middle-class living standards but of the intricate ethnoracial interplay and inequality that both unites and divides the American people.

The first chapter in this book is a demographic survey of what I call the central districts of Los Angeles, the neighborhoods where working-class, immigrant, and African American newcomers to the city settled during the early twentieth century. Lured by a variety of economic and social forces, these settlers entered a culturally diverse environment where they encountered neighbors of many different backgrounds. Chapter 2 examines the response of Anglo city officials and reformers to the emergence of these neighborhoods. Their efforts to reconstruct and reorder these districts and their inhabitants into a controlled, "American" environment established the foundation for modern city making in ways that, over the long term, had crucial consequences for immigrant and African American city residents. Chapter 3 looks at the Church of All Nations, one of the more celebrated attempts by middle-class reformers to remake the lives of central city residents. Yet All Nations ultimately failed, in the eyes of its founder G. Bromley Oxnam, to infuse its parish with a pan-ethnoracial community spirit, revealing the limits of even the most liberal social welfare programs of the period.

The next two chapters explore the dynamics of everyday social relations among central city residents themselves. Chapter 4 delves into the lives of central city children, Angelenos who proved the most willing to develop trans-ethnoracial friendships during the early twentieth century. As they grew older, however, these youths faced increasing resistance to such relationships from within and outside their neighborhoods. These pressures, and the decision of many children to accede to them, revealed the profound social pressures operating against inter-ethnoracial bonds, even in integrated environments like the central neighborhoods. Chapter 5 extends this analysis to adult sexual relationships. While numerous

Angelenos defied proscriptions against extraethnic dating and marriage, the ridicule and, sometimes, ostracism they endured ensured that they would remain in the minority through the 1930s. In the end, it was the sex industry that proved most conducive to mixed relationships, a sphere of interaction that, by virtue of marginal and legal status, both fed and fed on the taboos against inter-ethnoracial liaisons.

The final two chapters explore the political alliances that attempted to bridge ethnic communities in the central districts. Chapter 6 explores the vibrant street-speaking culture that several organizations used in an effort to develop a working-class coalition movement in the first two decades of the twentieth century. Though all of these organizations suffered significant flaws, they demonstrated the potential for radical organization in the central city neighborhoods, a potential that city officials attempted to squelch with increasing force. By the 1920s the Los Angeles Police Department (LAPD) had managed to repress most public demonstrations, but as Chapter 7 demonstrates, the battle for the streets of Los Angeles returned with a vengeance with the onset of the Depression and the emergence of the Communist Party of Los Angeles (CPLA). The LAPD-CPLA conflict marked, in many ways, the fullest expression of the central neighborhoods' potential for inter-ethnoracial political expression. The CPLA's fading presence on the city streets by 1940 indicated that the reconstruction of central Los Angeles, begun decades earlier and accelerated by World War II, was beginning to transform these neighborhoods into the isolated, monoethnic neighborhoods that came to characterize the postwar city. Such a transformation facilitated the incorporation of ethnoracial groups as separate, unequal members of the Los Angeles civic polity and set the stage for the conflicts that reverberated through Los Angeles, and many other American cities, during the last decades of the twentieth century.

CHAPTER I

The Familiarity of "Foreign Quarters"

The Central Los Angeles Populace

A SHORT TOUR THROUGH THE CENTRAL NEIGHBORHOODS

Passengers arriving in Los Angeles by train around 1925 received an introduction to the city's diverse working-class neighborhoods. Approaching downtown from the north, the train passed Lincoln Heights, a neighborhood of modest homes, shacks, small businesses, and "car shops" where Italians and Mexicans mixed in with a "poorer class of Americans." From there it crossed the Los Angeles River, the major artery bisecting the districts where much of the city's laborers resided. To the left, the industrial heart of the city fanned south along the banks of the river. Here was the manufacturing base of a booming metropolis that some boosters proclaimed a "second Chicago," complete with smog, pollution, and grit.[1] On the east floodplain lay the Flats, one of the poorest and most ethnically diverse districts in the city. Its residents, like many working-class Angelenos, lived in shacks and small homes scattered among the industrial developments that had sprouted like cottonwoods along the river. Writing in the early 1930s, Pauline Young described the neighborhood in words that could apply equally to areas on the river's west bank:

> The atmosphere of the Flats is heavy. Factories, warehouses, small industrial plants of all kinds and description, contribute their share of pungent smells. Feed, fuel, and livery stables, a wholesale drug company, a co-operative bakery, a firecracker factory, a granite-works establishment, a creamery, a garment-manufacturing concern, are some of the varied types

of industrial establishments which hem in the district to the north, south, and east, while the railroads define the western boundaries. Noisy engines, clanking over a maze of tracks, puffing steam in spirals, and emitting volumes of black smoke, spread a pall over the region.[2]

Over the bluffs that framed the Flats lay Boyle Heights and Belvedere, residential districts stretching east on higher ground past the city limits. These areas were home to a thriving population of Mexicans, Jews, Japanese, and Russians, to name only the largest groups, who inhabited housing stock that ranged from converted mansions with views of the city to crude shacks nestled in flood-prone gullies.

Out the right window one might catch a glimpse of pedestrians climbing the hill to Chavez Ravine, a small, almost rural Mexican enclave tucked into Elysian Park. The park looked down on the neighborhood settled by the Spanish and Mexican founders of the pueblo. Los Angeles's oldest district, dubbed "Sonoratown" by nineteenth-century Anglo newcomers, held many of the "house courts," apartment structures sharing a common open yard or court, that appalled middle-class reformers. Though the area's original Mexican inhabitants still maintained a presence, by the 1920s Sonoratown had attracted a broader spectrum of inhabitants: a substantial number of Italians, smaller numbers of Asians, and a smattering of African Americans and Anglos. The new arrivals did little to change the area's relentless poverty. In 1927 the normally more tolerant Louis Adamic dismissed North Main Street, its primary thoroughfare, as "a moron stream, muddy, filthy, unpleasant to the nose[,] . . . an awful stew of human life."[3]

Past Sonoratown, the train entered Chinatown and its environs, the city's traditional vice center. A quarter century earlier, prostitutes of various races who worked along Alameda Street sometimes accosted passengers on inbound trains. In 1897 riders on one train witnessed a shootout between local vice operators. By the 1920s much of this illicit activity had left the area, and remnants of the "crib district" visible from the train housed single workers and families.[4] But post–World War I arrivals to Los Angeles were not spared the spectacle of vice, for the Arcade Station at Fifth and Central lay at the entrance to the city's Skid Row and all the activities associated with it. After disembarking at the depot, they would encounter streetwalkers who "openly solicited" soldiers, sailors, and other men of all races. Couples retired to nearby cottages, dark alleyways, and vacant lots, and runners directed men to "houses" for a drink and female company.[5]

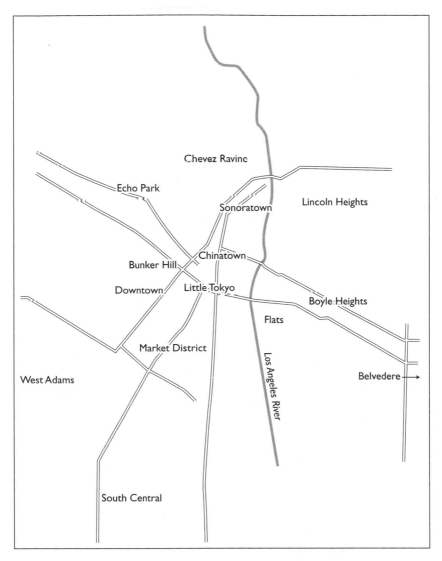

MAP 1. Neighborhoods of Central Los Angeles, Early Twentieth Century

Running west of the station toward downtown, Fifth Street catered to the most immediate needs of poorer Angelenos. Along either side of the street an array of missions, employment agencies, and saloons offered various solutions to the homeless and out-of-work. "Cabaret music, cowboy band's wild discord, [and] forced laughter" emanated from the livelier spots as one passed through crowds of street speakers, police officers, prostitutes, church people, alcoholics, laborers, and cross-dressers.[6] On Sixth Street, a block south of Skid Row, neighborhood children of various backgrounds converged on the Church of All Nations for boys' and girls' club activities. Proceeding up toward Main Street and Broadway, pedestrians encountered a central entertainment district, where movie theaters and burlesque shows beckoned to the multiethnic throngs. Looming over the western edge of the downtown corridor was Bunker Hill, a once-prestigious neighborhood of elegant mansions now subdivided into apartments and rented out to motley collections of bachelors and the elderly. In the late 1930s and 1940s the faded glory of the hill would become the setting for a series of John Fante novels about down-and-out Angelenos.

Across Main Street toward Bunker Hill lay Pershing Square, formerly Central Park, renamed for the military leader in the patriotic euphoria following World War I. Anglo residents established the park in the nineteenth century as an alternative city center to the Spanish- and Mexican-era plaza several blocks to the northeast. In subsequent years, both areas became nodal points for a vibrant street-speaking culture that drew audiences and participants from all areas of the city. During the war, government spies eavesdropped on these gatherings in the hope of thwarting anti-American alliances of Germans, Mexicans, and Japanese.[7] By 1925 officers lay ready to remove anyone engaged in "subversive" new entertainments, but visitors could still hear more acceptable speakers hold forth at the plaza.

If one wanted to get away from the bustle of downtown, one could hop on one of the streetcars headed south on Central. Crossing Ninth Street, the streetcar passed through the market district, whose wholesale produce businesses were owned and staffed by Anglos, Europeans, Asians, and Mexicans. Middle-class Anglos had built the homes in this area during the late nineteenth century, but sometime around 1900, according to one resident, a "progressive" real estate salesman willing to sell to "anybody" set up an office at Eleventh and Central and began to integrate the neighborhood. South of the market district lay other neighborhoods that had likewise been "opened up" to nonwhite Angelenos by aggressive home buyers and renters, Anglo landowners desperate to sell, and brokers willing to exploit the shortage of housing for immigrants and African Americans.[8] The city's black population was concentrated in these neighborhoods, and the entertainment district that would become famous during World War II was already flowering along Central Avenue. Yet African Americans, though prevalent, by no means dominated the district; it was home also to Japanese, Jews, Italians, Mexicans, and Anglos. At Slauson Avenue one crossed a line where Anglo residents to the south temporarily halted the residential expansion of mixed neighborhoods. But continuing into Watts, one once again entered an integrated community of bungalows inhabited by Anglos, African Americans, Mexicans, Japanese, and others who had been lured by affordable real estate and employment on the railroads. Bordering farmland that remained under cultivation well into the twentieth century, Watts remained a relatively sleepy community of working-class Angelenos until World War II. Jazz saxophonist Cecil "Big Jay" McNeely recalled his childhood home in a way that perhaps belied a more complex set of ethnic relations: "[It was a] mixed community, all nationalities were there. It was complete peace at that time. Spanish kids, Orientals, and whites. We all went to school together, no problem." Robert Van Meter made a similar comment about the Watts nightclubs. "They were places where black and white mingled," he recalled. "In the twenties there were a lot more activities together."[9]

From Lincoln Heights to Watts, working-class Angelenos of various ethnic backgrounds built up, worked in, and moved through a collage of industrial, commercial, and residential spaces at a time when the city was poised to vault into the ranks of the most powerful metropolises in America. The story of this phenomenal rise has been told many times, but as numerous scholars point out, many narratives obliterate non-Anglos from the landscape. More than a few historians have suggested, in fact, that the very success of Los Angeles depended precisely on an image, cultivated by a phalanx of dedicated boosters, of the city as a refuge from the industrial and racial "pollution" of modern industrializing urban America, a project of cultural cleansing that included the construction of a mythical "fantasy past" based on romanticized misconceptions of Californio rancho culture.[10] Yet within this ingenious advertising strategy lurked an irreconcilable contradiction: building such a city required a labor force far too extensive and varied to be staffed solely by Anglos. Asians, Mexicans, Europeans, and African Americans were drawn to Los Angeles by the same utopian promises, as

well as by the coarser solicitations of employers and labor contractors
seeking a pool of manual and domestic labor to build and run the new
urban oasis. Thus the often celebrated waves of Anglo migration—the
1880s land rush prompted by the arrival of the Santa Fe Railroad, the
1920s boon of midwestern transplants that stoked the regional economy, and the more problematic pilgrimage of dust bowl refugees during
the depression—also washed up other newcomers of darker complexions and different accents on the banks of the Los Angeles River.

It was this latter collection of migrants that by 1925 populated the
districts covered in this hypothetical tour. For the sake of convenience,
I have encapsulated these varied neighborhoods under the term "central
Los Angeles" or "central neighborhoods." *Central* is admittedly mis-
leading. While some of these districts, like Chinatown, Sonoratown, and
the Market District, bordered the commercial and industrial center of
the city, others, like Watts, lay miles from downtown in terrain more
rural than urban. Though pervasive, the poverty of these areas differed
in quality and origin from the post–World War II inner cities generated
by white flight and deindustrialization.[11] An alternative appellation is
"immigrant districts" or "foreign quarters," phrases that Anglos often
used to describe areas where they constituted a minority. Yet these terms
mislead as well, for Anglo and African American residents of central Los
Angeles were not immigrants, nor should one classify as foreigners those
Mexican and American Indian residents whose families predated Anglo
conquest. Anglo outsiders may have viewed these districts as foreign,
but for their inhabitants the neighborhoods were anything but. Indeed,
because other parts of the city remained effectively off limits to poor,
immigrant, and African American Angelenos, the integrated areas in
which they could live, work, and play were "central" to their lives.
These residents had other options; Pasadena, Hollywood, San Pedro,
and other towns drew substantial numbers of non-Anglos, and peripheral agricultural communities lured Asians and Mexicans as both permanent residents and migrant workers.[12] Yet their larger concentrations
of immigrants and African Americans tended to make the central neighborhoods the economic and cultural meeting point for many ethnic
groups. Moreover, to the extent that these districts harbored certain
recreational activities not sanctioned in other parts of the city, they
remained central to the lives of all Angelenos who wanted to participate
in them. Even Anglos who lived outside these districts often came to
them for work or passed through them on their way downtown.

A MIXED HERITAGE: LOS ANGELES TO 1886

In a certain crucial sense, the integrated central districts of early-twentieth-century Los Angeles continued a long tradition. From its inception in 1781 as a Spanish pueblo, El Pueblo de Nuestra Señora la Reina de los Angeles de Porciuncula had harbored a mixed population of American Indian, Spanish, and African ancestry.[13] A year later ethnoracial relations became an official issue when Father Junípero Serra, founder of the California missions, arrived to denounce the pueblo's residents for corrupting the indigenous population. Within a short time the landscape of the pueblo was inscribed with the racial heterogeneity of its inhabitants. South from the plaza at the center of town stretched a road known as el Calle de los Negros, later anglicized to "Nigger Alley." The *calle* funneled those Angelenos conducting activities not sanctioned by the church into the surrounding area. Into the 1830s, for instance, more than a dozen prostitutes operated just to the east in a residential zone set aside for American Indian residents.[14]

By the time U.S. forces captured Los Angeles in 1847 and ended California's involvement in the Mexican-American War, the calle had flowered into a wide-open entertainment district. Americans who drifted into town gawked at the raucous conglomeration of revelers who frequented the area. Horace Bell, for example, painted an evocative if exaggerated picture of the scene in the 1850s: "The crowd from the old Coronel Building on the Los Angeles Street corner to the plaza was so dense that we could scarcely squeeze through. Americans, Spaniards, Indians, and foreigners, rush[ed] and crowd[ed] along from one gambling house to another. . . . There were several bands of music of the primitive Mexican-Indian kind." Bell marveled that such a scene existed within the borders of the United States, for in his eyes "the town [was] plainly not an American community."[15]

The decades after statehood witnessed the first major transformation in Los Angeles's ethnoracial demography—an influx of Anglo settlers who by the end of the 1860s eclipsed the Mexican population as the majority. In their efforts to assume control of the town, these newcomers began to build away from the original pueblo settlement centered on the plaza and to reorient the town toward an Anglo core. Also, in 1877, they officially changed the name of el Calle de los Negros to Los Angeles Street, thus eliminating, in Harris Newmark's words, "a designation of the Los Angeles early gambling district long familiar to old settlers." Such actions marked the first steps toward constructing the vision of a

"white" Los Angeles that would resonate so strongly with their descendants.[16]

The late-nineteenth-century physical construction of white Los Angeles proceeded in concert with its social construction, projects that
strained the tenuous bonds connecting the various ethnoracial groups.
Before Anglo conquest non-Mexican newcomers to Los Angeles adapted
to the existing political and social conventions if they hoped to succeed
in their new home. Wealthy American businessmen, for example, frequently married daughters of elite Californio families, in part to cement
their relationship with those in power. For a time after the war such
unions remained common, especially since Anglo Angelenos had few
alternatives for mates.[17] Religious observance also united residents of
different backgrounds. The early years of Anglo rule occasioned a
notable if uneasy degree of interfaith cooperation among Jews, Catholics, and Protestants, reflecting their equal lack of political dominance.
During these years, residents of different faiths often worshiped together.
An early African American resident named William Ballard, for instance,
recalled that he attended a Catholic church at the plaza along with his
Mexican neighbors.[18] But the late-nineteenth-century Anglo ascendancy
to political and numerical dominance undercut many of these traditions.
Interfaith cooperation faded as Protestants established their own
churches. Likewise, intermarriage rates declined after the 1870s as the
population of Anglo women increased (see table 1).[19]

These trends prompted some observers to write out other races from
contemporary and future regional narratives, but underneath the ava-
lanche of Anglos other migrations were establishing a foundation for
the twentieth-century diversification of working-class Los Angeles. Chinese, lured across the Pacific by the gold rush beginning in the 1850s,
began to appear in the city by the end of the decade. Shut out of most
goldfields by recalcitrant Anglo miners, discouraged from truck farming
(in which they possessed considerable ability), and frustrated with the
low pay and backbreaking work of railroad construction, some began
to drift into Los Angeles. By 1870 they had established a Chinatown
surrounding el Calle de los Negros and the town's traditional entertainment district.[20]

For better or worse, Chinatown became one of Los Angeles's most
recognizable districts during this period. Like their counterparts in other
cities, Anglo officials allowed prostitution, gambling, drugs, and other
vice industries to pool in Chinatown as a way to keep them out of
"respectable" areas. The neighborhood's resulting reputation alter-

TABLE I
Population of Los Angeles, 1850–1930

Year	Population (in thousands)	Percentage Increase over Previous Decade
1850	1.6	—
1860	4.4	172
1870	5.7	27
1880	11.0	95
1890	50.0	351
1900	102.0	103
1910	319.0	212
1920	577.0	81
1930	1,238.0	115

SOURCE: Robert Fogelson, *The Fragmented Metropolis: Los Angeles, 1850–1930* (rpt. Berkeley: University of California Press, 1991), 21, 78–79.

nately attracted and repelled Angelenos. The patronage of Anglos, Mexicans, and others in Chinatown businesses contributed to the district's eclectic atmosphere but also fueled ethnic tensions. On October 24, 1871, a scuffle between police officers and suspected Chinese vice dealers erupted into gunfire that killed an Anglo bystander. In one of the ugliest incidents in the city's history, a gang of Anglos, Europeans, and Mexicans rampaged through Chinatown, shooting and lynching a total of eighteen Chinese Angelenos. Several prominent Angelenos subsequently blamed the event on "hot-headed" Mexican and Irish laborers, but other accounts suggested the rioters included members of all social strata. Judges handed out short jail sentences to a few perpetrators, a meager response that deepened the pall over the city's race relations.[21]

Strangely enough, however, the late-nineteenth-century experience of Chinese Angelenos compares favorably to that of their counterparts elsewhere in California. The massacre aside, Chinese in Los Angeles endured milder versions of the vitriolic hostility spewed by Denis Kearney and the Workingman's Party during the 1870s in San Francisco. Nor did the broader campaign against Chinese immigration that culminated in the 1882 and 1886 Exclusion Acts receive notable support from Los Angeles.[22] Historians have often located the source of this apathy in the feebleness of the city's labor movement, but other evidence suggests that Chinese integration into the local economy played a role as well. In 1886, for example, local exclusionists called for a boycott on Chinese labor and began to harass Anglos who hired Chinese "to do work a white man could do." Chinese truck farmers, already well established in the city, easily crushed the action by threatening a counterboycott of related businesses.[23] Exclusion, however, did affect Los Angeles's Chinatown by drastically reducing immigration from China after the 1880s. The city's Chinese population, dominated by bachelors, slipped by 1900 to just two thousand.[24] The decline perhaps contributed to the softening tensions between Chinese and Anglos. As a community that seemed headed toward extinction, Chinatown posed little threat to the white Los Angeles springing up around it.

Anglos invested in the vision of a white Los Angeles had reason to feel optimistic in 1886. The most problematic nonwhite populations in the city, Mexicans and Chinese, appeared to have crested. Anglos had consolidated their control over the city's political and social structure and had begun to lay the groundwork for what Robert Fogelson calls the "good community" of native-born Protestants. Yet the city's subsequent explosive and almost uninterrupted growth would introduce new residents and create new environments inconsistent with this vision. In attempting to channel what Harry Carr called "the last trek" of the "Aryan race," these boosters created another city of integration, diversity, cooperation, and conflict that would come to epitomize modern American urban development.[25]

ALL TRACKS LEAD TO LOS ANGELES

The arrival of the Santa Fe Railroad in 1886 ignited the first in a series of land rushes and advertising blitzes that brought immigrants and tourists alike streaming into Los Angeles. This first boom collapsed by the end of the decade, but beginning in the 1890s, the population of the city began to accelerate at a steadier pace. Between 1890 and 1930, Los Angeles metamorphosed from a town of 50,000 into a major metropolis of 1.2 million (2.3 million including metropolitan districts). The largest and, from the boosters' point of view, most eagerly anticipated contingent of newcomers consisted of middle-class and elite Anglo midwesterners dissatisfied with their lives in the country's interior. From 1890 to 1910 the proportion of native-born white Angelenos grew to over 76 percent of the city's total, surpassing that of other major American cities. Yet the invasion of middle-class white Protestants concealed smaller but substantial migrant streams that would eventually outstrip Anglo migration rates. At the turn of the century, about 23,000

Angelenos living within the city limits were nonwhite or foreign-born whites. By 1930 that number swelled to more than 360,000, a fifteen-fold increase, compared to a twelvefold increase for the population as a whole. [26]

Most likely, the first signs of these alternative migrations escaped the notice of the wealthier tourists and settlers who arrived in Los Angeles by train around the turn of the century. Their eyes may have passed over, for example, the cluster of shacks along the riverbed beneath what would become Lincoln Heights. Nicknamed "Dogtown" by Angelenos, the settlement housed Mexicans and Italians who worked the railroads that connected Los Angeles to the rest of the world.[27] Dogtown's residents illustrated the impact of the railroad network that had been constructed during the forty-year regime of the Mexican dictator Porfirio Díaz. This network transported peasants and villagers expelled from *ejidos* (communally owned farms), towns, and cities by Díaz's stringent modernization policies. U.S. railroads, desperate for cheap labor after the Exclusion Acts eliminated their sources in China, enticed Mexican workers across the border with the promise of steady work. In the process, they helped to launch what Douglas Monroy calls the "great migration," the Mexican repopulation of California and the American Southwest.[28]

The first settlements of Mexican railroad workers began to appear in the last decades of the nineteenth century along the corridor of tracks on each side of the river from Dogtown and the Flats down to Watts and south to the new harbor at San Pedro. Within the chain of storage yards, workshops, and other facilities, these workers found ample opportunities for employment, if not high wages. The area around these developments teemed with residents who worked or had worked on the railroads. Some companies housed Mexican employees in abandoned boxcars strung along idle tracks near work sites. Many of these "Boxcarvilles" lay in the river's floodplain on property of questionable value and, in the companies' eyes, suitable for laborers, Mexican or otherwise.[29]

Analogous forces drew African Americans to Los Angeles via the railroad industry. The late 1880s price wars between the Southern Pacific and Santa Fe Railroad companies made cross-country tickets affordable even to working-class blacks, who in the aftermath of Reconstruction found plenty of reasons to leave the South. Word of Los Angeles traveled east via porters and railway workers who had found in the city affordable living conditions and land available for purchase. Enticements like these attracted modest numbers of blacks in the late nineteenth century, setting the stage for an accelerated rate of growth after

1900 and the institution of Jim Crow legislation. A mere 1,250 in 1890, the black population in Los Angeles jumped to almost 39,000 forty years later.[30]

Mexicans and African Americans were the most visible populations of non-Anglos drawn to Los Angeles directly by the railroad industry, and the neighborhoods they created formed the backbone of central Los Angeles. The sleepy community of Watts, located several miles south of downtown, perhaps constituted the most dramatic example of a multiethnic, railroad-generated settlement. On the surface, Watts did not resemble a typical central city neighborhood. Abundant open space allowed residents to cultivate gardens and keep farm animals. Not withstanding its rural appearance, Watts remained tied to the industrialization of the Los Angeles basin and the immigration patterns associated with urban growth. The Pacific Electric Railway effectively established the town in 1902 when it completed a depot there. Real estate promotions promising "a dollar down and dollar a week" lot purchases immediately attracted settlers. The first Mexican inhabitants occupied a "Latin Camp" of tents and shacks set up for railroad workers outside of town, but the community gradually expanded into Watts's southern district. African Americans also settled in this swampy land they named "Mudtown," joining an assemblage of other arrivals that included Germans, Scots, Italians, Greeks, Jews, and Japanese.[31]

In his novel *God Sends Sunday*, Harlem Renaissance author Arna Bontemps described Mudtown as an isolated African American settlement: "Here, removed from the influences of white folks, they did not acquire the inhibitions of their city brothers. Mudtown was like a tiny section of the deep south literally transplanted." The district's far-flung location separated its residents from the majority of Anglo Angelenos, but Bontemps probably overemphasized its racial homogeneity. In fact, a later scene describes a picnic sponsored by Pullman porters in which Mexicans, "Gypsies," and several whites join the African American celebrants.[32] As the Mexican and African American populations in Watts expanded, inter-ethnoracial contact became more common but not necessarily as civil. Residents of South Gate, east across Alameda Street, maintained a defiant "whites only" policy through World War II and perhaps joined Watts Anglos in a growing backlash against other populations. The Ku Klux Klan staged several rallies in Watts during the 1920s, and in 1923 or 1924 an alliance of African American and Mexican residents petitioned the County Board of Supervisors to remove the police chief "due to his ceaseless harassment" of their communities.[33]

Such conflicts, however, masked an alternative current of tolerance and association between the town's various ethnoracial groups. Watts resident and African American activist Eusebia Small acknowledged: "The first black family that bought on East Main Street, on the north side, brought on a sudden rash of For Sale signs. Yet the white people had joined with us to fight the Klan. They used to come from across Main Street to our meetings."[34] Some white residents remembered little tension after African Americans moved into nearby homes. "There was a colored couple who moved on our street, and they were the nicest family you ever saw," one reported. "And I remember when I went to school, my best friend was a colored girl called Julia." Another white resident claimed to have associated with a number of African American friends, including one who maintained a "resort" around a "lake" patronized by both white and black families. One white family rented part of their ranch near Watts to a Japanese family, with whom they remained friendly, and noted that their tenants occasionally took them to dinner in Little Tokyo.[35] Several African Americans likewise recalled their childhoods in Watts with affection and identified a notable lack of racial tension. "In Watts you didn't run into racial problems," Britt Woodman remembered. "People got along, and everybody was beautiful." Britt's brother, William, was even more effusive: "The environment there was almost all races, and we all got along very well. There were whites, Mexicans, Orientals, Jewish people. That's why, at that time, I didn't really understand about prejudice. I said, 'How could this happen? Right here, we get along so beautifully, all of us together.' Everything was just beautiful. The environment was great."[36] It is tempting to dismiss such statements as romanticized childhood recollections softened by time, for even the social worlds of children in Watts did not entirely escape ethnoracial tension. Most likely, however, the spectrum of the community's race relations was as diverse as its residents. In learning to live with each other, early-twentieth-century Watts residents played out in microcosm the larger story of the central neighborhoods.

DOWN BY THE STATION

If the railroads spawned instant communities like Watts in undeveloped areas, they inscribed even greater changes closer to downtown. Beginning with the 1880s rush, the train stations disgorged thousands of new residents into the commercial and industrial center of Los Angeles every year. Many of the wealthier Anglo passengers continued to the hotels around Pershing Square or to outlying residential districts reserved for whites by higher land values and restrictive covenants, that is, clauses in property deeds that restricted sales to white buyers. Many less affluent Anglos headed to working-class suburbs such as South Gate that bordered remoter areas of industrial development where native-born whites complemented legal means with intimidation and violence to keep out inhabitants of darker complexions. But immigrants and African Americans, as well as some Anglos, who arrived in Los Angeles by train or other means often stopped, if only for a short time, in the areas directly adjoining the stations. Set among the factories, foundries, and warehouses of the city's industrial core, these districts became the port-of-entry neighborhoods for the central city and thus harbored some of the most diverse and desperate elements of the Angeleno population. Though a 1935 survey by the *Los Angeles Times* dismissed these areas as "the poorest consumer market" of any in the city, opportunities abounded for working-class newcomers seeking jobs, affordable goods, or recreation.[37]

Before the 1880s Mexican newcomers and the occasional African American usually headed, especially if they were single men, to the lodging houses and house courts around the plaza district and Sonoratown. As Mexican immigration ebbed, however, the area began to absorb a more diverse group of settlers. Many of Los Angeles's first working-class Italian residents, an extension of the migrant streams that fed the Little Italys of the urban Northeast, settled into adobe dwellings around Sonoratown. After 1910 Asian immigrants and a few poor Anglos joined them.[38] Even the plaza, Los Angeles's Mexican center, began to exhibit a more diverse array of denizens and passersby. In 1914 a USC student conducted head counts of visitors to the plaza over several days. He identified Mexicans as the majority, but by no means the totality, of visitors there. His figures for Mexicans ranged from 35 to 75 percent of the total, with an average of about 50 percent.[39] By the end of World War I, observers reported that Portuguese, French, Filipinos, Greeks, and Austrians had joined the aforementioned groups. One sociologist in 1920 categorized the 2,446 Angelenos residing in an area of Sonoratown just a few blocks north of the plaza as 60 percent Mexican, 20 percent Italian, and 20 percent "other."[40]

Of the original Mexican districts in and around Sonoratown, only Chavez Ravine avoided the trend toward integration. The three neighborhoods of Chavez Ravine, Palo Verde, La Loma, and Bishop, remained so isolated from the rest of the city that even after residents built their own dirt road to link the region to downtown Angelenos continued to refer to the area as "the lost colonies." Into the 1940s Chavez Ravine's sole industries consisted of a brickyard and a tortilla factory, and many residents cultivated large gardens and grazed farm animals on the hillsides. Though photographer Don Normark, who visited the area in 1949, found a smattering of African American, Anglo, and Austrian residents, and a few Czechoslovakian and Italian students at the nearby elementary school, it remained a predominantly Mexican community.[41]

But Chavez Ravine was the exception to the rule of gradual ethnic and racial diversification in the neighborhoods around downtown. The changing demography of Chinatown exemplified this trend. Of all the neighborhoods in central Los Angeles, Chinatown perhaps came closest to re-creating the type of crowded, grimy, and impoverished tenement neighborhood characteristic of northeastern cities. The district covered only a few square blocks, bounded on the east and north by Southern Pacific yards and on the south and west by downtown. Despite its central location, Chinatown languished without basic infrastructure improvements and regular garbage collection into the twentieth century. Streetlights were not installed until about 1913, and as late as 1922 the neighborhood had only two paved roads. The twenty-seven streets within Chinatown's borders traced what Nora Sterry, principal of the nearby Macy Street School, called in 1923 a "veritable maze" of narrow alleyways with looming tenement buildings that shut out the light. "The buildings were erected before the housing code and were patterned after houses in southern China, which are constructed with a view to warding off evil spirits rather than ensuring physical comfort, the belief being that spirits dislike darkness and cannot turn corners." The tortuous, overbuilt nature of Chinatown may have had more to do with landlords' attempts to maximize usable real estate at minimum cost than with thwarting spirits, but others spoke of the seeming impenetrability of the district's structures.[42]

Despite its foreboding appearance, Chinatown remained notoriously congested at all hours of the day, due in no small part to the thriving vice industry. Illicit businesses drew visitors of all ethnic and racial backgrounds, diversifying the public spaces of the district. By the turn of the century, as the Exclusion Acts strangled further immigration from China and city authorities cracked down on vice (see chap. 5), growing numbers of non-Chinese lodgers, mostly single men but occasionally families with children, moved into hotels (such as the notorious Ballerino Hotel), apartments, and stalls, or "cribs," that had formerly housed prostitutes. Clarence Yip Yeu, who immigrated to the United States in 1921, remembered the inhabitants of 1920s Chinatown as mostly Italian and Mexican.[43]

Just south of Chinatown, the area around the intersection of First, San Pedro, and Los Angeles Streets attracted an even more cosmopolitan array of residents. Dubbed "Five Points" by the turn of the century, the district was noted, or notorious, for its "several 'social clubs' of several nationalities and varying degrees of 'cussedness'" and numerous other saloons, gambling dens, and parlors. African Americans had moved into the area by the 1880s, and its subsequent classification as a "Negro district," referring more to the presence than the predominance of blacks, opened the door for other immigrant populations. By 1900 substantial numbers of Jews, Irish, Germans, and Chinese had moved in as well.[44] Although an early center of African American culture in Los Angeles, the area around and south of Five Points maintained a multi-ethnic character through the early twentieth century, as the pan-racial Azusa Street revival in 1906 demonstrated (see chap. 3). In 1925 a Japanese resident described the residents of the rooming houses and apartments along East First Street as "motley, including Japanese, Mexicans, and many other white immigrants." Anglo reformers disparaged the area as the worst of Los Angeles neighborhoods. "Everywhere there is bad housing, frightful overcrowding, congestion of peoples in houses and houses on lots," noted one report. "Nothing except the social agencies . . . bring [sic] any American influence into this neighborhood."[45]

After 1900 the burgeoning Japanese population made their commercial and cultural presence felt along First, Second, and Third Streets, and the area soon became known as Little Tokyo. Japanese immigrants had begun to trickle into Los Angeles toward the end of the nineteenth century. The 1900 census counted 150 in the city, although much larger numbers had already settled in Hawaii and parts of northern California. The 1908 "Gentleman's Agreement" between the United States and Japan dampened immigration from Japan, but subsequent internal migrations of Japanese augmented the population in Los Angeles. The first influx occurred after 1906, when Japanese in San Francisco abandoned homes decimated by earthquake and fire for Southern California.[46] By 1910 the Japanese population in Los Angeles had climbed to 6,000, and more than 21,000 lived in the city twenty years later. This growth registered most visibly in the environs of Little Tokyo. As late as 1911 a Japanese restaurant on San Pedro near Second Street served primarily an African American clientele. But Japanese newcomers were already replacing the Jewish stores and black residents from Five Points down to Azusa Street, even as their businesses continued to cater to the multiethnic residential population. By 1920 Little Tokyo was the undisputed center of Japanese cultural life in Los Angeles and Southern California, but substantial numbers of non-Japanese Angelenos, particularly newcomers to the city, continued to appreciate the district for its proximity to places of employment and commercial establishments. As late as 1940, according to John Modell, census tracts of the area counted a population only 29 to 36 percent Japanese, with substantial numbers of whites, African Americans, and Mexicans.[47]

South of Little Tokyo, a similarly eclectic collection of residents congregated along Fifth Street between Main and the Southern Pacific Depot. Middle-class Anglos had built many of the homes here during the nineteenth century, but encroaching industrial development drove them out of the area, leaving it for new settlers of more modest means. The denizens of Fifth Street lent the area a seedy reputation, but many working families inhabited the deteriorating homes around Skid Row. At the turn of the century, African Americans constituted one of the area's largest populations, and two-thirds of the city's 2,500 Jews lived there as well. Over the next two decades immigrants from around the world joined them, and a 1917 survey, identifying members of forty-two nationalities within its boundaries, declared it "the most cosmopolitan district of Los Angeles."[48] Rapid in-migration and population turnover after World War I ensured a changing constellation of ethnic groups, but as a 1939 survey by the Works Progress Administration demonstrated, no one group dominated the district before World War II (see table 2). Available evidence suggests that through the early twentieth century this area maintained notably high levels of integration. A number of rooming houses and apartment buildings, for example, held tenants of many backgrounds. The 1939 survey, for instance, revealed that one thirty-one-unit building at 843–5 Maple housed thirty "whites," nine Asians, eight Mexicans, two African Americans, and three "others." A nearby apartment building at 1016 E. Seventh Street housed nine whites, seven Mexicans, and three Asians. The survey's length of residence figures suggested that it did not capture buildings in the midst of rapid transition from one ethnoracial group to another. Few tenants had spent more than a decade in their apartments, but several tenants of various races had resided in each building for a number of years.[49]

Some of the residents in these survey areas worked in the markets that clustered around San Pedro and Ninth Streets, at the southern end

TABLE 2

Nationality-Race of Residents of Survey District South of Fifth Street,
as Percentage of Total Sample Population, 1920 and 1939

Nationality-Race	1920		1939	Expanded Zone
"Americans"	46.5	"Whites"	33.4	35.7
"Spanish"/Mexicans	18.5	Mexicans	47.6	42.7
African Americans	12.6	African Americans	1.6	4.0
Japanese	5.2	Asians	15.1	16.0
German	3.9	Other	2.3	1.4
Jews (all nationalities)	3.9			
Italian	1.6			
Other	7.8			

SOURCE: 1920 figures from "Special Facts Regarding Church of All Nations Parish," Jan. 1, 1920, 1, in Box 56, "misc. notes," G. Bromley Oxnam Papers; 1939 figures compiled from data cards in Boxes 56 and 57, Works Progress Administration, 1939 Survey of Los Angeles, Regional History Center, University of Southern California. Survey area was 21-block neighborhood between Sixth, Eighth, San Pedro, and Central Streets. Expanded zone extends several blocks south and west into the market district. For both surveys figures are samples that likely do not constitute the entire population of the district.

of the district. During the nineteenth century, Anglo residents had kept nonwhites north of Seventh Street, but this barrier collapsed soon after 1900.[50] At this time the Central Market, several blocks north on Third and Central, was controlled by Italians and Anglos. Growing demand for fresh produce, however, soon outstripped the market's capacity, and around 1909 a consortium of Chinese and Japanese produce sellers shut out of the Central Market banded together with Anglo investors to finance the Los Angeles City Market at San Pedro and Ninth. Several years later Southern Pacific established the Terminal Market at Seventh and Central, and the area became the produce center of the city. Though workers at these markets often remained segregated by firm, they included scores of Chinese, Japanese, and Mexicans who moved into nearby homes and apartments, further diversifying a district already populated by African Americans and European immigrants.[51] A 1917 survey concluded that the area "contains every nationality, the Mexicans and Italians predominating, and has the added complication of large numbers of Americans of the lowest class economically, as well as a great many negroes." Twenty-five years later the Chinese-owned restaurants in the area still attracted a multiethnic clientele, prompting one sociologist to observe, "The workers in the market, be they colored or white, frequently hang around these restaurants where they can chat, laugh, and yell freely as if there were no racial barrier between them."[52]

ACROSS THE RIVER

Districts east of the river possessed less of the frenetic, congested quality of their counterparts closer to the train stations. Though not necessarily more prosperous than other central neighborhoods, these areas more closely resembled suburbs in layout. Instead of apartment buildings, rooming houses, and house courts, dwellings were more likely to be single-family homes with open yards, even if the houses themselves were somewhat makeshift. Often, individual lots held several structures that landlords rented out to individuals or families. Some of these neighborhoods, especially those in Boyle Heights, acquired a stability that Angelenos of later generations would point to with pride. Yet despite these differences, many districts east of the river developed populations as heterogeneous as their counterparts to the west.

In the late nineteenth century Anglo settlers built many of the eastside's first dwellings on the bluffs and high ground overlooking the river. Lincoln Heights, for example, began as an enclave of native-born white skilled workers. To the south, Andrew Boyle purchased property along the Paredón Blanco, or White Bluffs, and well-to-do Anglos erected spacious homes with views of the river in what they renamed Boyle Heights.[53] But these early settlers were not alone for long. Along the floodplain below the bluffs railroad companies soon established Boxcarvilles for Mexican and other workers in Dogtown and the Flats. East of the bluffs, a series of gullies riddled a landscape that undulated by property value as well as elevation. Into low-lying areas like Fickett Hollow and Bernal Gully, where the constant threat of flooding depressed property values, moved settlers of modest means and various ethnicities.[54]

By the early 1900s Angelenos of all backgrounds were migrating in large numbers to the eastside districts. Japanese residents seeking an alternative to the congestion of Little Tokyo and downtown moved into the area around Evergreen Cemetery. Through the 1920s the community expanded to the north, south, and west, and a 1927 study counted about fourteen hundred families living there among other ethnic groups. Another survey of the five-block area bounded by First, Second, Mott, and Soto Streets revealed 25 Jewish homes, 20 Japanese, 7 Mexican, 2 "Spanish," 2 "Anglosaxon," 1 French, and 2 of unknown ethnic origin.[55] African Americans, a number of whom secured jobs at Evergreen, began to purchase the somewhat swampy and inexpensive land just to its west. By 1926 approximately fifteen hundred African Americans lived in the district. Anglos derisively referred to the area as "Pecktown" after the first landowner to sell to blacks, but residents, black or otherwise, found it convenient and affordable. As Japanese and African American settlements merged with those of other residents, the area became integrated block by block, and at least a few black landowners rented out rooms and dwellings to Mexicans and Japanese.[56]

Other ethnic groups moved into adjacent districts. Beginning in 1905, for example, a small but notable contingent of Molokan Russians arrived in Los Angeles. A clannish sect of observant, pacifist Christians whose religious practices marginalized them in their home country, the Molokans fled military conscription for the Russo-Japanese War and the social upheaval of the 1905 Revolution. The first arrivals settled on Vignes Street between Chinatown and the Los Angeles River, but they quickly relocated across the river to the Flats. The community expanded into nearby Salt Lake Terrace, and a number of Molokans moved southeast into Fickett Hollow, one of the gullies transecting Boyle Heights. In 1918 approximately 3,300 Molokans resided in the city, and by the early 1930s that number doubled. Despite the reclusive tendencies of more orthodox believers, the Molokans lived among various ethnic communities, and home owners within the group often rented to other Angelenos when they could find no tenants of their own kind.[57]

Italian Angelenos also established their strongest local presence on the eastside. A handful of Italians had made their homes in Los Angeles by the 1820s, and enough more had arrived by the middle of the century to establish a definite if ephemeral presence around the plaza. What some observers identified during the 1880s as a "Little Italy" evaporated by the end of the century in the face of Chinese and Mexican immigration. No more than two thousand Italians lived in Los Angeles in 1900, but their numbers ballooned with the opening of the Panama Canal in 1913, which established a cheaper and faster route between Europe and California. Even after immigration laws virtually halted the influx in 1924, the Italian population in Los Angeles continued to grow, reaching an estimated 36,000 by 1934.[58]

The early-twentieth-century Italian population in Los Angeles spread out over many districts in central Los Angeles, from Sonoratown south to the market districts, down Central Avenue, and southwest into West Adams. The closest thing to a Little Italy appeared in the Lincoln

Heights district, where Italians and Mexicans joined the Anglos who had built up the area. Compared to other immigrant communities, the Italian migration contained higher numbers of skilled workers, mostly from northern Italy, who were able to achieve a noticeable degree of social mobility. This difference may have allowed many Italians to leave the central neighborhoods for wealthier areas, although substantial numbers of them remained through the 1930s.[59]

The two groups that would ultimately make the strongest impact on the social landscape of the twentieth-century eastside were Jews and Mexicans. The 1850 census listed eight Jews living in Los Angeles, but by 1880 more than five hundred called the city home. The relative wealth and small numbers of early Jewish Angelenos encouraged tolerance from Anglos, who invited them to participate in "white" community activities at all income levels. The city council of 1850 included a Jewish member, and Jewish Angelenos such as Abel Stearns and Harris Newmark were among the city's most prominent businessmen. Some historians claim that the willingness of Jewish businessmen to deal with non-Anglos meant they endured little or none of the resentment directed at Anglos, and a few have even termed the nineteenth century a "golden era" in Jewish Los Angeles.[60]

To whatever extent these idyllic conditions prevailed, they began to fade by the 1890s when alternative migration patterns transformed the city's Jewish population. By that decade the exodus of poor Jews from eastern Europe had already relocated huge populations into neighborhoods such as New York's Lower East Side. Responding to some of the same advertisements and word-of-mouth that drew Anglos to Los Angeles, numerous Jews dissatisfied with the poverty and crowding of eastern cities began to make their way west. Like other European migrations, Jewish migration to Los Angeles accelerated with the opening of the Panama Canal and the flaring of anti-Semitism that accompanied World War I and the Russian Revolution. In 1900, 2,500 Jews lived in the city; there were 20,000 by 1920. Though federal immigration quotas passed in the 1920s sharply curtailed immigration from eastern and southern Europe, migration patterns within the United States continued to feed Los Angeles's Jewish population, which grew to more than 70,000 by 1930.[61]

Unlike their wealthier predecessors, this second migration of proletarian and, often, Yiddish-speaking Jews settled primarily in working-class neighborhoods among other poor immigrants. The early-twentieth-century geography of Jewish settlement included districts west of the

river from Temple Street down into South Central, but by the 1910s newcomers increasingly flocked to the area along Brooklyn Avenuue between
the bluffs and the cemetery, after a local realtor began to advertise heavily in New York Jewish communities. By the mid-1910s observers noted
that the new immigrants were "crowding out" the Anglo population,
and by the late 1920s the vicinity of Brooklyn and Soto Streets constituted one of the few sections in central Los Angeles that might reasonably be called monoethnic.[62]

The Jewish influx was accompanied by a Mexican resurgence on the
variable terrain of the eastside. Through the last decades of the nineteenth century the Mexican population in Los Angeles remained relatively stable and mostly confined to its traditional districts around the
plaza and Sonoratown. The appearance of railroad workers and Box-
carville residents just before 1900, however, foreshadowed the dislocations and repression of the Porfiriato and the outbreak of the Mexican
Revolution that induced a hemorrhaging of political and economic
refugees. In Los Angeles, their population skyrocketed from about
5,000 in 1910 to 30,000 in 1920 and at least 90,000 by 1930.[63]

The impact of this migration reverberated through the central neighborhoods. From Chavez Ravine and Chinatown to South Central and
Watts, Mexican immigrants settled in virtually any area where racial
covenants and Anglo hostility did not keep them out. But it was on the
eastside that they concentrated in the greatest numbers.[64] Aside from
the boxcar settlements along the railroad yards, the first Mexican ham-
lets east of the river probably emerged in Belvedere, the unincorporated
area east of Boyle Heights. Working-class Angelenos of various ethnic
backgrounds found its inexpensive land and the absence of municipal
taxes and building regulations ideal for self-constructed homes. An early
Mexican enclave, what one observer called "the worst kind of shacks,"
grew up at Maravilla Park, or el Hoyo Maravilla. From these beginnings
the Mexican population expanded rapidly into other parts of Belvedere
and City Terrace, a somewhat more prosperous district to the north. By
1930 an estimated 30,000 Mexicans resided in Belvedere and associated
areas east of the city limits.[65]

The eastside Jewish ghetto and barrio did not spring fully formed
overnight, and through the 1930s the area between them blurred into a
more multiethnic landscape. Between the Brooklyn-Soto intersection
and Evergreen Cemetery, for example, many ethnic groups shared the
neighborhood with Jews and Mexicans. Morris Kadish depicted his
childhood neighborhood around Malabar and Evergreen Streets in the

twenties as "maybe 75% Jewish," and bordering the "Mexican neighborhoods" to the east. Emilia Castañeda de Valenciana, who grew up
not far from Kadish, described the area as a "'United Nations' of Mexicans, Chinese, Japanese, African Americans, Filipinos, Jews, and
Greeks."[66] South of Brooklyn and Soto, the resident population became
much more diverse. Fickett's Hollow contained several ethnic groups,
most notably Mexicans and Russian Molokans, and Bernal Gully, to the
east, held a predominantly Mexican colony dubbed "La Barria." A
1936 Federal Writers Project abandoned any attempt to map the racial
groups of East Los Angeles, concluding that "they are so intermingled
that an exact segregation has not been attempted."[67] A Works Progress
Administration survey conducted three years later revealed that one section south of Brooklyn Avenue and west of Evergreen Cemetery was
40.2 percent Mexican, 31.6 percent "White" (including Jews and other
European immigrants), 22.5 percent Asian, and 5.6 percent African
American. Different ethnic groups had higher concentrations in differ
ent sections of the sampling area, but most blocks housed residents from
at least three racial-ethnic groups (see table 3).[68]

SOUTH AND WEST: EXPANDING CENTRAL NEIGHBORHOODS

By 1910 the city's booming economy fueled a rapid suburban expansion
of Anglos, who began to abandon older neighborhoods for newer, more
distant districts. The vacuum drew Angelenos of other backgrounds into
the older areas, thereby expanding the dimensions of central Los Angeles. Streetcar systems eased this growth, providing working-class Angelenos with inexpensive transportation to the industrial districts near
downtown and the river. African Americans were among the first non-
Anglos to move into the area south of the market district where Los
Angeles's major avenues dog-eared toward Watts. Two nodes of black
settlement in this region appeared soon after the turn of the century, one
at Thirty-third and Hooper and another along the Furlong Tract between
Fifty-first and Fifty-fifth Streets just west of Alameda. From these
footholds black Angelenos gradually moved into the intervening districts. According to Max Bond, one of the first chroniclers of black Los
Angeles, they had little trouble surmounting the racial covenants erected
to bar their migration. With plenty of alternatives for housing, many
Anglos preferred to depart rather than enforce the deed restrictions. In a
preview of the "blockbusting" strategies that became popular after
World War II, black buyers discovered that their very appearance in a

TABLE 3
Nationality–Ethnic Groups in Eleven Central City Districts, by Percentage of Total in Survey, 1917

	District											Total
	1	2	3	4	5	6	7	8	9	10	11	
Austrian-Hungarian	2	2	4	1	—	7	1	1	—	5	—	2.1
British	5	—	2	5	3	5	1	2	—	3	—	3.1
Chinese	1	—	—	—	—	—	—	1	—	12	1	1.6
French	2	1	2	3	2	1	2	1	—	—	2	1.9
German	2	—	2	2	2	8	5	1	1	5	—	2.5
Italian	5	26	46	5	1	3	1	5	17	2	12	9.2
Japanese	—	—	2	—	—	3	—	1	—	17	11	3.1
Jewish	19	—	—	42	16	7	11	2	—	2	—	12.0
Mexican	10	55	30	12	21	35	38	26	38	19	59	30.1
Russian	1	—	—	2	9	2	17	—	—	—	—	2.9
Turkish	—	1	2	—	9	—	3	—	—	—	3	1.8
U.S.	42	9	4	24	31	12	5	51	37	25	2	24.9
Other	5	2	2	1	2	11	11	4	2	2	2	4.1
No report	5	4	11	1	3	—	—	1	1	3	—	2.8

SOURCE: CCIH, Community Survey of Los Angeles, 37.
NOTE: Most columns do not total 100 percent.

neighborhood could often induce a wave of panic selling. This trend accelerated during economic downturns, when cash-strapped whites became less particular about who they sold to.[69] In this vein, most of the neighborhoods south of the market district, north of Slauson Avenue, and west of Alameda, where white resistance to further expansion solidified, became integrated by the mid-1920s. This area emerged as the focal point for new black settlement. By the mid-1930s an estimated 27,000 blacks lived along the South Central neighborhoods.[70]

Far from comprising a monolithic African American ghetto, however, pre–World War II South Central neighborhoods housed European, Asian, and Mexican immigrants in addition to blacks and the remaining Anglos. African Americans who grew up along South Central Avenue before World War II almost always described their neighborhood as multiethnic. Marshal Royal, for example, remembered the districts from Thirty-eighth Street to Vernon in the twenties as a mixture of African Americans, Jews, some Italians and Asians, and a few Anglos.[71] Japanese were among the first to take advantage of the new housing options opened by the settlement of blacks in formerly all-white areas.[72] Bond's analysis of the changing racial geography of Twenty-ninth and Thirtieth Streets between Arlington and Western from 1926 to 1933 noted the immigration of Japanese and Mexicans in addition to African Americans. Likewise, a survey of the Thirty-sixth Street neighborhood in 1926 revealed that Japanese and African Americans constituted the majority, with smaller numbers of whites, Chinese, and Koreans. By 1931 at least one sociologist was referring to mid–South Central as a second "Chinese" neighborhood in Los Angeles, with Mexicans, Japanese, African Americans, and eastern Europeans interspersed among the Chinese.[73] Pockets of Jewish settlement had formed in the area by 1910, and through the 1930s the number of Jewish families there fluctuated between several hundred and two thousand.[74] Over time, the African American portion of this population increased at the expense of the other groups. But like the growth of the eastside barrio, the emergence of the South Central ghetto took place over decades, with other ethnic groups lingering in the district for years. In short, early-twentieth-century South Central encompassed within its emergent black majority a diverse collection of ethnic groups typical of other central city neighborhoods.

West of South Central, smaller numbers of more prosperous African Americans, Asians, Mexicans, and European immigrants began to settle in wealthier Anglo areas. Though sometimes separated by class from their blue-collar neighbors to the east, these residents were also of diverse ethnic backgrounds. The West Adams district, for example, originally housed middle- and upper-middle-class Anglos. Wealthy Jews and Mexicans, such as the actress Dolores del Rio, however, began to move into the area by the 1920s. As Anglos vacated the area, African Americans were among those who replaced them.[75] By the mid-twenties other middle-class neighborhoods attracted multiethnic populations as well. Along Madison Avenue and West Tenth Street near Vermont, for example, African Americans and Japanese lived among whites. Relatively prosperous African Americans also moved into areas along Washington Boulevard, Western Boulevard, and Thirty-sixth Street.[76]

Bunker Hill gradually became part of central Los Angeles during the early twentieth century. Like Boyle Heights, it began its life as a wealthy neighborhood. Though the first building on the hill was an African American church, by the late 1870s ornate mansions were springing up so quickly that their upper-middle-class owners had trouble finding construction workers. After the turn of the century, however, elites began to look to other neighborhoods farther from downtown, and Bunker Hill shed its well-heeled residents. By 1920 construction in the area came to a virtual halt, and absentee owners began to convert the celebrated mansions into apartment houses, which they rented out to less affluent Anglos, Europeans, and Mexicans.[77] North of Bunker Hill, the neighborhoods running along Temple Street also drew substantial numbers of immigrant and nonwhite Angelenos. Temple Street between Rampart and Reno Streets had housed a number of African Americans in the nineteenth century, and a few "pioneering" blacks remained into the 1930s.[78] Jewish immigrants also moved into the area. Some Angelenos regarded Temple as the Jewish "Main Street" in the 1910s before the center of Jewish settlement shifted to Boyle Heights. As late as 1926, however, about 3,500 Jewish households still existed in the area. A wide variety of ethnic groups made their homes along Custer Street between Temple and Echo Park. Social workers there counted significant numbers of Jewish, Italian, "Spanish," Slovenian, and other European immigrants, in addition to native-born Americans.[79]

CONFLICT, TOLERANCE, AND FRIENDSHIP

Recalling her childhood in a mixed South Central neighborhood, jazz singer Florence Cadrez Brantley painted an idyllic picture of relations between residents. "There was never any feeling of racism or alienation on Twenty-First Street," she said. "We were always in and out of one another's homes all the time."[80] Brantley's contemporary, pianist Hampton Hawes, was more circumspect:

> Our neighborhood at 35th and Budlong was a mixture of whites, blacks and Orientals with a few Mexicans around the edges. Negroes were niggers to both whites and themselves, and whites were peckerwood trash to Negroes and themselves. The Mexicans kept to themselves and ate tacos; the Negroes kept to themselves and ate collard greens. . . . The Japanese mowed lawns and I don't know what else 'cause they were as mysterious to me as the Chinese who had laundries and grocery stores. . . . And the strange thing was, there was a peaceable mood in the country, a feeling of satisfaction and ease that people my age and older think of now as "the good old days."[81]

The disparate tones of these recollections suggest different evaluations of local ethnic and race relations, yet they share a common theme. Hawes may have described widespread ethnoracial isolation, but he echoed Brantley's interpretation of South Central as a place where conflict was rare. Each statement oversimplified the more complex interactions and barriers between ethnic groups.

Much of the racial tension in central Los Angeles before World War II emanated from Anglo residents resentful of the growing number of Asian, Mexican, African American, and sometimes European newcomers. "The niggers are taking over this town," one churlish white man exclaimed to an interviewer in 1936.[82] Such sentiments could be translated into more concerted resistance. In Boyle Heights, for example, recalcitrant Anglos sometimes used intimidation and racial covenants to harass Mexicans and Asian residents. In 1920 one group organized an aborted attempt to evict Japanese tenants and businesses from their neighborhood.[83] Likewise, when K. H. Shimizu bought a home just east of the city limits in Belvedere sometime in the mid-1920s, Anglo neighbors threatened him, vandalized his property, and set fire to the home. The intimidation worked; Shimizu sold out and moved to a more diverse and tolerant area near Evergreen Cemetery. Another Japanese Angeleno reported that neighbors advised him to leave after he purchased a Belvedere home during the same period. Frustrated and confused by what he considered an un-American attitude ("I suppose [the objectors] were Jewish, Italians, Russians, and low-class Europeans") the man also sold his house and moved to Boyle Heights, where he rented from a Jewish landlord.[84] A few years later, in 1927, white residents of City Terrace and north Belvedere attempted to have the area incorporated into Los

Angeles. Indignant Mexicans condemned the petition as an attempt to drive them out of the area by raising taxes to prohibitive levels. County officials eventually ruled that the taxation proposal constituted an unjust taking of property and voided incorporation.[85]

Such actions exacerbated ethnoracial tensions in central Los Angeles, but Anglos could exhibit tolerant and even friendly attitudes toward their neighbors. One white Angeleno admitted to Bond that he first opposed the arrival of African Americans into his neighborhood but soon changed his mind: "I have found them to be fine people. Sometimes I take my family next door and we eat supper with the Negroes whom I once fought. They come over to our house and eat with us in return."[86] Not all Anglos living in the central neighborhoods were so forthcoming, but those who chose to stay through the 1920s and 1930s came by necessity to some accommodation with their new neighbors, and a number joined middle-class reformers in reaching out, formally or informally, to immigrants and African Americans.

Friendships and alliances between non-Anglos of different backgrounds were more common. This tradition of cooperation drew much of its strength from shared discrimination at the hands of middle-class and elite Anglos. In certain contexts marginal groups found it convenient or even necessary to stick together. An African American woman, for instance, claimed that before World War II blacks traveling to a new city went to Chinatown for lodging because "the Chinese would always let you stay anyplace where other people would not accept you." In mixed-ethnic neighborhoods around the country African Americans sometimes learned European or Asian languages to communicate with their neighbors, and reformers in Los Angeles noted that even non-Mexicans living near the railroad stations learned some Spanish in order to participate in neighborhood life.[87] It is also likely that economic considerations at least occasionally trumped ethnic solidarity. In West Fresno, "a sociological melting pot of the most diverse sort," one observer noted that Japanese businesses secured "much of the Mexican and Filipino trade, even though a number of businesses run by [Mexicans and Filipinos] blare out Mexican and Spanish music day and night to attract trade."[88]

Historians have established that immigrant home owners often took families and friends from their own ethnic group into their homes, especially during periods of economic depression, and Los Angeles was no exception.[89] In integrated areas, however, a dearth of ethnic kin may have combined with other factors to encourage mixed households. A study of Japanese Angelenos found a Japanese family sharing a flat with an Italian family, a Korean and Japanese family sharing an apartment, and nine instances of Japanese and African Americans sharing homes. Keong Lee recalled that his family shared a frame house in the market district with an African American family in the late 1920s and that the two clans "got along well."[90] More common if not typical were separate structures on the same lot rented out to residents of different backgrounds, such as the African American landowners on Savannah Street in Boyle Heights who in 1939 rented out adjacent dwellings to four African American, four Asian, and two Mexican tenants. Other observers reported similar examples in the early twentieth century.[91] In general, it appears that such living situations generated little tension or conflict. A Mr. Joyce, a black grocery store owner and landlord on Thirty-sixth Street, recalled that some blacks objected when he rented two of his dwellings to Japanese. But the complaints quickly died down, and Joyce claimed that his black neighbors soon accepted the Japanese newcomers and that other local Japanese people began to patronize his store.[92]

These sorts of living situations were not typical in Los Angeles, nor can we assume that the majority of central Angelenos willingly reached out across ethnic and racial lines. Some of the same observers and scholars who reported instances of interaction also cited tendencies toward social segregation and isolation.[93] But ethnoracial isolation and distrust existed alongside alternative currents of interaction and friendship, creating a complex matrix of social relations in the central neighborhoods. It was in this landscape that many non-Anglo Angelenos grew up, a landscape that generated no small measure of anxiety for Anglos increasingly uncomfortable with central Los Angeles's rapid growth.

CHAPTER 2

Building the White Spot of America

The Corporate Reconstruction of Ethnoracial Los Angeles

WHITE SPOTS AND *PUNTOS NEGROS*

Harry Chandler liked to call his adopted city the "white spot of America." The bombastic publisher of the *Los Angeles Times,* a newspaper whose popularity waxed with Los Angeles's economic fortunes, was referring most directly to what he perceived as intense local economic development unfettered by labor unrest. The phrase also alluded to a belief, widespread among Chandler's circle, in the aesthetic, political, and moral purity of the city. Los Angeles, he insinuated, possessed none of the blight, decay, civic corruption, or criminal activity that plagued other urban areas.[1] But for others the term came to assume a third meaning as well, one likely connected to the tradition of attributing crime and political radicalism to "foreign" elements. The white spot was seen by some Angelenos as a racially pure space, a city built by white Americans for white Americans. During the 1920s, for instance, a group of Anglos attempting to block Japanese from moving into their neighborhood adopted the slogan "Keep the White Spot White." In 1927 the Spanish-language paper *La Opinión* accused Anglos of slurring the Mexican settlement in Belvedere's Maravilla Park as "el punto negro," the black spot, of the city.[2]

In retrospect, it is difficult for historians to see, even by squinting, any of the white spots envisioned here. The open shop remained in force throughout Chandler's tenure, due in no small part to a concerted campaign of intimidation by the police department. But the infamous 1910 bombing of the *Times* building by radical unionists dispelled any doubt that labor disturbances occured in Los Angeles. The vision of civic purity was even more fantastical: from 1900 to 1940 the municipal government generated a steady stream of scandals and corruption cases comparable to those in other American cities.[3] Finally, Chandler's career at the *Times* coincided with the very period when new arrivals from Asia, Mexico, Europe, and the southern and eastern United States were substantially broadening the city's ethnic and racial diversity. By almost any standard, the white spot of America existed only in someone's imagination.

Yet for all its obvious inaccuracies, the "white spot" idea evoked a broader transformation in the early-twentieth-century economic and social fabric of the United States. Los Angeles, emerging as a major metropolis in sync with this sea change, perhaps epitomized this fundamental reconstruction of American social relations. The key lay not in the "white" but in the "spot," for to identify a white spot in America meant that there were other spots that were not white. Often ignoring the polyglot nature of the central neighborhoods' ethnic communities, residents invested in Los Angeles as a white spot envisioned immigrant and nonwhite populations as distinct, bounded ethnic communities that could either be isolated from white populations or incorporated, one ethnic group at a time via Americanization programs, into the broader urban community. Though this ambitious social project failed on the terms of its architects, it ultimately exerted a profound influence on the ways that central neighborhood residents reconciled their ethnic background with the cultural diversity of their surroundings.

CORPORATE LIBERALISM AND URBAN DEVELOPMENT

To understand the significance of the white spot concept, one must place it in the context of a broader transformation that Martin J. Sklar has termed the "corporate reconstruction of American capitalism." For Sklar, the early twentieth century witnessed the sanctioning of large-scale corporate capitalism over the competitive capitalism of independent producers that had characterized a former republican ideology. This ratification entailed more than mere market regulation. It also meant endorsing a new political structure in which "independence," the sine qua non of republicanism, gave way to a corporate liberal concept of interest group politics. Before this transformation, the independent (and by extension, white) male producer was the building block of republican society. Wage earners, because they depended on employers, were thought to lack the political independence necessary for republican

citizenship. The rise of big business in the last half of the nineteenth century, however, ensured that most Americans, of any race, would remain
employees for life. Corporate liberalism resolved this dilemma by trans-
lating the stigma of dependence, or bias, into the virtue of interest. In
other words, advocates of corporate liberalism began to see American
society not as a collection of disinterested citizens or independent producers but as a collection of groups and corporations with specific interests. This paradigm shift allowed for the unprecedented collection of
power in the hands of a few, but it also permitted the mobilization of
different political groups whose agendas had not been sanctioned under
republican principles.[4]

The impact of this change for race and ethnic relations was simultaneously monumental and unclear. Before corporate liberalism, non-
Anglos had often been marginalized or excluded as inferior or dependent members of the republican community.[5] But because corporate
liberalism rendered independence irrelevant, these individuals could
organize, at least in theory, along ethnoracial lines.[6] Yet corporate liberalism was not inherently emancipatory. The grouping of individuals,
by political affiliation, class, race, ethnicity, and so on, could also allow
for their segregation and marginalization, for corporate liberalists did
not necessarily note the unequal relations of power between different
groups. Thus neither the "separate but equal" fiction of Jim Crow laws
in the South nor the residential segregation of Anglos and non-Anglos
was inconsistent with corporate liberal principles.[7]

The ramifications of this reconstruction extended throughout the
social landscape of Los Angeles. Modern industrial capitalism, epitomized in the railroad tracks paralleling the river, encouraged or even
required large numbers of working-class, immigrant, and African American Angelenos. But many Anglos viewed these populations and the
neighborhoods in which they lived as an increasingly vexing problem.
The white spot of America needed them, yet their presence undermined
the principle on which Los Angeles, as envisioned by Anglo boosters,
supposedly thrived.

This dilemma, less obvious in the workplace, appeared more pressing
in the sphere of residential and social relations. Throughout the early
twentieth century Anglos generally managed to partition, by virtue of
their economic dominance, ethnic communities into "appropriate"
careers. Though a 1926 National Urban League study of African Americans in local industry identified numerous instances of racial intermin-
gling on the shop floor, the data overall painted a picture of a city work-

force segregated by race and ethnicity. Even plants with mixed work-forces often parsed out assignments in ways that limited interaction. African Americans thus were concentrated in low-paying, unskilled labor, and remained largely isolated not only from whites but from Mexicans and Asians as well.[8] These findings support other studies of "ethnic economies" in working-class Los Angeles. Excluded from many types of work, central city Angelenos tended to funnel into those careers sanctioned by Anglos. Mainstream labor unions furthered this trend by excluding or segregating nonwhites and sometimes even European immigrants. Employment opportunities compartmentalized by race and ethnicity not only limited economic opportunities for central city Angelenos, they also allowed employers to play groups off each other. Thus when Mexican laborers struck the Pacific Electric Railway in 1903, the company found African American and Japanese workers willing to cross the picket line.[9] Not all workplaces were homogeneous, but Anglo dominance ensured limited interaction among workers of different backgrounds and, correspondingly, a limited threat to Anglos' higher economic status.

Maintaining this segregation became more difficult, however, in other kinds of social relations. Disease, vice, crime, and political radicalism were not as easily contained. For some Anglos, the mixed ethnic residential districts thus presented a pernicious threat to the city's social health. Beginning in earnest by the early twentieth century, these individuals embarked on a series of efforts to resolve the problem. These efforts were not uniform and reflected a diversity of opinion within Anglo Los Angeles that frequently erupted into open conflict. Some, for example, embraced an assimilationist point of view, believing that non-Anglo populations and their neighborhoods could, through careful intervention, come to approximate Anglo communities. Others veered toward a more segregationist stance, hoping to isolate these populations, both physically and socially, from their Anglo counterparts. But a common theme prevailed among the various strategies. Each involved an attempt to identify, classify, contain, remake, and, in some cases, remove the areas inhabited by immigrants and African Americans. Each presupposed and endorsed a spatial scheme of the city whereby different groups of residents inhabited different districts. A number of strategies actively sought to rebuild these districts in ways that removed their populations, while others represented a sincere if paternalistic desire to ameliorate the living conditions of existing populations. But even the most liberal strategies forecast an eventual "whitening" of the districts under scrutiny—

either by the assimilation of residents into Anglo cultural mores or by the physical replacement of residents with Anglo, or perhaps European, settlers. Much like efforts by wealthy Brazilians to whiten or "civilize" Rio de Janeiro and São Paolo during the same period, these corporate liberal approaches sought to maintain Anglo dominance over a rapidly changing environment.[10] The vision of a corporatized urban geography invoked in the City Beautiful movement, housing commissions, and zoning plans seemed to provide a strategy for reconciling Anglo dominance with America's industrial future. These programs had a profound impact on residents of the central neighborhoods, though not necessarily in the ways their architects intended.

SOURCES OF ANXIETY

What would the white spot look like? According to regular references in the *Times,* a "city of homes." "Homes" were detached, single-family dwellings, surrounded by open space in an environment that supported the cultivation of gardens. Residents in the city of homes formed the backbone of the "good community," a collection of families with established middle-class, Christian values. The aesthetic attractiveness, bucolic setting, and thorough cleanliness of their residences represented and contributed to the social and moral purity of the good community. Such qualities would ensure the continued economic success of the region by attracting other migrants and tourists longing for such an environment. The city of homes was simultaneously beautiful, ethical, prosperous, and, by implication, white.[11]

Given this vision, Los Angeles's spectacular and largely unregulated growth beginning in the late 1880s induced ambivalent responses from many middle-class and elite Anglos. While celebrating the city's emergence as a major commercial and industrial center, they feared that success would threaten the city of homes. Many of those most invested in the concept had, after all, abandoned eastern cities that were suffering from what they saw as excessive industrialization, overcrowding, crime, and ethnoracial diversity. Unchecked growth in Los Angeles threatened to recapitulate aspects of eastern urbanization that might spill over into the good communities. Such stains on the white spot of America would undermine its very existence.[12]

Middle-class and elite Anglos located much of their anxiety about unchecked growth in the districts populated by the poor, immigrants, and African Americans. The problem was fundamentally one of containment. Various policies and social forces worked to segregate these latter populations from the members of the good community. In the eyes of some Anglo Angelenos, however, the boundaries were insufficiently sealed. The environments of these districts, they reasoned, cultivated epidemics of disease, vice, crime, blight, pollution, and radicalism that could spread into the city at any time. Whether Anglos cared about the welfare of central neighborhood residents or not, many of them wondered whether the Pandora's box of urban ills would respect the barriers of higher rents, racial covenants, and vigilant policemen.[13]

Social reformers could find reasons to worry about almost any area populated by Asians, Mexicans, African Americans, or European immigrants. Conflating the environmental problems of the central neighborhoods with the cultural practices of their residents, reformers identified virtually every working-class neighborhood near downtown and the Los Angeles River as a target for rehabilitation.[14] Central neighborhoods, riddled with poorly designed lodging houses, crude shacks, dilapidated house courts, and rickety single dwellings, did suffer from lower health and safety standards compared to Anglo areas. House-court residents often used the courtyard, the location of the water supply, as kitchen space, laundry, garden, animal pen, and washing area. Few central city Angelenos owned their own homes, and landowners frequently maximized profits and the density of housing by building on rear lots. Often several families had to congregate in a single dwelling to afford the rent. The drive to maximize rents through concentrated development led to poor sanitation and ventilation in central city dwellings and little open space for social gatherings and children's activities.[15] Racial covenants and exclusionary practices in other parts of the city inflated central city rents, and Angelenos priced out of the market sometimes slept in coal yards or cow stables. Skyrocketing growth rates in the early twentieth century exacerbated the general housing shortage, especially after World War I. A social worker in Sonoratown reported in 1920 that even those families with income sufficient for the area often could not locate housing. She claimed to have found "six families in one block living in sheds in back yards because they are unable to find rents."[16]

The proximity of many working-class neighborhoods to industrial development and the Los Angeles River did little to ameliorate living conditions. Neighborhoods located in the floodplain endured the stench of raw sewage, the devastation of periodic floods, and the hazards of industrial machinery, moving trains, and air pollution. In 1924 Nora Sterry derided the neighborhood's environment:

> In recent years . . . the surrounding packing houses have so polluted the
> air with poisonous gasses as to stunt all vegetation and to make the
> process of breathing at times disagreeable because of the disgusting odors.
> There is always a heavy cloud of smoke hanging low over the district from
> the ever-passing trains, making the air full of soot and all things grimy to
> the touch.[17]

Not surprisingly, conditions like these contributed to high rates of disease among central city residents. Tuberculosis, for example, remained a persistent problem on both sides of the river. In 1924 a plague outbreak east of Main Street prompted health officials to quarantine the area and underscored Anglo fears about the potential threat of central neighborhood conditions to the rest of the city.[18]

Health concerns represented only one facet of more general fears of urban contamination. Boosters and real estate speculators believed that unsightly slums would repel tourists and wealthier migrants, drive down property values, and tarnish the utopian white spot image of Los Angeles. Some employers worried that the vice industries associated with the central neighborhoods would sap the productivity of the workforce. Many more fretted that radical organizations would take advantage of conditions in central Los Angeles to recruit Angeleno workers.[19] The districts' diversity itself was a problem. Ethnoracial mixing, some Anglos feared, undermined the ethnic institutions that could bridge immigrant and Anglo communities. Surveyors, having engaged in futile efforts to draw physical boundaries between ethnic communities, wrote off large parts of the central neighborhoods as a "congested foreign lump, unassimilable," an incubator for a mongrelized, illegitimate culture. In such areas, one report concluded, "we show immigrants Americanization at its very worst."[20]

For many Anglos, this last threat encapsulated all the other dangers posed by the central districts. As they saw it, neutralizing this and other threats entailed more than urban reconstruction. It also meant remaking central neighborhood residents. It was this last goal, as much as any, that drove the reformers who sought to change the built environment of the central districts.

BUILDING A BETTER HOME: HOUSING COMMISSIONS AND GOVERNMENT INTERVENTION

The City Beautiful movement was the first to address the concerns about urbanization in Los Angeles. A national phenomenon that achieved currency around the turn of the century, the City Beautiful movement assembled a collection of loosely affiliated planners, reformers, and politicians who sought to inoculate American cities against the virus of runaway growth. They venerated park designers such as Frederick Law Olmsted, and looked to exposition fairgrounds, such the Chicago World's Fair of 1893 and San Francisco's Pan-Pacific Exposition of 1915, as idealized models for urban landscapes.[21] In Los Angeles, City Beautiful advocates specifically contrasted their vision of urban utopia with the crowded streets and congested populations of eastern cities. For Rev. Dana Bartlett, the city's most fervent local champion of City Beautiful principles, the squalid, cramped, and dangerous tenements of eastern cities represented the nadir of urban development. Rather, acceptable neighborhoods consisted of detached single-family dwellings with open yards or gardens. Such a residential layout, as Bartlett argued in his 1907 treatise, *The Better City,* soothed the moral character of urban residents by emphasizing family unity and home ownership. Bartlett cheerfully asserted that Los Angeles was well on its way to achieving this ideal:

> There are no slums in Los Angeles in the sense that a slum is a vicious con-
> gested district. . . . For the most part the poor live in single cottages, with
> dividing fences and flowers in the front yard, and oftentimes with vegeta-
> bles in the backyard. Even in the most congested districts children can be
> kept within the yard, if so desired. Homes for the people; pure hearts for
> pure hearth stones, are the mottoes for a city like this.[22]

Bartlett's paean to pastoral cottages notwithstanding, other Angelenos recognized that housing quality in the central city left much to be desired. A number of philanthropists tackled the problem after 1900. Marshall Stimson, a prominent lawyer and local Progressive, for example, helped to subsidize a tract in Chavez Ravine in 1913 that relocated, by his count, two hundred fifty Mexican families from the river's flood-plain. Stimson reveled in the community's apparent gratitude. He claimed that when he made trips to the settlement, with bags of candy for the children, residents hailed him joyously with cries of "el patrón!" Stimson also made available a tract of affordable land in Watts for African American home buyers. In 1927 the estate of William Mead, a local real estate developer and state assemblyman, left $1 million to pro-vide housing for "worthy wage earners" at cost.[23]

Few of those familiar with the central neighborhoods, however, believed that private philanthropy was a systematic solution. A 1905 visit to Los Angeles by Jacob Riis, whose depictions of eastern urban poverty had shocked a generation of middle-class and elite Anglos, dispelled Bartlett's fantasy of a slum-free city. After a short tour Riis concluded that "slum conditions in New York might be more extensive but . . . certainly were no worse than those in Los Angeles." Outraged boosters, whose advertising campaigns turned on the city's favorable comparison with other urban areas, clamored for a municipal agency to address the problem.[24] Within a year the city council established the Los Angeles Housing Commission (LAHC) to oversee the enforcement of housing standards and the removal of unacceptable dwellings. In 1908 it appointed Bartlett to the board of directors. To ensure that the LAHC did not hamper construction in more prosperous parts of the city, the city council gave it jurisdiction only over house courts. The new commission thus received a mandate to conduct a protean form of urban renewal. The directors hired two male and two female inspectors (on the argument that immigrants were more likely to welcome women into their homes) to investigate and condemn, if necessary, house courts in the central districts.[25]

The LAHC represented only a tentative first step by local government to bring central Los Angeles into something approximating the city of homes. Despite condemning and demolishing dozens of house courts in its first six years, LAHC members maintained that the court, properly constructed, provided a superior environment for the moral character of its residents compared to tenements, shacks, and lean-tos.[26] As often as not, the LAHC conceived its task as a cultural mission. Ridding the "foreign" population of "ancient customs and superstitions," they believed, would eliminate both the house court "problem" and the cultural deficiencies associated with it. For many inspectors, heeding Bartlett's call to "ruralize the city" meant educating residents in domestic skills and encouraging the cultivation of gardens as much as enforcing building codes or punishing slumlords.[27] Commission literature made few references to economic inequality, poverty, or discrimination in the housing market. When LAHC officials attempting to relocate an evicted Mexican family in 1911 encountered resistance from prospective white neighbors, they simply looked for another site.[28] This accommodationist stance extended to the vagaries of the real estate market and progressive industrialization. One Sonoratown landlord complained to the *Times* that the LAHC had told his tenants to withhold rent payments until "unreasonable" improvements had been made on the house court, advice the landlord deemed "superfluous to this class of tenants."[29] But in general the LAHC adopted a nonconfrontational strategy. After an owner evicted a group of Mexican tenants from their shacks so that he could build a warehouse on the site, for example, the LAHC arranged to have the shacks transported by wagon to other lots with comparable monthly rents. A report commented brightly that most of the residents had secured jobs at a nearby brickyard for $1.50 to $2.50 a day, a minimum subsistence wage for the period.[30]

On the heels of the LAHC followed a state movement born of international developments and a swelling immigrant population. In 1912 the impending completion of the Panama Canal convinced newly elected Governor Hiram Johnson and a prominent Sacramento businessman named Simon Lubin that the new shipping route would redirect large numbers of Jewish, Italian, Russian, and other European migrants from the eastern seaboard to the West Coast. Johnson and Lubin feared that without preemptive measures San Francisco, Los Angeles, and other parts of the state would breed the same crowded slum conditions afflicting eastern cities. In 1913, to forestall these developments and ensure the proper "distribution" of immigrants to California, Johnson established the California Commission of Immigration and Housing (CCIH), with Lubin at its head.[31]

The CCIH epitomized a corporate liberal policy toward immigrant populations and immigrant neighborhoods. Echoing Riis, who compared social reform to healing the sick, it adopted a comprehensive plan to rehabilitate and "Americanize" both the physical spaces of central neighborhoods and the social practices of its residents.[32] The CCIH sought to instill in the immigrant population of California a respect for authority, the industrial order, and American laws by convincing them that they could become part of that system. This campaign involved two paternalistic strategies: prescriptions for proper behavior and efforts to improve the material lives of immigrants.

At its inception the CCIH reflected the preoccupation of many Anglo Californians with European immigrants. Much of Lubin's early correspondence as director consisted of inquiries to European consulates regarding immigration patterns to America and to eastern officials regarding their strategies for dealing with European immigrants. One of the CCIH's first acts in Los Angeles was to establish an "immigration station" at San Pedro Harbor to handle the swarms of Europeans they expected would arrive via the canal.[33] Some boosters anticipated a European influx with relish, provided they could, in the words of one member of the chamber of commerce, "render foreign immigration advantageous to our communities" by selectively enticing the "better class" of migrant to their city.[34] Along these lines, several organizations conducted extensive advertising campaigns in European nations directed at wealthier migrants. A group called the American Colonization League, for example, "propose[d] to bring the most desirable people, as to money, health, intelligence, and skill for agriculture, factory, and business vocations to the State of California." "What we need and what we want is a desirable class of citizens," they said.[35] Not all Anglos were as sanguine about the prospect of migrants streaming through the Panama Canal, even if they were white. The exodus of Europeans from the devastation of World War I, for example, prompted speculation about hordes of working-class war refugees descending on the state. To counter these concerns, the CCIH launched a nationwide publicity drive in 1915 stating that there was no work in California for "outsiders" and that relief efforts would only serve the destitute already in the state.[36] The commission did not exhibit the same concerns, at least initially, about the Mexican border. It assumed that the vast majority of new immigrants would come from Europe.

The CCIH also turned its gaze to immigrant communities already living in central Los Angeles. Paralleling other Americanization organizations in operation during this period, the CCIH in 1915 initiated a series of social programs to teach English, domestic skills, and "the fundamental principles of the American system of government and the rights and duties of citizenship." As numerous historians have pointed out, classes in English, "American" cooking, housecleaning, and sewing and other programs directed at women, the presumed keepers of the domestic sphere, strove to eradicate many elements of immigrants' cultures and to eliminated any dissent that might erupt into civil disobedience.[37] "Those who use violence or advocate the use of violence to secure changes in business, living conditions or government, violate the laws which a majority of the people have made," read a CCIH pamphlet handed out to newcomers. " . . . If you wish to help in the government of the United States, study carefully its customs, obey its laws, respect its officers, become naturalized, and do your best to help the rest of its people to work constantly for its improvement." One commission member acknowledged confidentially, "We are not making Americans, primarily; we are making people who hold the views or the institutions that we believe to be the best."[38]

The CCIH's more direct attempts to improve the material conditions of immigrants included protecting newcomers from fraud and abuse, which involved the establishment of "complaint departments" throughout the state.[39] Initially, the CCIH envisioned the complaint department as a way to collect statistics, not distribute "individual justice." As one official admonished the Los Angeles office, "The complaint department [is] not an agency for relief but a piece of machinery to standardize the immigrant problem."[40] By 1919, however, the Los Angeles office, under the supervision of a veteran social worker, Adele Calhoun, had evolved into a welfare and interpretive bureau for immigrants with a variety of work-related and neighborhood disputes. Programs such as these operated under the assumption that they would not only alleviate social problems but also serve as booster advertising for the "right" kind of immigrant. Under a "rain follows the plow" argument, commission members contended that "good conditions attract good immigrants . . . while fraud and degradation attract criminals and freeloaders hoping for an easy existence."[41]

The most curious project espoused by the CCIH involved the proposed dispersal of urban immigrants into outlying agricultural regions. Reasoning that immigrants from rural areas were unprepared for industrial labor, it suggested bestowing on them, via settlement programs and loans, the republican dream of independence as landowning farmers.[42] The CCIH acknowledged that immigrants did not necessarily share this dream and its prospect of social isolation. "The immigrant today is not a pioneer," Lubin admitted in 1915, "but goes where there are others of his kind."[43] Yet investigating this proposal led the commission to take a closer look at the economic limits affecting immigrants to urban areas such as Los Angeles. A 1919 CCIH report blamed speculative landholding and racial discrimination for raising central city rents above their natural market value.[44] Employing uncharacteristically strong antibusiness rhetoric, the report commented on the disparity between the immigrants that state business interests hoped to recruit and those who actually came: "California wants immigrants—with money enough, earned somewhere else, to buy our land [from] us. . . . California wants customers. . . . What we really need is human beings, to work, to transform the latent resources of the state to active wealth, for their own good and ours." The report even endorsed Henry George's controversial "single tax" on property—the transfer of all government taxes to property owners—as a means of breaking up large landholdings.[45]

As provocative as it was, "large landholdings" remained the exception to the commission's more centrist political stance. Like the LAHC, the CCIH preferred to recruit business interests to their cause rather than challenge them. Often it tried to sell reforms as measures that would benefit the economy as a whole. It argued that rents from "good" housing exceeded those from slums and that better housing would encourage a more content and productive workforce. It cited, for example, the benefits accrued to a railroad company that had established education programs and improved the housing of the workers. The superintendent of the yard, they claimed, noted a "steadier" labor supply and "better care of the track."[46]

Like the LAHC, the CCIH sometimes sparred with real estate interests or government officials over its efforts to improve housing conditions—and often backed down in the face of strong opposition. Despite achieving several legislative victories over housing standards, the commission had a negligible impact on the central neighborhoods.[47] Chief CCIH housing investigator Leo Mott had to admit to colleagues that the commission had little enforcement power and often had to resort to exerting "pressure on the owner of the building from various state and city agencies so that he [would] decide to demolish the structure."[48] Even an optimist like Dana Bartlett acknowledged by 1920 that enforcing housing ordinances was impossible given the drastic housing shortage. Even in a normal market, he concluded, the housing commission could make little headway with landlords who thought "anything was good enough for the Mexicans."[49]

Over time, these setbacks began to wear on CCIH officials, and by the 1920s commission publications were betraying their frustration with the organization's lack of progress. However, disappointment was directed not at funding and enforcement problems but at those immigrants who seemed least willing to follow the commission's Americanization precepts. Even after their assumption that European immigrants would become predominant in the central city proved incorrect, CCIH workers continued to demonstrate a preference for white immigrants and a belief in their superior ability to "Americanize." As the population of Asian and Mexican Californians grew, the CCIH redeployed hierarchical systems of race, placing ethnic European immigrants and, occasionally, Japanese closest to the "American" ideal and Mexicans, Chinese, and African Americans at the bottom. For example, the CCIH noticed that Europeans were more successful securing work, especially higher-paying manual labor, in central Los Angeles industries. The success of Japanese merchants also drew praise, and a few observers placed them above Europeans in ability to perform skilled labor. Mexicans, Chinese, and African Americans, in contrast, tended to hold more menial positions. CCIH members and other reformers noticed a similar discrepancy between the dwellings and housekeeping skills of European and non-European residents. Mexicans and Chinese appeared most likely in the eyes of the CCIH to foment diseases and other ills that might spread beyond the central neighborhoods. But when the 1916 influenza epidemic hit the city's Russian community harder than the Mexican community, the commission turned its own logic on its head. Mexican homes, a report stated, "are so full of chinks that the fresh air fans through undisturbed, and the predilection for sunning themselves—they crawl out just as instinctively as the lizard—provided heaven sent medicine." In contrast, the relatively snug, well-built houses of Russian immigrants helped to spread the disease among them.[50]

Perhaps because of their cultural superiority, some commission publications implied, Europeans seemed more receptive to Americanization programs and housing reforms than other ethnic groups.[51] Mexicans and Chinese, in contrast, were noticeably uninterested. While Mexicans increasingly used the commission's complaint department through the twenties, the directors noted that the bulk of these complaints related to labor contracts and "family disputes."[52] Substantive transformation of living conditions, the directors implied, had not become a priority for Mexican Angelenos. One social worker asked the rhetorical question "Do Mexicans desire better homes?" and replied "Yes and no." Their concept of improvement, she elaborated, was primarily aesthetic; they remained ignorant of the social and moral benefits of cleaner and more open dwellings. Likewise, Anglo observers singled out Chinese Angelenos for their reluctance to accept CCIH overtures. Despite their earlier recognition of the impact of economic forces in the central neighborhoods, commission members stubbornly clung to ethnic stereotypes as an explanation for living conditions in the "immigrant" districts.[53] By the mid-1920s proponents of Americanization were losing faith in the ability of their programs to assimilate nonwhite immigrants and their neighborhoods into the city's social landscape.

The decline of Americanization programs and the CCIH underscored the growing pessimism regarding immigrants of color. New immigration restrictions culminating in the National Origins Act of 1924 sharply curtailed the possibility of a European "invasion." Fading European immigration rates stood in sharp contrast to the rising number of immigrants from Mexico. Even some liberal Anglos concluded that Mexicans were "unassimilable." In 1926 CCIH directors, who previously had refused to make recommendations regarding national immigration policy, called for an end to unrestricted Mexican immigration.[54]

For their part, by the 1920s, immigrants were losing patience with Americanization proponents. *La Opinión,* for instance, pointed to the discrepancy between the promises of reformers and the continued discrimination against Mexican Angelenos. An angry letter from a Mexican woman only seemed to confirm the CCIH's implicit admission that its strategy to remake immigrants into "good Americans" had failed. Mexicans, the woman maintained, "will always be considered foreigners by you people. We don't mind it. What do we care to be U.S. citizens?" A Chinese resident likewise cited the contradictory messages embodied in Americanization: "Americans do not want us to live close to them even though they want us to become Americans. The Americans do not practice what they preach." Carol Aronovoci, a CCIH official and respected immigration scholar, echoed this sentiment. In a scathing indictment of Americanization programs, she castigated reformers for failing to live by their own principles of tolerance and for further alienating immigrants from the "American community."[55] Such self-criticism, however, remained rare among reformers, who generally preferred to blame immigrants' failure to assimilate on the immigrants themselves.

A resurgence of political conservatism in the 1920s curtailed many CCIH Americanization programs. In line with national trends, California voters swung sharply to the right, electing a wave of politicians who hacked away at government spending, regulations, and other impediments to the free movement of capital. A nationwide revival of Anglo nativism, embodied in the Palmer raids of 1919, the notorious Sacco and Venzetti trial, and the renaissance of the Ku Klux Klan—all unleashed a virulent strain of xenophobia. Friend Richardson, California's new Republican governor in 1923, dismissed the CCIH as a waste of taxpayers' money, as a threat to the state's real estate interests, and as government aid to subversives. Soon after taking office, he fired Lubin and commission member Paul Scharrenberg, a caustic American Federation of Labor (AFL) leader from San Francisco who had clashed repeatedly with established politicians.[56] The resignation of prominent Los Angeles social reformer Mary Gibson a short time before eliminated the commission's most dedicated founders. Though progressive politicians rebounded somewhat in the mid-1920s, the commission entered a period of dormancy from which it did not revive until 1938, when newly elected Governor Culbert Olson appointed the dynamic Carey McWilliams as its director.

The waning influence of reformers, California's new conservative political climate, and the indifference of central city residents marked the failure of Americanizationists to achieve their goals. For many Anglos, the persistence of poor sanitation practices, vice operations, labor turmoil, non-English speakers, and foreign nationals meant that central city residents had refused to live up to their end of the bargain. This apparent lack of cooperation justified at least the partial abandonment of "social reform" policies and suggested alternative strategies to remake the central city that did not depend on the cooperation of its residents. Zoning ordinances and city planning projects of the 1910s and 1920s indicated that industrial development might eliminate through displacement what reform could not.

(WHITE) SPOT ZONING: ERASING CENTRAL NEIGHBORHOODS

In Los Angeles, the conservative, pro-business political trends of the 1920s accompanied an economic boom that dwarfed prewar growth rates and doubled the native-white population. While the *Times* trumpeted Los Angeles as the "Chicago of the West" city planning organizations mobilized to protect white residential communities and ensure that current development would not compromise future industrial expansion.[57] The City Planning Commission (CPC) and other government bodies focused on building an efficient transportation infrastructure for the Los Angeles basin and zoning open lands for industrial development and adjacent residential districts that would supply the labor for the businesses that located there. Like their associates in the housing commissions, CPC members demonstrated an implicit belief that whites would comprise the bulk of this workforce, especially if affordable, high-quality housing were available. Not surprisingly, their vision closely resembled the type of urban growth the CCIH had recommended in a 1915 publication:

> The city should have a plan for streets, parks, playgrounds, and buildings. If possible the plan should provide for detached or family houses, with lawn and room for rear garden. A plan for additions to a city or for making changes in housing in manufacturing centers should provide space for homes of working people. Laboring people should live near their work. A ride of a laboring man to and from his work of more than fifteen or twenty minutes consumes time and money that he cannot afford. If he is in a good location, the nearer he is to work, the more time he will have for home work and leisure, and in addition save money in transportation.[58]

To varying degrees, new residential development in the central city during the 1910s and 1920s reflected these principles, but immigrants and

African Americans could not necessarily settle in these neighborhoods. Whether through prohibitive rents or racial covenants, many neighborhoods in Los Angeles remained effectively "zoned" white.[59]

In 1908 Los Angeles had become the first city in the country to establish laws regulating the kinds of development that could occur in specific areas. This legislation, refined in subsequent years, succeeded in protecting many middle-class and elite neighborhoods and helped to check industrialization that could have aggravated environmental conditions and traffic congestion. It also, however, channeled industrial growth into central city areas inhabited by immigrants and African Americans. By keeping the interests of business owners and more prosperous Angelenos at the forefront of their policies, zoning officials placed a burden on working-class residents of the city who found themselves living in neighborhoods earmarked for industry. Whether or not they intended to drive out these populations, zoning officials and their supporters demonstrated little inclination to include central city residents in their socioeconomic equation.[60]

In the early 1910s the city council had established an "industrial district" stretching east of Main Street to the Los Angeles River, encompassing Chinatown and the immigrant neighborhoods to the south.[61] A 1915 amendment extended the district east of the river into parts of Boyle Heights and included two subregions just west of the industrial district where certain less "offensive" industries were permitted (see map 2). Property owners could appeal for exemptions from the ordinances, and throughout the 1910s and 1920s the city council approved hundreds of "spot-zoning" changes. Tenants had no say in the designation of their neighborhoods.[62] Additional zoning changes in 1921 continued to channel light and heavy industry into the central districts. The new ordinances squeezed the central city housing supply by encouraging nonresidential development and speculative selling and discouraging upkeep on existing dwellings.[63]

As the decade progressed local business interests began to look to areas east of the river as the region's new frontier for industrial expansion. In the early 1920s the city council and the Los Angeles Regional Planning Commission established the broad region east of Main Street all the way to Whittier as the "East Side Industrial District." Subsequently, members of the chamber of commerce, the Merchants and Manufacturing Association, and the Los Angeles Realty Board (LARB) formed the East Side Organization (ESO) to supervise development. Perhaps alluding to the immigrant communities in Boyle Heights, Belvedere,

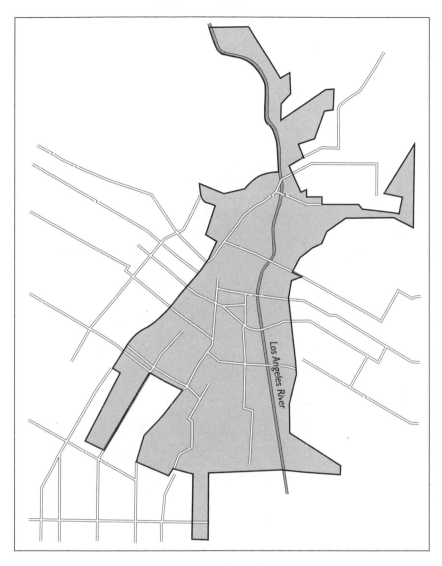

MAP 2. Central Los Angeles Areas Zoned for Industry, 1915

and City Terrace, the *Times* instructed the ESO to "clean house" in preparation for construction in what was "the least developed section of the city." Chandler's paper predicted that by the end of the decade the region would become "a combination of Gary, Pittsburgh, and Chicago, minus the smoke and soot."[64] Although the ESO's plans called for industry to dominate the district, it also recognized the need for residential neighborhoods to house its workforce. Existing neighborhoods in East Boyle Heights, City Terrace, and Belvedere, however, would apparently not suffice. Accordingly, in 1922 the ESO sponsored the creation of Belvedere Gardens, a five-thousand-home tract east of Belvedere around the "new industrial city" emerging along Whittier Boulevard, a tract designed by implication for Anglo home buyers.[65]

In effect, these zoning ordinances constituted an indirect effort by government and business to erase the "immigrant" neighborhoods they considered undesirable. These interests believed that the rapid economic growth of Los Angeles would entice enough native-white migrants to eclipse the immigrant and nonwhite population. The chamber of commerce's 1924 "Industrial Report," a tool for attracting new businesses to Los Angeles, revealed the vision if not the reality that many Anglo Angelenos held of their city's working classes and the neighborhoods in which they resided:

> There is an abundant supply of labor, both male and female, and it is 90% American born, and practically entirely English speaking. A percentage of the available labor is of Spanish decent—a class which has for generations been engaged in the making of various clothes and fancy work, and hence is very nimble and deft with the fingers. Open shop methods prevail, there is no labor strife, and strikes are unknown. Each man has his little bungalow, with flowers blooming the year round; his family is healthier; and hence he takes more interest in the job that enables him to live here. There is no such thing as a tenement in Southern California.[66]

Such propaganda, while not a statement of fact, revealed both the continuing identification of the city of homes with a happy, productive, workforce and the expectation that Los Angeles's economic development would serve to whiten the city. By Europeanizing the city's Mexican population as "Spanish," the report implied that these residents did not compromise the white spot of America. The continued influx of Mexican and other immigrants made little impact on the chamber's position, and the 1929 report omitted the statement concerning the "Spanish" element altogether.[67]

FROM THE WHITE SPOT TO THE "MEXICAN PROBLEM"

The development directed into central Los Angeles by the ordinances did not immediately eliminate existing residential neighborhoods. Even during the economic boom of the 1920s land remained plentiful enough that wholesale displacement was unnecessary. Over time, however, industrialization accelerated the migration of residents out of certain central city neighborhoods, especially those near the Los Angeles River and downtown. Throughout the early decades of the twentieth century this migration encouraged the expansion of immigrant districts into new parts of the city, particularly east of the river and along the South Central corridor. The extension of streetcar lines into these areas made commuting a viable option for their residents and helped to alleviate at least one drawback to displacement from the industrial district. Mixed development in central neighborhoods allowed many others to continue to walk to work. In addition, the escalating price of industrial land near downtown made the cheaper rents and land prices in outlying districts such as Watts and Belvedere more attractive to working-class Angelenos.[68]

Zoning may have facilitated industrial expansion, but it did little to alleviate Anglo concerns about "foreign" populations. By the mid-1920s this anxiety manifested itself most clearly in what some Angelenos termed the "Mexican Problem." What many Anglos had dismissed just a few decades before as a population on the verge of extinction had rebounded in dramatic fashion, more than tripling between 1920 and 1930. Belvedere provided an excellent example of this rebirth. The area's cheap housing (in part a result of its location outside city limits and, therefore, city regulations) had attracted a mix of European immigrants, native-born whites, and Mexicans since the turn of the century. Though developers had hoped to attract native-born whites to the area, Mexicans constituted the majority of the area's residents by the 1930s.[69]

Growing Anglo anxiety about California's Mexican population prompted Governor C. C. Young to authorize a government study in the late 1920s. The extensive report pointedly refrained from making policy recommendations, though it stated: "Mexicans are likely to become the most preponderant foreign-born peoples in California as compared with immigrants from European countries."[70] Ironically, Governor Young's report indicated what few Anglo Californians seemed willing to acknowledge—the dependence of the state's industrial growth on Mexican labor. The report noted that Mexicans constituted a significant, though undetermined, percentage of industrial, construction, agricultural, and railroad workers in Southern California. In addition, many employers had favorable impressions of Mexican workers, and some even preferred them to laborers of other backgrounds.[71] In short, the benefits of Mexican immigration far outweighed any burden they placed on the state.

Young's report, however, failed to quell a growing conviction among Anglos that the United States should take steps to restrict the immigration of "unassimilable" workers from south of the border. The 1927 call for restrictions on Mexican immigration by the CCIH demonstrated growing opposition, even among many liberals, to an open border.[72] By this time Mexican Angelenos were registering complaints with the CCIH against police officers who had harassed them on the street. Ygnacio Garcia, who lived just east of Chinatown, alleged in January 1928 that the LAPD was conducting sweeps of the plaza and arresting Mexicans "by the hundreds" for vagrancy. Many of those arrested found themselves "put to work by the city" until they made enough money to pay the fee at an employment agency. The emotional strain placed on family members who did not know what had happened to their relatives, Garcia concluded, was devastating the Mexican community. A short time later Andres Carranza, a Watts resident, filed a complaint charging that officers had arrested him while he was looking for work and threatened to deport him if he failed to find a job.[73] Apparently, police were not the only public officials pressuring Mexican Angelenos. A social worker reported that the County Charities Department tried to deport a Lincoln Park resident named Luisa Naranja as a "public charge" after illness forced her to stay at the hospital for an extended period.[74] These reports may not have embodied a systematic effort to harass Mexicans, but they did prefigure the notorious repatriation campaigns of the 1930s. Confronting mammoth increases in welfare and charity expenses during the depression, city and state officials decided that deporting ethnic Mexicans, irrespective of citizenship status, south of the border would help to alleviate the relief burden. Historians estimate that at least several hundred thousand ethnic Mexicans returned to Mexico during the decade, some voluntarily, some after enduring various forms of pressure from police and other officials.[75] The campaign against Mexican Angelenos indicated that many Anglos no longer saw the city of homes as a means to assimilate nonwhites but rather a space to be protected for Anglos and acceptable kinds of Europeans.

To the extent that they acknowledged the presence of nonwhites on the Los Angeles landscape, many Anglos preferred to contain, sanitize, and commercialize it for their own consumption. In the 1920s and 1930s, for instance, several prominent Anglos embarked on a campaign to preserve a caricatured cultural remnant of Mexican and Chinese Angelenos. The first project, supervised by a local socialite, Christine Sterling, spruced up the plaza as a historic district and established neighboring Olvera Street as a tourist bazaar. This commercial development preserved not Mexican culture but a largely mythical "Spanish Fantasy Past" for the benefit of Anglo tourists. Olvera Street represented Mexican culture as an idealized, Europeanized relic of the past rather than as a viable and growing element of Los Angeles's cultural landscape. Contemporary Mexican culture, like the contemporary Mexican population, seemed to have no role in the city's mainstream cultural life.[76]

The second project, also overseen by Sterling, was the construction of a caricatured version of Chinatown as a sanitized environment for Anglo tourists to observe another "dying" community.[77] By the 1910s, perhaps because of its aging and less active population, Chinatown no longer elicited purely negative reactions from white Angelenos. Although its reputation for illicit activity remained, middle-class tourists felt secure enough to enter the area. In 1913, however, a group of Anglo business interests purchased much of the property in Chinatown from the Sepulveda family under mysterious circumstances after a Chandler-led business consortium decided to lobby for a new railroad station there.[78] Though he had no qualms about razing the neighborhood, Chandler printed a number of elegiac articles in the *Times* "advertising" for a new Chinatown site.[79] By the 1930s demolition for the station had expelled most residents, and Sterling was supervising the construction of "China City," another tourist destination along the lines of Olvera Street, a few blocks north and west of the old Chinatown. Like Olvera Street, China City functioned primarily as a commercial and recreational area for Anglos. Apparently, Chinese Angelenos did not gravitate to the new development. They preferred New Chinatown, a less sentimentalized commercial area built near China City by the Chinese businessman Peter Soo Hoo. Few of them grieved when a fire burned Sterling's creation to the ground scarcely a year after its completion.[80] While less publicized than Olvera Street, China City represented the same romanticization of a mythic ethnic past untouched by the contradictions of contemporary ethnic culture.

THE UNCERTAIN IMPACT OF CORPORATE LIBERALISM

Around the time Sterling was assembling plans for Olvera Street, a group of University of Chicago sociologists was gathering material for what would become the seminal work of the academic version of corporate liberal urbanism. In *The City: Suggestions for Investigation of Human Behavior in the Urban Environment,* published in 1925, these scholars postulated an "ecological" model in which urban space became differentiated into various economic and social uses through a process of benign competition. In their view, this process of segregation and inequality produced a natural, symbiotic relationship between the various districts, as each region made its own special contribution to the life force of the city. The Chicago school model of urban development coexisted with a model of immigrant assimilation in which newcomers to the United States, through the immigrant neighborhoods in which they settled, would gradually become absorbed into the social and economic life of American cities. Each group would contribute, in its unique and bounded way, to the vitality of the metropolitan environment, yet the barriers between these groups, a natural and necessary expression of the ecological urban process, would mitigate disruptive events or processes that might compromise the growth of the city.[81]

Zoning ordinances, Olvera Street, and China City represented one attempt to impose this kind of corporate liberal vision on the landscape of modern Los Angeles. By attempting to subdivide these cultures into bounded, nonthreatening, urban spaces, many Anglo Angelenos sought to reconcile the persistence of nonwhite populations in the city with their vision of the white spot of America. Like the Americanization programs and housing commissions that classified "problem" districts and attempted to neutralize those characteristics that threatened the rest of the city, these projects displayed a superficial concern for immigrant populations that masked an underlying sense of dread. Many of these programs betrayed a hope that through controlled measures Los Angeles could grow out of its *puntos negros* and replace them with white spots more conducive to building the city of homes. Even as the surging numbers of Mexican, Asian, and African American newcomers counteracted those assumptions, many Anglos continued to cling to the ideal of a city simultaneously modern, prosperous, and homogeneous.

In one sense, the goal of these strategies, programs, and policies to whiten the central city, whether by demography or cultural identity, indisputably failed. The Belvedere Gardens project, for example, fell short as a bastion of Anglo homesteading in East Los Angeles. Housing commission surveys still referred to the neighborhood as an "American" district in 1925, but reports filed shortly thereafter indicated that Mexicans had begun to settle within its limits.[82] Nor did the central districts come to resemble the city of homes advocated by social reformers. Poverty, pollution, substandard housing, crime, and radicalism persisted in these areas through the depression, and many residents, especially those of color, exhibited scant desire to conform to the precepts of Americanization. Even the persistent diversity of central city neighborhoods seemed to counteract corporate liberal, Chicago school models of assimilation based on cohesive ethnic neighborhoods.

Yet despite their formal ineffectiveness, these efforts to reconstruct the central city had other consequences for the residents they targeted, not only in their relations with Anglo Angelenos, but with each other. To a certain extent, paternalistic discrimination in Americanization programs and housing commissions affected all residents of the central neighborhoods equally. Economic pressures generated by zoning further destabilized neighborhood settlement patterns and thereby enhanced the integration of working-class neighborhoods. In other words, the economic and social forces working on central Los Angeles fostered inter-ethnoracial contact and provided a context for coalition building. At the same time, however, the uneven categorization of white and nonwhite immigrants and the identification of immigrant groups with distinct neighborhoods (even if it did not reflect their actual geographic dispersion in the city) implicitly encouraged central city residents to organize, socially, politically, or otherwise, along ethnoracial lines.

Campaigns for the corporate reconstruction of Los Angeles thus encouraged central city residents to look to the ethnic community as the primary force for social organization and political expression. Yet within the integrated spaces of urban regions like central Los Angeles there also emerged competing visions that altered and even challenged the corporate reconstruction of modern America. Rather than accept the existence of white spots and dark spots, these visions sought to build a different kind of Los Angeles not bounded by racial or ethnic barriers. Often stillborn, half-formed, or incompletely expressed, they offered up another reconstruction of social relations and political structure, a reconstruction that in its specific time and location was every bit as American as the traditions of ethnic activism supported today.

CHAPTER 3

The Church of All Nations and the Quest for "Indigenous Immigrant Communities"

A SOURCE OF "INDIGENOUS COMMUNITY ACTION"

Sometime in 1927 G. Bromley Oxnam, the founder and first pastor of the Church of All Nations, granted an interview to a student researching the institution. In many ways Oxnam's creation resembled the dozens of other missions, settlement homes, and Americanization programs that dotted the central neighborhoods of early-twentieth-century Los Angeles. Oxnam had founded All Nations under the auspices of the Methodist church in 1918 one block south of Skid Row in a church building abandoned, along with the increasingly diverse and proletarian district, by its middle-class Anglo parishioners. His timing had not been auspicious. World War I had unleashed a torrent of nativism and Red-baiting in U.S. cities that proved toxic to many reform institutions. By 1918 many of them languished in a political climate no longer amenable to social welfare programs for "foreigners." But Oxnam's creation flourished in the late 1910s and the 1920s, drawing thousands of participants to its welfare programs and Sunday services. Even as right-wing groups sought to discredit the young minister, city officials and prominent Anglos trumpeted his church's impact on what they considered one of the most squalid districts of the city. In less than nine years, under less than ideal circumstances, Oxnam had built one of the most popular institutional expressions of Progressive-era reform principles the city had seen.

FIGURE 1. The Church of All Nations, founded in 1918. Security Pacific Collection/Los Angeles Public Library.

But as the interview progressed, Oxnam appeared less than ecstatic about his creation. Foreshadowing his imminent resignation, he admitted that the church had failed to achieve the goals he set for it. He expressed this failure in primarily spiritual terms; neighborhood residents took advantage of All Nations but not in all the ways he hoped. They did not "adopt" it as their own institution, and the church never developed into a source of "indigenous community action."[1] This phrase highlighted a philosophical difference between All Nations and many of its counterparts that attempted to impose the political identities and cultural trappings of American identity on the residents of central Los Angeles. Oxnam, to the contrary, envisioned a bottom-up process whereby the church would enable its parishioners to formulate their own political and spiritual "impulse." By gathering Angelenos of forty-two ethnoracial backgrounds (according to parish surveys) under the umbrella of a relaxed, nonsectarian spirituality, All Nations sought to bridge the cultural distances separating central city residents and promised a kinder, gentler incorporation into the American political and social system compared to other institutions of its type.

The failure to achieve this goal demonstrated certain contradictions between the church's principles and practice that may have escaped its architect. But it also demonstrated larger contradictions in Anglo efforts to reconcile the mounting diversity of the country's population with their principles of American patriotism and identity. Historians have castigated early-twentieth-century missions, Americanization programs, and settlement homes for whitewashing the cultural practices and identities of immigrant populations. But even an institution that downplayed religious conversion and blind patriotism in favor of cultural autonomy and political empowerment could not generate the kind of institutional allegiance that reformers demanded of immigrants. Oxnam's experience at All Nations exemplified the failure of one concept of urban corporate reconstruction, a failure that shed light on the difficulty of unifying culturally disparate populations and on the complicated ways in which central Angelenos internalized, challenged, and subverted calls for spiritual and social unity.

THE EDUCATION OF G. BROMLEY OXNAM

Oxnam was born in 1891 on a street a few blocks west of the future site of All Nations, in a neighborhood his biographer described as a "comfortable" Anglo middle-class enclave. Oxnam's father, a Cornish immigrant and mining engineer, put his skills to good use in his adopted country. The prosperous family owned one of the first cars in the city and enjoyed the privileges of a telephone and maids. Yet Bromley's parents were also devout Methodists, his mother a member of the Women's Christian Temperance Union, and young Bromley inherited the belief that building a Christian community entailed social as well as spiritual work. Oxnam was still a child when the family relocated to the wealthier Westlake district, but as he grew older he visited downtown often enough to observe the momentous transformation in the neighborhood of his birth.[2]

The transformation exemplified the post-1900 evolution of districts along the railroad routes, when the encroachment of commercial and manufacturing businesses began to erode the area's residential quality. As wealthier residents evacuated the district, immigrants and laborers

FIGURE 2. G. Bromley Oxnam, founder of the Church of All Nations, 1944, almost two decades after he resigned as pastor. Herald Examiner Collection/ Los Angeles Public Library.

who worked in nearby shops, yards, and factories replaced them. While industrialization reduced the living spaces and public streets of the neighborhood, the area's population continued to increase as newly arrived African American and immigrant families doubled or tripled up in dwellings designed for single families. Many landlords, anticipating an imminent sale to industrial concerns, neglected repairs. The neighborhood thus rapidly acquired a run-down and dilapidated appearance, despite the best efforts of some residents to maintain their homes and streets.

The exodus of middle-class Anglos translated into a marked decline in the fortunes of mainline Protestant churches. Surveying the situation, a local pastor, D. F. McCarty, concluded that a traditional church no longer had a role in the neighborhood. "I feel that one of the greatest difficulties in the field is the floating population of the community," he noted. "The people are here only for a short time and then are gone, sometimes nobody knows where. Our converts go and members go and hence the difficulty to build a strong church. The church should be made a mission, and have the full moral and financial backing of Los Angeles Methodism." In 1906 McCarty's church, just a few blocks from the future All Nations site, closed its doors. The Methodist leadership decided to rent the building to the Salvation Army and moved its Deaconess Home and Hospital out of the area, claiming that excessive industrial pollution had made the neighborhood unsuitable.[3]

If certain Methodists recoiled from the district's environmental decline, impoverishment, and ethnoracial diversification, however, others saw a social and spiritual challenge. They pointed to the proliferation of saloons and pool halls filled with drunks who accosted churchgoers on their way to services.[4] They pointed to soaring rates of juvenile delinquency, exacerbated by working parents who left their children unattended, and to gangs of "pavement boys" who ran wild in the streets and railroad yards, vandalizing property and stealing from residents and businesses. And they pointed to the heterogeneity of the new residential population itself as a prime obstacle to uplift and Americanization. Amid such disorder, they concluded, there was no practicable way to incorporate residents into the larger social structure of the city, and the area's inhabitants therefore developed socially predatory inclinations. "This congested foreign lump, unassimilable, was left largely to its own devices," noted one observer. "The East side 'Dead End' was a crime incubator."[5] In the eyes of these reformers, such conditions sapped the spiritual life of central city residents. Immigrants, one noted, "find themselves in a new and strange environment, utterly different from that which even their ancestors ever knew. Often they are surrounded by other foreigners as strange to them as they are to this new land of choice. . . . In these conditions they are apt to break away from their old religious life and lapse into a sort of modern paganism."[6] For a number of Anglo reformers, restoring the moral and social fabric of such populations represented the ultimate challenge to Christianity in modern America.

Oxnam became one of these reformers. As a young student at the University of Southern California in the early 1910s, he internalized the plight of the neighborhood of his birth. Searching for a solution to what he saw as a vicious cycle of spiritual and social decline, Oxnam turned to the renowned USC sociologist Emory Bogardus, who would later serve on All Nations' board of directors. A protégé of Chicago school cofounder Robert Park, Bogardus was one of Los Angeles's most eminent urban sociologists. Oxnam found Bogardus's interest in Americanization as a bridge between the "social distances" that divided ethnoracial groups particularly intriguing. He too came to believe that the incorporation of immigrants into the United States citizenry required not just an education in political allegiance but also a broad-based effort to alleviate the "un-American conditions" that perpetuated economic and social inequality.[7] Like other Bogardus students, Oxnam used class assignments as a springboard for his interest in social reform. Sometime around 1913 he secured an unpaid post with the City Housing Commission conducting surveys of central neighborhoods. "I spent the afternoon at the housecourts," he wrote in his diary after one excursion. "Truly the problem almost overwhelms me. . . . This is the beginning of something bigger, I feel."[8]

Oxnam's religious convictions required more than just a secular response; the spirituality of the central neighborhoods was also at stake. The young college student found inspiration in the Social Gospel movement sweeping the country. Epitomized in the writings of Walter Rauschenbusch, a second-generation German immigrant who grew up in New York's Hell's Kitchen, the Social Gospel gathered thousands of adherents in the early twentieth century, especially among the young Protestant ministers of Oxnam's generation. Its proponents reoriented the focus of salvation away from the afterlife and toward an earthly vision of Christian community that empowered marginalized populations. For more leftist reformers like Oxnam, this vision extended beyond spirituality into the economic and social spheres. Improving the material lives of the working classes, adherents predicted, would encourage greater commitment to God and church and leave more time for religious activities. This two-part process of social and spiritual development, the Social Gospel preached, would stave off the divisive and atomizing effects of modern urban life and provide a social and religious foundation for community building. The ultimate vision of the Social Gospel, at least as expressed through Rauschenbusch, involved an evolution toward both socialism and a kind of socialized Christianity (or, perhaps, Christianesque spirituality), what Oxnam would later call "fellowship developing the spirit."[9]

Rauschenbusch's followers believed that modern urban environments had dissipated the Christian impulse. Movies and other commercial attractions, for instance, drew the populace away from religious observance. Some mainline Protestants ruefully noted that lively "radical" churches and cults in Los Angeles were poaching members from their congregations. The obvious example was the Pentecostal Apostolic Faith Mission on Azusa Street near Little Tokyo that had been founded in 1906 by William Seymour, an African American preacher. The "Azusa Street revival" drew thousands of worshipers of all races to its feverishly boisterous services and spawned the modern Pentecostal movement. Condemned by many Anglo Christians for its antistructuralism, "emotionalism," mixed congregation, and preponderance of nonwhites in leadership positions, the mission at first seemed to symbolize an inter-ethnoracial alternative to established churches. Racial tensions soon crippled Seymour's church and split the congregation into segregated institutions, but the enormous popularity of its antiauthoritarian message troubled many traditional Christians.[10] Yet even more Angelenos seemed to have abandoned church altogether, defections some attributed to a decline in institutional Christianity's spiritual resonance. Churches had become "mere social clubs," they concluded, ill adapted to the challenges of an industrial, multiethnic urban environment. Even for secular reformers this trend had ominous implications, portending a breakdown of social relations that might kindle immorality and violence.[11]

The Social Gospel's antidote to these ills entailed a more comprehensive idea of ministry that addressed material as well as spiritual welfare. The strategy raised an obvious political question. If ministries were to advocate on behalf of the poor, what limits should be placed on their radicalism? Some prominent Angelenos followed the moderate reformism

of Social Gospel champion William Dwight Porter Bliss, who advocated
the gradual dissemination of the "brotherhood of man" message into
mixed ethnic working districts by enlightened, presumably Anglo, proponents.[12] But Oxnam joined some Social Gospel adherents in flirting
with more radical politics. While at USC he studied Marxist theory and
attended speeches by noted leftists such as Emma Goldman. Though not
completely taken in by these arguments, he internalized a respect for the
rights of the working classes that would color his subsequent career.[13]
Speaking at a YWCA banquet in 1912, the precocious twenty-one-year-
old took his audience on an imaginary stroll down crowded Skid Row
(where "at each corner a great group is gathered fighting over some social
or religious problem") to the corner of Fifth and Maple, where "a great
building stands, right where a saloon is today."

> [It shall be] an inspiration center for constructive social action, and so far
> as is practicable a participatory factor in that action. It shall bring the
> Gospel of Jesus to bear upon both the social and individual living, believ-
> ing in a thorough-going evangelistic policy, seeking the redemption of the
> community from community sin, and the individual from individual sin.
> It shall so align itself with all groups struggling for justice so as to infuse
> the spirit of Jesus into all the activities.

The center would not merely provide charity for the destitute; it would
"bring the force of the community to bear upon these problems and to
remedy them."[14]

In spring of that year Oxnam took his first step toward this goal
when he started a boys' club in the central city. Reasoning that boys had
a proclivity for "hero worship," Oxnam organized the group around
the King Arthur legend. He dubbed the club members "knights" and
established a "code" for proper behavior that included "doing right,"
being kind to women, keeping themselves and their homes clean, telling
the truth, and "loving each other." Initiates pledged: "We will not fight
except for what is right, and when we do we will never give up."[15]
Though the group apparently dissolved after Oxnam left Los Angeles
for divinity school at Boston University, the Order of the Knights provided a blueprint for the children's clubs that reemerged after 1916,
when the now-ordained minister returned and resumed his campaign
for a central city social center. Many of Oxnam's superiors remained
skeptical of the plan, especially his downplaying of formal Christianity.
"All he knows is social service," an anonymous Oxnam detractor had

commented sometime earlier. "He does not believe in evangelism."[16] But the superintendent of the Methodist church in Los Angeles, Dr. E. P. Ryland, liked the idea, and in fall 1918 Oxnam received the go-ahead to found All Nations.[17]

THE SPIRITUAL AND SECULAR
GENEALOGY OF ALL NATIONS

The Church of All Nations appeared at the tail end of a generation of social and religious reform in central Los Angeles. The roots of these ambitious projects began after the Anglo conquest of California eliminated the religious monopoly that the Catholic church had enjoyed under Spanish and Mexican rule. Subsequent decades witnessed a notable if uneasy degree of interfaith cooperation among Catholics, Protestants, and Jews. Not until the 1870s, when Anglo migration gave Protestants numerical and political hegemony in the city, did different denominations become more active in evangelizing to the central neighborhood populations. Many Anglos viewed Christian evangelism as the vanguard of the Americanization movement. By the early twentieth century missionaries were almost tripping over each other in their quest for converts. One social worker claimed that a group of Chinese girls attended four separate meetings over several days, with each social worker for the respective denomination presenting the girls as under their supervision.[18] Middle-class Anglo women were crucial to this movement, adopting important roles in the spiritual and secular reform institutions that spread through central Los Angeles in the 1900s and 1910s. These activities constituted one of the few acceptable avenues of endeavor for middle-class Anglo women outside the home, and many flocked to the work as a way to escape (or broaden) the confines of the domestic sphere. Although gender mores usually dictated that men direct such activities, these women formed the shock troops of Christians proselytizing in the central districts.[19]

Among the various institutions that appeared in the central neighborhoods by the early twentieth century formal religious missions predominated. The 1922 City Directory listed more than forty missions under different Protestant denominations, many of them clustered around Skid Row and other downtown areas frequented by the most destitute. Though sometimes providing social services, they tended to focus on spiritual salvation. The Fifth Street Mission that operated on Skid Row from 1908 until All Nations absorbed it in 1921, for example, required indigents seeking a meal or shelter to sit through extensive sermons.[20] The hard-sell evangelism of these institutions alienated many poor Angelenos who entered them only as a last resort. One recovering alcoholic bitterly recounted "sitting in some lousy mission hall for two hours listening to some crackpot preacher reciting high sounding phrases from the Bible, that [one] may receive a cup of coffee that falls from the hand of sympathy."[21]

The sheer heterogeneity of Skid Row made parsing beneficiaries by ethnic background impossible, but in other parts of the central neighborhoods missions preferred to target a specific ethnic group rather than a mixed-ethnic community. Methodists, for example, operated both a Japanese church and a Korean mission. By the 1920s five missions sponsored by different denominations were ministering to Chinese, and numerous others focused on Mexican Angelenos.[22] The Union Church in Little Tokyo was notably successful in drawing Japanese to its services and Americanization programs. It also actively opposed other religious institutions in the area and campaigned in 1920 against the establishment of a Buddhist temple near its site, which the church worried would go after its members.[23] The YWCA established two branches for nonwhites, one for African Americans on Twelfth Street and one for Japanese in Boyle Heights. In both cases local leaders gradually took over day-to-day operations. The Boyle Heights branch established a number of clubs and even purchased a residence house on East Third Street with money they raised themselves.[24]

Some of these missions managed to recruit a congregation and to groom a few "ethnic leaders" from the central city. But many residents rejected their overtures, and converts often faced derision from their ethnic communities. Kango Kunitsugo, for example, claimed that his parents joined a Christian church because its Anglo evangelists "were the first to treat Issei well," despite vociferous objections from their Japanese friends.[25] Sometimes conflicts between Christian evangelists and Catholics or Buddhists flared over the allegiance of Mexican and Asian Angelenos. Immigrants, especially from Asia, occasionally resolved the tension by improvising syncretic religious services or by maintaining memberships in two different institutions. In more than a few cases conversions created divisions within families. Japanese Angeleno Roy Taketa, for instance, converted to Protestantism but had a brother and sister who belonged to two different Buddhist temples, another brother who was Catholic, and a Buddhist wife.[26] In other words, early-twentieth-century Los Angeles missions achieved at most a series of small victories and never truly redefined the eclectic and variable religious orientations of central neighborhood residents.

The broadening evangelization efforts of middle-class Protestant urban residents during this period overlapped with more secular settlement house and Americanization programs. Like missionaries, supporters of these institutions varied widely in political orientation, ranging from ultraconservative groups like the Better America Federation to mainstream government officials on housing commissions or the Board of Education to moderate socialists like Oxnam. In essence, however, they all hoped to incorporate immigrants, if only in a subordinate role, into a larger "American society" anchored in Anglo-American traditions, language, living standards, patriotism, and, sometimes, Christian beliefs. Settlement houses, epitomized by Chicago's Hull House, placed reformers (generally female) as full-time residents in immigrant neighborhoods to give them comprehensive knowledge of the social conditions affecting specific districts.[27] Advocates hoped that daily contact between middle and upper classes and workers would alleviate class antagonisms and ameliorate living conditions. Even when they forsook religious affiliation, settlement houses shared the same goal of resolving the social divisions generated by modern urban life.[28]

By 1910 various groups had established settlement houses in Los Angeles, including the Catholic Brownson House, the Jewish Stinson Memorial Industrial School, the Episcopalian Neighborhood House, the Methodist Toberman Settlement, the Bethlehem Institute, and two secular institutions, the Municipal Settlement House and the College Settlement.[29] All offered an array of services for immigrants, including health care, interpreting, children's programs, English classes, and, if evangelical, religious instruction.[30] One of the most innovative was the YWCA's International Institute in Boyle Heights, which hired five full-time and seven part-time secretaries who spoke a total of twenty-two languages. In addition to running English classes, the secretaries ran a clearinghouse that informed immigrants of employment opportunities, naturalization procedures, educational requirements for children, health care opportunities, and ethnic organizations in their neighborhoods.[31]

Settlements provided immigrants and workers with important services that were often unavailable from ethnic community organizations, but their role in central Los Angeles rarely extended beyond the level of service provider. Many reformers who held concurrent positions on government commissions, progressive clubs, or national religious groups mobilized on behalf of immigrants or the working poor, but they rarely included the people they were serving as participants in their endeavors.[32] Furthermore, with the exceptions of the Brownson House, the Stinson School, and the International Institute, most of the employees and volunteers at these institutions were middle-class and Anglo. On occasion, central city residents went on to organize work or volunteer in settlement houses. The International Institute, for example, helped a Russian immigrant, Mildred Sandler, who spoke no English when she came to Los Angeles in 1922, graduate from high school and enroll at USC. In her first year at college she organized fifty women to expand the English program at the YWCA.[33] Sandler proved the exception to the rule, however; most immigrants left the settlements once they had received the assistance they needed.

The troubled history of All Nations' most immediate ideological predecessor, the Bethlehem Institute, suggested that many settlements suffered from precarious finances and anemic local support. Inaugurated in the early 1890s by the energetic Dana Bartlett (for whom the All Nations Foundation named its library), the institute established a number of operations, including a settlement house, a church, a hotel, an employment center, and a bathhouse, in various areas near downtown.[34] By the 1900s Bartlett's activities earned him a sterling reputation among reform-minded Angelenos as an expert in urban social and spiritual reform among immigrant populations. In positing the "city as a social settlement," Bartlett went beyond most mainstream reformers and Americanizationists to question the fundamental supremacy of Anglo culture in the United States, noting "there has never been a time when there was a white man's country with common ideals and a universal language. The nation, its people, and its language have always been in the making, for new elements have been constantly introduced."[35] Central Angelenos of all backgrounds flocked to the institute's social programs, but Bethlehem Church languished in the apathy of neighboring residents to Protestant worship. One observer claimed that the institute was "powerfully equipped to . . . win the foreigners through their many auxiliary agencies. But as for Bethlehem Church, it has been surrendered to the foreigners, all the English-speaking families having gone from the neighborhood." These "foreigners" proved less than taken with the church, and by the 1910s attendance at services had fallen off considerably.[36]

In 1913 a strange sequence of events precipitated the downfall of Bethlehem. That year the city council passed legislation forming the Municipal Charities Commission (MCC) to combat a rash of fraudulent charity scandals. The new law required that all organizations soliciting in Los Angeles receive authorization from the MCC. In fall, after Bethlehem applied for the permit, a disgruntled former employee protested the application. In what the *Los Angeles Times* called a "Bombshell for Dana Bartlett," the employee leveled a series of sensational allegations against the institute, including poor management, health violations, and graft. He accused the bathhouse operators of flushing the pools only once a week, despite the fact that the city donated 85 percent of the water. He contended that "boys of all colors" shared the pool with "persons with running sores" and men suffering from venereal diseases, and girls swam "clad in wrappers which float up round their shoulders so that they are virtually nude" in the presence of male instructors. He also alleged that one of the men's hotels was renowned as a "drunkard's retreat" and that management declined to discipline inebriated lodgers. Furthermore, the employee charged that accounting practices in the institute were virtually nonexistent and hinted that Bartlett handled most of the incoming funds with little or no oversight. Most surprising, the MCC discovered that the Bethlehem directors had gradually sold off or leased the various components of the institute to private contractors, to the point where it "no longer engaged in charitable work of any substantive value." Apparently, most board members did not attend meetings and had not visited any of Bethlehem's operations in years. Bartlett could not produce many of the institute's financial records, and his weak explanation that Bethlehem's endeavors were "experimental" and not meant to be self-sustaining elicited little sympathy. The MCC rejected the application, and the city assumed control of the institute's remaining operations. Bethlehem vanished with little fanfare and almost no protest from the central city population.[37]

The downfall of the Bethlehem Institute set a troubling precedent for Oxnam and underscored the failure of most settlements to generate support from the central neighborhoods themselves. Dependent almost entirely on outside funding, many of these institutions saw their fortunes rise and fall with the vagaries of local politics. In the tense years between Bethlehem's demise and the end of World War I many reformers elected to scale back their efforts on behalf of immigrant populations. Under attack by red-baiters and nativists, many gave way to programs that muted campaigns for social justice or welfare and concentrated on indoctrinating newcomers into American patriotism. Across the country, social reform and immigrant aid efforts lost much of the dynamism and political commitment that had characterized them before World War I.[38]

It was in this hostile climate and suspect legacy that the Church of All Nations launched its operations in 1918. Oxnam's institution reflected the heritage of its predecessors, but in bucking the conservatism of the period, it also departed from them in several significant ways. At a time when the social gospel was in retreat, Oxnam continued to support unionist and socialist causes while simultaneously building All Nations into one of the largest and most ethnoracially diverse social centers in central Los Angeles. In the process he created an institution that more than any other Anglo-created settlement or mission provided not only desperately needed services to central city residents but also the potential for broad social mobilization.

Oxnam began his campaign with a grueling speaking schedule that sometimes averaged six appearances a week. During one exhausting month, he delivered fifteen lectures, ten sermons at various churches, and sixteen "addresses" to different groups. The immediate dividends from this work included a steady growth in church membership, which doubled from 43 to 90 in All Nations' first two years, and a Sunday service attendance that ranged from 75 to 150. Though it did not rival larger churches, the growing congregation helped Oxnam to placate the more skeptical Methodist leaders.[39] Oxnam tried other methods to lure neighborhood residents into All Nations. He set up boys' and girls' clubs for children of a variety of ages, and he stretched the church's limited facilities to accommodate a playground and a library. The young minister sponsored weekly lunches for women working in the neighborhood laundries, generally providing a speaker or musical performance at each gathering. All Nations also undertook more conventional charity programs, including Thanksgiving food donations to destitute households.[40]

The establishment of "movie nights" at All Nations constituted by far the most effective recruiting tactic in its early years. Like other middle-class Anglo reformers, Oxnam and his employees were troubled by the cultural impact of movies on urban audiences. The theaters dotting Main Street on the western edge of the parish and in various other nearby locations showcased lurid films and drew patrons of suspicious character and various ethnicities.[41] One All Nations–sponsored study of

fifteen "delinquent girls" found that most spent several hours a week at
the theaters viewing films that "appealed to basic instincts." To counter
what it saw as the corrosive social influence of movies and other commercial amusements, All Nations brought movies into the church,
where they could ensure a proper environment and films of acceptable
content for children. Oxnam used these screenings as a means to advertise the other activities of All Nations.[42]

In January 1920 Methodist leaders authorized funds for a movie pro-
jector for All Nations. The results were dramatic. Attendance at the
Sunday school, which preceded the film, more than doubled to 160.
Oxnam canceled the sparsely attended Sunday evening service in favor
of movies and bragged that the gatherings drew "Catholics, Jews, [and]
foreigners of all sorts." One attendee reported sitting next to Japanese
and Mexican families who were enjoying *Old Mexico* and *Big Trees of
California*. In contrast to commercial fare, All Nations ran "clean come-
dies, dramas with moral lessons, educational films, dramatizations of
the classics, news reels and patriotic films." Oxnam mused that if the
church had enough money for daily showings, "literally thousands of
children would be kept from the sinister influence of the streets, and the
high juvenile delinquency rate in this section largely abated." Oxnam
developed multimedia presentations to complement the movies, adding
theater group performances, comedy routines, collective singing, and
lectures to the evening schedule.[43]

All Nations soon outgrew its meager facilities, and in 1921 the
Methodist leadership sold the building and purchased two adjoining
structures (which a reporter described as a "trainman's boarding house"
and an "out-of-date gray double storied building in plain sight of the SP
[Southern Pacific] yards") and a small lot on Sixth and Gladys Streets.
Simultaneously, they consolidated All Nations Church, the Fifth Street
Mission, and the Deaconess Friendly House on Agatha Street into a single body, the All Nations Foundation, under Oxnam's direction.[44]
Methodists then embarked on a $300,000 campaign for the foundation
and for a new "Plaza Center" catering to Sonoratown residents. The
Plaza Center's architects dubbed it a "Tuskegee Institute" for training
"ministers, industrial leaders, and Christian citizens" to rescue the district from the "white slave den" it had become. The Plaza Center also
embraced a multiethnic congregation, albeit in an indirect manner.
Though claiming to target "Latin Americans," the center explicitly included Italians, Portuguese, French, Filipinos, and other residents of the
neighborhoods around north downtown as members of this "practically

homogeneous" ethnic group.[45] For All Nations, the greatest immediate
dividend of expansion was a new medical clinic, which by the mid-1920s
treated several thousand patients a year. Augmenting the paid staff with
USC student volunteers, the clinic provided a crucial service for poor
Angelenos who came from all over the central city, though doctors were
periodically cited for drinking on the job, using antiquated anesthetics,
and accepting kickbacks from an eyeglass company.[46]

BUILDING THE SPIRITUAL COMMUNITY

Oxnam's goal for the All Nations Foundation extended well beyond
social service. For him, such programs marked only the first step in the
construction of a "community conscience, sadly lacking now; a knowledge of community problems, and a keen sense of individual responsibility to God, country, city, home, and self." Oxnam collapsed the project of restoring religious morality to the urban populace with the project
of Americanizing immigrants. Echoing the Social Gospel, he bemoaned
the immigrant who "flings aside the restraints of the old world, but fails
to lay upon the moral restraints of the new. In a word, they accept the
freedom of America but fail many times to appropriate the morality
which makes freedom safe." Rejected both by the culture of their parents
and by prejudiced white Americans, Oxnam feared, the immigrant
would develop antisocial and even destructive tendencies.[47] The solution
lay in restoring a moral code that accounted for the spectrum of freedoms
and cultures immigrants encountered, yet remained grounded in fundamental values. "Americanization," Oxnam averred, "was not an arith-
metical problem with its answer in terms of percentage Americanism,
but . . . a Christian problem with its answer in terms of character." For
him, Americanization entailed the creation of a "common family" ideal
based on the "fatherhood of God" as much as the reorientation of everyday practices.[48]

Oxnam tried to mesh his spiritual vision with his political views.
Though he decried "conflict" in the country's economic structure, he
leaned toward a socialist solution rather than preservation of status quo
capitalism and corporate welfare. Though he advocated Americanization, he defined the term more by living standards and tolerance than by
Anglo cultural forms and blind patriotism. Though he preached Christianity, he defined the term more by moral commitments to cooperation
and self-respect than by the formal observance and liturgy. In this sense
Oxnam invoked a coalition of diverse groups rather than a cultural and

religious homogenization of the American workforce, a coalition committed to material equality as much as spiritual communion. Tracing the American promise of "equal rights" back to Jesus, Oxnam declared that all humans should have the right to "be well-born" (that is, to health care, especially for childbirth), the right to a home, the right to an education, the right to work, and, for children, the right to "play" or freedom from labor.[49] He even championed the nascent government in the Soviet Union, stocked the foundation's library with Marxist literature, and speculated in a series of lectures that the "Russian radical" would play an important role in attaining world peace.[50] Oxnam's political activism drew the attention of the federal government, which placed him under surveillance beginning in 1918. Five years later an alliance of conservative extremists thwarted Oxnam's campaign for a seat on the school board by portraying him as a Communist. By 1951 his four-hundred-page FBI file earned him an interview before the House Committee on Un-American Activities.[51]

As his relationship with the city's battered labor movement demonstrated, however, Oxnam also tried to draw radicalism into the fold of Christian morality. He saw unionization as a "religious advance" that would ensure social justice and equality as well as social stability. "The union is the greatest influence for Americanizing the foreigner, save only the public school," he asserted in one sermon. "It's an influence for law and order, and is a chief influence for international peace." Yet Oxnam cautioned labor activists not to forget the religious and moral aspects of their crusade and tempered pro-union rhetoric with what his biographer called "nonrevolutionary leanings." He therefore condemned violence and sabotage by strikers even as he blamed these acts on the recalcitrance of employers.[52]

Oxnam's balancing act approach to labor relations exhibited the limits of his radicalism. His successor, Robert McKibben, recalled, for example, that Oxnam challenged a group of Industrial Workers of the World (IWW) speakers who had set up shop near the church by undertaking his own speaking campaign across the street. According to McKibben, Oxnam undercut the Wobblies' destructive militancy by "proclaiming a Christian emphasis on the need for adequate jobs and adequate pay for a job well done. His competitors soon sought other locations." Oxnam did not like to associate with Wobblies, whom he dismissed as "fascists," but he came down more firmly on the side of labor during the contentious 1919 Pacific Electric Railroad strike.[53] In offering the unionists the use of the foundation's auditorium, Oxnam provided what at least one anonymous striker described as a valuable morale boost. When an Irish nationalist sparked ethnic animosities, Oxnam stepped up to the podium to restore order. "When he had finished there was neither race nor creed, 'border nor breed nor birth,' to divide us," the unionist concluded. "Out of the total ministry of that church there came a conviction to many of the strikers that they were really playing a part in a great program. They became aware of the fact that they had a part in bringing the Kingdom of God." While this narrative almost certainly overstated the sentiments of most unionists, they did, according to church reports, pack All Nations to capacity for a series of Oxnam sermons on the relationship between church and labor.[54]

Oxnam built on his work with the strikers to publicize the inauguration of the "Open Forum," which he hoped would become a "real force for Americanization in [the] community." The weekly meetings consisted of movies, community singing, and a one-hour address by a "leading authority."[55] The speaker at the first meeting, Upton Sinclair, promised both to "drive all reds from our midst" and to bring about "the establishment of a republic of industry, in which all the workers shall be free and equal citizens, in which they shall all have a free and equal voice in determining the conditions of their labor, in which their products shall belong to them all alike." Among the other lecturers were a Baptist clergyman, whose topic was "The Origin of the Social Idea," and a USC professor, who lectured on the "Japanese Question." Combined with Oxnam's own sermons, the Open Forum meetings became a principal means for the church to advocate the extension of religious principles into the political arena.[56]

Oxnam's spiritual commitment was manifested even more strongly in his pleas for interethnic and international cooperation. The family of God, he believed, did not respect national borders, and the expanding economy around the world only increased the interdependence of nations. The young pastor frequently lectured on social conditions in Europe, Asia, and other continents, supplementing his sermons with accounts of his frequent overseas trips. "The idea that America can live to herself alone is utterly false," he admonished one audience. "This world is a unit, and it is a unit economically. . . . Some day we are going to see that the conditions that affect Asia, that affect Africa and South America sooner or later affect America."[57] For Oxnam, this global interconnectedness extended to local ethnic communities. Outside All Nations, even non-ethnic-specific social reform programs often isolated single ethnoracial groups under the argument that it was more practical and that immigrants preferred to remain with their own kind.[58] But Oxnam deplored this strategy and its implication that Americanization entailed a one-way process of acculturation from "foreigners" to "Americans." Believing that Americanization programs should seek a "contributory fusion and not annihilating assimilation," Oxnam saw no reason to homogenize classrooms of students from integrated neighborhoods. The cultural basis of "Americanism" should center on contact with and appreciation of different ethnicities rather than on Anglo-American mores. True Americans, Oxnam maintained, required a sense of cultural difference and exchange.[59]

To this end, publicity for All Nations consistently emphasized the multiethnic character of its programs. Pamphlets advertising an "All Nations Kindergarten," for example, depicted African American, Mexican, Asian, and white children mixing freely and gently poking fun at cultural differences.

> Ben Potter (Negro), entered excitedly one day,—"I brung a new girl." Out in the hall we found Cheyona Nakai (Japanese). . . . Salbador Zuniga (Spanish), says "Jes" for "Yes" and when bidding us "Goot bye," seriously but with quaint courtesy, shakes hands. His friend, Naomi Iwasaki (Japanese), now does likewise. . . . Ben Jordan (Mexican) is a manly little chap and quite bright, even though he does call a camel a canamil. . . . Humberto Morales (Mexican) could speak no English when he came to us six months ago. Now he is often our interpreter to mothers in the Day Nursery. But when called a Mexican one day before company, he emphatically denies the charge,—"I'm American!" And so we all are, no matter where our parents may have been born.[60]

Oxnam was careful to specify that citizenship promised equal access to American social space, not simply access to a segregated space of "ethnic" Americans. Unlike most other Anglo social reformers, for instance, Oxnam supported intermarriage as a natural and desirable part of Americanization. He rejected concepts of racial purity and celebrated the cultural amalgamation of mixed families. After presiding over the mixed marriage of two parish members, for example, he mused in his diary, "And so the races fuse, and the American of tomorrow emerges."[61]

Oxnam balanced his utopian melting pot with a respect for traditional ethnic and cultural practices. Nowhere was this more evident than in his approach to religious evangelism. Its pastor may have been Methodist, but All Nations devoted scant effort to convert parish residents and instead encouraged Jews, Catholics, and Buddhists who came through its doors to attend religious services at their own institutions.[62] Oxnam emancipated his concept of Christianity from the institutional operations of the church, maintaining that one did not have to practice Protestantism to be a "Christian." Thus he countered sectarians by maintaining that those outside one's faith may simply be "serving god in another way." At one point Oxnam considered instituting Catholic services at All Nations, though he abandoned the idea for fear that more orthodox Catholic priests might undermine the "family" ideal. He did, however, actively court non-Protestants as allies in the church's welfare projects and studied the teachings of other faiths.[63] He was also willing to speak at non-Christian religious gatherings. At a 1922 Buddhist festival, for example, he fervently argued for an interfaith campaign against racism and the "commodification of labor."[64] At its best, Oxnam's ecumenical concept of Christian community accepted parish residents into a "family of God" without demanding the erasure of cultural or religious differences.

Oxnam's faith in cooperation and community, however, overlooked other divisions in the parish and the church that worked against his family of God. In part the problem resided in Oxnam himself. His socialist and internationalist leanings were tempered by a fondness for professional expertise and rationalism, as he remained suspicious of what he viewed as the frenzied appeals of extremists on both the left and the right. "Give me a good conservative by conviction any day," he wrote in his diary, "but deliver me from the emotional reactionary." In the same entry he declared an almost technocratic faith in the principles of expertise: "I am coming more and more to see that our rebuilding is to be done by those technically qualified, pushed on perhaps by the urge from below and a growing social consciousness."[65] Oxnam did not belabor these points in his diary, but in managing the church, he implicitly privileged Anglos and elites as the active directors of social reconstruction and immigrants and working classes as passive recipients of elite benevolence. The distinction began at the top. Like many talented and motivated persons, the young pastor possessed a high degree of self-confidence and a corresponding authoritarian streak. When underlings initiated policies contrary to his earlier instructions, for example, he admonished them that all operations should "be run under one hand."[66]

This authoritarian streak embedded itself in the larger relationship between a staff of providers and a congregation of recipients. Though All Nations drew a multiethnic population to its services, it seldom offered influential positions in the foundation to parish residents, especially those of color. Throughout Oxnam's tenure at All Nations both the workforce and the financial contributors remained predominantly Anglo.[67] Oxnam appeared to endorse this division by aiming many of his moral precepts at middle-class and elite Anglos rather than at parish residents. During one sermon titled "The Builders of Tomorrow," for example, he challenged "those of you here who have power and influence in circles of public health to insist tomorrow upon the right to be well-born."[68] Many of Oxnam's projects peripheral to All Nations likewise targeted wealthy Anglos rather than working-class Angelenos. In the mid-1920s he organized a series of bimonthly "International Relations Suppers" designed to educate "American" (i.e., Anglo) participants in different cultures.[69] All Nations periodicals such as the *Modern Samaritan* and the *Young Citizen,* published to "quicken . . . the interest of men and women of influence in the problems growing out of our modern conscience," implied that the life of "service" was the proper province of the privileged. The poor existed more to receive welfare than to contribute to its distribution.[70] Perhaps as a result, attendance at Sunday services reflected Oxnam's popularity among middle-class Anglos rather than among residents in the parish. Even by 1924 the official church membership remained primarily "native white," and 60 percent of the membership lived more than two miles from the All Nations neighborhood. Some of this group included former parish residents who had moved to the expanding neighborhoods southwest of the All Nations district. But observers noted the comparative wealth of church members versus the boys' and girls' club members, almost all of whom lived within a half mile of the church, especially between Fifth and Ninth Streets.[71]

Within this disjuncture church rhetoric occasionally lapsed into more explicit racism. In the early 1920s, for instance, All Nations presented a pageant titled "These Things Shall Be," written by a foundation supporter in collaboration with Oxnam, in wealthy Pacific Palisades. The script celebrated the broad social basis of the church's activities ("It's a lot of other things besides a church") and the commitment of its Anglo workforce. In one scene, an almost incoherent Mexican woman presents her child to the clinic for a desperately needed operation. ("Señorita, no money—no money; My Tony—operation.") Told she does not have to pay for the operation, the mother pathetically thanks the reformers:

> *Mrs. Mendoza (Dumbly trying to show her appreciation):* Oh gracias, gracias, señorita: some day, maybe, I pay.
>
> *Vivian (Nurse):* Poor Soul! We let them pay us a little when they can; it makes them feel more independent. But in a case like that where it's an absolute impossibility, we don't hold them to a payment.

The finale calls for a multiracial gathering of children representing the nations of the world. In a revealing indication of the author's concept of geography, an Anglo worker points to the representatives of Africa and Mexico. "Fortunately, Africa and Mexico are the smallest and therefore can take the end positions which make it possible to carry out the idea of the ends of the earth meeting." Taking place under the auspices of adult Anglo providers, the pageant narrative offers virtually no role for adult parishioners.[72]

Other accounts suggest that some foundation employees indulged in the same kind of racist paternalism, especially when highlighting their perceived achievements in rehabilitation. One boys' club director, for instance, told an interviewer that many of the Mexican boys under his charge remained "indolent and lazy" despite his efforts to groom them for "leadership positions." Another boys' worker was even more condescending, describing various non-Anglo charges as "a purveyor of smutty stories and salacious literature," "evasive, deceitful, light fingered, a snake in the grass," and "discouraged, moody, indifferent, with suicidal tendencies."[73] Such statements in no way characterized every social worker at All Nations, but they reveal that the foundation was not immune to the discrimination that undermined other social work. Despite their professed support for immigrant cultures, church workers sometimes betrayed a suspicion that immigrant and African American children lacked the moral integrity of Anglos.

BOYS' AND GIRLS' CLUBS

The valorization of mainstream Anglo mores appeared most clearly in the operation of the boys' and girls' clubs. Children's work, which evolved into All Nations's forte, naturally reinforced the paternalist role of the reform institution, especially when neighborhood adults were absent from the administration of the children's programs. The parenting All Nations elected to do often fit squarely within principles celebrated by Anglos much more conservative than Oxnam. Gender roles provided an obvious example. Boys' clubs, with names such as Indians, Pioneers, Comrades, and Trojans, received manual training and lessons on "good citizenship, self-reliance, and manliness." Girls' clubs focused on housekeeping skills and preserving ideas of "beauty and grace." These efforts reflected reformers' beliefs that such values would improve the material conditions of central Los Angeles. They also reflected a desire to curb practices the reformers deemed subversive to the existing social order.[74]

In its work with boys, All Nations hoped to supplant the delinquent behavior it attributed to inadequate supervision with a supportive group structure that would encourage "productive" activity. Church workers identified gang affiliation as a dangerous perversion of the natural desire for socialization. As one boys' club organizer put it, "There is an influence and an attitude specially generated in the gang—oftentimes for evil, but potentially for good." The violence, vandalism, and vice resulting from gang activity ("the child drug and liquor addict makes his appearance along with the useful sex victim") represented the negative consequences of inadequate family and social bonds. All Nations could channel this energy to more productive ends, its supporters believed, by providing the boys of the parish with constructive and structured activities. The success of the boys' clubs, perhaps the most popular of the foundation's offerings, apparently testified to that sentiment. By the mid-1920s All Nations was boasting about the district's plummeting juvenile delinquency rate and claimed to be "pushing gang territory off the map."[75]

The structure of the boys' clubs borrowed heavily from civil institutions and fraternal orders in ways meant to highlight interethnic cooperation and good works. Initiation ceremonies for the Phi Gamma fraternity club, for example, included a celebration of the Bible as the "highest ideals of man" and the globe as a symbol of brotherhood among all nations.[76] Club members elected officers (president, vice president, treasurer, chaplain, secretary, and sergeant-at-arms) by ballot, and potential initiates needed a recommendation from a standing member before they could join the club.[77] Requirements for the resurrected King Arthur Club for young boys included six weeks of good conduct, reading one book, knowing one King Arthur story, passing a fitness test, and attending Sunday school. The "page laws" required that members be clean, honest, truthful, patriotic, helpful, and reverent. Pages had to "work for [the] end of war," denounce racism, and "love and obey their parents happily."[78] Members who violated club rules could face expulsion, subject to a three-fourths vote of the membership. After police arrested a Spartan Club member for an unspecified infraction, his peers voted to recommend a sentence at a reform school. For the Spartan club director, the social aims of club activities were fairly obvious: "Social control was exercised in the light of collective interests. As the club became conscious of its status as a group and desirous of achieving the top through competition, it also became conscious of its control of individual members through the exercise of collective action. Shirkers were forced to fulfill their obligations to the group."[79] A reporter concurred, noting that All Nations boys soon learned "life is very much like chess— you've got to play according to the rules, and use your brains."[80]

Other club activities drew more direct connections between formal politics, civil obedience, and patriotism. One year Oxnam organized a study project on city government for the Phi Gamma club. After delivering several lectures on city planning, street management, lighting, housing, and sanitation, he reorganized the club on the basis of the city council, with each member assigned to committees and duties. Two of the boys then ran for mayor and debated in front of the Thursday movie group, which elected a winner.[81]

Despite the foundation's avowed interest in integration and equality, class and racial divisions sometimes infiltrated the children's program. A group of Jewish Girl Scouts whose existence predated the establishment of All Nations did not want to mix with Gentiles, and the foundation allowed it to stay intact.[82] In addition, the church maintained parallel boys' clubs, one for those of "better rearing" and one for the "tough" type from broken homes. Racial distinctions between the clubs were not absolute, but white children were the majority in the former, and nonwhites the majority in the latter (see table 4). The class distinction carried over into club activities as well. While the Phi Gamma club participated in civics studies and government operation, the Spartans Club for "tough" boys learned the importance to securing and maintaining a job of personal appearance, industriousness, and dependability.[83] According to an account of a summer Bible school class with a racial makeup similar to the Spartans, the children helped to manufacture a number of items (towels, sink protectors) for the foundation and then attended a church-sponsored picnic at which an LAPD officer gave a talk on "kids and police being friends."[84]

Girls' clubs received far less attention than the boys' clubs and drew significantly fewer members. While boys learned civics and "manliness," girls learned about the traditional activities of Anglo middle-class womanhood. The deaconesses conducted classes on dressmaking, sewing, housekeeping, domestic science, and nursing. Though the girls elected officers for their clubs, civic politics did not otherwise enter their activities. The initiation ceremony for the Sigma Tau Beta sorority, the counterpart to Phi Gamma, for example, focused on maintaining and cultivating "beauty." It did not mention the internationalism that was the main theme of the Phi Gamma initiation, nor was the sorority included in the city government project.[85] Girls' programs also remained physi-

TABLE 4
Membership of Selected All Nations Children's Clubs, by Ethnoracial Background, Early 1920s

	Phi Gamma Fraternity	Spartans Club	Daily Vacation Bible
Anglo	5	1	11
Spanish	1		
Jewish	2		9
Armenian	1		
German	4	1	1
Austrian	1		
Mexican		15	14
Italian		3	1
Japanese		2	12
African American		1	6
Bohemian		1	
Norwegian		1	4
French		1	
Irish		1	
English		1	1
Irish-Spanish		1	
French-Mexican		1	
Anglo-Japanese		1	
"Black-Hindu"			1
Anglo-German			4
French-Irish			1
Anglo-Mexican			1

SOURCE: "Phi Gamma Frat. List," in "CAN II," Box 57; Charles Sheldon Thompson, "Democracy in Evolution: The Natural History of a Boys Club Group" (Los Angeles: G. Howland Shaw, 1940), 10–11, in "Boys Work" file, Box 58; "Daily Vacation Bible School Report for the Year 1926," and "Memo: Nationalities in DVBS," in "CAN misc. 3," Box 58, G. Bromley Oxnam Papers.

cally separated from those of the boys. Generally run out of the Deaconess House, the girls' clubs had to borrow the boys' club facilities one day a week for athletics and other activities.[86]

Claims from many foundation workers and outsiders obscured the clubs' limited effectiveness in curbing delinquency. In the early 1930s a city probation officer claimed that the "formerly delinquent" All Nations area now had one of the lowest rates in the city. He advocated extending "the Oxnam plan" to other parts of Los Angeles. A wholesaler at the Terminal Market on Seventh and San Pedro Streets likewise noted that thievery of produce had subsided after the foundation opened its doors.[87] But Wes Klusman, the first director of the boys' clubs, painted a more complex picture. As a structured environment for learning, the boys' clubs in his view left something to be desired. Klusman described his first meeting as "a cross between a Democratic Convention and a Haymarket Riot." Gradually, he managed to impose some discipline on the clubs but struggled to extend that discipline into the boys' everyday lives. He admitted, for example, that his charges constantly stole from local stores (their fathers supposedly sanctioned the thefts as retaliation for the high prices charged by the store owners). His efforts to curb these activities met with only limited success. Klusman remembered that when the motometer (an instrument that measured radiator temperature) disappeared from his car, outraged club members vowed to retrieve the device. Sometime later several boys returned to the church with three motometers stolen from other vehicles. Klusman likewise described the Sunday school sessions, when the boys generally acted out biblical scenes, as entertaining, chaotic, and not entirely effective in their moral preachings. "We could never be certain as to action, verbiage, or moral," he concluded. "Undeniably, however, it was fun."[88]

Despite these setbacks, the boys' and girls' clubs exerted a measurable degree of influence over the lives of parish children. A number of them found an effective setting in which to develop social relations and skills that would benefit them later in life. One boy acknowledged he never had had any non-Mexican friends until he joined the club.[89] Club directors trumpeted the long-range influence of the clubs. Checking his charges ten years after they joined the Spartans, a boys' club worker bragged that twenty-nine of thirty were gainfully employed and that several credited the foundation with making them useful "citizens" and deterring them from a life of crime. Ed Barger epitomized the possibilities of the foundation. Orphaned twice (his foster parents died when he was a boy, apparently of complications from syphilis), Barger earned a reputation for troublemaking early in his life. In the years before the church's arrival, he presided over the notorious Seventh Street Gang, whose members engaged in a variety of illegal activities, including robbing a local store at gunpoint and burning down the Seventh Street School. On joining the boys' club at All Nations, Barger reformed his ways, and soon the Phi Gamma fraternity elected him president of their organization. In the mid-1920s the church supported him and his wife when one of their children was born with severe deformities. In 1927 observers proudly cited his presence, along with his family and another former Seventh Street Gang member, at the dedication of the new foundation buildings, directly across the street from the gang's former gathering place. Barger remained a church member and supporter well into his adult life, even after he moved away from the district.[90]

But Barger was not typical. The church's focus on children and its failure to open up its leadership to the neighborhood meant in practice that youths who passed through the foundation programs often left the church when they reached adulthood. The implications of this loss appeared painfully obvious to at least one former boys' club member: "Being a Spartan taught me to be happy, forget troubles and enjoy myself while I could. I knew things would change in the future but I didn't think they would change so quickly and for the worst. . . . Away from the club members, I've always been the same. You ought to know what that means."[91] However successfully the clubs preached cooperation, tolerance, and hard work to participants, the foundation provided no institutional mechanism for carrying these principles into their adult lives. Young adults graduating from the clubs entered an urban environment where, as Oxnam was the first to admit, these principles did not necessarily operate. Even if the graduates maintained their faith in the lessons of All Nations and sought to bring them into larger fields of social relations, they could only pursue such activities outside the foundation. In short, the structure of All Nations as it evolved by the mid-1920s undercut Oxnam's broader goal by shutting out the very sort of social mobilization it hoped to cultivate.

THE FAILURE OF SPIRITUALITY

By the mid-1920s signs of troubled lurked beneath the surface of All Nations' successes. The Open Forum ceased to meet, and though Oxnam still spoke on diverse topics of social justice, fewer outside orators came to the foundation. A Central Labor Council–sponsored Workers College program, established at the foundation in 1922 to educate laborers in organizing skills, likewise vanished after just a year.[92] Given the predominance of Anglos on the All Nations staff, the evaporation of these programs left few opportunities for adult parish residents to participate in the social programs of the church. Even in the popular boys' and girls' clubs all was not well. At the outset Oxnam had deliberately deemphasized religion and spirituality to sidestep accusations that All Nations wanted to steal children from their parents' faiths. He was mindful that the original 1918 parish survey revealed that more than 3,300 of 5,000 residents were "hostile" to the prospect of another religious organization operating in their neighborhood. Oxnam attributed these responses to mainstream Protestantism's traditional apathy to issues of "social justice" and to excessive directives regarding personal behavior. Accordingly, Oxnam avoided the role of puritanical crusader, particularly with regard to the religious and social practices of children. While he worried about the influence of "blind pigs" and other "vice resorts" on parish youth, for instance, he preferred to contribute to antivice campaigns led by others rather than lead them himself.[93] He also downplayed religious instruction in the children's programs. One social worker noted that saying Grace and the occasional religious song constituted the extent of devotional practices at the All Nations nursery. She claimed that the out-of-work mothers, many of them Mexican and Japanese, who visited their children at the nursery never objected to such practices. Another official maintained that there was no effort to proselytize in the boys' and girls' clubs, though "the whole spirit of the club[s] is to incarnate as nearly as possible, the true spirit of Christianity. The authorities have confidence that if such a spirit is thoroughly manifested the boys will acquire it without much preaching of the creed." The girls' club manager acknowledged occasional religious teachings under her direction but denied they constituted an integral part of the program. A deaconess, pointing around the room to various Jewish, Japanese, African American, and Scandinavian children under her charge, noted that few attended the Sunday school.[94]

Oxnam had hoped that this soft-sell would gradually encourage the parish to develop a greater spiritual investment in the church, but by the mid-1920s this scenario appeared more and more far-fetched. The Sunday school program, which had grown so remarkably during the church's early years, now rapidly lost momentum. By 1923 observers, noting both stagnant enrollments and the difficulty of retaining competent teachers, ruefully concluded that the school was "not progressing."[95] A year later, as attendance in their central city churches continued to slip, Methodist authorities consolidated six parishes under a single "City Parish." All Nations became the leading service provider but also discontinued religious services and transferred its congregation to another church.[96] Two years later the Methodist leadership terminated the experiment after three churches shut their doors and the congregation of another petitioned for withdrawal to restore its autonomy. But the secularized status of All Nations persisted. When the new Community House and Boys Club opening in 1927, the foundation had virtually ceased to perform traditional religious services.[97]

Despite these struggles, the Methodist leadership remained committed to All Nations and in 1927 funded a major renovation and expansion of the foundation's facilities. Yet by this point the institution's flagging spirituality was beginning to wear on its minister. Diary entries began to betray a sense of frustration with his creation and an ambivalence about its future prospects. Sermons from this period—"Has the Church Failed?" "Is it a Class Institution?" "Can the Church Take Sides?"—revealed a pastor struggling with the basic role of religion in modern society and its capacity to effect social change.[98] Oxnam's fervent belief that the next great religious "Awakening" would involve the "socialization" of religion, that its expansion into the everyday practices of humanity and its obliteration of social distinctions would simultaneously follow from and reinvigorate religion's spiritual forces, seemed to have waned. In a 1925 diary entry he commented on the "apparent disintegration" of the local Epworth League (a Methodist organization for young adults) and the Board of Sunday Schools. Wondering whether Christianity had "reached the end of its institutionalized form," Oxnam offered up a Weberian analysis of the church's evolution that perhaps betrayed misgivings about All Nations: "Institutionalism is like a machine in one sense, and like a coffin in another. The life of Christianity—its body is in the coffin of ecclesiasticism, form, etc., and like most bodies in a coffin, it is nearly dead. Yet that is not true, for Christianity is a vital force—and will burst forth alive elsewhere. It is what we think Christianity to be that may die. . . . I wonder whether we will have churches as such tomorrow, or whether we will have fellowship developing the spirit."[99]

In the 1927 interview with the student, Oxnam finally brought his misgivings about the church out into the open. He admitted that if he had it to do over again, he would have started with the social settlement and then built the church. Citing the hostility to evangelism revealed in the initial survey of the neighborhood, he claimed, "If the Church is already there you super-impose the Church upon the community, as a ready-made institution. You don't really know whether the community wants it or not, or rather with us, we knew it wasn't wanted. . . . They saw an institution existing of which they were not a real part, the people who called themselves Christians who over and over again showed themselves to be the very persons who caused anxiety and heartache and trouble to the laboring classes." If the church had emerged out of the settlement, he concluded, it would have been more "indigenous," a "natural group expression." Oxnam himself admitted that All Nations had "no place for adults" but blamed the absence on an older generation's adherence to the "old evangelistic idea," on its inability to grasp the significance of his church's social orientation. Oxnam also acknowledged that his more secularized sermons in part represented a response to audience demand, and he lamented the relative lack of interest in traditional religious preaching at the foundation. While attendance at his sermons on playwrights averaged 250, for instance, he admitted, "Just as soon as I preach a real sermon the attendance drops to about 150."[100]

The interviewer's paper later quoted a Mexican girl's response to a Catholic priest who castigated her for joining an All Nations club. "I don't go to All Nations for religion," she replied. "I go for recreation." Such a response encapsulated Oxnam's dilemma. By the time the student completed her paper, All Nations' founder had already announced his intention to leave the foundation for a faculty position at the Boston University School of Theology, where he had studied a dozen years before. Oxnam subsequently became the youngest bishop in the church's history, supported New Deal programs and other liberal principles, and even landed on the cover of *Time* magazine. But he never returned to Los Angeles for any significant period.[101] Robert McKibben, the associate pastor who assumed control of the foundation in 1927, indicated that he shared his predecessor's concerns about All Nations. "Dr. Oxnam has city-wide appeal," he told the student, "but it has been primarily in behalf of these people, not to them." He hoped to keep All Nations scaled down, to "increase oneness." Over the next several decades he shepherded the foundation through a gradual narrowing of its focus to youth programs and, after industrialization drove out the parish population, relocation to Boyle Heights.[102]

THE LIMITS OF CHRISTIAN AMERICANIZATION

In 1924, when All Nations was at the height of its popularity, a Japanese Angeleno vented her frustration with American churches to an interviewer. "One thing I have noticed about American churches, I think foreigners, who need something from them, like charity, are more welcome than others," the young woman observed. "But if you are a foreigner and are able to stand on your own feet, you are not so welcome. I have been very much disappointed in the church."[103] There are any number of other reasons why adult residents of All Nations parish may have avoided the church. Some may have viewed it as a threat to the religion of their birth. Others may have found the spirituality too staid compared to the more emotional revivalism blossoming throughout the country. Some may have felt intimidated by the foundation, like one neighborhood father who refused to attend a luncheon for his daughter's girls' club because he did not have a good suit to wear.[104] Yet the young woman's response perhaps summed up the primary reason All Nations remained a resource for central city residents to draw from, rather than a community and spiritual center to invest in. Unlike other missions and settlement homes, the foundation did not demand that those availing themselves of its services make a formal religious conversion, abandon their own languages and customs, or disavow radical politics. And yet Oxnam and All Nations did expect something in return: they expected a diverse group of urban residents to come together as a single body under the auspices of an institution created by middle-class Anglos and to invest at least part of their social and spiritual identities in that body. Such a stance implied that parish residents could not stand on their own feet, that they needed to be told how to act and relate to one another in their adopted country.

In many ways this stance reflected broader expectations common to diverse proponents of corporate liberal principles, and Oxnam's failure recapitulated the failures of missionaries, Americanizationists, and other Anglo reformers during the twenties. The story of All Nations raised serious questions about the larger ethnoracial aspect of corporate reconstruction in the United States. On what basis was it possible to nurture a so-called indigenous movement of faith centered on what could only be termed, from the point of view of the neighborhood involved, an exotic institution? Likewise, on what basis could immigrants develop an affinity for an Americanism defined and imposed, however benevolently, from outside?

If Oxnam's approach brushed up on the limits of Christian Americanization as a solution to these quandaries, it also pointed to a vibrant political and social culture that escaped many middle-class and elite Anglos who ventured into the central neighborhoods. Within these districts a plethora of indigenous community actions were emerging, albeit often outside the institutional realm of reform organizations. In confronting neighbors of different ethnic and racial backgrounds, residents formulated different strategies for socializing and organizing and instigated the kinds of activity Oxnam wanted to nurture. In the complicated relationships and conflicts that followed, some central city residents implicitly attempted to build social structures that incorporated the diverse communities of their city into a rational whole. In such ways they entered into a dialogue with other Angelenos that alternately internalized, challenged, and transcended the corporate reconstruction of Los Angeles.

CHAPTER 4

"So Many Children at Once and So Many Kinds"

The World of Central City Children

KIDS ON THE CORNER

Kango Kunitsugo grew up in the market district of Los Angeles during the Great Depression. In the streets near his home he played with African American, Mexican, Chinese, and Japanese boys. "I don't think we ever consciously thought of being American or Japanese," he recalled some decades later.

> Your home was another world. . . . I guess we formed a security island kind of thing. I remember days when there was only one non-minority family living on that block. A fellow named Thomas Stone was the only white living there. I guess because we were kids we never did have the feeling that he was a white man. In fact, we used to chase white people from the neighborhood, and Tom used to be right with us; I could never figure it out. . . . But I think in those days we were less conscious of the thing; you weren't exposed to too may things. You went to school and came back, went to Japanese school and came back, and played football out in the streets.[1]

However sheltered his childhood, Kunitsugo was certainly exposed to people of widely different cultures and backgrounds. His remembrance reveals awareness of existing racial divisions, affiliation with an ethnocentric institution, and willingness to transcend, selectively at least, ethnoracial boundaries. For adult residents who came to Los Angeles from relatively homogeneous communities with more cohesive ethnic traditions, the complex, multiethnic environments may have seemed strange, even foreign. But their children were not necessarily aware that the integrated streets, playgrounds, schools, and other public spaces of early-twentieth-century central Los Angeles constituted a new kind of urban setting.

The idyllic picture that older Angelenos often paint of their youth in the central neighborhoods may have several sources. Adults may romanticize childhood in light of subsequent experiences, omitting or forgetting the more troubled aspects of their upbringing. At the same time, fond memories of youth may accurately reflect a period in which awareness of injustice and burdens of responsibility weighed lightly on one's shoulders. It is doubtful that many central city children, or those of any other neighborhood for that matter, had a sophisticated grasp of the profound social and economic forces shaping early-twentieth-century Los Angeles or of the intricate distinctions between ethnoracial groups in their neighborhoods. As Kunitsugo suggested, even the general question of American identity did not necessarily arise. But the rose-colored character of his comments also emerged from a more specific historical context and reflected interaction not as evident in postwar Los Angeles. In the schools, playgrounds, and other public spaces where they played and learned, children of these districts enjoyed opportunities to cultivate cross-cultural relationships that often were unavailable to (or undesired by) their elders. Kunitsugo's notion of a "security island" describes a cultural space in which central city children of his generation could associate irrespective of their ethnoracial backgrounds.

Yet to whatever extent it existed, the halcyon days of central city childhoods went unchallenged for only so long. Preadolescent children may have forged inter-ethnoracial friendships in at least partial ignorance of their social implications. As they grew older, however, they encountered more resistance to such relationships from both within and outside their ethnic community and became more aware of the distributions of power that traced racial, ethnic, gender, and class boundaries. School, dating, and work successively introduced new barriers to social interaction. Many children rapidly internalized a respect for ethnic boundaries and hierarchies and imposed them in their own social circles. But others bucked conventions and continued to transcend the social boundaries that confined many adults. The conflicts, large and small, that almost inevitably followed revealed the profound consequences of these relationships for urban ethnoracial relations. These encounters influenced the cultural transmission of meanings about race, class, and ethnicity in American society to the newest generation of

American citizens. In various situations, a child's response to peers of different backgrounds could highlight the contradictions of structural and cultural racism, the possibilities of overcoming such divisions, or the re-formation of ethnoracial boundaries. As those of Kunitsugo's generation grew into adulthood, they entered the informal ranks of social educators for the next generation, renewing a volatile and contested cycle of cultural transmission.

STREETS, YARDS, THEATERS:
THE NEIGHBORHOOD OF THE CHILD

By the twentieth century the growth of permanent Mexican, Japanese, African American, European, and other minority communities in Los Angeles began to register in the city's population of children. Some of these children had been born abroad and immigrated with their parents. Their first view of the city could be jarring. "Angelita Avila," a young girl born in a small village in Mexico, recalled of entering her elementary school for the first time: "I really believe I had never seen so many children at once and so many kinds."[2] Kazuo Kawai, the Tokyo-born son of a Christian minister who came to Los Angeles as a young boy, was shocked at the appearance of white people—"the strange people who had red hair, blue eyes, and white skin, just like the pictures of the ogres in Japanese fairy-tale books"—and felt intimidated by the "hordes of dirty little Mexican, Negro, Italian, Greek, and Jewish children" at the Ninth Street School. But second-generation immigrant children likely had no memories of their countries of origin. Central Los Angeles constituted for them the sole setting in which they learned about the world. Even newcomers caught on, however, and Kawai himself admitted he "learned all the ways of the east side, and very soon . . . became one of the regular gang."[3] Like Kawai's, the lives of many central city children were saturated with multiethnic encounters.

Central city children confronted possibilities for cultural interaction every time they left their homes. The streets and other public spaces of their neighborhoods presented ample opportunities for children engaged in what reformers derisively referred to as "unsupervised play." The congested districts around downtown provided a plethora of pedestrians, street life, and social practices for children to observe. Movie theaters, for example, proved a popular site of social interaction for all races, despite the exclusionary or segregationist policies of certain establishments. Even children from very poor families could afford a ticket to a downtown or neighborhood movie at least occasionally. Unsupervised congregations of children both inside and outside the theaters became common by the twentieth century.[4] Areas bordering commercial and industrial operations provided more active opportunities for unsupervised play. One boy enthusiastically noted there were "lots of dark alleys and stores and boxes to hide in" for youths in his neighborhood. A Chinatown resident remembered that his peers used to gather in an abandoned barn. Some youngsters frequented the produce market area on Central Avenue, prompting periodic complaints about children pilfering food from the trucks and storage bins.[5] The railroad yards bracketing the riverbed, with their abundant hiding places, meeting areas, and climbing opportunities, also were popular. Children played on idle cars, and the older or more adventurous might hop rides on outgoing trains. In one case, two boys inadvertently locked themselves in a car and were not found until several days later, by railroad workers in Fresno. Other children used the open spaces extending north along the river and east and south of developed areas for games and exploring.[6]

As reformers ruefully acknowledged, many central city children whiled away hours in these public spaces outside the purview of their parents. They noted that working-class mothers, particularly those of color, entered the workforce at higher rates than did middle-class or elite mothers, removing them from the home for extended periods.[7] In addition, social workers disparaged the number of "broken" immigrant and African American families of the central districts and attributed instances of juvenile delinquency in these homes to lack of oversight. Certainly work demands placed a strain on child care among central Angelenos, as the popularity of nurseries and child care facilities established by reformers or the city indicated. In the absence of other alternatives, older siblings or neighborhood children often assumed responsibility for watching their little brothers and sisters. This practice became prevalent enough that at least one central city school briefly allowed its students to bring younger siblings in their care to class. Enough disruption resulted that the school quickly revoked the policy and established a nursery.[8]

Whatever the cause, many central city children, especially boys, spent time free of adult supervision. Parents as a group seemed more reluctant to allow their daughters to be unsupervised. Not surprisingly, this gendered protective impulse jumped dramatically when girls reached puberty. Julie Suski was one of many central city children who chafed under parents' strict policies about unsupervised play, and Kunitsugo, recalling the paucity of girls on the streets, joked that their parents were hiding them.[9] Nevertheless, many girls got the chance to play outdoors. A study of fifteen All Nations girls between the ages of nine and thirteen concluded that they engaged in "unsupervised play," frequently with friends of different ethnoracial backgrounds, between ten and twenty hours a week. Almost all of the girls surveyed also went to movies unaccompanied by adults. In fact, a reformers' census of central city playgrounds in 1918 found no appreciable gender imbalance. While many of these playgrounds were supervised, and perhaps therefore more acceptable to parents, they provided spaces for young girls to play with neighborhood friends. Like the female child "gang" members in San Francisco described, and perhaps romanticized, by Herbert Asbury, these girls actively participated in the street life of Los Angeles.[10]

For both boys and girls, the public spaces of the central neighborhoods presented innumerable opportunities for inter-ethnoracial contact. Many Angelenos who grew up in these areas before World War II recalled a virtual absence of racial animosity between children (and often between children and adults), and many cultivated at least one or two interracial friendships. Leo Carillo, the son of a well-to-do Californio family who spent his early childhood years in the plaza district, had a number of Chinese friends and interacted enough with the Chinese, Indian, and Californio "loafers around the Plaza" to acquire a variety of language skills. He noted: "In their relations with the other nationalities who lived around the Plaza, the Chinese were extremely friendly and constant in their friendship. . . . It was perfectly natural for me to pick up the sing-song sibilant language of the Cantonese, and I would find myself at home switching from Spanish to Cantonese to English without any conscious effort."[11] Emilia Castañeda remembered the "United Nations" neighborhood of Mexicans, Japanese, Chinese, African Americans, Jews, Filipinos, and Greeks in Boyle Heights where she grew up as relatively free of discrimination: "There was a mixture, and we got along fine. Of course, we kids used to tease each other, but not really get into fights. I can recall that it was a pretty happy neighborhood when I lived there." Milton Quan likewise remembered teasing between children in the market district but claimed "it was not meant to be abusive, just kid stuff."[12] A number of aspiring jazz artists from South Central and Watts recalled harmonious relationships between ethnic groups. Football star and actor Woody Strode, looking back on his childhood in the Furlong Tract area where African Americans, Germans, Italians, and Mexicans lived together, commented: "All the kids would play together on the street. We didn't have any problems like they have now. . . . We fought some, but then we'd back off, shake hands, and go eat at the other guy's house." Saxophonist and Watts resident William "Brother" Woodman recalled that white, African American, Mexican, Asian, and Jewish children of the neighborhood all got along very well: "That's why, at that time, I didn't really understand about prejudice. I said, 'How could this happen? Right here, we get along so beautifully, all of us together.'" Of course, this conviviality did not always extend to parents and adult relations, and reminders of racial segmentation reappeared consistently. Woodman's brother, Britt, for example, associated with white and Mexican kids in Watts but claimed that white friends living east of Alameda could not invite him to their neighborhoods because of objections from their parents and neighbors.[13] And yet the intrusions of racism, however prevalent, existed alongside an alternative culture of association and friendship that flourished among the newest generation of central Angelenos.

CHILDHOOD INSTITUTIONS: GANGS, PLAYGROUNDS, LANGUAGE SCHOOLS, AND MORE

Like other Anglos around the country, Angeleno reformers abhorred the prospect of minors running rampant through the streets and industrial areas of the city. Physical safety was the foremost concern. Automobiles, streetcars, and trains injured and killed numerous Angelenos every year and presented a real threat to children, especially on the crowded boulevards of the central neighborhoods.[14] But reformers also feared for the moral well-being of central city youth. They worried about the saloons, dance halls, theaters, and pool halls that beckoned unsuspecting children. "Some city environments, such as those associated with rooming house districts, railroad yards, and the older industrial districts, are dangerous to boys' welfare," Bogardus reported. "Older boys, immoral women, dope peddlers, abound in these districts."[15] Another social critic noted that "undirected street play has a tendency to develop disrespect for law and cunning in social relationships. This is especially true when crowded streets permit only disorganized fooling in the place of play." In short, for most reformers, the street was an unacceptable site of learning. "If . . . the child is crowded into the streets and left to its own resources with no opportunity for wholesome play," one concluded ominously, "then we must expect the results of the street's training."[16] Central city parents may or may not have agreed. Some Ange-

lenos from less boisterous parts of central Los Angeles, such as Boyle
Heights residents Archie Green, Morris Kadish, and Michio Kunitani,
remembered that their parents felt secure releasing them into the neighborhood. Others, however, may have agreed with an African American
who commented, "Los Angeles ain't no place to raise a kid. All he does
is get in trouble playing around the streets."[17]

For central city boys (and occasionally girls) of all ethnoracial backgrounds, "trouble" often took the form of the gangs that congregated
everywhere, from streetcorners to public libraries. Many gangs functioned solely as social clubs, but others, like the Seventh Street Gang
that plagued the All Nations parish, engaged in violent and destructive
acts.[18] In certain cases, violence indicated ethnoracial antagonisms. Like
the juvenile gangs that terrorized Chinese in San Francisco, some Angeleno children targeted politically defenseless Chinese and Japanese. An
ethnic Japanese doctor living in Boyle Heights, for example, claimed to
have been assaulted by a group of "European" boys, perhaps because
he was married to a white woman.[19] Gang fights sometimes erupted
along ethnoracial lines. One reformer repeated to Bogardus rumors of
an impending fight between black and white gangs "down there among
the pipes" (in an industrial yard) to settle an argument that began outside a movie theater. Another central city boy of undetermined ethnicity
recalled, "We fought gangs of Mexican kids down in the river. . . . We
fought other gangs around closer if they ever bothered us any." Chinatown resident Allan Chan also remembered that the neighborhood
served as a popular site for interracial gang fights because police there
seldom interfered.[20] Gang affiliation did not necessarily break down
along ethnoracial lines. Neighborhood bonds, as Kunitsugo's gang suggested, could also play a role. One boy commented, "The reason we
formed into a club was primarily to defend ourselves against the other
gangs that were on the different streets. Almost all the fellows around
there were organized into gangs, and we had to be too, in order to be in
things." In such contexts gangs could blur ethnoracial boundaries as
much as reinforce them, and it was not uncommon to find in early-
twentieth-century Los Angeles cosmopolitan predecessors of the
pachuco gangs of the 1940s.[21]

Before World War II gangs lacked the sustained, predatory criminal
activity that decimated the central neighborhoods in the late twentieth
century. In part this was because prewar gang members were much
younger than their Cold War counterparts and often left their gangs
when they joined the workforce around the age of fifteen.[22] Yet con-

temporary reformers still worried about the pernicious influence of street life and gang activity. Though ethnoracial relations did not necessarily top the list of their concerns, one solution to gang activity indirectly addressed the issue. The playgrounds that began to appear in the central districts by the early twentieth century offered controlled environments and supervised clubs in place of gang society and street life. They constituted a new kind of recreational space where children were taught to resolve conflicts and forsake bigotry.

The middle-class and elite architects of what came to be called the Playground movement viewed their projects as more than just athletic facilities. They suggested "recreative centers" as a more fitting term. Through these centers, supporters argued, they could appropriate the social structure of the gang, an institution they understood as a misdirected response to social disorder, toward wholesome ends. "Gangs," wrote one commentator, "represent the spontaneous efforts of boys to create a society for themselves when none adequate to their need exists." The playground, another argued, "captures the gang spirit and sets it to interesting and diversified activity [and] prevents the gang and his own boy from becoming predatory."[23] The men and women who created the recreative centers believed they could engineer a productive social network binding the central city children. Reformer Bessie Stoddart, for example, mused, "On the playground fair play must be constantly practiced, self-control constantly maintained. This is the very essence of democracy. For to know how to associate, how to cooperate with one's fellows is the foundation of our national form of government."[24]

The Playground movement in Los Angeles began in 1904 with the establishment of the City Playground Commission, the first of its kind in the United States. A year later the commission completed its first project, the Violet Street Playground near the future site of All Nations. The facility covered two acres and included fields, playgrounds, clubhouses, a gym, and a director's residence. More projects followed: a playground in the Echo Park neighborhood that accommodated up to seven hundred children a day, the Salt Lake Playground in the Flats, and the large City Recreation Center in Sonoratown.[25] The efforts of the commission did not end with the playgrounds' completion. Rejecting the idea of unsupervised play time, officials warned that the recreation centers did not "operate themselves" and instituted a battery of programs for their "crucibles of citizenship." Paid directors oversaw organized athletic and arts programs and, like the All Nations clubs, attempted to inculcate in their charges a sense of civic responsibility for their facility. The Echo

Park Playground, for example, maintained a "Playground Republic," consisting of an elected "government" of voluntary members who paid a monthly "tax" of five cents, made rules, and maintained equipment. Also like All Nations, directors segregated girls into activities and spaces more "suited" to their gender and designed to promote feminine characteristics and skills.[26]

The Playground movement had an ambiguous impact on central city children and ethnoracial relations. On the one hand, neither delinquency nor gang activity nor children's street culture disappeared from the neighborhoods. Many children lived too far from the sites to visit them regularly, and some neighborhoods, like the Custer Street district near Echo Park, struggled for years to get approval for construction of a local playground.[27] Nor did "open" public playgrounds mean that all groups used them equally, or that harmonious ethnoracial relations prevailed. A 1918 census of the major playgrounds suggests that the they reflected the diversity of the neighborhoods around them, but some ethnic clustering most likely occurred (see table 5). Observers of the Chinatown playground, built in 1924 on an old Southern Pacific lot, claimed that only Chinese children patronized it. An observer of a Watts playground asserted that white children rejected African American playmates and associated with Mexican children only if they were "finelooking" and well dressed.[28] On the other hand, the centers did draw youngsters of all races and ethnicities from the center city, and other playground workers noted with enthusiasm that the structured environment seemed to mitigate tensions of all sorts. The children "come here to play together," one commented, "and the narrow spirit breaks down." Woody Strode was even more effusive: "Our business was in the playgrounds. That's where we grew up; we were never into school. . . . After school, during the summer and practically every night of the year, all the neighborhood kids would gather."[29] Though they might not have eliminated ethnoracial antagonisms, playgrounds at the very least presented, in a more structured fashion, the kinds of opportunities for ethnoracial interaction so prevalent in central neighborhood streets.

The integrated environment of the playgrounds stood in contrast to the ethnoracial restrictions placed on other Los Angeles recreation facilities. Nonwhites, for example, were barred from certain public beaches and swimming pools in and around the city. One ordinance, passed by a unanimous city council vote in 1920, banned Japanese from public tennis courts and golf courses. The bill's authors claimed that Japanese were crowding out whites on the tennis courts.[30] The YMCA segregated some

TABLE 5
Census of Selected Playgrounds in Los Angeles, by Race or Ethnicity, 1918

	Violet	Salt Lake	Temple	Hazard	Echo	Recreation Center
"American"	59	153	443	569	706	155
Mexican	829	661	54	16	5	651
Spanish*	36	129	67	66	30	12
Italian	415	33	65	237	27	438
"Jewish"	15	251	443	215	167	
Russian	15	877		8	1	
African American	217	12		13	33	1
Japanese	18	8			14	1
Chinese	5				2	
German	1	32	5	38	20	5
French	23	13	9	49	8	11
Greek	15	17		3	1	2
Swedish	7			2	14	
English		3	27	27	27	2
Irish	5	2	5	55	8	1
Romanian		4	3			
Syrian		23				
Armenian		238	3		6	2
Polish		18		3	1	4
Hungarian					6	1
Servian		3	14			
Belgian		2	1	19		
Indian		5				
Austrian		5	26	8	6	26
Canadian		3	10		5	
Lithuanian		4		1		
Austrian-Hungarian		10				
Scottish		2	2	3		3
Bohemian			4	4		
Croatian			5			
Egyptian			3			
Norwegian			1	1		
Danish				4		
Portuguese				2		
Dutch					4	3
Assyrian						14
Slavonian						3
Swiss			1			
Welsh	1					

SOURCE: From "Summaries of Playground Surveys" (no author), fall 1918, "Interchurch Movement" file, Box 102, G. Bromley Oxnam Papers.
*May refer to Mexicans who identified or were identified as "Spanish."

of its facilities, and some movie houses either refused admission to patrons of color or confined them to certain sections.[31] Some swimming pools admitted nonwhites only after they submitted to a humiliating "health" exam and then presented an authorization card at the entrance. Chinese Angeleno Walter Chung, for example, recalled that the Lincoln Park pool turned him away for that reason. His white companions supported their friend by refusing to enter the establishment.[32] Not all recreational facilities practiced discrimination, and a number of interracial social clubs existed, including the All Nations Club and a well-known Boy Scouts troop in Boyle Heights.[33] Yet children of color who ventured beyond the streets and playgrounds for amusement were more likely to encounter discrimination and segregation.

Central city parents often complemented these segregationist policies by sending their children to ethnic-specific social and educational institutions. As numerous other studies have chronicled, these institutions functioned to preserve cultural practices and to encourage intraethnic ties among younger generations. Language schools, which children attended on weekends or in the evening, constituted the most obvious examples. Chinese and Japanese Angelenos maintained several such schools throughout the early twentieth century, and Russians, Jews, and Mexicans funded at least one school each to teach their children the mother tongue.[34] Gauging the response of the students is difficult. For some, they served as a respite from the unfamiliar and alienating mixed-ethnic neighborhoods they lived in. Others, however, found the atmosphere of language schools stifling and rejected the skills and values taught there as irrelevant to their lives in America. Conflicts between parents and children over attendance at language schools formed part of the broader generational division that historians have identified in immigrant communities. A child's rejection of language school did not necessarily indicate a rejection of his or her ethnic community but could suggest a longing to interact with other children on equal terms. At least some young central city Angelenos felt that ethnic-specific institutions did not help them to develop the ability to interact with outsiders, an ability that would be necessary even if only used on occasion.[35]

Not all parents condoned their children's desire to mingle with peers of other ethnoracial backgrounds. Anglo parents, not surprisingly, as a group proved most reticent. Future Los Angeles mayor Tom Bradley sadly recalled a childhood friend he had in the West Temple district. One day the Anglo boy told Bradley his mother and father had forbidden him to associate with the "colored" children on the block. The two boys continued to meet but had to do so out of sight of his friend's parents. In an interview from the mid-1920s a Filipino worker castigated white Americans who would not let their children play with immigrant children. He felt it contributed to foreigners' sense of isolation and their unwillingness to assimilate.[36] But such hostility was not limited to Anglo parents. Noting that "the contacts children make in school may alienate them from their parents," Bogardus identified one teacher who had endured complaints from a number of fathers and mothers about their children's classroom associations. He worried that parental influence might contribute to racial friction at school. A few years later, Beatrice Griffith noted that some parents and leaders of an unnamed "Mexican colony" had forbidden their children to associate with white and African American peers. The edict "bewildered" their children and non-Mexican friends, until a more "alert" leader stepped in to remedy the problem.[37] Some objections voiced by central neighborhood parents suggest that class concerns motivated them as much as racial concerns. One study of the period argued that Chinese parents, especially those of the middle class, worried about the mixed-ethnic environments in which they lived. "The native-born Chinese imitate the bad from the two countries, because many of the Chinese here do not give the younger group a good example as they are of the laboring class," it concluded. "Because of the lack of contact with high class Americans on account of the attitude of the Americans towards them, they do not have a good example there either. They imitate those who live in the neighborhood of the Chinese community who are largely immigrants and low-class Americans." Tom Gubbins, an Anglo with long connections to the Chinese community, claimed that middle-class Chinese sometimes sent their children back to China for school after the age of fourteen, allegedly because "at this age they begin to get the rough stuff of the Americans and also the Chinese community."[38]

Of course, not all central city parents objected to inter-ethnoracial association, and at least a few actively encouraged it for their children. Archie Green, the son of Russian Jews, recalled that his parents subscribed to a principle of "internationalism" and escorted him to various ethnic events to develop his appreciation for other cultures. Ying Wong Kwan, who grew up in the Bunker Hill and Temple Street areas, claimed her mother worked hard to develop ties with their neighbors and told her to ignore children who called her names. Internalizing these efforts, and claiming that "being open to all nationalities was typical for Chinese," Ying cultivated friendships with children of all nationalities.[39]

Many others, if not enthusiastic about the cosmopolitan circles in which their children traveled, tolerated it as an inevitable part of central city childhood.

NEIGHBORS, STRANGERS, AND CLASSMATES: THE SCHOOL ENVIRONMENT

Parental control had its limits. At some point, even those central city children who remained in relatively homogeneous ethnic enclaves and avoided integrated playgrounds and institutions had to confront peers of other races in a social setting. If streets and playgrounds provided opportunities for ethnoracial interaction, most central city schools, in one form or another, imposed it.

For most working-class children of any background during the early twentieth century, regular school attendance was a new phenomenon. Their predecessors might have attended sporadically, and some skipped school altogether to go to work. California passed its first compulsory education law mandating attendance up to age fourteen in 1874, but enforcement in Los Angeles remained lax through the turn of the century. As late as 1907, playground directors recognized the reality of child labor by keeping some playgrounds open into the evening "for the benefit of working boys and girls." Such nonchalance, however, soon evaporated under protests from reformers and socialists, who claimed to have found young boys and girls working ten-hour shifts in factories.[40] Progressives eventually managed to push through municipal legislation enforcing the attendance laws, hiring truant officers, restricting the working hours of minors, and requiring work permits for children. Thereafter the school population mushroomed, prompting a rash of school construction, especially in integrated working-class districts. By the 1910s over 90 percent of Angeleno children were attending school. Between 1908 and 1916 the total number of pupils in Los Angeles jumped from 33,422 to 54,796. Attendance figures stabilized during World War I, but according to one school official, the system added 20,000 new students a year during the early 1920s.[41]

Though accurate and consistent data are scarce, available evidence suggests that high rates of growth and population turnover in these districts virtually ensured some degree of diversity in central neighborhood schools. In certain cases, schools in formerly all-Anglo neighborhoods diversified as new immigrants replaced departed residents. A school in Lincoln Heights northeast of downtown, for example, witnessed a drop

FIGURE 3. Girls' class picture, Twentieth Street School, 1921. Shades of L.A. Archives/Los Angeles Public Library.

in the number of "American" students from 85 percent in 1913 to 53 percent by 1921 and a corresponding increase of Italian and Mexican students from 8 to 22 percent and from 4 to 20 percent, respectively.[42] A 1924 census of twenty-two primary schools in mixed ethnic districts revealed a student population that was 52.3 percent "white" (including European immigrants), 35.0 percent ethnic Mexican, 6.9 percent African American, 5.3 percent ethnic Asian, and 0.6 percent "other." To be sure, these students were not distributed evenly throughout the schools, but on eleven of the campuses no one racial group constituted more than 60 percent of the student body. Of the five campuses where one racial group made up more than 80 percent of the student body, four were dominated by whites of unspecified ethnic background, and in each case the white majority declined or disappeared over the next twelve years (see table 6).[43] Several new intermediate (later junior high) and high schools constructed in working-class districts during the 1910s and 1920s attracted an even more cosmopolitan array of students, in part because they drew from larger areas than primary schools. Michio Kunitani, for instance, recalled that the football team at Roosevelt High School in Boyle Heights, which he attended in the mid-1930s, included Jewish, Russian, Armenian, Mexican, and Native American players in its starting lineup. A 1936 survey of the school recorded a student body that was 28 percent "American," 26 percent Jewish, 24 percent Mexican, 7 percent Russian, 6 percent Japanese, and 9 percent Italian,

TABLE 6

Population of Selected Los Angeles Primary Schools,
by Race or Ethnicity, 1924

School	Total Enrollment	"White"	Black	Asian	Mexican	Other	Non–English speaking
Ninth St.	891	229	139	226	278	19	273
Amelia St.	543	14	0	219	310	0	361
Hewiit St.	393	22	5	191	167	8	96
Coronel	741	92	17	21	608	3	708
San Pedro St.	893	481	87	41	271	13	241
Cornwell	1,426	1,313	1	17 ,	103	0	251
Breed St.	744	607	1	37	91	8	70
Second St.	1025	657	0	4	364	6	313
Bridge St.	1,299	699	14	2	577	7	515
Echandia	55	54	1	0	0	0	51
Marengo	694	559	0	0	133	2	161
First St.	841	464	93	123	158	3	273
Malabar St.	1,689	1294	41	13	341	0	196
Soto St.*	(684)	238	0	0	466	6	334
Utah St.	2,012	883	5	22	1,102	0	958
Alpine St.	650	438	0	2	207	3	171
California	582	298	0	62	211	11	177
Castelar St.	631	226	0	9	395	1	284
Nevin	868	184	559	10	114	1	96
Staunton	582	157	95	0	330	0	246
Wadsworth	973	641	254	11	62	5	46
Murchison	679	341	1	0	342	13	213

SOURCE: From "Intensive Study of Representational City Churches: the City Parish," Institute of Social and Religious Research, New York, 1926, in "CAN misc. 1917–1927" file, Box 56, G. Bromley Oxnam Papers, Library of Congress, Washington, D.C.
* Figures in parentheses do not add up.

Armenian, or other ethnic background. While Roosevelt perhaps epitomized the multiethnic Los Angeles school, the student bodies at most other schools in the working-class districts east and south of downtown during this period were characterized by varying degrees of what Douglas Monroy terms "meaningful diversity."[44]

Within these districts, integration among the student body translated into at least some integration in the classroom. While schools in other parts of Los Angeles County followed California's long tradition of segregating Mexican and Asian children, attempts to segregate schools in mixed ethnic areas of the city during the 1910s and 1920s generally remained rare and ineffective, especially in light of those districts' rapid demographic changes.[45] A 1918 petition by Austrian residents of the Belvedere district to segregate Mexican students, for example, became pointless given Mexicans' subsequent predominance in the area. One exception to this rule of official apathy occurred along the neighborhoods bifurcated by Alameda Street south of downtown. As other groups settled the area, white residents in 1927 pressured the school into establishing Fremont High School for children in the remaining white districts while placing adjacent integrated neighborhoods in the Jefferson High district.[46] In subsequent years the percentage of African Americans and immigrants at Jefferson rose considerably, but a few students found ways around the board's policy. Kango Kunitsugo and some of his Asian, Mexican, and African American friends submitted fake addresses placing them in a school district of their choice. Likewise, Tom Bradley avoided Jefferson by borrowing the address of the family for whom his mother worked as a domestic to attend the more rigorous Polytechnic High. Rodney Chow also remembered that some principals used to "grill" students suspected of submitting false addresses and would expel students who "broke."[47] Despite these efforts, false address filing at least partially undercut attempts to segregate school populations.

The amalgamation of children of all backgrounds produced a dynamic, sometimes volatile environment. Teachers and adult observers reported that students alternately demonstrated their internalization of dominant ethnoracial divisions and their willingness to transcend them. Nellie Oliver, an elementary school teacher, recalled that the Mexican children in her class "tried for some time to drive the Japanese and Chinese out of the school by calling them names and throwing stones at them." However, she continued, "conditions have . . . become greatly improved as of late." Prejudices usually faded as students became accustomed to their peers, she explained, and though some students tended to collect with those of their own race on the playground, they still had good relations with one another.[48] Another teacher described friendly relations among Mexican, Chinese, Japanese, African American, and Jewish students but noted that one of two Anglo boys, the most "troublesome" boy in school, claimed he was picked on because of his race. And one scholar identified a disproportionate number of "problem" African American students from Twentieth Street Elementary, a discrepancy he attributed to resentments generated by "color distinctions" among the student body.[49]

FIGURE 4. Roosevelt High School Spanish Club, undated photo. Many high
school administrators encouraged student participation in ethnic-specific
clubs. Shades of L.A. Archives/Los Angeles Public Library.

Former students acknowledged that racial tensions sometimes flared
in the schools, though not necessarily on a consistent basis. Rodney
Chow, for instance, remembered that some Japanese students would
"push around" Chinese kids at Ninth Street School, but he said he also
had Japanese friends. A Japanese girl who attended the Hewitt Street
School avoided the Mexican and Russian children, though she claimed
there was no racism at the school.[50] Louise Leung Larson, the daughter
of well-to-do Chinese merchants and later a prominent Los Angeles
journalist, recalled that neighborhood children sometimes jeered her on
the walk to school. Other Chinese and Japanese students also recalled
jeering, although at least one of them suggested the kids were only "jok-
ing." Teru Miyamoto, a Los Angeles High School graduate living in Little Tokyo, remembered that she experienced both rejection and acceptance from her peers: "Sometimes some girl who didn't like the Japanese
very well would go with you because her friend liked you and then after
she got to know you she would like you too."[51]

These comments suggest a tense network of conflict and tolerance,
but they existed alongside other interpretations of school environments
that emphasized accommodation and friendship. Indeed, some students
and teachers painted an almost idyllic picture of ethnoracial relations. A
teacher at the California Street School, for example, found "no apparent discrimination" between Mexican, Jewish, and Asian children, nor

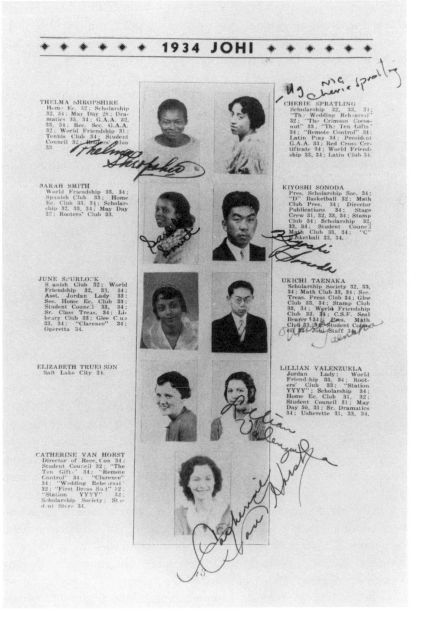

THELMA SHROPSHIRE
Home Ec. 32; Scholarship 32, 34; May Day 28; Dramatics 33, 34; G.A.A. 32, 33, 34; Rec. Sec. G.A.A. 32; World Friendship 31; Tennis Club 34; Student Council 32; Rooters' Club 33.

CHERIE SPRATLING
Scholarship 32, 33, 34; "The Wedding Rehearsal" 32; "The Crimson Cocoanut" 33, "The Ten Gifts" 34; "Remote Control" 34; Latin Play 34; President G.A.A. 33; Red Cross Certificate 34; World Friendship 33, 34; Latin Club 34.

SARAH SMITH
World Friendship 33, 34; Spanish Club 33; Home Ec. Club 33; Scholarship 32, 33, 34; May Day 32; Rooters' Club 33.

KIYOSHI SONODA
Pres. Scholarship Soc. 34; "D" Basketball 32; Math Club Pres. 34; Director Publications 34; Stage Crew 31, 32, 33, 34; Stamp Club 34; Scholarship 32, 33, 34; Student Council Math Club 33, 34; "C" Basketball 33, 34.

JUNE SPURLOCK
Spanish Club 32; World Friendship 32, 33, 34; Asst. Jordan Lady 33; Sec. Home Ec. Club 33; Student Council 33, 34; Sr. Class Treas. 34; Library Club 33; Glee Club 33, 34; "Clarence" 34; Operetta 34.

UKICHI TAENAKA
Scholarship Society 32, 33, 34; Math Club 33, 34; Sec. Treas. Press Club 34; Glee Club 33, 34; Stamp Club 33, 34; World Friendship Club 33, 34; C.S.F. Seal Bearer 34; Pres. Math Club 33, 34; Student Council 34; Johi Staff 34.

ELIZABETH TRUELSON
Salt Lake City 34.

LILLIAN VALENZUELA
Jordan Lady; World Friendship 33, 34; Rooters' Club 33; "Station YYYY"; Scholarship 34; Home Ec. Club 31, 32; Student Council 31; May Day 30, 31; Sr. Dramatics 34; Usherette 31, 33, 34.

CATHERINE VAN HORST
Director of Reception 34; Student Council 32; "The Ten Gifts" 34; "Remote Control" 34; "Clarence" 34; "Wedding Rehearsal" 32; "First Dress Suit" 32; "Station YYYY" 32; Scholarship Society; Student Store 34.

FIGURE 5. Jordan High School yearbook page, 1934. Shades of L.A. Archives / Los Angeles Public Library.

did any ethnic group behave in a "cliquish" manner. One Japanese girl
claimed to associate with a "sort of melting pot group because there
were all kinds of racial backgrounds among us." Louise Leung Larson
recalled that her closest friends in elementary school were a Jewish girl
and an African American girl. [52] Archie Green made friends with Japanese, Mexican, Jewish, and other students while attending several
schools in Boyle Heights. Herbert Leong, Julie Suski, and James Chan
likewise remembered mingling freely with the other children. William
Chew Chan had mostly Chinese friends but also a very close Mexican
friend at Macy Street School. And former Polytechnic High student
Allan Chan recalled that "most of the minority students stuck pretty
close regardless of whether they were Black, Mexican, or Chinese."[53]

DRAWING WITHIN THE LINES:
LEARNING ABOUT ETHNORACIAL BOUNDARIES

Whatever degree of tolerance and interaction existed in Los Angeles
schools, these conditions did not go unchallenged for long. As they grew
older Angeleno youth encountered various forces that influenced their
social relations with each other. Teachers and administrators, almost all
of them Anglo, alternately reinforced and undercut the promise of egalitarian, integrated social relations, imposing on students a multitude of
often contradictory lessons about the meaning and significance of racial
and ethnic categories.[54] These mixed messages could confuse students
who were unable to reconcile the inconsistent application of ethnoracial
categories with the social structure of the school.

   By the early twentieth century, school administrators began to recognize that the diversifying student population in California cities required
changes in local education. Their innovations both drew from and contributed to the Americanization campaigns popular at the time. The California Home Teacher Act of 1915, spearheaded by CCIH board member Mary Gibson and implemented in Los Angeles by a cadre of
administrators with ties to the settlement movement, encapsulated many
of their strategies. The act authorized the creation of "neighborhood
schools," immigrant-targeted campuses combining traditional education with social programs and adult education classes as engines of cultural and political assimilation. Despite resistance from nativists and fiscal conservatives, who managed to curb Americanization programs after
World War I, these administrators and activists exerted a substantial if
not dominant influence on educational policies in Los Angeles.[55]

Neighborhood school curricula emphasized what administrators termed "internationalism" studies and to some extent anticipated the ethnic studies movement of the Civil Rights era. Sue Kunitomi Embrey, looking back at her education at the Amelia Street School, made an explicit comparison: "People say that things like Chicano Studies or Black Studies are innovations in education. We had all that. . . . We actually had a cultural program all year round that emphasized the different ethnic groups."[56] Internationalism studies differed from postwar ethnic studies in that it focused more directly on relations between nations than on ethnic relations within America. The "World Friendship" clubs established by several schools to promote "cultural understanding," for example, addressed the legacy of World War I more explicitly than they did mixed student bodies and neighborhoods. Nevertheless, reformers noted that international relations could serve as a metaphor for local interaction, what one writer termed the "brotherization" of the diverse student population.[57]

Students soon learned, however, that the egalitarian rhetoric of internationalism studies did not necessarily extend to school policy. Educators might have promoted cultural understanding, but they did not necessarily treat ethnoracial groups themselves equally. Tracking, whereby schools divided students by ability or educational goal, removed many students of color (and some immigrants from southern or eastern Europe) both from their Anglo peers and from academic and professional classes. School officials acknowledged that remedial classes tended to draw large numbers of immigrant children, especially Mexicans and Russians, who scored low on intelligence exams. Some observers asserted that the tests discriminated against children with poor English skills and mirrored the prejudices of local teachers. One student claimed to have witnessed several instances in which Chinese students who scored an A had to repeat a test because of incredulous teachers.[58] But Anglos who admitted the shortcomings of the tests sometimes endorsed segregation anyway. Emory Bogardus, for example, maintained that even English-speaking second-generation Mexican students seemed "handicapped" compared to "American" students at school. He advocated separate classes for immigrants so that they would not become discouraged by their poor performance in relation to native English speakers. A few non-Anglos endorsed segregation for the same reason.[59]

Tracking, remedial classes, and discrimination went a long way toward redistributing student populations along ethnoracial lines, but they did not homogenize Los Angeles classrooms. Diversity, limited school resources, and individual teacher policies often precluded monoethnic or monoracial classes in mixed central neighborhood schools. One teacher at Temple Street School, for example, inaugurated an Americanization class for Japanese and Mexican students and gradually returned some of the better students to the "regular" class. A teacher at the California School grouped her students by language type, placing Romance-language speakers together while establishing a separate class for Chinese, Japanese, and Yiddish speakers, whom she taught phonetically. However, she forced students in these classes to converse with those of different ethnicities to prevent them from lapsing into their mother tongues.[60]

But if these classes preserved some opportunities for inter-ethnoracial contact, they also introduced children to the social stratification they would encounter as adults. Designed to teach practical skills that would make them employable, vocational training effectively partitioned students of different ethnicities into "appropriate" careers.[61] Segregation under tracking policies did not anger every student or parent in the system. As Judith Raftery points out, working-class Angelenos of the period, including Anglos, generally had "modest expectations" for their careers and embraced the practical skills they received in vocational training.[62] And yet for some students tracking could frustrate career aspirations. Esperanza Acosta (later known as Hope Mendoza Schechter, a labor organizer) recalled the response of her guidance counselor at Belvedere Intermediate when she asked to switch from home economics to an academic track so that she could pursue a nursing career: "She said what made me think that anyone who was sick in bed would want anyone as black as me to take care of them." Denied the transfer, a frustrated Acosta let her grades slip and eventually dropped out of school.[63]

As Acosta's story suggests, some Los Angeles teachers augmented the ethnoracial stratification of vocational and remedial education with less formal methods of discrimination. A number of former students charged that teachers withheld educational opportunities from them. Clarence Johnson, an African American, remembered that his teachers discouraged students of color from pursuing professional or skilled work, and Tom Bradley sadly recalled all the "gifted people with no outlet" at Lafayette Junior High, where teachers pointed Asians toward gardening and clerking careers and African Americans and Mexicans toward service jobs.[64] Sometimes children protested when teachers did not show them enough respect. One principal admitted that a group of disgruntled students had rebelled against a teacher who had "said something that made them think she looked upon them as dirty Mexicans," forcing him to transfer the teacher to another school. A Chinese woman claimed she dropped out of high school because of hostile treatment from teachers. Beatrice Griffith, examining the experiences of ethnic Mexican children during the 1940s, found school officials who subscribed to more ruthless strategies. One intentionally made work for Mexicans so complicated that they quit, and a principal claimed to have found a simple solution to the "Mexican problem" at his school: "We just see that none of them get to the tenth grade."[65]

In several cases, school officials even sought to remove minorities elected to leadership positions by their classmates. Students at one high school, for example, elected Sophie Yamanaka editor in chief of the school paper, but the faculty decided they did not want a Japanese student in a leadership position. They put a white student in the chief position and demoted Yamanaka to associate editor. In Hollywood the election of Japanese John Aiso as student body president ignited a protest from several white students, leading the school principal to dissolve the student government and institute "temporary faculty rule."[66] Such incidents did not necessarily characterize schools closer to downtown Los Angeles. Roosevelt High, for example, elected a Japanese student body president and an African American female class president without objection in the early 1930s, and Jordan High elected a Mexican student body president. But incidents of discrimination contributed to some students' education in the realities of American racial meanings.[67]

It would be a gross exaggeration to state that all school officials discriminated against nonwhite students. Numerous teachers took a genuine interest in their pupils' welfare and developed supportive relationships with them. Kango Kunitsugo recalled that his teachers always encouraged him to pursue his education despite the racial exigencies of the job market. "I really think they didn't realize what the outside world has to offer—or not to offer," he allowed. Enrique Vega claimed that most teachers had the respect of the students and exerted a good degree of influence over their thinking. Although his family repatriated to Mexico during the depression, he returned frequently to Los Angeles for work and always took the time to visit his favorite teachers. A Chinese boy counted Macy Street School principal Nora Sterry and a Mr. Weinstein, his teacher at Ninth Street School, among his good friends. Sue Kunitomi Embrey also remembered that there was a very low turnover of Amelia Street faculty and that the teachers established good relationships with the students and their families. And despite enduring numerous racist educators, Tom Bradley recalled at least one white teacher who supported his scholastic and career ambitions.[68]

Yet this sympathy seldom translated into meaningful efforts to help overturn the socioeconomic barriers confronting immigrant and African American students. More often, teachers sought to accommodate students' desires with available opportunities and to reconcile them to the limitations imposed by their backgrounds. One teacher, for example, claimed she was only being realistic in acknowledging that African American, Mexican, and Japanese children were "handicapped vocationally." "I never tell my boys that by going to high school they can make more money," she admitted. "I tell them that they will enjoy life more by going to school, but that is all. Otherwise, they will come in and say, 'Look at Manuel, Miss M. He went to high school, and he works in the brickyard the same as Pedro, who never went to school.' But I tell them that Manuel enjoys life more, for he can read and appreciate things more."[69] Archie Green recalled learning a similar lesson while attending Bridge Street School. On the day of Herbert Hoover's inauguration the principal called a school meeting.

> [She] wanted to re-enact the inauguration. We had one boy in our school named Billy Adams. Fortuitously from Miss —'s perspective he was named after a president. . . . So she asked Billy to come up, and she explained to us that it was unlikely that any child who was born abroad or had parents who were born overseas, whether the name was Gutierrez or Finklestein or Shubin or Yamamoto or whatever, would get to be president, but Billy Adams was already on his way.[70]

The principal may only have meant to point out the realities of the American political structure, but the lesson on the limits of political opportunity for non-Anglos could not have been lost on the students.

Segregation in school environments did not emerge solely from the efforts of school administrators. Parents anxious to preserve ethnic ties encouraged students to associate with peers of their own ethnicity as they grew older. Some Anglo parents hastened the process by transferring their children out of neighborhood schools.[71] Growing social pressures began to register in the social interaction of students at higher grades. Alfred Lee claimed that white and Mexican children at Sixteenth Street Primary School treated him "as equal" but that he began to notice social segregation thereafter. "The higher an education a person gets the more discrimination one encounters," he concluded, echoing the comments of other students.[72] Roosevelt graduates Morris Kadish and Michio Kunitani recalled that by high school the social lives of most

Jewish students concentrated in Jewish clubs, that Mexicans kept to themselves and spoke Spanish outside the classroom, and that Japanese segregated themselves as well. Kunitani rebuffed a teacher's efforts to get him to join the Japanese Club, which he felt was an institutional attempt to divide the student body. His insistence on associating with peers of different backgrounds was admirable but not necessarily common, even in a school noted for its diversity and tolerance.[73]

Not all interethnic and interracial friendships ceased by high school, but children who maintained such relationships after puberty frequently endured ridicule from their families and ethnic communities. Louise Leung Larson confessed that she began to distance herself from friends of other backgrounds after hearing racist remarks from some Chinese friends. A number of other Chinese students noted that grammar school friendships with "Americans" did not last into high school. According to a Chinese parent, "The boys and girls of grammar school age will mingle with each other with no thoughts of any discrimination: When they have attained high school age, some of their parents object to such association, and some of them begin to discriminate because of such influences."[74] A Japanese girl who had several Anglo friends at school began to feel uncomfortable there after she and a "spanish" girl were the only two students not invited to a classmate's birthday party. In 1925 Lincoln High student Chiyoe Sumi acknowledged her apprehension about mingling with non-Japanese: "I always feel that maybe they wouldn't want me. . . . I never felt that way in grammar school, it is just since I started high school that I feel different. I don't think it is because of a change in the American girls, because some of the girls who were my friends in grammar school are still my friends in high school."[75] Regardless of their origin, the new pressures accompanying impending adulthood, in particular, the sexual awakening of adolescence (see chap. 5), began to take their toll on inter-ethnoracial relationships.

OUT OF THE FRYING PAN:
FROM SCHOOL TO THE WORKFORCE

Economic forces also played a role in eliminating the diversity in secondary schools. Despite the increase in school attendance, poorer students continued to face periodic pressure to leave school in order to contribute to family incomes. Work permit programs often allowed them legal means to circumvent attendance requirements. The decision to drop out cut across racial and ethnic lines, but immigrants and African

Americans, who faced less resistance from truancy officers and school officials than their Anglo counterparts, left in disproportionate numbers.[76] They were also more likely than Anglos to have one or both parents unemployed, absent, or deceased. Social reformers tended to attribute these "broken" homes to personal or cultural failings, but numerous surveys suggested that the most common cause was death of a parent. A survey of five hundred children in the All Nations district revealed that of 140 "broken" families, 77 were from death of a parent, 45 from divorce or separation, and 18 from desertion, findings echoed in other studies.[77] These surveys did not list the cause of death, but environmental pollution in the central neighborhoods and industrial accidents almost certainly accounted for some of these fatalities.

Whatever the cause, broken homes increased the pressure on immigrant and African American children to contribute to the family income and aggravated the problem of truancy and attrition. Even if both parents were present and working, children might find themselves encouraged to work during at least part of the school year. Several frustrated reformers and school officials claimed that central city parents looked on their children as "economic units" and often removed them from school during harvest periods or other times when work was available. Thousands of children continued to apply for work permits "out of economic necessity."[78]

In part as a result, ethnoracial compositions of central Los Angeles classrooms changed as students moved into higher grades. Figures from a 1908 federal survey of the Los Angeles school system revealed that 59 percent of kindergartners had native-born white fathers, versus 74 percent of high school seniors. Even accounting for the larger number of elementary versus high school grades, the survey identified a precipitous decline in the number of Chinese, Jewish, Italian, Russian, and African American students from primary to secondary schools and the virtual disappearance of Mexican students by high school grades. Only Japanese students (of which there were barely more than one hundred) maintained a somewhat consistent population from kindergarten to high school. During the 1910s and 1920s, the numbers of immigrant and African American high school students increased dramatically, but attrition rates among these groups continued to outstrip that of Anglos.[79]

The depression exacerbated this trend, forcing many poor, immigrant, or nonwhite students to exchange schoolbooks for paychecks. According to Michio Kunitani, Mexican students left Roosevelt for the workforce in especially high numbers during the 1930s. Likewise, Marshal

Royal recalled that among African American Angelenos "it was quite a fashionable thing to quit school during [the depression], because of the financial condition of most of the families around," and Keong Lee remembered that few Chinese attended school after junior high because, with all of their work responsibilities, "there was no time" for class.[80] Paradoxically, disproportionate dropout rates may have preserved diversity in certain schools by decreasing the demographic impact of a group that was coming to dominate a specific neighborhood. Thus Roosevelt High School in the 1930s maintained its renowned ethnic balance, even as Mexicans began to predominate in parts of the school district.[81] In most cases, dropout rates increased the Anglo or white population of high schools beyond their representation in the surrounding neighborhoods.

Regardless of the specific impact on each school, however, students who dropped out exchanged the somewhat integrated environment of the classroom for the more ruthlessly segregated world of the Los Angeles workforce. This was particularly true for adolescents. Younger children who worked, especially boys, often engaged in what reformers called "blind alley" jobs—selling newspapers, delivering items, shining shoes, and so on—and toiled alongside peers of different backgrounds on the cosmopolitan streets of downtown. The newsboy trade, for instance, hired substantial numbers of Jewish, Italian, German, Mexican, and Anglo boys and, by the 1930s, a few African American boys.[82]

Yet older students and former students had no illusions that the lessons of tolerance preached by internationalism studies operated in local employment. Indeed, awareness of limited opportunities prompted some young Angelenos to abandon education as a pointless exercise, even if their fiscal situation did not immediately demand it. "Sure I quit school," one Mexican boy told a reformer. "What difference would it have made if I'd finished? I would have become a laborer anyway. I can be that without going to school." "Look at José," said another boy. "He graduated from Roosevelt, yet he's digging a ditch. I will do the work I am learning now when I graduate."[83] Chinese and Japanese Angelenos complained that even with college degrees they could only find work as cooks or at produce markets. Some therefore abandoned their educations as a fruitless enterprise. An African American boy underscored his dim prospects by referring to a friend who worked as a delivery boy despite his skill as a trained mechanic. The boy claimed repair shop owners would only hire him to wash cars.[84] Even children who stayed in school generally recognized their limited employment options in

America. Sun Lee, for example, told an interviewer that he planned to pursue a degree in electrical engineering but hoped to find a job in China, since firms in the United States "d[o] not hire Chinese."[85] Not all Angelenos denounced the segregated workforce. One sociologist, for example, claimed that many Molokan Russians preferred the lumber yards that employed 75 percent of Molokan men and the laundries and candy factories that employed Molokan women to integrated schools where their children might "Americanize" too quickly.[86]

The transition from adolescence to adulthood in central Los Angeles during the early twentieth century suggests that while integration may have been necessary to achieve inter-ethnoracial cooperation, it was not sufficient to do so. Persistent stratification and division, whether instituted by school officials, parents, or peers, often eroded children's willingness to cross ethoracial boundaries. The virtues of mixed school environments identified by some Angelenos suggest recognition of both the promise and the problem of forging new social bonds in a multiethnic community. As one African American parent commented, "If my boy goes to school where there are only Negro boys, he is not prepared to get out into the world and get along with the white, the Oriental, the Jew, and the immigrant." But in an integrated school, "when he graduates he does not have to make the transition which would be so hard for him later in the business world."[87] Some former students, having endured failure and discrimination in their adult lives, separated the nostalgic world of their childhood from what they encountered afterward. Kazuo Kawai, for example, remembered that as a student at Ninth Street School he was "an integral part of that cosmopolitan eastside population that was being molded by the zealous school teachers into good Americans. . . . [A]t that period of my life, everything which I learned in school about America took root, and I felt I was American." Subsequent experiences embittered Kawai, however, and by adulthood he had abandoned the optimism of his youth. "At present," he said, "I never speak of America as my country. . . . America made a foreigner out of me."[88]

CHAPTER 5

Mixed Couples

Love, Sex, and Marriage
across Ethnoracial Lines

THE MANY COLORS OF LOVE

Of the possible kinds of inter-ethnoracial contact in the central neighborhoods, those involving sexual or romantic relations perhaps prompted the most visceral reactions. Whether in the context of prostitution, dating, or marriage, they seemed to pose an immediate threat to established racial and ethnic communities. Historians have already chronicled the tremendous anxiety that afflicted Anglo-Americans during the late nineteenth and early twentieth century, when the movement of white women into the workforce and the growing population of nonwhites stoked fears of racial amalgamation. Crystallizing in fits of hysteria like the "white slave" panic, these anxieties resonated with broader concerns about the impact of commercial culture, modern industrial labor practices, and urban living on traditional gender roles and ethnoracial relations.[1] In this climate many Anglos in Los Angeles and around the country reaffirmed the taboo against mixed-race couples, especially those involving white women. Even liberals who argued fervently for "understanding between the races" often drew the line at intimate relations. But Anglos were not the only ones confronting this specter of amalgamation. Immigrants and African Americans, many of them new to urban environments like those in the central neighborhoods, expressed concerns about the consequences of inter-ethnoracial sex and its potential dilution of their communities. In short, few communities in Los

Angeles were amenable as a group to intimate liaisons that extended beyond their boundaries.

And yet this resistance, however effectively asserted, faced strong countervailing forces. The expansion of integrated districts in early-twentieth-century Los Angeles increased the possibility for romantic, or at least lustful, connections between partners of different backgrounds. Moreover, the lopsided gender ratios of certain immigrant populations meant that some Angelenos seeking companionship had no choice but to look outside their ethnic community. In such contexts, instances of inter-ethnoracial contact became almost inevitable. Many of the mixed couplings that took place in Los Angeles at this time were casual liaisons between prostitutes and clients in central city neighborhoods. Others involved romances between adolescents and young adults who met in school, on the street, in dance halls, or at the movies. Finally, a small but not inconsequential number of Angelenos managed to construct long-term mixed relationships and to raise families despite ostracism from certain quarters. One would certainly not identify this last group of relationships as common, but they held a social importance out of proportion to their numbers. They embodied the challenge of a modern, integrated social geography to traditional ethnic and racial boundaries and to traditional concepts of social order. Struggles over the nature and extent of "race-mixing" represented in large part attempts to reconstruct the meaning of race and ethnicity in a multiracial environment and a modern, corporate liberal social system.[2]

RED-LIGHT KALEIDOSCOPE:
THE ETHNORACIAL GEOGRAPHY OF PROSTITUTION

In the early 1930s a University of Southern California sociology student, J. MacFarline Ervin, interviewed a white prostitute who catered to African American clients. The woman explained that black men would pay more for her services than whites. "It ain't that I'm so crazy about Colored men," she told Ervin, "but I can make more money here among them." Other white prostitutes agreed. "I could make no money hustling with our [white] men so that accounts for me being here," one allowed. A third financially strapped Anglo girl entered the trade along South Central after she "heard that Negro men would give almost any price for contacts with white girls." In contrast, Ervin noted that pimps often directed African American prostitutes to concentrate on the more lucrative white clientele. A black prostitute confirmed this sentiment. "I like to have white trade because they will pay more," she concluded. Ervin and other observers found that many Los Angeles residents—Mexican, Asian, and European immigrants in addition to Anglos and African Americans— involved in the sex trade during this period engaged in relations with partners of different ethnic or racial backgrounds.[3]

Residents of pre–World War II Los Angeles recognized the close relationship between prostitution and the broader structure of ethnic relations. The relative affluence of Anglo men, the relative poverty of immigrant and African American women, the skewed gender ratios of some immigrant populations, and cultural mores that placed higher values on sexual access to Anglo women all contributed to a proliferation of interethnoracial liaisons in the sex trade. Other studies of mixed-ethnoracial sex districts in late-nineteenth- and early-twentieth-century American cities have emphasized the alternative social relations that emerged within them.[4] But these activities could have other, less emancipatory effects as well. By allowing Angelenos to transgress ethnoracial boundaries in a setting of marginal legality, prostitution reinforced restrictions against such behavior in more legitimate contexts. Those who dated or married outside their community could face hostility from outsiders who associated their relationship with illicit activity. Moreover, the concentration of prostitution in districts populated by immigrants and African Americans convinced some Angelenos to associate all female residents of those districts with the sex trade. Presumptions about sexual availability made immigrant and African American women in these neighborhoods vulnerable to approaches by men and further marginalized them in relation to Anglo women.

The heterogeneous nature of the Los Angeles sex trade revealed the complicated and often contradictory interplay between ethnoracial relations and the new urban environments that emerged during the industrial revolution of the late nineteenth and early twentieth century. Different ethnoracial combinations of participants (prostitute, client, pimp) in sex for money exchanges might hold different meanings for various observers with respect to ethnic, racial, and gendered power relations. But the threat to ethnoracial cohesiveness remained at least somewhat consistent no matter what the specific relationship of actors in a given exchange.[5] In each case the structure of the sex trade underscored the social forces that separated groups even as they shared neighborhoods and public spaces of the city. Because it often concentrated in these same

districts, the sex trade played an important role in the way that ethnoracial communities and individuals established relations with and
boundaries between each other.[6]

Between the 1880s and World War II the geographic center of the sex
trade in Los Angeles wandered, but it always remained within a zone
between downtown and the Los Angeles River. The location of the sex
trade reflected in large part the moral priorities of middle-class and elite
Anglos, many of whom sanctioned prostitution during this period as
long as it stayed out of Anglo neighborhoods. This policy acknowledged
the sex trade's seeming inevitability while attempting to separate prostitutes both geographically and morally from "respectable" women.[7] It
also predated Anglo rule. Before 1848 Spanish and Mexican officials
maintained a red-light district in various areas populated by Native
Americans and other residents of non-European ancestry. After statehood American officials pursued a policy of containment with regard to
the sex trade and other vice industries. One 1874 law, for example,
expelled bordellos from the central business district but not from other
areas of the city. The founding of the LAPD in 1876 accompanied ordinances excluding vice operations from wealthier Anglo districts and lim-
iting their hours of operation, and at the end of the nineteenth century
the city council briefly established a legal vice district in Chinatown. Not
until 1902 was legislation passed outlawing prostitution in the city
limits.[8]

Containment policies increased the ethnoracial diversity and interaction of those areas where vice operated. Reduced police interference in
red-light districts encouraged both workers and customers in the sex
trade to converge on those neighborhoods regardless of their ethnoracial backgrounds. Anglos who might have segregated themselves in
other social contexts came much closer to other Angelenos when they
bought or sold sexual favors. A few nineteenth-century brothels strung
along New High Street may have confined themselves, either through
price or policy, to Anglo customers and Anglo or European prostitutes.
Many others, however, sustained a more diverse workforce and clientele. Within such environments, the potential for crossing ethnoracial
lines increased substantially, both in customer-client relationships and in
the business structure of the sex trade.[9]

Chinatown was the city's principal red-light district from the 1850s
through the turn of the century. Twentieth-century reformers, looking
back on the neighborhood's "open" era, recalled with little nostalgia the
days when Chinatown housed "all the brothels and one-third the saloons

of the city" and where "opium and gambling dens thrived unmolested."[10] Observers noted that the neighborhood drew visitors from all over the city to its bars, opium establishments, gambling houses, and brothels. Marshall Stimson recalled trips to gambling dens in Chinatown while attending high school. During one visit, a police raid interrupted their activity. An officer who knew Stimson's family let him go, but as the young boy was walking back to school, "two (police) wagons passed loaded with a miscellaneous lot of Chinese, Mexicans, and Negroes, and three [Anglos] of the high school group" from the raid.[11]

If Chinatown's sex trade in the late nineteenth century attracted a mixed clientele, its workers were similarly diverse. Since the 1860s Chinese entrepreneurs had transported "slave women" (sometimes young girls sold by their parents) from mainland China to cash in on the shortage of Chinese women in the United States.[12] Brothel owners often housed these women in cribs, rows of stalls that faced a street or alleyway. But non-Chinese prostitutes also moved into the cribs and into larger houses such as the notorious Ballerino's Plaza on Chinatown's "Nigger Alley." According to some eyewitness accounts, by 1900 the majority of prostitutes operating in the cribs and houses in the area were white (newspapers made vague references to an "American section" of the red-light district), along with substantial numbers of Chinese and African Americans and smaller numbers of Japanese.[13]

The publicity surrounding a 1903 campaign led by three Protestant clergymen to eliminate the crib district uncovered the cosmopolitan nature of Chinatown's sex trade. In December of that year dozens of supporters invaded the neighborhood, papering the alleyways with flyers written in several languages (including Spanish, Portuguese, German, and French) that advertised "safe houses" for repentant sex workers. Among other avowed achievements, reformers claimed to have rescued a sixteen-year-old Japanese girl from a brothel owner's "jail."[14] But like others caught up in the white slavery panic, these activists were most concerned with the plight of white prostitutes. They conjured up elaborate scenarios of underground networks designed by foreigners to lure white women into the sex trade. Especially in the western United States, these sensational stories fed on the specter of Asians' supposed "deviant" sexuality. In 1910 this broader campaign would culminate in the passage of the Mann Act, which prohibited the transportation of women across state lines for "immoral purposes."[15] Anticipating that legislation in his antiprostitution polemic, *Queen of the Red Lights*, reformer Rev. Sydney Kendall solemnly reported a story about a note

FIGURE 6. The "crib district" in Chinatown, the center of prostitution in Los
Angeles, 1891." Security Pacific Collection/Los Angeles Public Library.

scribbled on the back of a Chinese lottery flyer and sent to a local newspaper. The note read, "I am a white girl kept by Chinamen. . . . I am
writing this with my blood and a fish bone." The LAPD, Kendall
assured his readers, subsequently rescued the girl.[16]

In retrospect, these captivity stories lack credibility, and reflect a common Anglo preoccupation with the sexual purity of white women. But
they drew on more plausible observations about the diversity of male
clients and "macs" (pimps) who frequented the crib district. Few pimps
or "keepers" deigned to confront the reformers, and Kendall may have
been speculating about their ethnic backgrounds in his narrative. A list
of brothel owners arrested during the crackdown, however, included
Chinese, French, Italian, Irish, and other surnames and suggests a diverse
array of top-level operators.[17] Reformers were more explicit about the

cosmopolitan hue of the crib district's customer base. Kendall's partner, Rev. Wiley Phillips, later recalled that most patrons of the crib districts were Chinese, Mexicans, and African Americans. He described the whites who patronized the district as young men and boys of the "lowest economic and social class."[18]

Kendall, Phillips, and their supporters eventually convinced the LAPD to shut down the crib district, but their victory did little to stop the city's sex trade or to keep immigrant and African American men away from Anglo prostitutes. Part of the problem lay with police officers and city officials not entirely comfortable with the new policy. They feared that prostitutes expelled from Chinatown might move into wealthier Anglo districts where they would solicit on the streets and walk, as Mayor Meredith Snyder put it, "side by side proper women." A recalcitrant LAPD chief reportedly declared, "I won't interfere with the crib district. It is the best place in the city to catch a criminal in."[19] Unable or unwilling to eliminate the sex trade, the LAPD instead instituted a "south of First [Street]" policy that relocated prostitutes from the environs of Chinatown to the mixed-use industrial and residential neighborhoods near the river and along Central Avenue.[20] Prostitutes spread out into multiethnic neighborhoods where they mingled with other residents. Police reported streetwalkers operating as far south as Thirtieth Street and as far west as Grand Avenue.[21] The new setting did restructure the sex trade in certain respects. Rather than concentrate in cribs or large brothels, many women in the sex trade began to operate individually or under the loose direction of pimps. Some solicited clients on high-traffic streets, while others took referrals from business partners working the streets, saloons, and dance halls. A few even approached men on streetcars and jitney buses that ran through working-class districts.[22]

Throughout the early decades of the twentieth century the sex trade thrived in the districts east of Main Street and south along Central Avenue. Notes from a 1918 survey of the All Nations district, for instance, indicate that prostitutes operated there more or less free of police interference. Surveyor June Barth reported that streetwalkers clustered in the area around the Southern Pacific Depot on Fifth Street, where they openly solicited soldiers, sailors, and other men of all backgrounds. Couples retired to small nearby cottages or repaired to dark alleyways and vacant lots. One interviewee identified a "notorious sport house" run by African Americans on Merchant Street. The house allegedly employed black and white women and attracted men of all races. The interviewee maintained that after a series of neighborhood complaints officers had investigated the establishment but concluded it was "on the square." Its operators avoided detection in part by flashing lights and placing pieces of paper in the windows to signal customers. The majority, though by no means all, of the prostitutes operating in this district were African American. Residents identified a house run by Hungarians, for example, that had developed a substantial customer base in the neighborhood.[23]

Although they often exacted bribes for the privilege, local police generally treated sex workers in the central neighborhoods leniently. Officers even allowed nonwhites to purchase the favors of white women. One All Nations district resident recalled a plainclothes detective who called in a raid on a nearby house after observing a white woman enter with an African American man. The witness reported that six officers broke down the door and entered the building. Sometime later, however, two cases of beer were delivered to the house. The officers eventually left, "shook hands all around," and neglected to make any arrests.[24] With such arrangements in force, inter-ethnoracial sex continued to flourish in the city's sex trade.

The geography of this trade became clearer in 1919 when a county grand jury indicted Mayor Frederic Woodman for accepting bribes from two African American vice operators to sanction a "protected area" within the east-of-Main neighborhoods for gambling operations, liquor sales, and prostitution. A published record of prostitution arrests over a two-month period revealed sex workers operating from Temple Street north of downtown through the districts stretching south and east toward the river (see map 3).[25] These records did not note the race or ethnicity of prostitutes or clients, but they firmly located the sex trade in mixed-ethnic districts. They also suggested that prostitutes had returned to Chinatown, a statement subsequently confirmed by observers.[26] The indictments, legislation, and sweeps that hit the sex trade during the 1920s failed to deliver more than glancing blows. Streetwalkers, "both amateur and professional," continued to solicit in neighborhoods east of Main Street and down South Central Avenue into the 1930s.[27]

Prostitution may have encouraged inter-ethnoracial contact, but this does not mean that it challenged conventional racial and ethnic boundaries of sexual interaction. More often the structure of prostitution reinforced those boundaries by exploiting cultural and economic differences between ethnic or racial groups to generate profits. For white prostitutes, this exploitation began with the higher value that social conventions placed on their sexual favors. Their actions mirrored the practices

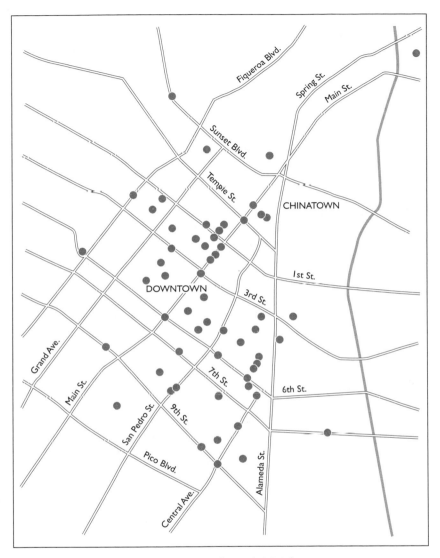

MAP 3. Prostitution Arrests: January 1 through March 5, 1919

of some brothels in late-nineteenth-century San Francisco that, according to Herbert Asbury, based fees on the prostitute's race. One establishment, for instance, charged 25 cents for sex with Mexican women, 50 cents for African American or Asian women, and 75 cents to a dollar for white or European immigrant women.[28] This type of fixed pricing structure may or may not have operated in Los Angeles, but white prostitutes recognized that their skin color entitled them to charge more than other sex workers, especially to immigrant and African American clients. A number of taxi-dance halls catering to immigrant (especially Filipino) men, for instance, employed substantial numbers of white women in the early twentieth century. Owners of these establishments charged patrons 10 cents (and sometime more) a dance, and some women sold sexual favors to clients at even higher prices. Recognizing that these men had few other options for social contact with women, many employers and employees of the taxi-dances seized the opportunity to gouge their patrons.[29]

White prostitutes outside the dance halls also understood the value of their skin color. After the dispersal of prostitutes from Chinatown, a number of them set up shop in "Negro" sections of the city along South Central and in the West Adams district. According to Ervin, almost three hundred such women were operating in these areas by 1930. As the statements he recorded suggest, these sex workers recognized that immigrants and African Americans would pay more for their services. In granting these clients access, the women required that they acknowledge that the "wages of whiteness" extended to the sex trade.[30]

At the same time, other prostitutes had economic incentives to pursue Anglo clients, who generally had more money to spend than other johns. As Ervin reported, African American pimps often directed their prostitutes to concentrate on more lucrative Anglo clients. But he also identified strategies employed by black women in the sex trade to subvert this preference for white men and to exploit mainstream white opposition to interracial sex. Ervin claimed that African American prostitutes frequently blackmailed Anglo clients by threatening to expose their activities to family members or the public. These stories perhaps represent an imagined rather than fulfilled revenge. But Ervin also noted that a few African American prostitutes made a point of charging white customers more than black customers, indicating at the very least a degree of consciousness regarding the gendered nature of ethnic and racial inequality in America.[31] These assertions underscored both the willingness of prostitutes to capitalize on ethnic or racial distinctions and the ways in which the structure of prostitution helped to perpetuate those differences.

THE SEX TRADE AND CENTRAL CITY WOMEN

Inter-ethnoracial contacts augmented the revenues of some prostitutes, but they also exacted a price on other women who lived in the districts where the street walkers operated. The establishment of formal or informal red-light districts encouraged some Angelenos to identify neighborhoods and their residents with the sex trade. Simply by residing in certain areas, women could find themselves mistaken for prostitutes. Because the police restricted vice industries to working-class, mixed-ethnic areas, immigrant and African American women bore the brunt of this stigmatization. The 1903 crusade exacerbated this problem by driving prostitutes into areas with larger residential populations. Female residents of these neighborhoods subsequently became more susceptible to advances and harassment by men who assumed they were both available and promiscuous.

Because prostitutes operated so visibly in these areas, male Angelenos sometimes felt free to proposition any unaccompanied women they encountered on the streets or in other public spaces. One young Japanese woman, for instance, confessed she was often intimidated by aggressive suitors: "At times, while I have walked along the street, particularly in the downtown sections, men have ogled me and called out 'Hello, cutie,' 'Oh, baby' and similar vulgar expressions. Occasionally, strange American men who have sat by me on the street car have attempted to be familiar."[32] Middle-class observers noted that men often solicited women in these areas and sometimes attempted to recruit them into lives of prostitution. Several moral reformers claimed that certain jitney and streetcar drivers, especially those operating in the working-class neighborhoods east of Main Street and along South Central Avenue, approached female passengers with promises of easy money and a luxurious lifestyle. Juvenile court judge and reformer Miriam Van Waters recounted the case of "Consuela," a seventeen-year-old Mexican girl seduced by an Anglo pimp she met on a streetcar. The man soon "put her to work on the streets."[33]

Assumptions about their sexual availability also rendered immigrant and African American women vulnerable to unscrupulous or racist policemen. In the early decades of the twentieth century, officers periodically arrested unaccompanied women in public for "vagrancy," a code word for prostitution when applied to females, even if the suspects were not actively soliciting. In 1908 Dorothy Johns, a Socialist Party member jailed for violating a public speaking ordinance, submitted a report to a party paper on one of her cellmates, an African American girl named "Bernice." The teen-aged Bernice had been picked up on the street and given a "sixty or sixty" (choice of a $60 fine or sixty days in jail) sentence for vagrancy. In Johns's eyes, however, she was clearly not a streetwalker. While other "regulars" paid the fine and left "to ply [their] trade unmolested until such time as [they] would have more money for the city," the insolvent young girl remained incarcerated. According to Johns, the officers' assumptions about the girl eventually became a self-fulfilling prophecy. To pay off the debts she incurred while in prison, Bernice allegedly joined a parlor house near Chinatown.[34] Stereotypes about unaccompanied women emanated not only from police and aggressive men. One well-to-do African American recalled that while waiting for a streetcar she was accosted by another woman, who yelled, "You little yellow ——— what are you doing on my corner. . . . I pay six dollars every week for this corner and I ain't letting no ——— cut in on me."[35]

The presence of white prostitutes in red-light districts also encouraged men to make assumptions about white women who resided in or ventured into these zones. Male residents of color often assumed these women were selling sexual favors and felt free to disregard Anglos' restrictions on their association with the women. Several Anglo residents of the All Nations district, for example, complained in 1918 interviews that African Americans and other residents of color would tip their hats to, wink at, or openly proposition white female pedestrians. Certain female Anglo reformers refused to enter Chinatown for fear of being mistaken for prostitutes.[36] In one sense, these conditions demonstrated that the impact of the sex trade on Angeleno women transcended race or ethnicity. Yet while Anglo (and some European immigrant) women could escape such ascriptions by leaving multiethnic districts, African American and many immigrant women often could not. This double standard ensured that the latter more often remained defined as sexually promiscuous, subject to solicitation, and therefore unfit partners for "legitimate" relationships, at least in the eyes of Anglo Angelenos.

Numerous immigrant and African American Angelenos who opposed prostitution in their neighborhoods recognized the ways in which the sex trade, especially when it involved mixed relations, lowered the social status of a district and its residents. Some opponents specifically objected to the presence of Anglos, especially Anglo men. Asian and African American Angelenos frequently made known their contempt for Anglo men who ventured into Chinatown or Central Avenue in search of female company. Several African American writers, for example, complained that the integrated Central Avenue nightclubs frequented by prostitutes were giving the area a "bad name." They chastised visiting Anglos lured by the promise of intimacy with "dark-skinned" women during "periodic color fads." A white prostitute noted that she had some difficulty securing a room from an African American landlord, who claimed that "she did not keep white roomers, [because] the people might suspect there was something wrong in her house." In the early 1930s an alliance of African American elites, including *California Eagle* publisher Charlotta Bass, undertook an unsuccessful campaign to eliminate the sex trade and other illicit industries from the nightclubs.[37] In his unpublished novel, *Brothers,* Harold Bruce Forsythe wrote about some young African Americans who "buncoed" (mugged) two drunk whites who came to South Central looking for African American women. "If a damn ofay ain't got no better sense than to get drunk and come down to Joke Town looking for tail, he deserves what he gets," commented one character.[38] Forsythe's account may have been fictionalized, but it spoke to the resentment some African American youths felt about the unequal racial structure of the sex trade.

Likewise, residents of Chinatown and Little Tokyo often kicked out rowdy middle-class Anglos who ventured into their places of business. In particular, they detested the "slumming parties" that toured the brothels, opium parlors, and gambling houses of Chinatown during the late nineteenth and early twentieth century.[39] Chinese and Japanese leaders believed that the sex trade and other vice activities tainted legitimate businesses in the neighborhood. When their attempts to drive these industries out of their neighborhoods failed, however, they instead tried to segregate their community from interaction with outsiders. Chinese elites, for example, pressured owners of brothels, gambling houses, and opium parlors to set up surveillance systems to watch out for police and to restrict admission to Chinese patrons.[40] For their part, Japanese community leaders created their own vice establishment, the Tokyo Club, to lure Japanese men away from Chinatown and other integrated entertainment venues.[41]

Mexican Angelenos also condemned the presence of prostitution in their neighborhoods. In 1923, for example, a Mexican woman from Sonoratown filed a complaint at the local office of the California Commission of Immigration and Housing. She claimed her neighbor was selling marijuana, morphine, and sex out of her house-court dwelling while her ten-year-old son guarded the door. Numerous other women who complained about neighborhood prostitution expressed concerns about the potential exposure of neighborhood youngsters and the damage to the districts' reputations.[42] Generally, these complaints did not cite interethnic relations as particularly objectionable aspects of the sex trade. But they insinuated that the presence of prostitution affected the social status of every neighborhood resident, especially women in public places. These were problems that residents of wealthier Anglo neighborhoods did not have to address.

Despite their objections, residents of red-light districts generally lacked the political power to drive out the sex trade. They also had to contend with members of their own communities who viewed prostitution as a profitable enterprise. In 1929, for example, the African American journal *Flash* wryly noted the small fortunes made by owners of Central Avenue clubs who solicited white clients with the promise of a "Harlemidic" recreational experience of music, dancing, and dark-skinned women.[43] Potential whistle-blowers knew they might incur the wrath of the vice operators they fingered. One ironic and tragic instance of this dilemma occurred in 1923, when an African American called in a complaint against a brothel operating in the All Nations District. The man mistook responding police officers for agents of the brothel owner and pulled out a gun. The shootout that followed killed Charles P. Williams, the first black LAPD officer to die in the line of duty. Though not a typical event in Los Angeles, this story illustrated the resistance antivice activists could face from members of their ethnic community. The alliance between these operators and police or government officials on the take generally made it difficult for residents of red-light districts to remove the sex trade from their neighborhoods.[44]

The structure of the sex trade stigmatized Angelenos of all backgrounds who chose to pursue intimate mixed relationships in more "acceptable" contexts. Commensurate with the perceived impact of these relationships on the integrity of the ethnic or racial community, inter-ethnoracial couples found themselves tainted by associations with illicit behavior. This stigmatization could justify the ostracism of individuals who married outside their ethnoracial community. Moreover, as historian Peggy Pascoe has shown, nonwhite women could find it difficult to inherit property from their white husbands because the courts assumed their relationships were primarily commercial in nature. An 1880 state law prohibiting interracial marriages, applied almost exclusively to couples that included a white woman, underscored the obstacles to legitimating such relationships.[45] In short, the connection between prostitution and mixed relationships helped to reinforce social mores that advocated dating and marriage within one's ethnoracial community.

Anglos were not the only Angelenos to deprecate mixed dating and marriage, though they were the only ones with the power to give their condemnations legal force. Immigrants and African Americans also felt uncomfortable about legitimate inter-ethnoracial relationships because they had the potential to dilute the communal structures that were so crucial to their welfare. These communities were not free of tensions with other ethnic groups. One 1930 incident in the Central Valley town of Stockton, where a Filipino-Japanese marriage sparked consumer and employment boycotts between the two ethnic communities, dramatized the possibilities for conflict in any multiethnic district.[46] If immigrants and African Americans recognized that laws or customs forbidding interracial marriages legitimized racial and gender hierarchies, they did not necessarily endorse racial and ethnic amalgamation as a solution to discrimination and social inequality. For these reasons, the taboo against interethnic and especially interracial sex extended well beyond Anglo communities. Many Angelenos opposed such relationships, especially if they extended beyond the short-term contacts of the sex trade.[47]

A story told by Jesse Kimbrough, an African American police officer, illustrates the marginalization of mixed relationships in Los Angeles during this period. In 1916 Kimbrough joined the Los Angeles Police Department as one of approximately sixty black officers (out of a total force of six hundred fifty). In *Defender of the Angels,* his fictionalized recounting of his career in the LAPD, Kimbrough writes about the fate of African American officers assigned to a "north side" beat near the plaza. According to Kimbrough, white superiors transferred black officers there in order to get them fired. Soon after arriving, the target would find himself approached by an attractive Mexican woman. The conspirators hoped to catch the officer in a compromising position with a "white" woman. Though in the eyes of most Anglos a Mexican woman qualified as white only in a legal sense, the ethnoracial difference apparently would have indicated an illegal sex-for-money exchange. The conspirators felt their plan, if successful, would justify the expulsion of their colleague from the force.[48]

Two other stories demonstrated how some Angelenos in mixed relationships found their activities stigmatized by associations with the sex trade. The first, from a 1906 account in the *Los Angeles Times,* concerned a troubled marriage between an African American man, Andrew Johnson, and his Anglo wife, Lillian. The article implied that though she "truly loved" her husband at the beginning of the relationship, Mrs. Johnson agreed to the marriage primarily because of a promise of financial support (the article does not mention how they avoided the antimiscegenation law). The sight of the couple, especially outside the downtown area, apparently traumatized many Angelenos. "They [the Johnsons] used to go to the coursing matches when they were held at Baldwin's Ranch," the writer reported. "Waiting for the cars back to the city, horrified crowds would stare at this prettily dressed young girl walking under the escort of a typical 'sporting coon.'" The article used the term "sporting" or "sportive" several times to describe Andrew, a thinly veiled allegation of participation in the sex trade. This allusion became more explicit when the article revealed that Lillian had sued for divorce because her husband had enjoyed the company of several "noisy negro women." By insinuating a connection between the husband and prostitutes, the article simultaneously condemned the marriage and explained how such a "sorry match" came about. For the *Times,* the interracial nature of the union remained inextricably linked to the sex trade.[49]

A second story pointed to the specific legal problems that this association with prostitution could cause legitimate mixed couples. One night in June 1899, a police officer witnessed Jim Wong Fook, a half-Chinese half-Japanese U.S. citizen, and Juliette Roberts, the daughter of French Canadian immigrants, entering a rooming house. Assuming Roberts was a prostitute, the officer broke into their room and arrested the couple. When prosecutors discovered that Roberts was underage, they switched the charge against Fook to attempted rape. Roberts told the court she wanted to marry Fook, and her parents agreed to the match, but the county clerk, citing the antimiscegenation law, refused to issue a license. The testimony eventually earned Fook an acquittal, but he remained unable to marry Juliette in California. Police and prosecutors continued to imply that the relationship was illicit.[50]

DANGEROUS LIAISONS: DATING AND MARRIAGE
ACROSS ETHNORACIAL LINES

The stories of Kimbrough, Fook, Roberts, and the Johnsons illustrate the powerful forces arrayed against inter-ethnoracial relationships in legitimate contexts. After all, these sorts of liaisons portended more permanent attachments, marriages, and families that blurred the lines between ethnic communities and produced offspring of nebulous social and ethnic identities. Teenagers perhaps absorbed the impact of this opprobrium most directly, and issues associated with sexual maturity may have had much to do with the spread of social segregation in Los Angeles high schools.

Of course, concerns about mixed relationships among central city Angelenos constituted only part of the larger issue of adolescent sexual practices. To varying degrees, parents of all backgrounds sought to control the recreational activities of their teenage children. These efforts generally began with restrictions on the mobility of daughters. Women who grew up in the central districts during this period often remembered pervasive, even suffocating, parental surveillance. "As soon as I was sixteen," one Mexican girl from Belvedere recalled, "my father began to watch me and would not let me go anywhere or have my friends come home. . . . The way it is with the Mexicans, the bigger a girl is, the farther they pull her into the house." One Molokan parent admitted, "I don't let my children go anyplace," especially the dance clubs that her daughter's friends patronized.[51] Central city parents also attempted, with less vigor and success, to control the sexual activities of their sons. The traditional prerogative of men to move about the public spaces of the city for school, work, or recreation, however, generated among boys a greater sense of entitlement to such freedom and more opportunities to evade surveillance. Social workers described the case of an Italian boy who lived in the central city during the 1920s. One of seven children of a candy factory worker (and, allegedly, a part-time bootlegger) father, the boy managed to stay "out all hours" despite the father's attempts to lock him in the house.[52] Miram Van Waters, a Juvenile Court referee and reformer, also noted that punishment often failed to restrict the movements of adolescent boys. One Russian father sadly recounted to her his inability to keep his son off the streets of Los Angeles: "I beat him to death,—then they say—it is against the law. The teacher comes and says; 'Let Fred come to the playground.' I let him go—he never comes home."[53]

Such stories demonstrate the futility of many parental attempts to control children's behavior. Dances and other social functions remained popular among teenagers of the period, and even adolescents who avoided dance halls, movie theaters, and other commercial amusements could find opportunities for "delinquency" on the street, at school, or in the workplace. One sociologist expressed concern, for example, for an

Italian girl whose parents kept her home at night but who also worked (without a permit) eight-hour days stitching gloves at a clothing factory. Apparently, the unwholesome influences of fellow workers threatened the girl's moral upbringing.[54] The parents of a Mexican girl discovered to their horror that she had begun dating a Greek man while working as a waitress at a café. An African American girl took a live-in job as a domestic because her employers, unlike her mother, allowed her to go out at night.[55] Faced with such defiance, certain central city parents felt compelled to resort to more drastic measures, as the statutory rape trials and forced marriages that dot the court records and reformers' files of early-twentieth-century Los Angeles attest.[56]

In the cosmopolitan central districts, many parents worried not only about their children's sex lives but also about the ethnoracial backgrounds of their partners. In the public spaces of these districts, some adolescents continued relationships begun at school or initiated new ones. One sociologist related a story about a sixteen-year-old Jewish girl who, her parents claimed, often met boys at movies and dances. One night she sneaked out of her house and went to a "cheap Mexican dance hall" with an Anglo girlfriend. Her distraught mother eventually tracked down the girl and dragged her home "by her hair."[57] Another sociologist reported the case of a fifteen-year-old African American girl who became involved with an Italian boy she met at a movie theater. After six months she became pregnant and eventually gave birth to a daughter.[58] To some degree, the content of movies and other popular culture fashions may have encouraged cross-cultural contact. In her history of her mixed Chinese-European family, Lisa See reported that the young men in her family became much more popular with white women after Rudolph Valentino made "exotic sensuality" more fashionable.[59]

Teenage participants in a mixed relationship often faced censure from their respective ethnic communities and hostility from other Angelenos if they appeared together in public. Chinese parents, particularly those of the middle and upper classes, for example, tended not to approve of non-Chinese dates for their children. Several Chinese women recalled that Chinese fathers often rebuked not only daughters who dated non-Chinese but their dates as well. Some adolescents met their dates away from home and the view of parents and neighbors. "Jennie," the daughter of Molokans, had her dates drop her off on a corner a few blocks from her house. In part she feared that her home ("the worst house on the street") and her Russian background (which she concealed) would discourage boyfriends, but she also felt the need to keep her parents in the dark about her "race-mixing."[60] But parents were not the only ones to object. Adolescents and young adults sometimes demonstrated the same hostility to cross-cultural couples. Boys, in particular, often sought to exert what they saw as their sexual prerogative over the girls of their ethnic group by attacking any outside suitors. Young Molokan boys, for example, were notorious for beating up the non-Molokan boyfriends of Molokan girls. To avoid attacks, these couples often had to meet some distance from the girls' homes.[61]

Resistance could also emerge from Anglo outsiders. Even when whites were not involved, reformers sometimes supported informal taboos on interracial dating in deference to what they saw as the wishes of central city ethnic communities and a "natural" social order of ethnic segmentation. As they did with their students' career alternatives, schoolteachers often sought to reconcile the romantic desires of their students with existing social realities rather than encourage relationships that might cause friction between groups. A Jefferson High School teacher, for example, recounted the story of a white student who developed a crush on one of his Japanese classmates. The teacher reported that she took the boy aside and carefully explained why he could not pursue the girl romantically.[62] Regardless, many central city children apparently acknowledged the realities of racial divisions and accepted the impact on their social lives. One Chinese boy admitted he had a crush on a white girl but allowed, "I know that I can't have her." A Japanese girl admitted that she dated Anglo boys but had no plans to marry any of them because "mixed marriages do not work."[63]

The array of social forces opposing cross-cultural teenage dating helped to dampen its frequency. Many central city youths chose to confine their search for romantic partners to members of their own ethnic group. Nevertheless, some adolescents and young adults continued to pursue mixed relationships, and a few extended them to longer-lasting unions and even marriage. Escalating social resistance, however, underscored a general commitment by many central city Angelenos to marginalize such families and the challenge they posed to racial and ethnic boundaries.

If inter-ethnoracial romances among teenagers and young adults remained anathema to large sections of Los Angeles's populace, mixed marriages and families provoked even more censure. Even same-race couples who married across ethnic or religious lines could face reprimands from their ethnic communities. Native-born and immigrant whites tended to maintain the highest level of resistance to such relationships, but disapproval and even condemnation could emanate from central Angelenos of all racial backgrounds. Children in these families could also face rejection from one or both of their ethnic parent communities. This tempered the willingness of many central neighborhood residents to embark on such relationships. Yet a number of Angelenos chose to marry across ethnoracial lines and to raise mixed families, even in the face of social ostracism. Life in these families could be difficult, and some relationships succumbed to tensions exacerbated by the cross-cultural nature of the union. Nevertheless, a few such families survived intact and without necessarily sacrificing all their previous ethnic ties. Their persistence, however uncommon, highlighted the possibility for enduring ties between the disparate communities that populated the central districts of early-twentieth-century Los Angeles.

The tradition of mixed marriages and families in Los Angeles stretched back to the multiracial founders of the pueblo and continued through the next century under Spanish and Mexican rule.[64] The Anglo conquest of California altered but did not halt this tradition. In the first decades after statehood, as the city's numerous ethnic communities struggled to build social and institutional foundations, inter-ethnoracial unions were common, especially for those male immigrants who, because of lopsided gender ratios in their ethnic community, had to choose between mixed marriages or celibacy. As a result, Angelenos who married across ethnoracial lines endured less ridicule than they would in later years, when ethnic social structures had matured. Wealthy Anglo newcomers, for instance, continued a prestatehood practice of marrying into prominent Californio families during the 1850s and 1860s. According to historian Richard Griswold del Castillo, one quarter of Mexican Angelenos who married between 1856 and 1875 married Anglos.[65] Some marriages among working-class Angelenos also crossed ethnoracial lines. Billy Lew recalled that a number of Chinese men of his father's generation, facing a dearth of eligible Chinese women, married African American or Mexican women. "People cared," Lew acknowledged, "but they couldn't say anything about it." Ah Seung, who sometimes went by the name Black Seung, was the offspring of a Chinese-black relationship. According to city residents, he spoke Chinese and moved freely between Chinatown and other mixed areas of the city. Likewise, William Ballard, one of the city's earliest African American residents, was born in what he called a "Mexican" neighborhood on First Street in 1862 and attended a "Negro School" taught by an African American who had a Mexican wife and two children.[66]

Tolerance for inter-ethnoracial marriages, to whatever extent they existed during these decades, diminished substantially toward the end of the nineteenth century. As women and family groups became more numerous in immigrant populations, many Angelenos no longer had to look to other communities for mates. Politically dominant Anglos, their numbers swelling from the economic booms of the late nineteenth century, took steps to buttress racial hierarchies and especially to insulate white women from nonwhite men. The signal event in this campaign took place in 1880 when the California legislature passed a bill outlawing marriages between whites and Asians, African Americans, or those of mixed blood. Even before the bill, Los Angeles County officials had sometimes refused marriage licenses to mixed couples.[67] As the Fook-Roberts saga indicated, the new law hampered mixed marriages involving whites and nonwhites. But local officials were apparently less vigilant with regard to unions between nonwhites of different races. In her study of Punjabi Indians in Imperial Valley, Karen Isaksen Leonard noted that clerks routinely approved mixed marriages between non-Europeans of any background, often listing Mexicans as "colored" even though the state supreme court had officially classified them as "white."[68]

Even with regard to eliminating white-nonwhite marriages, antimiscegenation laws were only partially effective. Some couples evaded official scrutiny by simply not registering the union. Fong See and his Irish wife, Lettie, for example, lived in central Los Angeles for many years and raised a family without ever having a formal ceremony. In 1918 an All Nations district surveyor likewise found a "white" woman and Mexican man who claimed to be married, though their neighbors expressed doubts about the legal status of the union. [69] Bernard Cohn, a Jewish city councilman and leading businessman, raised two families in the late nineteenth century, one with a Jewish wife and one with his mistress, Delfina Verelas de Cohn. Although he supported Verelas and their six offspring and even paid for the burial of two children who died young, Cohn never married her. Verelas lost a suit against Cohn's estate when she was unable to provide legal evidence of the union.[70] Other couples went to Tijuana or to states without antimiscegenation laws, and in 1897 a Chinese man chartered a boat on which he married his Anglo wife in international waters.[71] Racial classifications could also subvert the intent of antimiscegenation laws. During the first decades of the twentieth century, for instance, Filipinos frequently took advantage of their "white" status to marry white women. Between 1924 and 1933, 70 percent of the 299 marriages in Los Angeles involving Filipinos were interethnic; about half of these unions were to native-born whites, many of them taxi-dance girls. In addition, 11 Filipinos married foreign-born whites, 37 married African American women, 26 married Mexican women, 8 married American Indians, 2 married Japanese, and 1 married a Chinese woman. [72] By this time hostile Anglos were noting the frequency of such unions, especially in the context of the dance halls that young Filipinos frequented. A 1929 Commonwealth Club publication warned that "inter-marriage [with whites] appears to be common" among Filipinos, before claiming, erroneously, that "it cannot be legally accomplished under the laws of California." In 1933 the state reclassified Filipinos as nonwhite in an effort to eliminate mixed marriages. [73]

Despite legal and social restrictions, inter-ethnoracial marriages were an indelible part of early-twentieth-century central Los Angeles and of similar multiethnic districts around Southern California. Sociologists of the period often spoke of a smattering of ethnic combinations even in districts they did not consider integrated. [74] Yet they were also quick to identify the tensions that accompanied these unions. Accounts of mixed relationships from the early twentieth century often underscore local hostility to interethnic marriages and affairs even if the spouses were of the same race. A young Molokan told an interviewer that his mother believed his American girlfriend would not know how to say the vows in church and refused to sanction his marriage. He admitted that until he received his mother's blessing he would stay single. [75] Once married, couples often found that this tension persisted, and outside family members were not above attempting to sabotage the relationships. A Mexican woman, for example, claimed that the mother of her French husband "turned him against her." The couple, who had one child, got a divorce. [76] An Anglo man attributed his conflicts with his Mexican wife to their nationalities: "She is a Mexican, Citizen of said Country. I am a citizen of the United States." According to the man, his wife blamed his health problems on his military service "fighting for that dirty American flag," and his outraged in-laws treated him "as they would a dog" while attempting to break up the union. [77]

In more than a few instances, hostility extended to ostracism. After a Molokan girl married a Catholic boy (of unspecified race), her parents became so furious that the couple decided to move to a bungalow south of the Flats and outside the "Russian district." Expulsion from the neighborhood often entailed expulsion from the community as well. Molokan Angelenos seemed to have been particularly hard on this point. A Molokan mother said of her daughter who married a Mexican,

"She is dead to us." Mexican Catholics were known for banishing children who married Protestants. One young woman in such a marriage reported, "When we marry we have to live the life alone and stay away from our parents mostly."[78] Such tendencies, however, were not confined to any one group. Many Irish relatives of Lisa See's great-grandmother ostracized her after she married a Chinese man in 1897. Writing some thirty years later, a sociologist noted that a number of Anglo families in Watts had not accepted their Mexican in-laws and that many Mexicans likewise objected to relatives marrying Anglos. George Sanchez argues that many mixed couples involving a Mexican partner were compelled to relocate to areas in South Central and Southwest Los Angeles where neighbors were less hostile to such relationships.[79] For some Angelenos, exile was too difficult, and they abandoned their partners to return to the community. A Molokan girl reported that most of the twenty-seven Molokan girls she knew who married American, Italian, or Mexican boys were unhappy: "Most of these girls live with their husbands for six months or so and then they come home. They are looked down on, and nobody wants them." Rejection could engender redemption, however, and most "renegade" children who left their spouses were apparently welcomed back into their family homes and the Molokan community.[80]

It would be a mistake to characterize the attitude of central city residents to mixed marriages as invariably hostile. More likely, interethnoracial couples experienced a range of responses from friends, acquaintances, and strangers. One native born white woman who married a Japanese Presbyterian minister, for example, acknowledged that she lost some friends as a result of the marriage but that others, including her parents, accepted her husband. Neighbors exhibited a similarly diverse range of responses. After five years together and the birth of a daughter, the woman claimed her life was "getting better all the time."[81] Chinatown resident Tom Gubbin reported that an Anglo neighbor and her Chinese husband received regular visits from her in-laws. Even clannish Molokans sometimes extended their hands to married relations outside their group. One family, for example, took in an Italian daughter-in-law after their son had deserted her.[82] Acceptance appeared more likely in neighborhoods with new and especially diverse populations. George Weiss, who claimed Filipino, Jewish, and Spanish ancestry, reported in 1937 that the neighbors around his general store at Vermont and Sixty-seventh Street, an area open to nonwhites only a short time, displayed no hostility to him or his Mexican wife.[83]

Nevertheless, a study of mixed marriages in Los Angeles for ten years ending in 1933 revealed the small numbers of Angelenos who married across ethnic or racial lines. Though Constantine Panunzio concluded that intermarriage occurred more frequently in Los Angeles than in "comparable areas," only 12 of every 1,000 marriages that took place in the city were mixed. Filipinos had by far the highest rates of intermarriage, reflecting both their predominantly male population and their legal ability to marry whites. Mexicans also had relatively high rates of intermarriage. Of 11,016 marriages involving Mexicans during the period, 1,885 involved a non-Mexican partner. This latter group included 1,287 marriages (8.3 percent) to native-born whites, 437 (4.0 percent) to foreign-born whites, 115 (1.0 percent) to Central and South Americans, and 46 (0.4 percent) with American Indians, Asians, or African Americans.[84] Of 97 marriages involving Chinese during the period, 23 were interethnic, most of them between Chinese men and non-Chinese women. Fourteen involved marriages to Japanese, 5 to African Americans, 1 to a native-born white, and 2 to other "yellow-browns." Japanese, in contrast, married outside their ethnic community very rarely (2.7 percent of marriages involving at least one Japanese) by the 1920s. Panunzio found 23 such intermarriages: 14 to Chinese, 4 to African Americans, 2 to Filipinos, and 7 to whites. African Americans also married outside their group in low numbers, accounting for only 55 of 4,885 marriages. Thirty-seven married Filipinos; 5, Chinese; 4, Japanese; 4, whites; 1, Mexican; and 4, other "yellow-browns."[85]

These marriages, however uncommon, testified to the possibilities, at least, for central Angelenos to transcend ethnic boundaries even in the context of important familial relationships. Yet these possibilities existed alongside a more generalized hostility to unions that crossed ethnoracial boundaries. The pastor of Euclid Heights Methodist Church, a ministry in East Los Angeles that struggled to develop an interethnic congregation, acknowledged that mixed marriages lay outside the purview of mainstream cultural practices. Though allowing that he had presided over a few successful intermarriages, he nevertheless maintained that "young people of other races for the most part have drifted elsewhere for companionship with the opposite sex."[86]

ANGELENOS OF A DIFFERENT COLOR: MIXED FAMILIES

According to many middle-class and elite residents of Los Angeles, the marginalization of mixed marriages extended to their offspring, and antimiscegenation law advocates often justified their position by pointing to a "natural" desire for homogeneity in all ethnoracial communities.[87] Even liberal Anglos and social reformers often bemoaned the fate of mixed-race children, who in their eyes were burdened by isolation and ridicule. Some social workers concluded that mixed children were especially prone to delinquent behavior as a release for their frustrations.[88] Such conclusions certainly overgeneralized the more complicated experiences of these young Angelenos, but they were not entirely fabricated. Ethnic groups could marginalize or even banish those members who married across racial or ethnic lines and the children they produced. Not all mixed race children suffered rejection, but their experiences illustrate the limits of social tolerance to inter-ethnoracial families.

Numerous social workers described the struggles of children from mixed families to reconcile their liminal ethnic status with the variegated social landscape of central Los Angeles. Some children resolved the dilemma by choosing to identify with a single ethnic community. A social worker, observing two children of a Japanese man and an English woman, commented that the daughter "didn't want to be Japanese" but learned to accept it, while the son more quickly decided he preferred to associate with Japanese children.[89] A more unusual example involved an orphaned girl of Mexican descent who moved in with a Chinese family. The girl's mother had befriended the Chinese couple after they took her to a Chinese doctor who healed her sprained ankle. After the mother died the family adopted the daughter, who apparently adapted quite well to her new family. A social worker reported that the girl was a "leader of children in Chinatown, thought she was Chinese, and worked as a Chinese extra in movies.[90]

Other mixed children had more difficulty overcoming the dilemma of identification. The son of a Japanese man and a Mexican woman (the latter died when he was an infant) chose to associate primarily with Japanese, even though his Japanese stepmother did not like him. He felt that if he mingled with Mexicans, his Japanese friends would look down on him. According to an informant, the boy developed a truancy problem at school. When he reached the sixth grade his father, a driver for the Japanese consul (some of the people who were interviewed voiced suspicions that he moonlighted as a chauffeur for prostitutes), removed the boy from class to work for him. The interviewer concluded that the boy was an "outcast" from both Mexican and Japanese societies.[91] A Chinese Angeleno noted that a half-Chinese, half-Norwegian neighbor was ostracized from all social circles. For a girl of Anglo and Japanese parentage, the difficulties became most apparent when she began dating. If she dated Japanese boys people would "look at her," but she worried about how Anglo dates would react when they learned of her Japanese ancestry.[92] Another case concerned a boy whose Chinese father had died and African American mother had disappeared. Concerned social workers accused the foster parents of smoking opium and living behind a pool hall. They claimed that the Chinese community would not accept the boy and that the boy was unwilling to move in with blacks.[93]

When mixed marriages broke up, parents and relatives often quarreled over the upbringing of their children. One child of a Mexican mother and French father became the target of a dispute after the couple divorced. The father, who moved to Texas, wanted his son left in the foster home of a Mrs. Roth where he "could get proper care and learn English." The mother wanted to keep the child with her family. Another Mexican woman in Boyle Heights encountered a different sort of problem when she married a Japanese man and sent her (Mexican) daughter from a former marriage to visit her sister. When she found out about the marriage, the sister refused to return the daughter and "became hysterical" when the new husband came to her house.[94] A third family, composed of a Scottish father, a Japanese mother, and two children, had been expelled by the families of both parents. When the husband died, the wife's family took her and her daughter, who had more Japanese features, back. They left the red-headed, freckled son to be raised by his Scottish grandmother. These and other disputes indicated the cultural frailty of mixed families and the desire to claim a child for one's own community if the marriage went sour.[95]

The pressure among children of mixed background to choose (or to have chosen for them) an ethnic identity in many ways pointed toward a solution to the tensions engendered by cross-cultural families. For the children themselves, it resolved the identity crisis that "outcast" theorists believed would marginalize them from all ethnic groups. For ethnic communities it solved, to a degree, the problem of incorporating members with alternative possible ethnic affiliations. Thus the community and the allegiance of its members in theory remained intact. Of course, choosing an ethnicity constituted in no sense a final or total solution to the dilemma of mixed backgrounds. As Lisa See demonstrated in her eloquent account of her Chinese-Irish family, questions of ethnic affiliation and identification remained a perpetual part of a multiethnic family's history, and at least some Angelenos fought to assert a multiracial identity in the face of resistance from outsiders. Their struggles prefigured later efforts to emancipate ethnic and racial identities from rigid, essentialist definitions.

In one sense, the multiracial families that emerged in Los Angeles before World War II challenged the insularity of ethnic communities with a model of amalgamation that might have problematized racism and discrimination in American cities. By placing residents of different backgrounds in close contact, the integrated social landscape of the city enabled the formation of some relationships that potentially eroded ethnic distinctions and increased the population of mixed Angelenos. Their presence reminded Angelenos of the permeability of ethnic categories and of the possibilities and dangers attending this permeability. In another sense, however, these families lay outside conventional practices of intra-ethnoracial marriage, and the resistance to mixed marriages, with the active support of middle-class and elite Anglos, continued through World War II and the postwar years. Such trends seemed to indicate the persistence of proscriptions against inter-ethnoracial sexual relations even as certain Angelenos violated those strictures. If central city residents sought broader points of coalition building and cross-cultural affiliation during the early twentieth century, they would not find them in reproductive amalgamation. It would be only in more platonic realms where discrete ethnic communities could form alliances rather than bleed together, that alliances could flourish in a more general sense.

CHAPTER 6

Preaching to Mixed Crowds

Ethnoracial Coalitions and the
Political Culture of Street Speaking

THE SOAPBOX TRADITION

In the years before film, radio, and television enveloped mainstream American culture, public speaking was an important medium of political expression and entertainment in urban life. In cities across the United States, the harangues of soapbox politicians bled into the exhortations of religious zealots, the high-pitched cries of newsboys, and the verbalized, frequently melodious advertisements of street vendors to form the vocal contribution to the dissonance of the modern urban soundscape. These voices, rarely recorded, have largely been lost to historians, and one may dismiss a good portion of them as blunt commercial solicitations or the babblings of the mentally unstable. But prosaic and irrational street speakers shared the soapbox and streetcorner with agitators who exhorted the multiethnic populace of districts like those in central Los Angeles to challenge the dominance of middle-class and elite Anglos. Not all street speakers were political, but the culture of street speaking had fundamental political implications, appealing as it did, at least in theory, to all passersby regardless of race, ethnicity, gender, or citizenship.[1]

Street speaking was both a child and a casualty of modern urban development. Growing cities provided the crowded environments and diverse, working-class audiences on which street speakers relied. At the same time, street speakers clogged traffic, slowing pedestrians and automobiles and disrupting commerce. As the twentieth century progressed,

FIGURE 7. Soapboxer addressing a crowd in the plaza, c. 1920s. Security
Pacific Collection/Los Angeles Public Library.

street speakers were driven from downtown areas by new ordinances
and police enforcement. Physical marginalization accompanied cultural
marginalization, as modern technology introduced new media that rendered street speech increasingly unfashionable and irrelevant. These
dual forces ultimately proved lethal to the culture of street speaking, but
they did their work slowly, over decades. A far more immediate and visceral threat was posed by middle-class and elite Americans who feared
the political implications of inter-ethnoracial, working-class political
coalitions. The Red scares of the early twentieth century unleashed a
series of police actions against working-class groups who literally took
their message to the streets of America's cosmopolitan cities. Street
speaking thus represented the ultimate threat to the white spots of
America, portending a mongrelized uprising of minorities that could
swamp the "good communities" of Anglo urbanites.

Street-speaking culture in Los Angeles may not have burned as long
as its counterparts in older cities, but it ignited a series of political brush-
fires from the turn of the century through the Great Depression that
spooked wealthier Anglos and city officials. To varying degrees, organizations such as the Socialist Party, the Partido Liberal Mexicano, the
Industrial Workers of the World, and the Communist Party used street
speech to mobilize working Angelenos and to seize political power
for central city residents. In practical terms, all of these efforts eventually succumbed to external pressures and internal contradictions. Sustained campaigns of repression, incarceration, and violence by police
and municipal authorities silenced many protesters and intimidated

many more. Internal dissension also undermined organizations, and even those who were committed to equality and social justice struggled to contain the diverse agendas of multiethnic central Los Angeles within single institutional frameworks. But these failures tell only part of the story, for the street speeches and demonstrations sponsored by these organizations constituted an enduring part of central city culture for more than a quarter century and provided innumerable lessons to central city residents on the nature and consequences of political coalition building.

For many central city Angelenos, street speech was one of the few available forms of political expression with any potential effectiveness. Through the turn of the century groups of (usually western) European immigrants managed to influence some local elections via questionable ballot practices, but a reform movement led by middle-class and elite Anglos in the early 1900s eliminated the ward system and crippled the ethnic political machine.[2] African American Angelenos managed to elect Frederick Roberts to the California State Assembly in 1918 but exerted at most a minor influence in local politics. In a revealing moment, black voters in Watts endorsed the town's annexation to Los Angeles in 1926, despite the fact that it eliminated an African American presence in local politics that activists had fought mightily to secure. According to resident Eusebia Small, "We found that we didn't have any influence anyhow. We finally elected a Negro trustee . . . [but] his one vote didn't weigh much."[3] Ethnic groups with large numbers of noncitizens fared even worse. Mexican representation in Los Angeles government had vanished by 1900 and would not reappear until after World War II. Neither they nor Asian and eastern European immigrant populations could mobilize enough votes to make a dent in the overwhelmingly Anglo electorate. Like immigrants in other American cities, many of these Angelenos responded with apathy to opportunities for citizenship and voting rights that would give them little effective power. One South Central store owner, who claimed a Filipino, Spanish, and Jewish background, concluded, "I am not an American citizen and have never given the idea much thought. Maybe some day I will get around to it, but at present I have too much to do, to think about it."[4] In short, formal politics proved of little use to central city residents.

Street speaking, in contrast, offered an immediate voice to Angelenos regardless of cultural background, citizenship status, party affiliation, or financial means. Indeed, the only effective obstacles to interaction lay in language barriers and police repression. Street speeches and demonstrations thus provided a scaffolding for the articulation of working-class coalitions, the political extension of ethnoracial interaction in the central neighborhoods.[5] The organizations that adopted the soapbox tradition in early-twentieth-century Los Angeles made some of the first attempts to meld diverse populations of modern industrial cities into a cohesive political movement.

THE GEOGRAPHY OF STREET SPEECH
IN DOWNTOWN LOS ANGELES

Street speakers set up shop in many parks, lots, and sidewalks during the late nineteenth and early twentieth century, but they concentrated their activity in the arc of neighborhoods stretching from the plaza to Pershing Square. The plaza harbored the most vibrant and cosmopolitan array of speakers and listeners. Despite Anglo efforts in the nineteenth century to reorient the city around Pershing Square, the original center of the pueblo continued to play an important role in Los Angeles's cultural life, especially for nearby residents.[6] One of the few open spaces in a part of the city undergoing convulsive growth spurts, the plaza drew scores of people seeking refuge from the crowded streets of Sonoratown, Chinatown, Little Tokyo, First Street, and downtown each day. True to its heritage, the area remained most popular among Mexicans. In 1914 a USC student noted, "The top rows of benches leading from North Main Street are always occupied by Mexicans and a more or less heated argument is usually in progress among them, the usual topic being the Revolution in Mexico. Supporters of all factions are to be found among them and adherents of the Industrial Workers of the World and of the Mexican Liberal Party may be heard in the general discussion."[7] Nevertheless, Angelenos of all backgrounds made use of the plaza or passed through it on their way to nearby neighborhoods. The spectrum of activity in the park resembled that of its counterparts in other American cities and included a healthy tradition of public speaking and demonstrations. In 1912 city authorities, in a move that acknowledged this tradition and sought to contain it within that space, installed two concrete podiums there for speakers to use, thereby sealing the plaza's reputation as the Hyde Park of Los Angeles. Throughout the next two decades the plaza fulfilled this role despite periodic crackdowns against subversive rhetoric by the LAPD. As the depression emptied workers' pockets of money for commercial amusements, gatherings of Jews, Japanese, Filipinos, African Americans, Mexicans, and Anglos continued to converge on the plaza every Sunday to hold forth on various topics (see map 4).[8]

A somewhat different culture of public speaking materialized in Pershing Square during the same period. Like the plaza, the square lured an eclectic mix of Angelenos to its lawns and benches: white-collar workers on breaks from their office jobs, the elderly who descended each day from their rooms in Bunker Hill tenements, and refugees from the blighted sidewalks of Skid Row to the east. Because its immediate environs included financial establishments, commercial businesses, and hotels catering to wealthier Angelenos, Pershing Square drew substantially more police surveillance, and the speaking culture paled in comparison to that at the plaza. Nevertheless, on any given day crowds gathered to observe speakers of all sorts and to engage in lively debates. In 1905 a newspaper reporter said, "There is not a spot in any city of America that has been more completely monopolized by the common people than this park. . . . Anyone could go to [Pershing Square] and find a crowd to listen to his speech at any time."[9]

Pershing Square and the plaza bracketed the most populous and frenetic sections of pre–World War II Los Angeles and, correspondingly, the most frequent sites of proletarian street speaking and demonstrating. Stretching east from Main to Alameda Streets, Fifth Street formed the central artery for the city's raucous Skid Row, or the "Slave Belt" as some rechristened it during the depression, and cultivated a healthy street-speaking culture. A magnet for the city's homeless, alcoholic, unemployed, newly arrived, and otherwise marginalized inhabitants, Skid Row contained saloons, theaters, rooming houses, employment services, and rescue missions that ensured a continuous stream of pedestrian traffic and a dependable if not always polite audience for soapboxers.[10] Similar types of street life thrived along the boulevards running north of Skid Row, especially Los Angeles Street, through mixed residential-industrial areas up toward Little Tokyo and Chinatown. Among the throngs street speakers found a ready market for the exchange of ideas (and sometimes epithets) of a religious, social, or political nature.

The geography of street speech held another advantage that appealed to radical interests. The areas where street-speaking flourished were disproportionately populated by the working class and non-Anglos, but they were not otherwise isolated from wealthier areas of the city. Middle-class and elite Angelenos also labored in these districts or passed through them for work or recreation. The disruptions created by large gatherings forced even nonparticipants to acknowledge the presence of the speech

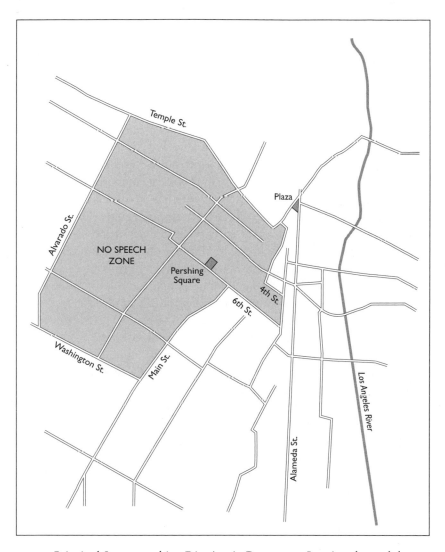

MAP 4. Principal Street-speaking Districts in Downtown Los Angeles and the "No-Speech Zone," 1920s

or demonstration. The proximity of these neighborhoods to Los Angeles's economic and political centers ensured that street speech audiences, particularly if directed into marches on city hall or other government offices, could rapidly make their presence felt among better-off Angelenos. It was even conceivable for a large and sustained public outburst to shut down the city center. Despite rapid expansion, the political and commercial activity of early-twentieth-century Los Angeles remained concentrated in these few blocks. City leaders were well aware that downtown demonstrations could snarl its public transportation system or hold its civic institutions hostage. In this sense, then, the mobilization of central city residents in the streets, whether sparked by speakers or some other catalyst, posed one of the greatest political threats to middle-class and elite Anglos during the early twentieth century.[11]

The specter of inter-ethnoracial, class-based protest touched off a war against street speaking that raged hot and cold from the early 1900s through the Great Depression. Political organizations that sought to mobilize via street speakers and demonstrations confronted a hostile municipal police force that, according to one observer, "express[ed] a theory of law enforcement more openly opposed to the Constitution than any [he] had yet encountered." Attempts to build inter-ethnoracial coalitions in the central neighborhoods thus took place under extreme duress and violence from authorities that "ceased to distinguish between the economic dissenter and the criminal."[12] The criminalization of these political efforts, especially when they explicitly invoked cross-cultural affiliations, represented the most repressive aspect of corporate liberal principles expounded by middle-class and elite Angelenos. In vanquishing radical, street-based political movements, these interests sought to channel the political impulse of central city residents into more formal structures, where middle-class Anglo majorities could muffle their voices. Yet the failure of coalition politics based on street speaking cannot be attributed solely to repression. As we shall see, organizations that mobilized along these lines struggled to overcome a variety of internal flaws. But the intensity of the campaign revealed the vital role street speakers played in the broader political battles of Los Angeles.

THE BATTLE IS JOINED:
SOCIALIST FREE SPEECH FIGHTS, 1900–1911

The Socialist Party was the first twentieth-century political organization in the city to make successful use of street speaking as a major tool of organization and propaganda. An insignificant force at the turn of the century, Socialists gathered enough strength over ten years to challenge the political parties for control of the city. The party achieved its greatest inroads among skilled and semiskilled white workers fearful of the threats that industrial development posed to their job status and security. Some of its leaders, however, recognized that broader support lay in the more diverse collection of unskilled workers residing in the central neighborhoods. From 1901 to 1911 they gradually built up support in these neighborhoods, primarily from native whites and European immigrants. Popularity among Asian, Mexican, and African American Angelenos remained elusive, in large part because of the leadership's reluctance to challenge the racist policies of the city's labor unions. Though it failed to recruit many central Angelenos, however, the Socialist experiment succeeded in demonstrating that street speaking could be effective for inter-ethnoracial political alliances. The lesson would be lost neither on subsequent, more inclusive movements nor on the vested interests that assembled to oppose them. The resulting free speech fights of the 1900s established streets and street speaking as the physical and political battleground between residents of the central neighborhoods and the rest of Los Angeles.[13]

The Socialist Party of the United States coalesced out of fragments and factions of several political organizations that had sprung up in the late nineteenth century. Embodied in the upbringing of its charismatic national leader, Eugene V. Debs, a midwestern railroad worker and union activist, the party lay anchored in both nineteenth-century republican principles of independence and the vibrant but uneven labor movement of industrializing America. Various parties with socialist inclinations were active in nineteenth-century Los Angeles, but they made few inroads into city politics until they converged under the Socialist Party banner.[14]

Soon after the turn of the century, Socialist speakers began to appear on the streets and in the parks of downtown Los Angeles. Party activists seized on a front-line strategy of regularly scheduled meetings at various high-traffic intersections along Los Angeles, Main, and Market Streets. The speeches targeted casual pedestrians on their way home from work, but the regular scheduling also established a framework for continuing participation. The visibility of the organization thereby increased with the size of its audience. Speakers supplemented this approach with informal solicitations at Pershing Square and the plaza. Small meetings gradually built up to large rallies and lectures held in rented halls or auditoriums, all publicized in the party's newspaper, the *Los Angeles Socialist* (later *Common Sense*). This strategy of accretion soon built up a base of support among central city residents.[15]

The spectacular success of the party's campaign soon drew the attention of municipal authorities. Recognizing the threat it posed, they took immediate steps to dismantle the Socialist soapbox machine. After the city council passed an ordinance in 1901 requiring police permits to speak in public parks, LAPD officers began arresting party activists in Pershing Square. Within two years, Socialists complained, they were arresting anyone who spoke publicly in the square on any topic whatsoever. In 1903 the city council extended the measure to cover public streets, and by early 1908 the police commission had rescinded speaking permits for the Socialists at the plaza and at two other popular locations, the intersections at Second and Los Angeles Streets and Seventh and Main.[16] A parallel crackdown on union pickets demonstrated the city council's and the LAPD's resolve to drive working-class protest from the streets. Police also began to enforce an ordinance prohibiting the distribution of handbills in downtown areas, which Socialists had done to publicize meetings in private halls. One police chief even called for the licensing of newspaper sellers, a transparent attempt, the party alleged, to remove Socialist literature from the streets.[17] While officers harassed Socialist street speakers, wealthier Angelenos launched a campaign of "business man's Christian meetings" along Skid Row, often directly adjacent to party gatherings. Outraged party members condemned the two-pronged effort as a "giveaway" of public streets to private interests and ridiculed the "fat tradesmen, garbed in expensive but shapeless clothes, urging hungry men to turn their minds to better things above." Through the Free Speech League, a party organization formed in 1903 to fight the crackdown, Socialists protested, in print and on the streets, the double standard that kept the streets open to "religious fakers" and businessmen but closed to proletarian organizations.[18]

The Christian businessmen's meetings soon petered out, but police repression did much more damage to the Socialist street-speaking network. At first, the party countered by renting vacant lots so that they could hold their meetings on "private" land. One lot at Fifth and Los Angeles Streets proved especially popular, drawing several hundred to each of the biweekly meetings held there. A hat passed at the end of each gathering generally collected enough money for the rent. The opposition responded by pressuring a local bank to call in a loan made to the lot's owner if he did not stop renting to the Socialists. The party lost the battle when the landlord decided to build on the site.[19] Their new tactics thwarted, Socialists decided to flood the prisons with activists in order to drain the city government's resources, tie up the courts, and publicize the free speech fight. Promising to "fill the jails with violators," the party, with support from the embryonic local IWW chapter, organized a battery of meetings, as many as twenty a week, in downtown streets. Speakers invoked the Constitution and the founding fathers, thereby grounding their protests in Anglo-American political traditions even as they called for a class-based coalition. As police arrested each speaker, another would arise, often reciting First Amendment rights as he or she took the stand. Ten or more protesters might thus earn a trip to jail in a single demonstration. Foregoing the right to post bond, the swelling crowd of incarcerated Socialists defiantly formed a party chapter at the city jail.[20]

Despite palpable tensions between activists and police, thousands of Angelenos continued to attend free speech demonstrations. In late February 1908 activist L. T. Fischer opened a meeting of five hundred on Franklin Street invoking his ancestors who "had fought in every war that was waged for freedom" in their thirty years in America. Rev. George Woodbey, an African American Baptist minister, "asked the belligerent police if they did not think they were violating their oaths to support the constitutions, state and national." Officers arrested him and the others who rose up to take his place, including a woman named Jessie Shuck, and smashed the soapbox. Undaunted, protesters marched down Spring Street through the heart of downtown, jeering at police ("Cossacks!") and singing the Marseillaise. Other protests followed a similar course. On July 18, 1908, several thousand paraded through downtown, drowning out the gathering of Democrats who had collected to endorse William Jennings Bryan's candidacy for president. Concluding their march at their stronghold at Fifth and Los Angeles Streets, the demonstrators gathered around a speaker, who began to address the crowd. When a policeman asked him if he had a permit, the speaker replied that it was "on file at the Library of Congress." Officers arrested him and several other speakers, but the tide was turning in favor of the demonstrators.[21] In August, facing persistent and widespread disobedience, an overwhelmed court system, and jail cells bursting at the seams, the city council brokered a compromise with the party. In return for the abolition of the permit requirement, Socialists agreed to respect a no-speech zone covering the white-collar districts of downtown west of Main between Commercial and Ninth Streets. Though the deal placed Pershing Square and the streets around many government buildings off-limits, the party claimed a victory and set about cementing its presence in its traditional speaking areas along Los Angeles Street and in the plaza.[22]

The subsequent rise and fall of the Socialist Party in Los Angeles is well known. With their speaking rights restored, the party rallied increasing numbers of Angelenos to its cause. In 1911, as opponents scrambled to abolish the ward system of elections and thereby dilute the vote of "proletarian" districts, local attorney and mayoral candidate Job Harriman captured a plurality in the primary and appeared poised to assume the city's highest office. Days before the election, calamity struck the party when Clarence Darrow convinced his clients James and John McNamara to plead guilty to the October 1910 bombing of the *Times* building. The Socialists' close identification with organized labor, which had taken years to establish, now proved its undoing. Disgraced by his support of the McNamara brothers, Harriman finished a distant second in the balloting. Whether Harriman would have won without the guilty plea remains unclear, but the scandal dealt an unmistakable fatal blow to Socialist aspirations for political power in Los Angeles. The party never again made a serious challenge in municipal politics.[23]

GAPS IN THE SOCIALIST COALITION

Some accounts represent the Socialist campaign as a lost opportunity for working-class Angelenos. It is far from clear, however, that all central neighborhood residents mourned its fall. For one thing, the ranks of party street speakers, dominated by the middle-class professionals who held most of the party's leadership positions, presented a primarily Anglo face in public demonstrations.[24] A few orators were of more modest means, including the flamboyant John Callahan, a megaphone-voiced Civil War veteran nicknamed the "Yellow Devil" for the gaudy uniform he wore when hawking party papers. Most others, particularly the more conservative members that came to dominate the party by 1910, worked in offices instead of factories. In some cases Socialists played up the prominence of their activists, perhaps to counter attacks that the party appealed only to uneducated laborers. *Common Sense,* for example, bemoaned the jailing of speakers, "women of gentle birth and men of refinement and education," in cells among common crooks. Most of the imprisoned party members, the writer continued, "were among the most prominent citizens of Los Angeles and almost all of them were property owners."[25] Such posturing did little to convince labor unions or central neighborhood residents that the party spoke for their interests.

Socialists' inclusion of women speakers constituted one notable effort to diversify the street campaigns, but it also reinforced the party's middle-class Anglo image. Before the escalation of the free speech fights, middle-class women sympathetic to the party had confined their participation to private meetings in their homes.[26] As arrests on the streets mounted, however, party officials began to accept female speakers, perhaps with the hope that they would temper police violence. By most accounts, the women embraced the opportunity with an enthusiasm rivaling that of their male counterparts. The female speakers who were arrested during the free speech fight even started a "social club" at the women's jail and invited others to come see them "via the soapbox" rather than as visitors.[27] Women tended not to address the same topics as their male counterparts but instead focused on the special concerns of their gender as dictated by middle-class mores. Invoking their role as protectors of the family, they promoted the benefits of Socialism to motherhood, education, and children. They thus carved out a sphere of public activity similar to that of middle-class social reformers.[28] The response of central city residents to the presence of female street speakers is difficult to gauge, but the absence of non-Anglo women among this group, and the absence of women as a whole from leadership positions in the party, suggests they had a negligible impact.

While claiming to speak for working Angelenos, Socialists omitted many nonwhite central city residents from their political equation. Asian Angelenos, who were excluded from the Anglo-dominated labor unions courted by the party, received little sympathy from Socialists. They did nothing, for instance, to protest the 1908 anti-Japanese campaign cosponsored by the Los Angeles Central Labor Council, in which supporters plastered the city with "fire the jap" posters. With Mexicans naturalizing at low rates, recruitment of immigrant populations via party-sponsored "foreign language" clubs focused almost exclusively on Europeans. Ignoring these Angelenos meant little on election day, but in the long run the party's failure to confront racism head-on helped to perpetuate open-shop policies and the weakness of organized labor in Los Angeles.[29]

Socialists' only explicit overture to nonwhite residents of the central neighborhoods involved their endorsement of the Partido Liberal Mexicano (PLM). Emerging in the waning years of the Porfiriato, the PLM was one of several political and military organizations opposing the dictatorship in Mexico. During the 1900s, the PLM operated largely in exile out of several U.S. cities, with Los Angeles a major stronghold of support. Like other refugees of Mexican government persecution, these dissidents did not necessarily find a hospitable political climate north of the border. During his tenure, Porfirio Díaz had established strong relationships with a number of prominent American businessmen, who funded many of his ambitious modernization projects. Thus when Mexican officials requested U.S. aid to suppress the PLM leadership, business leaders and municipal officials in Los Angeles and elsewhere were happy to help. In 1907 ethnic Mexican detectives in the LAPD, with intelligence support from the Mexican consulate, arrested the PLM's leader, Ricardo Flores Magón, his brother, and two other party leaders in Los Angeles.[30]

Sharing foes and ideologies, the Socialist Party and the PLM cultivated a symbiotic interest that subsumed, for a time, certain underlying conflicts. In the Díaz regime the Socialists saw self-serving elites similar to those in Los Angeles, and they sympathized with the plight of labor in Mexico. In championing the PLM, the party also jabbed at its avowed enemy, Harrison Gray Otis, the cantankerous *Los Angeles Times* magnate and one of the most powerful open-shop proponents in the city. It was common knowledge that Otis and a number of his colleagues had large property holdings south of the border and had a strong interest in preserving the status quo in Mexico. At the same time, Socialist contempt for Otis stemmed in part from his predilection for using Mexican labor to combat unionism. The party thus hoped that ameliorating conditions for Mexican workers would halt their migration north and thereby improve the political leverage of white workers. In coming to the aid of the jailed dissidents, they saw a relatively easy and effective way both to help fellow workers and to publicize their own cause. The contradiction between their support for the PLM and their disdain of Mexican immigrants, however, would soon strain the fledgling alliance.[31]

With Harriman representing the defendants, the party organized a series of public meetings and speeches excoriating local authorities for kowtowing to the alliance between the Mexican government and American business that repressed labor on both sides of the border. Mexican Angelenos flocked to these meetings, and Magón directed his followers to ally themselves with the Socialists and other leftists in the United States. These actions did not translate into any substantial influx of Mexicans into the party, though Socialists trumpeted the founding of a

half-dozen-member "Mexican branch" in Alhambra, a blue-collar suburb northeast of downtown.[32] Harriman managed to secure an acquittal for the PLM leaders, but scarcely a year later, Mexican LAPD detectives arrested PLM and Socialist Party member Lazaro Gutierrez de
Lara in the plaza for speaking against Díaz. Emboldened by their recent
free speech victory and surging popularity, Socialists saw a chance to
strike back at the LAPD. The all-white De Lara Defense Committee
secured the speaker's release, although attempts to bring charges of
abuse against the arresting officers failed. Once more demonstrations
drew Socialist and PLM members together on the streets of downtown
Los Angeles.[33]

Soon afterward, however, the relationship between the two parties
began to sour. One source of tension lay in the diverging fortunes of the
two organizations. Socialists, fixated on their growing influence at the
polls, drifted to the center at the same time that a struggling PLM was
flirting with more radical politics. Disillusioned with his allies in the
United States and frustrated by continual police harassment, an increasingly militant Magón began to alienate mainstream Socialists in the
United States. In 1911, at the height of Socialist power in Los Angeles,
Harriman tore open the rift by cutting off party support to the PLM. A
bitter Magón labeled the "white radicals" racist opportunists who sold
out their allies for their own interests.[34]

Magón's complaint pointed, if somewhat obliquely, to the heart of
the conflict between the PLM and the Los Angeles Socialist Party. While
sympathizing with the plight of workers in Mexico, party members
exhibited feelings about the Mexican people themselves that were at
best ambivalent and at worst openly hostile. More comfortable with a
political alliance than with social or workplace integration, they feared
that migrants from south of the border, like those from Asia, would
undermine the living standards of white workers. The party therefore
demonstrated much more support for workers in Mexico than for ethnic Mexicans in the United States. Though a few white Socialists made
impassioned pleas for a more inclusive industrial democracy, the majority did as much to alienate Mexican residents of the central neighborhoods as to attract them. Mexican Angelenos had to balance the legal
defense of the Magón brothers with the Socialist press's underhanded
referrals to Mexico as the "land of smallpox" and insinuations that
Mexican labor depressed wages for white workers.[35] These contradictions made it difficult for Mexican Angelenos to accept the calls for
unity proffered by party leaders and street speakers.

The Socialist Party in Los Angeles also stumbled in its appeal to African Americans. Nationally, blacks remained suspicious of Socialists and their ties to racist AFL unions. The local street-speaking campaign offered up a voice that promised to overcome this distrust. The emissary was Rev. George Washington Woodbey. The only notable Socialist speaker of color in Los Angeles, Woodbey challenged the racial and ethnic limits of the party organization and called for an aggressively inclusive coalition of city workers. Although he was an ordained Baptist minister, Woodbey spent much of the first decade of the twentieth century stumping for Socialism throughout cities in the American West, where he often had trouble finding hotels that would accept black guests. Despite regular stints in local jails, Woodbey spoke on the streets and in the auditoriums of Los Angeles as often as any Socialist. His skin color attracted a disproportionate share of police and vigilante violence. Local party members acknowledged both his commitment and his vulnerability by turning over part of the collections from some meetings to "Comrade Woodbey, who stands the brunt of the attacks in the firing line." In 1912 he was one of hundreds arrested in San Diego to protest the street-speaking ban against the IWW.[36]

On the soapbox Woodbey articulated the inter-ethnoracial possibilities of socialism. He supported the founding principles of the party while simultaneously attacking the racist hierarchies embedded in its structure and platform. He steadfastly opposed, for instance, the exclusion of immigrants, including Asians, from American soil and denied that newcomers reduced living standards for workers of any color. In a prescient observation, he dismissed the idea that such barriers would protect "American" labor. If capitalists could not import Asian workers, he reasoned, they would simply export jobs to Asian countries. In his support for immigrants Woodbey omitted the Americanization rhetoric on which so many Anglos hung discriminatory sentiments. At the Socialist Party's national convention in 1908 he summarized his views on immigration: "There are no foreigners, and cannot be unless some person comes down from Mars, or Jupiter, or someplace. I stand on the declaration of Thomas Paine when he said 'The world is my country.'"[37]

A few Socialists echoed Woodbey's call for racial and ethnic inclusion, but the party in general preferred to ignore such arguments for fear of upsetting its white majority, and it continued to pander to exclusionist labor organizations such as the AFL. Paralleling their treatment of Mexicans, Socialist Angelenos recruited African Americans only into segregated organizations that lacked full membership rights to the party.

A halfhearted endorsement of a black junk dealer named Frank Whitley for city council and platform announcements that the party favored economic, not social, equality did little to capitalize on Woodbey's goodwill. Reports after the 1911 election suggested that close to 80 percent of African Americans voted for Harriman's opponent, George Alexander.[38] In the aftermath of the *Times* bombing and Harriman's come-from-ahead defeat, a number of the party faithful shed their egalitarian, pro-coalition trappings and decided to start from scratch. The short-lived Llano Del Rio colony, founded in 1914 in the arid desert north of Los Angeles, represented for some party members an idealized vision of a proper Socialist community, but membership was restricted to whites. By 1915 Woodbey had lost the minister's position he held for twenty years at a San Diego church and disappeared from public life.[39] The impressive oratorical machine that Socialists had constructed on the streets of downtown Los Angeles ground to a halt.

SUPPRESSING "FOREIGN AGENTS": THE WORLD WAR I CRACKDOWN

In the years after the Socialists' fall, street-speaking culture in Los Angeles languished under the withering attacks of irate business interests and Red-baiting conservatives. Around downtown, economic expansion and traffic congestion prompted calls for more vigorous regulation of soapboxers and the disruptions they caused. International disruptions from the Mexican Revolution to World War I and the Russian Revolution aggravated fears of social unrest and radicalism, especially of those who promoted ethnoracial coalitions. Sensing broader support, elites and conservatives in the government and the private sector pressed the LAPD to muzzle leftist speakers in the streets and parks. In the 1910s and early 1920s, their efforts centered principally on remnants of the PLM and another loosely organized syndicalist organization, the IWW, or Wobblies. The soapbox gatherings and demonstrations these groups sponsored drew smaller crowds than the Socialist meetings but considerably more police violence, marking an escalation in the war against street speaking.

The IWW was founded in 1905 in Chicago by unionists fed up with the reactionary tendencies of the AFL and fortified in following years by Socialists dissatisfied with that organization's rightward trajectory. Wobblies exhibited little of the white bias and none of the middle-class aspirations characteristic of many Socialists. Although it officially renounced "violence" in an effort to forestall political persecution, the organization maintained a commitment to the direct action and civil disobedience that became its hallmark. Unlike the Socialist Party, Wobblies continued to support the PLM after 1911 as part of their plan for a pan-ethnic working-class movement. They even made up about 20 percent of the force that undertook an ill-fated attempt to seize Baja California for working-class Mexico in 1911.[40] Other aspects of the platform avoided the contradictions that had tripped up the Socialists and made the IWW, in theory at least, more appealing to residents of the central neighborhoods. Rejecting outright the "Americanism" cherished by Socialists, it dismissed all forms of nationalism as an obstacle to class consciousness. Members produced flyers in various languages to entice workers of all ethnic backgrounds into the fold.[41] They also condemned the conservative trade unionism of the AFL and instead appealed directly to unskilled industrial workers of the type who were coming to predominate in central Los Angeles. Finally, the IWW dismissed formal politics as an ineffective means to class emancipation, thus side-stepping the quandary of appealing to noncitizens while trying to build voting strength.[42]

Unfortunately for the IWW, however, it also departed from the Socialists in attracting nowhere near as many adherents, either to soapbox gatherings or to its membership rolls. Socialist meetings could draw hundreds to thousands of spectators, but IWW meetings often consisted of small groups huddled together after the evening traffic had subsided. Jesse Kimbrough, an African American police officer in Los Angeles, remembered the ostentatious display of Wobbly speakers: "Their strength lay in the power of their lungs. They could raise the roof off a hay barn when they thundered their rallying song. 'Hallelujah, I'm a Bum.'" But he also remembered the sparse attendance at the speeches.[43] IWW protests appeared sporadically through the mid-1920s, but the organization never achieved any significant, sustained following in downtown Los Angeles. Even on the free speech issue, the local chapter was overshadowed by more dramatic fights in San Diego and San Pedro.

Both internal and external factors played a role in dampening the IWW's appeal to central Los Angeles. For one thing, the traditional bases of Wobbly support, mining and farm labor, did not generally figure in the industrial landscapes of large cities such as Los Angeles. Moreover, Wobblies did not enjoy the support from other local groups that the Socialists had. At the outset of its formation in 1905, the IWW had maintained cordial relations with the Socialist Party both at the

local and the national level. Within a few years, however, even mainstream Socialists had become leery of the Wobblies' syndicalist leanings,
militant antiracism, and disdain for the Americanism that embodied so
much of the Socialist heritage. Conversely, the revolution-minded IWW
often disdained more moderate working-class organizations. In Los
Angeles, the local office's dearth of support was compounded by its isolation from the national organization, which directed little attention to
the struggles in Los Angeles. Not noted for their deep pockets in any
part of the country, Wobblies in Los Angeles suffered from an especially
acute shortage of money that hampered efforts to drum up support.[44]

While the IWW remained more ethnoracially inclusive than the
Socialists, it compared less well with regard to gender issues. Perhaps
because of its origins in heavy industry, the organization remained a
decidedly male-dominated group, providing virtually no voice for
women activists. In general, it appears that few women spoke on its
behalf in the streets or public spaces of Los Angeles. One exception
occurred at a 1919 rally in a Main Street auditorium held in defiance of
the LAPD crackdown. A government mole who attended the meeting
reported the presence of two female speakers, one an elementary school
teacher, along with "quite a sprinkling of women and young girls in the
audience." Women were not absent from IWW activities, but on balance the organization developed few visible female leaders or activists.
Its opponents found it easy to stigmatize the organization as a gathering
of rootless, dangerous single men.[45]

Bereft of adequate funding, political influence, and an established
social basis, Wobblies made easy targets for authorities itching to clamp
down on working-class protests, especially those involving ethnoracial
coalitions. An early indication of the impending conflict occurred on
January 5, 1913. Several hundred Wobblies, led by "two Mexican
women of Amazonian proportions" carrying a red flag, began a parade
from the Skid Row area up Los Angeles Street toward First Street. When
police attempted to confiscate the flag and disperse the procession the
marchers rebelled. Officers beat several demonstrators and arrested four
Anglo and Mexican Wobblies. The *Times* cheered the LAPD for quickly
dispersing the crowd of protesters and spectators who "had effectively
blocked all kinds of traffic."[46]

On Christmas of that same year, the LAPD extended the campaign
against unauthorized street parades to plaza gatherings. After government officials convened a hearing to discuss the city's unemployment
problem, a coalition of Wobblies, union members, and independent

workers held a series of meetings at the plaza to protest their exclusion from the hearing and to set forth alternative solutions to joblessness. Organizers then called together a larger protest for December 25. Several hundred people, mostly unemployed Mexican, Italian, and Anglo men, gathered in a cold drizzle that Christmas morning. For several hours a series of speeches and a general discussion took place without any apparent disruption. Some observers later recalled that the "mexican" portion of the audience gradually became the majority and that the speeches, in both Spanish and English, became increasingly vitriolic. At some point police moved in on the crowd and a riot erupted. An officer shot and killed one man, Rafael Adames, and wounded at least one other. Onlookers carried the dead body to the "Wobbly hall" on Los Angeles Street where police found him. Dozens of other protesters and several officers were injured in the melee. The *Times* excused the death of Adames by noting that he "had an unsavory reputation as an IWW and a troublemaker" who led a protest of unemployed Angelenos at City Hall some weeks before.[47]

Wobblies condemned the police action, and numerous witnesses denied the LAPD's allegation that the protesters had instigated the violence, but city authorities took advantage of the incident to ban future gatherings. The police began by "put[ing] the Plaza district under martial law" to ferret out other suspected agitators. They expelled "all curb-stone restaurateurs, fakirs *[sic]* and loafers" from the streets and raided pool halls, movie houses, and parlors to track down fugitive radicals and quell the "disturbances" that continued late into the night. Though they focused their efforts on Sonoratown, the police canvassed other neighborhoods in the central city and made arrests as far south as Seventh and Main. Of the seventy-three individuals detained, fifty-three were identified as Mexican. The *Times* played on nativist fears by quoting an alleged demonstration leader named Peter Castorano as saying, "I am against all government: I have no use for the American flag." In the following days, police arrested several others who came to speak at the plaza, including an Italian who, according to the *Times,* exhorted a group of two hundred Mexicans to exact revenge on the LAPD for killing Adames. City attorneys ultimately prosecuted forty-three for the Christmas disturbance, the largest number of prisoners arraigned for a common infraction in Los Angeles history up to that point. Job Harriman represented the defendants, but this time he managed to secure few acquittals, and the *Times* gleefully reported that several convicts were still in jail six months later.[48]

A subsequent city council investigation into the Christmas morning incident cleared the LAPD of any wrongdoing, but the political fallout continued to rain down on the central neighborhoods. The city council followed its acquittal by passing a resolution "warning away the unemployed" from Los Angeles. The *Times* and at least one councilman called for a ban on free speech at the plaza and a citywide ban on all soapbox speakers without American citizenship. Authorities also made a desultory gesture toward ameliorating the economic conditions that led to the riot. Forced to admit the existence of an unemployment problem, the city council hastily authorized the creation of a "Lot Cleaning" department at the Municipal Free Employment Bureau. Applicants would receive $2 a day for trash removal and cultivation of the vacant lots that dotted the downtown area. Within a couple of days, however, the city council cut the wages in half after thousands of Mexican railroad workers quit their $1.50-a-day positions for more lucrative employment. The *Times* fumed that the former railwaymen were "crowding out worthy white applicants." The city replaced the program with two Griffith Park work camps, one for Mexicans and one for whites, that quarantined some of the unemployed for the next three months.[49]

As the decade wore on, international events raised the threat, as some Anglos saw it, of a mongrel uprising against the white spots of America, prompting further crackdowns on mixed-ethnic public gatherings. The deepening Mexican Revolution, the PLM's embrace of revolutionary anarchism, and Pancho Villa's incursions north of the border aggravated Anglo insecurities about Mexicans. Compounding these worries, the outbreak of World War I, the Russian Revolution, and renewed concerns about the Japanese "yellow peril" led some reactionary Anglos to concoct elaborate scenarios of German, Mexican, Japanese, and American IWW conspiracies to invade the southwestern United States. The 1917 interception of the infamous Zimmermann telegram, in which Germany proposed an alliance with Mexico and a joint campaign to recapture territory lost to the United States during the Mexican-American War, prompted some Americans to cry conspiracy. A 1917 *Times* article ominously warned its readers: "If the people of Los Angeles knew what was happening on our border, they would not sleep at night. . . . German nationals hob-nob with Mexican bandits, Japanese agents, and renegades from this country. . . . Los Angeles is the headquarters for this vicious system, and it is there that the deals between German and Mexican representatives are frequently made."[50]

Amid such hysteria, any working-class political movements bridging ethnoracial boundaries came under immediate suspicion. The *Times*, for instance, deftly conflated class-based protest with political treason, implying that any popular workers' movement was the doing of outside subversives. Of alleged foreign agents stirring up "labor friction" in the city, the paper warned, "These aliens are too shrewd to appeal to a mixed population to side with Germans, Allies or neutrals—they are organizing on what they choose to term a 'patriotic basis.'" Fanning the flames of paranoia, the paper played off the ethnic uncertainties of mixed populations in modern urban areas:

> It is known that several governments employ hundreds of men and women in all walks of life to gather information. . . . Is the next door neighbor a loyal citizen or an enemy? The ordinary citizen cannot tell. . . . What American can tell the difference between a German, a Swiss, or a Frenchman born on the border of any of those countries? If all are dressed alike what American can pick out a Chinese, Japanese, Filipino, or Korean? . . . Thousands of Germans speak fluently languages not their own. America is said to harbor more varieties of spies than another nation on the face of the globe.[51]

To combat this alleged underground network, city and federal authorities launched a crusade against free speech and public demonstrations in the streets of Los Angeles, the medium by which, they assumed, treasonous plots spread. Wobblies, Mexican revolutionaries, and other radical speakers increasingly found themselves caught in its net. On the federal level, the effort began with the establishment of a counterintelligence program in the public areas and industrial zones of Los Angeles. In 1917 the Department of Justice assembled its own cadre of domestic spies, including Emilio Kosterlitsky, a Russian-born, former Mexican military officer who had served under Porfirio Díaz. Best known in the United States for his role in suppressing a strike of Mexican workers against an American mining company in Cananea, Mexico, Kosterlitsky fell out of favor with the U.S. government during the Mexican Revolution and spent a number of months in jail. Rehabilitated as a government spy, he passed much of World War I on a bench in Pershing Square, eavesdropping on conversations and trying to catch German agents in the act of recruiting Mexican Angelenos.[52] On the shop floors of factories associated with the war effort, the War Department instituted a "Plant Protection" program to guarantee steady industrial production and to protect the firms from sabotage, strikes, or other subversive activity. Department officials created a network of "loyal" workers in each plant to inform on traitors and any suspicious activities. The informants were categorized by military "rank" (captain, lieutenant, etc.) depending on their reliability, as established by the plant owner.[53]

Other federal workers preferred less subtle methods of combating dissent. On September 19, 1917, several months after the United States entered World War I, two hundred soldiers stationed in Arcadia, a whites-only suburb northeast of downtown, stormed the IWW headquarters on Skid Row, ostensibly in retaliation for an attack on two of their members the previous week. As impassive LAPD officers looked on, they destroyed the office and chased a handful of Wobblies down the street. According to the *Times*, thousands of spectators cheered the soldiers. In the wake of this assault, the IWW realized that Los Angeles authorities would not allow them to maintain a public presence. They therefore decided to cease downtown demonstrations for the duration of World War I and to abandon active recruiting. For the rest of the decade Wobblies confined themselves largely to "underground" meetings.[54]

PLM speakers and affiliated activists who continued to gather at the plaza faced similar treatment. On May 6, 1917, police dispersed a crowd of one thousand and arrested three speakers, including Ricardo Magón's son-in-law, Raoul Palma, widely known as the "boy orator of the Plaza." According to a jailhouse letter intercepted by federal investigators, Palma and his supporters were in the process of building a new "hybrid" organization called the Los Angeles Bureau of Workers Activities that would resurrect the ethnoracial coalition of the Socialist Party–PLM period. Palma hoped that a series of plaza speeches in Spanish and English would draw support for the bureau and ensure that "the labor organizations of the city are more in touch and harmony than they [have] been hereto."[55] City Attorney Thomas Woolwine subsequently brought up Palma on a questionable murder-robbery charge, eliciting a derisive series of letters from Kate Crane Gartz, a wealthy Pasadena socialite who provided financial and emotional assistance to numerous local leftists. She dismissed the prosecution's effort as "another Mooney case," a reference to the labor activist jailed, also under questionable evidence, for the 1916 Preparedness Day bombing in San Francisco.[56] Woolwine lost the case, but authorities deported Palma and another speaker to Mexico. Proclamations from the local PLM office on San Fernando Street condemned the arrests and called on Mexican Angelenos to unite against "the dogs who call themselves the guardians of public order."[57] Two weeks later Vicente Carrillo attracted the LAPD's attention when he started an antidraft registration movement around Sonoratown. Citing the poor wages paid to Mexican workers, Carrillo questioned their interest in fighting Germany. The *Times* did not appreciate his rhetorical question, "Why . . . not take 500,000 Mexicans and marry them to American girls, that we may have some interest to fight for?" Like Palma, Carrillo was sentenced to jail and eventually deported.[58]

Paralleling the counterintelligence spies loitering in city parks, conservative Anglos established counterpolitical speakers to replace the leftists expelled from the streets of Los Angeles. During America's involvement in World War I, for example, the city hosted an active chapter of the Four-Minute Men, a national organization devoted to drumming up support for the war effort. Led in the city by Marshall Stimson, the Four-Minute Men conducted a series of short talks at theaters and other public gathering places, and occasionally on the streets, concerning proper maintenance of the home front. Much of the speeches involved entreaties to obey rationing regulations or solicitations for widow and orphan funds, but they also spoke against pacifism and other "unpatriotic" union-protest movements that might undermine the wartime economy. A number of speeches were translated into different languages, including Armenian, Greek, Chinese, Japanese, Italian, Spanish, and Russian.[59] While rarely confronting the IWW or the PLM directly, the Four-Minute Men inaugurated a conservative public-speaking campaign that countered radical rhetoric on the street with a pro-business, pro-"American" message valorizing the social and political status quo.

Other efforts made more explicit attempts to quash dissent among central city residents. Administrators at the Plaza Center, for example, briefly established a series of "wisely directed" discussions on labor issues that they hoped would draw Mexicans and Italians away from the "cross-eyed agitators" who populated the plaza.[60] But it was the Better America Federation (BAF) that quickly came to dominate the rhetorical campaign against Wobblies, unions, and anyone else who sympathized with working-class or central city residents. Founded in Los Angeles in 1917 by private utility magnates to mobilize the "average businessman" against "class legislation," the BAF during the twenties and thirties was perhaps the most virulent Red-baiting private organization in Southern California. The group touted a zero tolerance policy against leftist street speaking and censorship of "subversive" publications and in the early 1920s succeeded in briefly banning the *Nation* from Los Angeles public schools.[61] At the same time the BAF organized its own Speakers Bureau to combat the "pernicious influences and propaganda" of leftist street speakers. Like the Christian businessmen's meetings that squared off with the Socialist Party a decade earlier, the Speakers Bureau organized a series of lectures and speeches on downtown streets and at private businessmen's and club meetings advocating a conservative, antiunion "Americanization" campaign for immigrants.[62]

Though they appealed in rhetorical terms to immigrants, African Americans, and other residents of the central neighborhoods, BAF speakers denounced virtually any criticism of free market principles or local employer practices as treason. Most BAF supporters were themselves middle-class and elite businessmen, but the organization managed to field one or two working-class immigrants as street speakers. One official, for example, commended Elek Markowitz, a naturalized "Roumanian [sic] fruit-peddler" and American Legion volunteer, for giving a speech on the superiority of American working conditions to those in Europe at the corner of Broadway and Mercantile in 1921. The Speakers Bureau held many of its meetings at Second and Los Angeles Streets, a popular site during the Socialist free speech fight and a resolutely working-class area.[63] Despite enthusiastic reports from organization members and unconditional police support, the speaking campaign apparently hit a few procedural snags. The BAF remained uncomfortable, for instance, with the interactive nature of street-speaking culture and the potential problems of input from diverse, working-class audiences. In 1920 BAF leaders circulated a memo directing speakers not to take questions from the crowd. Instead, questions should be submitted in writing and answered at a subsequent speech to ensure that they would be "correct and consistent." By this point some speakers also encountered more caustic resistance from unfriendly pedestrians, and the BAF newsletter issued a plea for police protection of their soapboxers from harassment by scurrilous Angelenos.[64] The BAF speaking campaign peaked in the early twenties and faded thereafter, when the virtual extinction of leftist street speech made the effort unnecessary. But the organization continued to hound the IWW and a new adversary, the Communist Party, well into the next decade.

Before 1919 the LAPD based their treatment of Wobblies and other leftists on loose interpretations of the law, but the passage of California's Criminal Syndicalism Act that year gave them a powerful weapon with which to terrorize their foes. Emerging in the wake of the Russian Revolution and the frenzied 1919 strike wave in the United States, the law jump-started the Red scare period that marked a sharp right turn in mainstream American politics. Like similar ordinances passed in other states, the act outlawed in vague terms all "subversive" activities and literature, effectively legitimating a blanket campaign against leftist groups.[65] When Los Angeles Wobblies took tentative steps toward reasserting their presence in the city's streets, the LAPD was ready. In October 1919 authorities raided IWW headquarters and arrested nineteen of the organization's leaders. A force of American Legion volunteers, armed with weapons provided by local industries, was deputized to form a "flying squadron" targeting subversive activity. One month later they once again raided IWW headquarters, wrecking the office and injuring several of those inside, all of whom were arrested. In the days that followed, Legion deputies shut down a "red" bookstore, arrested several individuals in Pershing Square for "disloyal conversations," and broke up at least one indoor IWW meeting.[66] The raids had the desired effect of wiping the organization off the face of Los Angeles. "There is nothing down here," one Angeleno Wobbly ruefully reported in 1921, ". . . not even a jail relief committee." Across California, more than 500 individuals were arrested under the Syndicalism Law by 1926 and 128 sent to prison, many of them IWW members.[67]

The last major conflict between the IWW and authorities over public speaking in Southern California took place not in downtown Los Angeles but along the dockyard neighborhoods of San Pedro, the bustling harbor community to the south. In 1923 Wobblies and striking dockworkers waged a violent battle with police and vigilantes who broke up meetings on the streets and in private homes. In one notorious incident, vigilantes stormed a meeting of families and scalded several children with hot water that had been set up for coffee. They also kidnapped and tarred and feathered several leaders of the walkout. In terms of Wobbly publicity, the high point of the struggle came when officers arrested Upton Sinclair and several others for reading the Constitution on Liberty Hill, a piece of high ground rented to the IWW by a sympathetic landowner. Realizing that the intensive police repression was sapping the strikers' resolve, organizers terminated it after five weeks.[68]

The decline of the IWW after the events at San Pedro left a void in the political street-speaking culture of Los Angeles. The Southern California chapter of the American Civil Liberties Union (ACLU), created in 1923 in response to the San Pedro fight, became the sole organization of any consequence to support free speech in downtown Los Angeles. The ACLU, however, operated primarily as a legal organization and conducted no public-speaking campaigns of its own. The mid-1920s witnessed the continued harassment of political speakers in Los Angeles, even when they confined themselves to parks, the traditional safe haven of the soapboxer and casual conversationalist. In 1923 an exasperated Kate Crane Gartz inquired of LAPD chief August Vollmer, "Has your department the jurisdiction over the plain clothes men, self-confessed criminals and stool pigeons hired by the District Attorneys office to hound innocent men standing or sitting talking together in Pershing Square, and arresting even a newspaper reporter who was interviewing them?"[69] In 1925 officers arrested Leo Gallagher, a radical civil rights attorney who would later become the Communist Party's chief local defender, for allegedly disturbing a Christian evangelist on a Sunday afternoon at the plaza.[70] These incidents, though demonstrating the continued blackout of political street speech, also underscored the absence of concerted, organized speaking campaigns. For the rest of the decade, police had few targets beyond isolated individuals such as Gallagher, and street speaking as a political tool virtually disappeared from Los Angeles.

BOXING OUT THE SOAPBOX: URBAN GROWTH AND ZONING

Despite the crackdown on Wobblies and leftists, other kinds of public orators continued to practice their art in central city neighborhoods in the late 1910s and 1920s. The no-speech zone established in 1908 as part of the city's compromise with the Socialists expelled speakers from the center of downtown, but they continued to congregate in other areas, especially along Los Angeles Street south of the plaza and along Eighth Street near Spring. A steady increase in pedestrian traffic, fueled by migration, housing shortages, and the boom-bust economy of Southern California during this period, provided substantial audiences for speakers. New entertainments such as movie theaters might have provided an alternative to open-air activities, but they also drew large crowds into downtown thoroughfares.

Urban growth, however, also had negative effects on street-speaking culture. The proliferation of streetcar and automobile traffic exacerbated the gridlock that already choked the downtown boulevards. Faced with constant traffic jams, a skyrocketing number of train and auto accidents, and outraged business owners, the city council gradually began to expand the no-speech zone east and south.[71] Despite protests citing the public street as "the only forum for the poor and oppressed" and an unsolicited study by the Socialist Labor Party that concluded traffic was "not excessive" in one proposed area of exclusion, the city council extended the no-speech zone through Eighth Street in 1915, pushing the speakers down to Tenth and Eleventh Streets. The concrete podiums set up in the plaza during the same period provided only a modest concession to street speakers. Those orators who persevered had to deal with traffic noise that threatened to drown out their voices.[72]

Expanding the no-speech zone did little to eliminate either congestion or the presence of "undesirables" on the street, and advocates of the new ordinances frequently betrayed a BAF-like paranoia about leftist mobilization. Yet in 1922 the chamber of commerce, of all groups, issued a report on the Second and Los Angeles Street area, known locally as "Drunk's Paradise," that concluded the presence of large numbers of urban poor resulted more from businesses, missions, and employment offices catering to the "laboring class" than from street-speaking. Maintaining that some street speakers might improve the area, the report suggested merely an increased police presence and better lighting to prevent crime.[73] In 1923 city officials even explored the possibility of reintroducing street speakers into the no-speech zone, as long as they were not political. Prodded by the Salvation Army, the city's Public Safety Committee recommended that the Police Commission be given the authority to issue speaking permits within the zone to "charitable, religious, and similar organizations," with the obvious intent of excluding Wobblies and other radicals.[74] The City Attorney, realizing such preferential treatment could not be written into law, amended the proposal to give the police authority to grant permits to any group. The final ordinance passed by the city council extended the no-speech zone along Fifth Street all the way to Central Avenue through the Second to Aliso stretch of Los Angeles Street and down to Tenth Street.[75]

By the mid-1920s legislation and police harassment had pushed street speakers to the parks and the fringes of the increasingly congested downtown area and to thoroughfares in outlying districts such as Brooklyn Avenue in Boyle Heights, where Jewish residents gathered on warm evenings to talk politics.[76] A 1926 sociological study of speakers in Pershing Square and the plaza concluded that their activities performed a definite social function but provided scant foundation for political movements. At Pershing Square, where organized gatherings were outlawed, street speaking in essence consisted of a "secret forum" where regular denizens, generally elderly white men, carried on extended conversations with an eye out for the police.

> One can hear men first in quiet conversation. Voices are raised. Passersby stop and listen. A crowd soon gathers. Words fly thick and fast. Antagonistic ideas clash; convictions are expressed in angry tones. The crowd

stirs about as it increases in size. The park officer approaches. The crowd silently and suddenly scatters, only to form again as soon as the officer gets out of sight.[77]

The arguments may have involved pressing social issues of the time, but according to the study, they operated almost exclusively as a recreational form of socializing for Angelenos with few institutional attachments. Speaking at the plaza was more organized but generally occurred only on Sunday afternoons. The speakers and the audience there were more diverse than at Pershing Square: Anglo, African American, Jewish, and Mexican participants, as well as a smattering of women. Many participants and audience members, the study concluded, were "hoboes" residing in nearby rescue missions. The author noted that though some speakers spoke on "political" subjects, there was a general absence of violence or police control.[78] Louis Adamic, writing in 1927, confirmed that plaza speakers could not broach any subject that was "economic heresy." He added that both Mexicans and Asians were gradually being driven out of the area by massive commercial development that would soon bury the plaza "culture."[79]

Angelenos who sounded the death knell of the soapboxer during the 1920s spoke prematurely. The onset of the depression and the arrival of the Communist Party ushered in a resurgence of street speaking, demonstrations, and police violence not seen since the heyday of the Socialist Party. The quality of this campaign was somewhat different, depending as much on the spectacle of violence as on the dissemination of information. Despite the Communist-driven renaissance, the trends of the twenties portended a cloudy future for soapbox culture. The dispersal of industries and residents into outlying districts meant that Angelenos, whether in or outside the central neighborhoods, shared less common ground than they had before. Furthermore, new commercial media such as film and radio introduced alternative sources of recreation and information not tied to public space. Regardless of police repression, these developments slowly rendered street speaking irrelevant to the political and social life of Los Angeles. They also marked the incipient erosion of ethnoracial contact that had characterized the central neighborhoods in previous decades.

CHAPTER 7

The Streets Run Red

*The Communist Party and the
Resurgence of Coalition Street Politics*

ONCE UPON A TIME IN THE PLAZA

Sometime in the 1930s veteran *Los Angeles Times* journalist Timothy
Turner penned a column titled "The Japanese Carpenter Who Got Religion." The protagonist, "none too bright, even as honest Japanese car-
penters go," wanders into the "Sabbath Eve bedlam" at the plaza one
day and becomes fascinated with the "cosmopolitan" crowds milling
about. Despite his negligible English skills, he is drawn to a sharp-
dressed Salvation Army preacher who plays a trumpet in the midst of
other orators. The carpenter returns the following weekend, sporting his
own uniform and blowing his own trumpet, "which he had mastered to
the extent of two hymns, barely recognizable." He soon becomes a regular performer, though few can make out his words or his music. One
Sunday he arrives to find a Communist demonstration in progress.
Spanish, English, and Yiddish fill the air. Without warning police officers descend on the gathering, and the angry crowd retaliates with fists
and sticks. The ensuing melee leaves the poor carpenter trampled and
alone in the street. Firemen arriving to clean up the area mercilessly
blast him with their hoses, ruining his uniform and trumpet. The carpenter's spirit is crushed: "Anyway, it was gone, that fine feeling he had
felt when he first got his soldier suit and his brass horn." He abandons
the plaza and his "public personage," although "he was sometimes seen,
dressed in a neat suit of black, entering the Buddhist Temple at First and
Central."[1]

Though probably fictitious, Turner's story illustrates what many middle-class and elite Anglos thought about the politics and population of the central neighborhoods during the early twentieth century: the condescending assumptions about immigrants' attraction to "American" culture and their failure to mimic it, the fear of the plaza and adjacent areas as mongrelized, unstable, zones of potentially violent protest, and the attribution of radicalism as cause, rather than consequence, of ethnoracial divisions. In the 1920s a consortium of public officials, private citizens, and business interests largely managed to squelch leftist street speakers in downtown public spaces via police control, legislative ordinance, redevelopment, or cultural programs. By the onset of the Great Depression, however, this battle, resuscitated by the local branch of the Communist Party of Los Angeles, returned to the streets with a vengeance, bringing with it all the political and social consequences Turner found so appalling. Like their ideological precursors, the Communists threatened the established, corporate liberal social relations of dominant political interests by pitting the eclectic working-class population of the central neighborhoods against the bearers of the white spot dream.

Although the Communist campaigns echoed the appropriations of Los Angeles streets by the Socialists, the PLM, and the IWW, they did much more than simply revive earlier issues and strategies. The party's presence in the central neighborhoods in the 1930s offered a basis for coalition building that differed in substantial ways from those of their predecessors. With a stronger organizational basis than the IWW and a more inclusive recruiting strategy than the Socialists, the CPLA made a more effective if ephemeral appeal to those central city Angelenos at the fringes of traditional urban politics. Of course, the Communist cause benefited in no small measure from the suffering wrought by the severe dislocations of the 1930s. Dire economic circumstances made its radical platform and emotional demonstrations more appealing to Angelenos who might otherwise have distrusted the organization or feared police retaliation. The climate of desperation masked, to a degree, the CPLA's considerable shortcomings: a rickety organizational framework, ill-defined goals, political ideology that shifted with the vagaries of the Comintern (the party's Moscow-based international body), and a predominantly Jewish and Anglo membership unschooled in appealing to other groups. Like the Socialist Party and the IWW, the CPLA's failure to sustain a viable, integrated front had as much to do with internal flaws as with external oppression.

Despite these shortcomings, the Communist-inspired street politics that erupted during the early years of the depression broadcast a new challenge from central city residents to the white spot of America. In Los Angeles as in other cities, police, public officials, and business interests acknowledged the threat by organizing the most extensive campaign to eliminate a political movement since the Red scare of 1919–21. The war between these two forces for the streets of central Los Angeles marked the culmination of a struggle that stretched back to the turn of the century.

THE GATHERING STORM: THE CPLA IN THE 1920S

Given the post–World War I Red scare, it may seem surprising that the national Communist Party (CPUSA), founded somewhat innocuously in 1919, escaped the crosshairs of conservatives for most of the 1920s. In Los Angeles, right-wing extremist groups like the Better America Federation continued to rail against a decaying IWW, anarchists like Sacco and Vanzetti, and local liberals like Bromley Oxnam. But the domestic "Reds" they targeted generally did not include Communists, who during the decade remained concentrated in the most heavily Jewish section of Boyle Heights. Both in Los Angeles and in the nation as a whole, the founding members of the CP had drawn from a disparate group of exiled Socialists, Wobblies, and other leftists. But the heart of the party lay in the new, largely foreign-born communities of Jews who saw in Communism a solution to centuries of economic marginalization and anti-Semitism.[2] During the 1920s, CPLA operations centered on the Co-op at 2706 Brooklyn Avenue in Boyle Heights, a multipurpose restaurant, office, barber shop, and meeting hall that hosted a variety of political, social, and cultural groups in the Jewish community. Most of their rallies and soapboxing in the 1920s took place not in downtown but in residential neighborhoods and outlying parks where they attracted less police attention. Some early members recalled the period as a tranquil, "unconflicted" time when the party functioned as much as a social organization as a political party.[3] Others, like Angeleno Peggy Dennis, who with her husband, Eugene Dennis, became one of the country's most visible Communists, felt the party needed to reach beyond the Jewish community if it hoped to influence domestic politics. By the late 1920s, many Jewish Communists like Dennis had changed their names, in part to evade police surveillance, in part to camouflage their Semitic backgrounds.[4] In 1928 the Comintern sanctioned this trend by issuing a new set of organizational directives, later identified as the Third Period strategy. The directives called for mobilization around the specific interests of different ethnic groups, especially African Americans, but also abolished "foreign-language federations" within the party in favor of a more integrated organizational structure.[5]

Third Period strategy, combined with the devastating onset of the Great Depression, transformed the CPLA from a provincial collection of eastside Jews into a dynamic political movement. Local and state governments' callous response to the economic fallout from Black October galvanized central city residents of different backgrounds into action. The signs of crisis were everywhere. Massive layoffs and a deluge of displaced agricultural workers from rural areas swelled the ranks of unemployed who wandered the central neighborhoods in search of work, handouts, and distraction from their suffering. Families evicted from homes clustered in camps, sheds, open spaces by the Los Angeles River, or wherever they could find shelter. Destitute residents formed long lines outside central city missions and employment bureaus. A local party-sponsored film from the period contrasted the sprawling, immaculate homes of patrician Los Angeles with the teeming streets and tortuous breadlines of the central neighborhoods.[6] Public officials tried in vain to stem the tide of economic refugees into the city, and regional boosters amended their literature to warn newcomers that employment was unavailable. The LAPD embarked on a decade-long campaign to expel "transients," culminating in a two-month blockade of California's borders by one hundred thirty officers in 1936.[7] Mexican Angelenos fared even worse after Anglos instituted the notorious repatriation programs to encourage or force ethnic Mexicans to relocate south of the border. Several hundred thousand left the Southwest during the 1930s.[8]

Within this turmoil the Communist Party seemed poised to channel the disparate radical traditions abiding in central neighborhood populations. Eastern Europeans, including Jews, brought the Communist movement from the region of its first victory. Former Wobblies and former industrial socialists kept alive the Anglo-American radicalism of earlier decades. A small but radical Japanese movement also flowered under the guidance of Sen Katayama, a world-traveling labor organizer, Socialist, and cofounder of the CPUSA and the Japanese Labor Association. The latter became the primary Communist organization for Japanese in Los Angeles.[9] Mexican Angelenos brought a variety of socialist, anarchist, and other radical traditions out of the Mexican Revolution, as well as an aggressive attitude toward unionizing agricultural and industrial industries.[10] African Americans had cultivated a variety of political organizations ranging from the National Association for the Advancement of Colored People (NAACP) to black nationalism to the emergent Sleeping Car Porters Union.[11] Each of these traditions had flowered in ethnic-specific contexts, but the Communist Party now proposed to unite them under the umbrella of a single organization.

THE SPECTRUM AND SPECTACLE OF PROTEST

In the early 1930s Communists looked to the street demonstration to fuse the various radical traditions into a common mass movement under their leadership. At their best, the loosely structured protests they developed highlighted the flexible strategy that organizers adopted to recruit Angelenos of different backgrounds. Historians have often portrayed the CPUSA as a tightly controlled, monolithic organization directed with almost dictatorial efficiency by the party's central office in New York, which itself reported to Moscow.[12] Conceptually flawed on a number of levels, this evaluation is especially problematic with respect to local Communist activity in Los Angeles. The party's philosophy of "democratic centralism," which gave elected officials broad powers and forbade public dissension from party doctrine, created a more hierarchical power structure than conventional American political parties, and the national leadership tended to privilege the interest of the party bureaucracy over that of rank-and-file membership. But this authoritarianism functioned imperfectly at best. Understaffed and chaotic party offices were not overly efficient in distributing information, and the party often did little to ensure that its directives were implemented. Dorothy Healey, who would eventually head the party organization in Southern California, claimed that few members bothered to read the ponderous, poorly worded directives issued by the Comintern or the national office.[13]

Los Angeles's geographic distance from the CPUSA's central office in New York exacerbated the communication problems, leaving local activists even more independent. National directives supposedly passed through the California regional office in San Francisco before proceeding to Los Angeles, but Southern California Communists often received instructions late or not at all. Of course, broad changes in party policy were felt in the city, but nuts-and-bolts operations often were left to the discretion of local members. With little oversight from higher-ups, motivated organizers in Southern California felt free to develop their own activities and strategies. Alice McGrath, perhaps best known for her role on the Sleepy Lagoon Defense Committee, recalled her prewar activities in the party: "I knew what I wanted to do, and I was just enough of an outlaw to make my own assignments." Likewise, Lil Carlson contrasted the freedom she enjoyed as an organizer in California with the "suffocating" control she endured when she moved to the New York office.[14]

CPLA activity thus involved less an extension of Soviet methods than an improvised and even culturally syncretic process of political mobilization. Young, inexperienced, and insolvent, organizers on the front lines of the party propaganda machine adopted a flexible, publicity-based strategy for appealing to the diverse interests of integrated urban neighborhoods. Their efforts fell far short of an unqualified success: internal racism, the periodic intrusion of ill-conceived directives, and miscommunications posed constant threats to the fragile multiethnic coalition germinating in the party. But the tensions between ethnic factions and the often myopic "party line" position on race that continually rattled the national leadership of the CPUSA did not always percolate down to far-flung jurisdictions such as Los Angeles.[15] When local activists took up the street demonstration as a basis of organization and protest and when they mobilized around specific issues rather than broad Communist principles, they often managed, for a time at least, to unite the diverse residents of the central neighborhoods under a common cause.

The CPLA organizing effort began with face-to-face contact on the shop floor and in residential neighborhoods. For most of the 1930s they had little success in the former venues. Open-shop conditions and recalcitrant AFL locals stifled attempts to infiltrate unions or factory workforces. According to local leader Ben Dobbs, the Trade Union Unity League (TUUL), the party's organ for intraunion recruitment, "never really took off in Los Angeles."[16] Rose Pesotta's bitter denunciation of party attempts to co-opt her AFL-sponsored strike of city garment workers the previous year underscored the cool reception that greeted many Communists on shop floors. Toward the end of the decade, the emergence of the Congress of Industrial Organizations (CIO) and the party's switch to a less sectarian Popular Front approach cooled tensions between Communists and unionists, but shop floor successes in Los Angeles remained elusive.[17]

The CPLA did much better in house-to-house and street organizing. Party activists combed the working-class neighborhoods around downtown to drum up audiences for demonstrations. This recruiting apparatus was divided into small neighborhood units that conducted an extensive series of private neighbor-to-neighbor meetings and smaller speeches in the central neighborhoods. Initial contacts led to larger demonstrations, often centered in the plaza, Skid Row, and other downtown locations. Soapbox speakers began to "build up" well-traveled streetcorners in certain neighborhoods, conducting meetings and passing out leaflets to establish a regular presence. Members of the Young Pioneers, a CP youth organization, also advertised meetings and demonstrations when they sold subscriptions of party periodicals door-to-door in working-class neighborhoods.[18]

In addition, this recruitment strategy often operated under the auspices of satellite organizations with target agendas or constituencies, membership in which did not require party membership. Thus, while available evidence suggests that the CPLA had just over a thousand members by 1935, satellite organizations included many more.[19] The Scottsboro Council, for example, contributed to the national campaign to free the "Scottsboro boys" (nine African American youths jailed in Alabama on spurious evidence for the rape of two white women) but also organized black Angelenos around civil rights issues, such as pressuring South Central businesses to renounce all-white hiring policies.[20] Other organizations pursued different constituencies. The Young Pioneers, for example, provided social activities for minors but also directed them to protest school conditions. The Young Communist League (YCL) did the same for young adults. International Labor Defense (ILD), the legal arm of the party, appealed to victims of police brutality or deportation proceedings. The Friends of the Soviet Union generated support for Stalin's regime, and the Friends of Ethiopia protested Mussolini's invasion. Many of these groups maintained formal if transparent independence from the party. But they operated alongside more openly Marxist institutions such as the Los Angeles Workers School, a short-lived effort that sought to bridge the gap between theory and practice by teaching Marxist principles and participating in local demonstrations and campaigns.[21]

Some of these groups did not maintain their original momentum, but the changing constellation of party-sponsored organizations made it more likely that central city residents would find one that spoke to their concerns. For larger rallies or demonstrations the party brought these different groups together, creating an eclectic mass of protesters who seemed to speak with one voice on a broad range of issues. African Americans rallying in support of the Scottsboro boys, Jews protesting Nazi Germany, Mexicans aiding striking Imperial Valley farmworkers, old-line union members supporting Tom Mooney, and Japanese protesting antialien fishing laws might all end up at the same meeting. The eclecticism of CP protest topics provided fodder for party jokes. Lil Carlson, who as a teenager organized and soapboxed in East Los Angeles for the YCL, recalled one perhaps apocryphal story about a landlord faced with a mob of protesters. The landlord agreed to all the demands except one, pleading with the protesters, "I can't free Tom Mooney."[22] Combining protest issues in a single demonstration not only increased attendance, it also encouraged members to draw connections between poverty relief, civil liberties, social justice, international politics, and the labor movement. In other words, the CPLA's public organizing strategy explicitly sought to establish a coalition politics that would unite the diverse residents of central Los Angeles. Organizers laid the groundwork for this coalition by fanning out through California, organizing and supporting strikes in both industrial and agricultural areas.[23]

Among the most active and successful of the satellite organizations were the Unemployed Councils. Established nationally in early 1930, the councils became for many a sort of informal neighborhood association and mouthpiece for the newly destitute. Under the mottoes "Don't Starve—Fight!" and "Work or Wages," Communist organizers canvassed neighborhoods door-to-door and set up initial meetings at sympathizers' homes. Once convinced to form a council, the residents elected their own leaders, and the organizer moved on to the next block. During the early 1930s, the Unemployed Councils conducted a battery of protests at the County Welfare Office downtown, as well as at numerous soup kitchens around Skid Row, which they claimed provided only a fraction of the "relief" workers deserved. They also established informal squadrons to reactivate utilities and return furniture to the homes of evicted families. Though the party sponsored the councils, organizers generally let the party's hand in them remain hidden. Most members were not in the CPLA, and it is likely that at least some participants did not realize they were involved in a Communist organ.[24]

The large demonstrations organized by the Unemployed Councils and other CP-sponsored groups during the 1930s inaugurated new trends in the political culture of street speech and the campaign to suppress it. The Socialists, the PLM, and the IWW viewed the soapbox first and foremost as a way to preach to central city residents and fought to restore that right when police intervened to stop them. Communists, in contrast, almost encouraged violent responses to their demonstrations as a way to make class conflict a visceral experience for central Ange-

FIGURE 8. Communist demonstration on Main Street, 1930. Demonstrations often disrupted the flow of downtown traffic. Herald Examiner Collection/Los Angeles Public Library.

lenos. This strategy began with deliberate attempts to disrupt the normal flow of downtown traffic, to force pedestrians to confront the demonstration. To this end, party members were willing to use the plainclothes officers and anti-Communist spies (from conservative groups such as the BAF, the American Legion, and the pro-Nazi Friends of New Germany) who shadowed their efforts to add to the apparent audience. The penchant of these moles for disrupting the proceedings lent a contentious tone to the demonstrations, especially in those meetings designed as actual debates between pro- and anti-CP advocates.[25] Even at solely party-sponsored events, hecklers were common, and street speeches could shift quickly from single soliloquies to open debates.[26] But for many demonstrators, this tension was an intrinsic, perhaps even necessary part of the spectacle.

The almost inevitable involvement of the LAPD during the early 1930s made violence at Communist demonstrations a virtual certainty. At the behest of BAF members and like-minded Angelenos, government officials created the Intelligence Division to deal with subversive activities. Dubbed the Red Squad, it soon became the enforcement tool of Los Angeles's antiradical elite. The squad's chief, Capt. William F. Hynes, cut his professional teeth as a spy who infiltrated the IWW during the San Pedro strike of 1923. With detectives, paid informants, and volunteers from the American Legion and the Silver Shirts, a pro-Nazi anti-Communist "Christian militia" group, Hynes set up an extensive surveillance system targeting Communists and other local radicals. The CPLA demonstrated little ability to uncover the moles, and many stooges funneled information to the police for years. CPUSA official Steve Nelson, who arrived in 1939 for a new assignment, claimed he had to root out almost thirty informants that had been operating undetected in local party organizations.[27] The Red Squad did not confine their activities to surveillance. Numerous companies paid officers directly for "strike protection" services as bodyguards for employers or scab workers and as strongmen to break up picket lines. Prominent businessmen could also receive access to Red Squad files on activists, and occasionally Hynes dispatched officers for duties specifically requested by elite members of the business community. He even hired himself out as a "consultant" to employers threatened by unionization efforts.[28]

The Red Squad adopted a proactive stance toward the Communist street campaign. Tipped off on large demonstrations before they occurred, officers often arrived early to clear the plaza or streets of loiterers and to prevent protesters from assembling. In other cases police-instigated violence broke up CPLA gatherings in progress. These crackdowns may have muzzled the speeches of soapbox Communists, but they also became incorporated into the spectacle of protest. By breaking up meetings, teargassing downtown streets, and clubbing demonstrators (including women and occasionally even children) the LAPD symbolized the oppression of Los Angeles workers. Furthermore, the dispersal of crowds into the surrounding streets, where "occasional outbursts," spontaneous speeches, arrests, and disruption of traffic might continue for hours afterward, served to expand the area of demonstration. In this manner, spectators sometimes became participants in ways they might not have planned.[29] Unlike the Civil Rights marches of the postwar period, Communists did not adhere to a policy of nonviolence, and demonstrators often fought back when attacked, if they had the opportunity. Women as well as men frequently retaliated against the police, and rants in the *Times* about the scratching, biting, and kicking of arrested demonstrators were probably not fabrications.

FIGURE 9. Communist demonstration at the plaza after the judicial decision gave the CPLA the right to hold public gatherings, 1934. Courtesy of the University of Southern California, on behalf of the USC Specialized Libraries and Archival Collections.

Dorothy Healey, one of California's leading Communist organizers in the period, recalled that one of the first things she learned when she joined the party was how to knee a cop at a demonstration.[30]

The violence accompanying CPLA demonstrations might have scared off a fair number of working-class Angelenos, but it attracted a significant number as well. Many undoubtedly came merely to watch, but other central city residents found in the protests an opportunity for political expression effectively denied to them in the formal political sphere. United against police and vigilante violence, participants came together in a common, visceral struggle that encouraged the transcendence of ethnoracial and other boundaries. Activist accounts of their experiences at demonstrations and the persistent willingness of participants to place themselves in the path of abusive police testify to the importance of CPLA street politics in building a sense of collective endeavor.

The 1930 Hunger March demonstrations perhaps epitomized both the LAPD's resolve to crush public protests and the Communists' determination to perpetuate the war for the streets of central Los Angeles. As the first coordinated demonstration of the newly formed Unemployment Councils, the CPUSA called for nationwide marches on February 26. Organizational snafus prompted the postponement of the march one week, but the Southern California office, in a prime example of the communication problems that plagued CPUSA bureaucracy, did not receive notice of the postponement until it was too late to call off the action. Ambitious leaders decided to hold two marches.[31] These were not the first party demonstrations to rumble through the streets of downtown, but for many Angelenos they became the archetypes—for conservatives, of the threat that Communists posed to the social order; and for the party, of the lengths that elites and their forces would go to protect their own interests.

The first demonstration began on February 26 with several marches starting at various points in the city. The CPLA's plan called for the parades to converge at the plaza and then proceed to city hall a few blocks away. This strategy, which became standard practice for larger demonstrations, allowed marchers to recruit pedestrians from a wider area and made it difficult for the LAPD to shut down the march before a critical mass had assembled.[32] As the plaza began to fill up, however, the Red Squad moved in with tear gas and billy clubs. The defiant protestors countered as best they could. Scores were injured in the melee that followed, and officers arrested at least twenty individuals of various ethnoracial backgrounds. Fumes from the tear gas canisters billowed out of the plaza, forcing many residents of Chinatown and nearby areas to evacuate their homes and businesses. Even after the original fighting had died down, smaller disturbances erupted like aftershocks for hours afterward. Well into the evening defiant protesters milled about the streets, and rattled LAPD officers raided known Communist meeting places in search of the event's architects.[33]

Scarcely a week later, in coordination with the national Hunger March, a crowd of between five thousand and ten thousand returned to reprise the previous march. Close to one thousand uniformed and plainclothes officers squared off against them. The trouble began when officers arrested Rose Padilla and Irving Manning at First and Main Streets. Cut off from the plaza by a phalanx of policemen, individual protesters began to make spontaneous speeches around the area. Few spoke for more than a minute before police dragged them away. Miriam

Johnson, who was a young girl when she participated in the march, remembered the violence against children as well as adults:

> Every time somebody tried to speak on the corner they would beat the shit out of them. We [girls] didn't wear pants then, we wore dresses, and they'd take their straps and smack us across the legs—we all came back with terrible welts on our legs. . . . Anyway, that day on one corner one of our people Max Olsen stood up to make a speech, and the Red Squad went after them. We came equipped. I had a hairpin and pepper. They opened his skull, and I was standing in the middle of the street and this skull was pouring blood, and I got wild. And I took the hairpin and I jabbed it into the cop's neck, yelling "let go of him!" And he turned around and let me have it. He knocked me out.[34]

By the end of the day some fifty demonstrators were in jail, including two schoolgirls who stuck out their tongues and "made faces" at police. In a rare display of restraint, officers decided not to employ the high-powered fire hoses loaned to them by the Fire Department.[35]

The 1930 Hunger Marches set the tone for subsequent encounters between the CPLA and the Red Squad. On May 1 of that year, as the CPLA called a set of protests for labor's traditional May Day holiday, police once again closed off the plaza and dispersed nascent gatherings along First and Main Streets. The local Unemployed Councils responded with a barrage of weekly demonstrations at the County Welfare Office on Second and Broadway. They also developed other strategies, such as tossing flyers out the windows of buildings overlooking heavily trafficked streets, in violation of the local handbill ordinance. Other organizers formed "flying squadrons," small groups of demonstrators who made quick speeches at factory gates and in various public areas. Some members joined theatrical groups and performed skits at meetings. Party members also began to canvass working-class neighborhoods outside the city limits, beyond the jurisdiction of Hynes's men.[36] The Red Squad, meanwhile, tightened its grip on "subversive" activities. Postulating that Communism was ipso facto illegal, they began to break up meetings not only in public spaces but in private halls as well. When the CPUSA's presidential ticket, William Foster and African American John Ford, arrived in Los Angeles on a campaign tour, officers arrested them preemptively and dispersed meetings in their honor at the Brooklyn Avenue Co-op.[37] The LAPD even showed up at the Roosevelt High School graduation ceremony to ensure that students expelled for protests were denied their diplomas. One of the students, Lil Carlson, appeared anyway, but officers barred her from the ceremony. When YCL members gathered outside the school to protest the expulsion of their peers, Red Squad members stood by while dozens of students ran off the demonstrators. Anti-CP policies intensified in 1934 when newly elected Mayor Frank Shaw reinstated James E. Davis, a former LAPD police chief removed under a cloud of corruption allegations several years earlier. His reputation restored, Davis kicked off his new term by proposing the fingerprinting of domestic workers to monitor subversive activity and the expulsion of all homeless and transient individuals from the streets of Los Angeles.[38]

The terms of the conflict between the Red Squad and the CPLA changed somewhat in 1933 when the party finally won some protection from the court system. That year Leo Gallagher, the ACLU attorney who was himself convicted several times for public speaking, brought a suit against the LAPD after they dispersed a meeting at the Co-op. A judge issued an injunction preventing the Red Squad from breaking up Communist meetings in private halls or areas that did not block traffic. With the ruling in place, the party, for the first time in several years, was actually able to run larger meetings at the plaza from start to finish without interruption.[39]

With some legal protection from the Red Squad, the full character of Communist demonstrations became more evident. Like the Socialists and the Wobblies, they put forth a series of speakers who spoke for a few minutes at a time in rapid succession. Unlike the Socialists, however, the Communists went to great pains to make these meetings inclusive, played up the multiracial nature of their coalition, and pointedly included speakers from a variety of ethnic and racial groups. Observers often cited the cosmopolitan character of the participants as one of the demonstrations' defining features. Karl Yoneda, who became one of the most active party organizers in the country, for instance, joined the party after witnessing a rally that included, in his words, "hundreds of whites, Mexicans, and Negroes, men, women, and children."[40] One unidentified observer at the 1934 plaza May Day rally reported "the speakers were of all races and nationalities, including several negroes and a japanese." Speeches and translations appeared in English, Spanish, Italian, and Japanese, and numerous signs and handbills in different languages circulated through the crowd.[41]

Anglos and Jews might have dominated party membership, but they convinced significant numbers of other Angelenos to participate in Communist-sponsored activities. A January 1931 police sweep of "asserted red chiefs," for example, netted individuals with Jewish, Italian, Japanese, and Spanish surnames.[42] Accounts and arrest lists of demonstrations published in newspapers suggest that Angelenos of all backgrounds participated in demonstrations, a fact often acknowledged by anti-CP forces. A number of Red-baiters focused on this feature of party-sponsored activities as evidence of their immorality. Implying that integration on such terms could not remain stable for long, they suggested that segregation of the races ultimately fostered a more peaceful and desirable social order. The State Police Officers Association, for instance, played on Anglo fears of miscegenation by accusing Communists of deliberately having white women "thrown into the path of Negro men." According to their reports, "within the Party's ranks there existed a situation in which white women openly consorted with negro men: white, black, Japanese, Mexican, and Filipino members had set up their own little personal alliances with the full approbation of the Party." Painting a picture of turmoil within party ranks after some "jilted negroes" attacked their former lovers, the association called on the leaders of each ethnic group that was "interested in preserving the purity of race" to fight Communism.[43]

If nothing else, the association correctly identified the ethnoracial diversity of party-sponsored activities in California. African Americans, for example, became attracted to demonstrations after the CPLA began holding street meetings at Eleventh and Central, near the northern end of the South Central corridor, in the late 1920s. By 1930 arrest lists from demonstrations routinely included at least one or two African Americans, and it was these demonstrators who received a disproportionate amount of abuse from the LAPD. James McShann, for example, led an Unemployed Council demonstration against the County Welfare Office in 1934 and was convicted of starting a riot when he allegedly exhorted the crowd to "hit the building." A fellow inmate at the Lincoln Heights jail later claimed that McShann ached so much from the beating administered by the Red Squad that he could not sleep at night. Paul Walton, jailed and convicted after police broke up a meeting near Pershing Square in 1931, absorbed numerous well-placed blows from LAPD billy clubs and walked with a permanent limp afterward. A year later officers broke his nose during a protest at Forty-sixth and Central following the arrest of vice presidential candidate John Ford. Despite their penchant for attracting billy clubs, a number of black Angelenos assumed leading roles in the regional Communist Party, including Lou Rosser (head of the YCL), Frank and Hursel Alexander, and Pettis Perry, who went on to become an influential leader in the CPUSA.[44]

Japanese Angelenos constituted a small but vital and dynamic component of CPLA activities as well. Their unofficial leader was Karl Yoneda, a *kibei* (American-born, Japanese-educated) radical who fled Japan to escape military conscription. At one point the only ethnic Japanese longshoreman on America's continental west coast, Yoneda spent his life organizing from Alaska to Los Angeles. Inspired by Sen Katayama, Yoneda was a fervent believer in coalition building and organized among Mexicans and African Americans in addition to ethnic Asians. Like black demonstrators he also drew a disproportionate share of police violence. At one 1931 demonstration, an LAPD officer knocked Yoneda unconscious after he held up a sign reading "Our Children Need Food." Two days later, after holding him incommunicado, Captain Hynes finally called on party members to pick up the disoriented "dying Jap."[45] While the official party membership of Japanese in Los Angeles during the 1930s hovered between sixty and one hundred, anti-Communist investigators listed several times that many in their reports, likely counting sympathizers and demonstration participants who elected not to join the party. Sufficient support for the party existed in California to maintain two Japanese-language Communist newspapers, *Doho* and *Rodo Shimbun*.[46] In addition to recruiting in Little Tokyo and the wider Japanese community in Los Angeles, the Japanese Workers Association took part in larger party demonstrations. Enosuke Yamaguchi, for example, was arrested several times, once when he tried to speak from a truck full of activists that had sneaked through a police blockade at an antiwar demonstration in the plaza. Government officials eventually deported him, along with a number of other foreign-born Japanese Communists. The Committee for the Protection of the Foreign Born, a party organization created to prevent deportations, succeeded in securing the right of these deportees to be sent to the Soviet Union, rather than back to Japan, where they would have faced persecution or even death.[47]

Communists also opened up significant new avenues of participation for women, who played important roles in the recruiting organization, spoke frequently both as organizers and at rallies, and went to jail along with their male counterparts. Dorothy Healey, for instance, was speaking on street corners in Berkeley by the time she was sixteen years old, and she continued to stump in Los Angeles and in other parts of the country during the depression. The presence of "jewish, japanese, and even chinese schoolgirls" at one 1930 rally in Los Angeles testified to the participation of women of all ages and backgrounds in party-sponsored activities.[48] Numerous women held leadership roles in the CPLA, among them Ida Rothstein, who directed the regional chapter of the ILD, and Louise Todd, briefly the head of the party in Los Angeles and eventually for all of California. Several other women in Southern California ran for office on the Communist platform. Among workers and party members at least, many of these women claimed to have rarely if ever experienced discrimination. Furthermore, unlike their Socialist counterparts, female Communists' political presence was not predicated on a sole or special interest in "the family." The topics of female speakers and the assignments of female organizers ranged as widely as those of men. Healey recalled that she disdained any suggestion that they played different roles in the party than men, and Carlson remembered feeling she "could do anything the boys do." After having her first child, Dennis continued her full-time work as an organizer despite the added strain.[49]

The participation of Communist women, in the face of the masculine imagery that drenched party rhetoric of the 1930s, enabled them to colonize a sphere of political activism traditionally reserved for men.[50] The strength of the CPLA in central city neighborhoods and its weakness in male-dominated blue-collar industries may account in part for its unusually dynamic female activists. It was not uncommon for the number of women arrested at a demonstration to equal or surpass the number of men. As they had in regard to the party's multiethnic alliances, many anti-Communists condemned the presence of women at demonstrations as a disruption of traditional gender roles that betrayed the illicit character of Communism. The Los Angeles Times, for example, depicted androgynous and hysterically violent women attacking police officers while male demonstrators "cowered in the crowds." Perhaps concluding that these female activists fell short of a middle-class feminine ideal, police officers often did not refrain from strong-arm tactics, intimidation, and violence against them. Numerous women sustained injuries at the hands of police officers. One seventeen-year old girl, Doris Clay, was allegedly beaten unconscious by members of the Red Squad for speaking to several unemployed at a downtown lot. When she refused to give up the names of other "working class leaders," the officers reportedly "cut" her more than thirty times.[51]

The inclusion of women in party activities did not cut evenly across ethnoracial lines. Most women in leadership roles were Anglo or Jewish, perhaps indicating patterns of racial discrimination or some resistance from nonwhites to women's participation in overt politics. Nonwhite women who became involved in Communist activities tended to remain more closely tied to their ethnic communities. Mary Hatsuko Imada, for example, a Japanese fish cannery worker who married a Filipino unionist, joined International Legal Defense in 1930 and went on to organize female Japanese cannery workers under the United Cannery, Agricultural, Packing, and Allied Workers of America (UCAPAWA) during the Popular Front period. Adele Young, an African American, likewise focused most of her efforts in South Central neighborhoods.[52] Mexican women remained notably absent from CPLA leadership, though they worked with party members and were quite willing to risk arrest during demonstrations and strikes.[53] But the dearth of nonwhite women in the party ranks suggested broader gaps in the CPLA coalition.

Despite these shortcomings, the personal and interactive nature of the party's recruiting strategy resounded strongly for many of those drawn into the Communist sphere. The story of Elaine Black Yoneda is perhaps unusual, in that she became one of the West Coast's most militant activists, but it highlights many of the dynamics of Communist cultural operations in downtown Los Angeles. Born in New York City into a family of Russian Jewish immigrants, Black met her first husband, the Irish American son of a Knights of Labor member, at a Young Workers' meeting her parents forced her to attend. Neither she nor her future husband were committed activists at the time and actually considered eloping to escape their more leftist elders. Then, on the night of February 26, the young couple came to the plaza to meet some friends for a night out and encountered the aftermath of the first Hunger March demonstration. Learning that one in their party had been caught in the LAPD sweep, the couple found their way to the nearby ILD office, where a group of Anglo, Jewish, and Japanese activists were congratulating a Japanese protester for manhandling an especially abusive officer. Just then the police burst in, throwing one woman across the room and arresting several of the activists. Dismayed by what she had seen, Black began to participate in ILD demonstrations and eventually joined the party. The next year, after the LAPD broke up a rally across from Pershing Square with tear gas, police arrested her when she tried to rescue a Jewish needle-trades worker from a beating at the hands of four officers. In the car on the way to the station the needle worker admonished the officers for handling Black roughly. One of them replied, "She's no lady," and punched her in the chest. Black, her husband, the needle worker, and Paul Walton were convicted of inciting the riot, despite the judge's recommendation to the jury for acquittal. Not long afterward Black divorced her first husband. In 1935 she married party activist Karl Yoneda in Washington, to avoid California's antimiscegenation law.[54]

Pettis Perry also joined the party after witnessing violent conflicts between police and activists. Ironically, he came to California in part to escape the violence of his Alabama childhood, where he saw the beatings and lynchings of a number of African Americans. Frustrated with life as a sharecropper, Perry spent several years hopping trains around the country, supporting himself with odd jobs and migrant agricultural work, before landing in Los Angeles. One day someone handed him a flyer for a CPLA-sponsored picnic in support of the Scottsboro boys. At the picnic, where about fifty of the several thousand in attendance were black, Perry watched whites surround a county sheriff who arrived to evict the black members from the park. The willingness of the demonstrators to confront the police over a "black" issue impressed Perry, and continued to do so as he watched officers beat white Communists at other rallies in support of racial justice. When a friend suggested that the party's stance on civil rights was "bait" to recruit African Americans for other purposes, Perry responded, "If this is bait, they've got a damn big sucker. If they're willing to get shot, willing to go to jail, willing to get beaten up, willing to pick a Negro for Vice President, just to get me into the party, then that's the bait for me." In 1932 he joined the ILD and began making speeches and selling party papers door to door, despite a salary so irregular that at times he was forced to sleep at party offices. With the help of several Communists and texts by Karl Marx and W. E. B. Du Bois, Perry taught himself to read and rapidly enhanced his qualifications for advancement within the party ranks. By 1939 he was chairman of the CPLA, and after World War II he continued to rise in the CPUSA bureaucracy.[55]

The stories of Black and Perry epitomized the possibilities for coalition building within the CPLA. Numerous personal and political contacts emerged in the charged context of demonstrations, whether they entailed common defense against the police, raising bail and finding legal representation for arrested demonstrators, or merely symbolic support for a foreign-language speaker whom many demonstrators might not understand. These contacts sometimes led to direct organizational efforts across ethnic lines—Perry, for example, helped to organize a boycott of Japanese products to protest military incursions into China—but at the very least they demonstrated the interrelated nature of disparate social movements in the multinational neighborhoods of central Los Angeles.[56]

CRACKS IN THE COALITION

Unfortunately for committed members such as Black, Yoneda, and Perry, the promise of a broad-based coalition under the CPLA never materialized. Street demonstrations drew Angelenos of widely disparate backgrounds into a common political practice, yet the party struggled to translate this energy and camaraderie into a broader movement.[57] In part, the problem lay in the party's inability, despite strict proscriptions against racism, to quell disputes that periodically flared among members. CPLA official Ben Dobbs, for example, recalled organizing a dance for young members of the Needle Workers Industrial Union that degenerated into a brawl when two black workers tried to dance with white and Mexican women. The party reprimanded Dobbs for "not handling the situation," and the youth group he had worked to build in the union dissolved. Incidents like these foreshadowed more vitriolic conflict after World War II, when Perry himself spearheaded a bitter campaign to purge the CPUSA of racism that led to the expulsion of several prominent leaders in the 1950s.[58] Such troubles did little to alleviate suspicions that Angelenos of color may have harbored about the intentions of white Communists.

While the CPLA succeeded in recruiting a number of "leaders" from various ethnic groups, many nonwhite Angelenos preferred a more informal alliance. Bert Corona, who went on to become a noted labor leader and Chicano rights activist, claimed that though Mexican activists often cooperated with Communists during the depression, few of them joined the party. Corona himself turned down recruiters because he "was somewhat aware that contradictions existed in the party in regard to sharing power with non-Communists." He opted instead to work with other organizations and draw on connections with party allies when the opportunity arose. Carlos Bulosan likewise resisted overtures from Filipino and Jewish Communists he encountered in Boyle Heights during the 1930s because they did not seem amenable to a separate "unit" for Filipinos in the party. Historian Josh Sides identified a similar sentiment among black Angelenos during the depression, concluding that "plenty of African Americans used what they could of the Communist Party's ideology and tactics and left out the rest."[59] In short, though many Angelenos of color appreciated the benefits of CPLA-sponsored activities and resources, they were wary of sacrificing their autonomy to the party structure. By maintaining an arm's-length alliance, they checked the efforts of some Communists to manipulate working-class protest toward ends that did not address the participants' priorities.

Of course, nonwhites were not the only ones concerned about the authoritarianism and discipline expected of party members. Many new recruits dropped out once they realized the demands on their time and the restrictions on their activities they had incurred. Members might be reprimanded, for instance, if they took a weekend vacation without approval from their superiors. Healey estimated that as many as one million people passed through the ranks of the CPUSA during the 1930s. "They didn't stay," she concluded. "They joined, but were turned off first of all by too many meetings, or just never were integrated into the party, for whatever the reason. There was an enormous amount of turnover." Committed members like Healey, who felt compelled to request party permission before having her first child, tended to come from Anglo and Jewish backgrounds. Others remained less willing to give up so much of their time and their traditional social activities for an organization to which their ethnic group had few ties. The party's enthusiasm for mixing assignments could be especially alienating to potential activists, since it might remove them from their own ethnic communities.[60]

These drawbacks were exacerbated by the dogmatic sectarianism of the party's Third Period platform between 1928 and 1935, which alienated some Angelenos not ready to give up on less radical organizations. Following party precepts, local Communists in Los Angeles condemned Upton Sinclair's End Poverty in America (EPIC) platform as "social fascism" and dismissed the NAACP as a "bourgeois" institution. They were also not above sabotaging other workers' organizations that they deemed insufficiently revolutionary. This conviction appeared most clearly in the party's refusal to cooperate with non-CP labor unions, and the parallel unions they established under the Trade Union Unity League clashed as often with other unions as with employers. The party-sponsored Needle Workers Industrial Union, for example, earned the lasting enmity of International Ladies Garment Workers Union organizer Rose Pesotta for its efforts to poach ILGWU membership during their heated Los Angeles strike of 1933.[61] This sectarianism preserved a commitment to radical protest at the cost of isolating Communists from many potential supporters unwilling to denounce less radical organizations.

Immigrant and nonwhite Angelenos could encounter more specific obstacles to joining the CPLA. Many faced resistance from ethnic leaders who viewed Communists as either a direct economic threat or competition for the allegiance of their people. Local and elite-controlled foreign-language newspapers, such as *La Opinión* and *Rafu Shimpo,* echoed the blue-blooded *Times* in condemning the party. In addition, for noncitizens (except Russians, since the Soviet Union refused to accept deportees), Communist membership carried the very real threat of deportation. Mexicans, perhaps mindful of the deportations of Mexican revolutionaries in the 1910s and 1920s, labored in the shadow of the "repatriation" campaign that sent hundreds of thousands south of the border in the 1930s. For them, endorsing a union in and of itself could draw the attention of authorities, even if the unionist had citizenship papers. These reasons convinced many party sympathizers to forgo party membership, and many who did join assumed another name to throw off anyone who might be tracking them.

These obstacles, combined with the party's anemic fiscal resources, created a fragile infrastructure with little ability to deliver on its long-term goals. Far from Red-baiters' nightmarish visions of highly disciplined stealth operatives, CPLA members conducted work more often characterized by inefficiency and poor coordination, and many projects died quietly if they did not achieve significant momentum in a short time. Miriam Johnson, for example, recalled a failed attempt to start a Young Pioneers group for Mexican students at Roosevelt High School. According to her, the organizers succeeded in teaching the recruits a few songs and then abandoned the project after about six months.[62] The experimental quality of the CPLA thus also had its downside, and the party could not always provide enough focus or effectiveness for their programs.

GETTING OUT OF THE STREET:
DEMONSTRATIONS DURING THE POPULAR FRONT

In 1935 the CPUSA exchanged its Third Period strategy for a more cooperative approach to political action. The new mandate, known as the Popular Front, encouraged party members to join other workers' organizations, cut back on restrictions and expectations for party membership, and reversed previous opposition to New Deal programs. Thousands of newcomers joined the party ranks, and a number of historians identify the period as the beginning of Communists' greatest influence.[63]

But the Popular Front had drawbacks as well. The party effectively threw out many of its existing organizations along with its sectarianism, and forsook the strident positions that appealed to many of its supporters in places like central Los Angeles. In Los Angeles and elsewhere activists began to spend more time on election politics, supporting platforms and candidates (most notably Democrat Culbert Olson, who won California's governor's seat in 1938) they would have denounced as "social fascists" only a few years before. Organizers increasingly shifted their attention from neighborhoods and public streets to the large rubber, steel, aircraft, auto, and other factories proliferating throughout the Los Angeles basin.[64] Public demonstrations still constituted a vital part of the party's activity, but its newfound endorsement of government programs diminished the urgency and conflict that had characterized earlier gatherings. After 1935 downtown demonstrations declined in both frequency and attendance. The *Times* chortled that the 1936 May Day demonstrations were the "quietest in years," having attracted only a few hundred spectators and no violence.[65]

The CPLA's fading presence on the streets of Los Angeles cost them visibility among residents of the central districts. To be sure, party members brought their experience and commitment to new organizations such as the CIO, but the Third Period coalitions of demonstrators with disparate agendas were not as easily replicated in the more industry-specific, workplace-centered framework of the CIO. The adoption of the Popular Front meant a decline in the independence of party-sponsored organizations popular with immigrants and African Americans, and the CPUSA increasingly channeled the political efforts of marginalized Angelenos into organizations more directly controlled by white men.[66] The continued growth of Communist membership in the late 1930s and the 1940s did not necessarily indicate concomitant growth in the party's influence. During the Popular Front, the party relaxed the selective requirements that previously had limited membership. New participants thus joined the party rather than one of its satellite organizations. Furthermore, in Los Angeles it appears that membership growth after 1935 occurred as much in outer neighborhoods as in the central city region. YCL recruitment, for example, continued into the 1940s but primarily in the new Jewish neighborhoods of West Los Angeles. Facing apathy and rampant vandalism in its multiethnic Boyle Heights centers, the YCL eventually abandoned them to focus on the westside. After the war, the CPLA and its opponents increasingly focused on Hollywood, where the blacklisting of film industry workers marked the onset of the McCarthy period.[67]

Shifting Communist strategies signaled the end of street speaking as a significant political practice in central Los Angeles. Many soapboxers disappeared in the face of increasing competition from new forms of media and entertainment and downtown's declining centrality to city life as a whole. Local government officials took steps to ensure they would not return. In summer 1935 officials abolished the free speech Sundays that had drawn orators to the plaza for decades. "Small audiences have been hearing the speakers each Sunday, packing the sidewalks on the south and east sides of the Plaza where the speakers line up the streets facing the curbs," Timothy Turner recorded in an article in the *Times Sunday Magazine*. But he expressed little sympathy for the Japanese, Mexican, Jewish, African American, and Anglo speakers photographed for the piece. "It is perhaps just as well" that the tradition ended, he concluded, "for plazas should of all places be peaceful places of rest." Officials were not done with the question of soapboxing. By 1939 they had extended the no-speech zone through most of downtown.[68] Working-class political coalitions by no means disappeared from the central neighborhoods, but they would no longer build through the medium of street speech, as they had in earlier decades.

Conclusion

From Central Neighborhood to Inner City:
The Triumph of Corporate Liberal Urbanization

On almost any level World War II was a watershed event in the history of Los Angeles. The bombing of Pearl Harbor unleashed a frenzy of development, from shipyards in Long Beach to steel factories in Fontana, which utterly transformed the region. City officials woke up to find defense plants clamoring for workers and reversed their decade-old harassment of Okies and Mexicans. The war had a similarly profound impact on the metropolitan population. In one fell stroke, the internment of Japanese Angelenos removed one of the city's major ethnic communities. Little Tokyo metamorphosed, virtually overnight, into an African American neighborhood called Bronzeville, and Chinese truck farmers took over the stalls vacated at the City Market.[1] Meanwhile, waves of African Americans, Anglos, Mexicans, and other newcomers flooded into the city to take advantage of an unprecedented labor shortage.

Aside from internment, war seemed to bode well for ethnoracial relations and to erode the barriers that had divided different groups of city residents. Moribund parts of the central districts sprang back to life. Central Avenue entered its golden age of popularity as a cosmopolitan generation of Angelenos, flush with wages, flocked to its jazz venues and nightclubs. Defense firms desperate for manpower relaxed, to varying degrees, local industry's long tradition of excluding women and non-whites. More broadly, the exigencies of America's self-avowed status as protector of the free world inspired new efforts to eradicate legal barriers to integration. Concerns about the ramifications of discrimination and harassment on wartime morale prompted the federal government to establish the Fair Employment Practices Committee (FEPC) to eliminate discrimination in defense plants. Though of limited effectiveness at best, the FEPC represented one of the most visible federal efforts to combat segregation and discrimination since Reconstruction, some seventy years earlier.[2] A number of postwar trends seemed to build on this quest for social equality. In 1947, after city clerks refused them a marriage license, a Mexican Angeleno and her African American fiancé initiated a legal challenge against the California antimiscegenation laws. In *Perez* v. *Lippold,* the state supreme court overturned legislation that barred interracial marriages. Two federal decisions, *Shelley* v. *Kraemer* in 1948 and *Barrows* v. *Jackson* in 1953, effectively outlawed the enforcement of racial covenants.[3] A long-standing barrier separating Anglo districts from the central neighborhoods appeared to have been breached. In the workplace, a number of energized unions, particularly those in the CIO, began to recruit Asians, Mexicans, and African Americans, groups that had until then been largely excluded from the local labor movement. At the same time, leaders of various ethnic communities launched several institutions to foster better race relations in the region.[4]

Yet the wartime euphoria of unity, equality, and integration was clouded by darker developments, of which internment was only the beginning. In 1943 tensions between Anglo sailors and Mexican pachucos boiled over into the notorious and misnamed Zoot Suit Riots, during which Anglo gangs of enlisted men rampaged through the central districts, pummeling Mexican youths they considered dangerous and disloyal. Along Central Avenue, LAPD officers harassed revelers, especially interracial couples, casting a pall over the neighborhood's vibrant nightlife.[5] And in the defense plants, as Chester Himes documented in two bracing autobiographical novels, race relations were anything but idyllic. Discrimination, intimidation, and violence against African Americans and, to a lesser extent, Mexicans, Chinese, and other ethnic minorities plagued the factories.[6] The CPLA continued to grow, but their most visible activities shifted away from the central neighborhoods to Hollywood and the westside, where the bulk of membership growth drew from middle-class Anglos and Jews with few connections to defense industries. Government officials registered this change and redirected their attention toward alleged "infiltration" of the movie industry and away from the working-class coalitions that had prompted so much concern since World War I.[7]

The countervailing increase in ethnic and racial tensions accompanied growing segregation in central neighborhoods. This trend reflected the maturing impact of policies and developments that predated the war. Zoning regulations established in the 1920s continued to erode the stability of central neighborhood populations. The federal government contributed to this strategy in the late 1930s when the Federal Housing Administration (FHA) established its guidelines for home loan distributions. The FHA redlined areas where even small numbers of nonwhites resided, disqualifying central city neighborhoods such as Boyle Heights (which it described in the late 1930s as "hopelessly heterogeneous" and "honeycombed with diverse and subversive racial elements") from assistance. These policies not only effectively restricted government loans to whites, it forced them to buy homes in white neighborhoods, encouraging European and Anglo residents of the central neighborhoods to relocate to outlying districts.[8]

Even before these policies went into effect, however, observers had begun to note incipient signs of a white exodus. Some Molokan Russians, for instance, were already leaving Boyle Heights and the Flats for South Gate and other all-white communities. Jewish settlements had likewise begun to diffuse beyond the central city districts by 1940. By World War II the geographic center of Jewish Angeleno life was drifting westward toward the Fairfax district and north toward the San Fernando Valley. After the war Jews gradually abandoned eastside areas of concentration such as Boyle Heights and City Terrace.[9] The exodus of Europeans and Anglos from the central neighborhoods reflected and contributed to a hardening of racial divisions. During the mid-1930s, surveyors commented on "a growing trend towards segregation" in Watts and by 1946 concluded it was "rapidly assuming the characteristics of a racial island." Also in 1946 observers reported incidents of racially motivated violence between students at several central neighborhood high schools and between Mexicans and African Americans in Watts and the Hollenbeck section of Boyle Heights. By the 1950s these outbreaks had abated, if only because the schools themselves were becoming increasingly homogeneous.[10]

Government redevelopment programs that erased or redistributed the residential populations of large sections of the central districts during the 1950s and 1960s likewise had roots in the prewar era. The razing of Chinatown to make room for Union Station in the early 1930s foreshadowed larger but fundamentally similar postwar programs.[11]

Turning their backs on federal public housing funds in the 1950s, city officials embarked on a series of projects that bulldozed working-class homes to make room for commercial establishments, office buildings, and industrial plants. The aging mansions of Bunker Hill gave way to high-rises, the ramshackle cottages of Chavez Ravine to Dodger Stadium. Warehouses and storage facilities replaced much of the working-class districts between Main Street and the river.[12] Japanese Angelenos returning from internment after 1945 found a steadily contracting housing stock in Little Tokyo/Bronzeville. A few blocks south, All Nations watched attendance at its programs dwindle with the surrounding population. The church relocated across the river to Boyle Heights but could not escape residential erosion there either. Freeway construction carved up western sections of the district and most of the Flats. The All Nations Foundation gradually shed its programs until only the summer camp, in the hills above the city, remained. Today the original buildings sit abandoned and moldering on Sixth Street amid the depressed environs of Skid Row.[13]

In those neighborhoods that escaped redevelopment, prewar demographic trends accelerated during and after the 1940s. With competition for housing at stratospheric levels, Anglo residents, buffered by conservative newcomers from the South, shored up residential barriers to nonwhites in areas bordering the central neighborhoods. For African American Angelenos, the 1940s witnessed what one historian calls "the maturing of the ghetto," as what formerly had been integrated became almost totally black. Pioneers who established footholds in all-white areas such as Compton and Leimert Park set off white flight panics repeated in cities across the United States. As a result, neighborhoods recently integrated soon became predominantly black, and a monoracial black neighborhood spread south and west from downtown into the 1970s.[14] Districts across the river witnessed a corresponding intensification of the Mexican population. The Brooklyn/Soto section of Boyle Heights remained an island of diversity into the 1960s, but areas to the east and south gradually merged into a monoethnic barrio. By the 1980s most white, Asian, and African American residents had left the eastside neighborhoods, and the student body at Roosevelt and other eastside schools had become almost entirely Mexican. Some middle-class Mexicans managed to follow job opportunities into Los Angeles's mushrooming suburbs, but those who remained found themselves increasingly cut off from the economic and social life of the city.[15] During and after World War II, city and county officials aided the siphoning of racial groups by segregating recipients of public housing—African Americans in South Central projects, Mexicans in eastside projects. A few developments, such as the Flats' Aliso Village, sheltered a diverse population of residents during their early years, but they constituted an exception to the broader rule of isolation and homogenization.[16]

These trends followed a concomitant dispersal of jobs and capital from the central districts as a whole, the urban decentering that became a Los Angeles hallmark. Once again, the war merely accelerated processes already under way by 1940. As early as the 1920s new plants and businesses had begun to appear outside the central neighborhoods, often in all-white suburbs such as South Gate that subsequently became their chief labor source. New suburban communities began to sprout up on the city's periphery during this decade, often near new industrial plants.[17] Wartime development spread industry more widely across the basin, forcing many central city residents to commute long distances to jobs in the shipyards and airplane factories. After the 1940s firms continued to set up plants in suburban regions where they drew from local workforces that were disproportionately white.[18]

In short, ethnoracial distillation and concentration fundamentally transformed the demography of postwar central neighborhoods, and the corporate reconstruction of Los Angeles reached fruition, though not along the lines envisioned by early-twentieth-century Anglos. Immigrants and African Americans had not assimilated into Anglo norms, nor had the city "whitened" itself into the urban ideal of the good community. What had occurred was the transformation of an eclectic collection of integrated neighborhoods into a compartmentalized city with racial and ethnic communities largely cordoned off into separate districts bordered by strips of "transitional" areas. The most immediate distinctions emerged between white and nonwhite districts. The former, gradually absorbing the European immigrants who had once resided in the central neighborhoods, devised increasingly sophisticated means to insulate their neighborhoods from the rest of the city's population. But even among nonwhite communities the lines of distinction were hardening, like the new concrete Los Angeles River bed laid down by federal funds during the depression. As early as 1946 Carey McWilliams commented that while Mexicans and African Americans "overlap in a few sections of the city, they live for the most part in separate districts and, to date, there has been relatively little collaboration between them." Within a short time one could reasonably speak of "Black Los Angeles" and "Mexican Los Angeles," not as ethnoracial communities spread through the central district, but as specific territories demarcated on the cultural map of the city.[19]

The impact of this transformation on central neighborhoods has not been entirely disastrous. Social segregation, after all, aided the flowering of ethnoracial consciousness that culminated during the Civil Rights era in the Black Power, Chicano Power, and Asian American movements. In the postwar ghettos and barrios (which some sociologists termed "spaces of freedom") many Angelenos enjoyed an unprecedented degree of local political autonomy. After the war, a new generation of nonwhite politicians flexed its muscle. On the eastside the Community Service Organization engineered the election of city council member Ed Roybal, the first ethnic Mexican to hold elective office in Los Angeles during the twentieth century. In the South Central districts, a burgeoning African American political machine elected policeman Tom Bradley to the city council and made its presence felt in numerous other municipal elections. In some ways, Roybal, Bradley, and other non-Anglo politicians represented an insurgent central neighborhood political influence that the white establishment could no longer ignore. Perhaps employing personal skills they had cultivated while growing up in the integrated districts of prewar central Los Angeles, Roybal and Bradley parlayed this influence into successful political coalitions with white Angelenos that eventually propelled Roybal into the House of Representatives and Bradley into the mayor's office.[20]

Yet the movement of limited numbers of non-Anglo Angelenos into political office, professional occupations, and middle-class status obscured the deepening impoverishment and isolation of the old central districts. These left-behind neighborhoods became part of a new "inner city," now further divorced from the more prosperous suburbs. A name change for the central districts was probably in order. After the war, they were no longer "central" to the lives of Angelenos the way they once had been. Less and less visible to other city residents who either crossed the neighborhoods by freeway or avoided them altogether, many South Central residents found that a few black leaders could not alleviate their voicelessness. The violent Watts riot of 1965 owed at least part of its impetus to this frustration.[21]

Of course, inter-ethnoracial contact did not disappear after World War II. African Americans, Asians, Mexicans, Europeans, and Anglos continued to come together in both old and new contexts. But these instances of interaction increasingly occurred in middle-class neighborhoods or between ethnic leaders, in social spheres outside the everyday life of the central districts. Intermarriage rates, for instance, began to register substantial increases during the mid-1950s, a few years after the overturning of antimiscegenation laws. But available evidence suggests that such unions tended to occur among upwardly mobile Angelenos able to move into middle-class suburbs.[22] The celebrated dance halls of 1950s El Monte, a farming community outside Los Angeles, brought young Angelenos of different backgrounds together, but historians have questioned the extent to which integration on the dance floor translated to interaction and understanding outside the clubs.[23] Tom Bradley's election to the mayoralty in 1973 led to more non-Anglo representation in local government and seemed to build on the race relations organizations begun during the war. But the relationships forged in these organizations had more often taken place among ethnic elites than among working Angelenos. The Watts and Rodney King riots showed that these alliances among leaders may not have reflected corresponding interaction on the streets and public spaces of the central neighborhoods.

The most visible evidence of ethnoracial segregation in the central districts appeared in the rising instances of conflict between groups that had formerly coexisted, if not easily, at least peacefully. Japanese returning to Little Tokyo/Bronzeville after World War II encountered African Americans not necessarily willing to give up their new homes, and several residents reported instances of violence between the two groups. Similar tensions emerged between returning white and Mexican veterans and the rapidly growing black population in Watts.[24] Such incidents, however minor, foreshadowed the more sustained conflicts that have followed the settlement of new immigrant communities in the central districts. As the violence between Koreans and African Americans precipitated by the Rodney King riots and the political battles between African American and Latino immigrants over various local agencies in South Los Angeles indicate, ethnic communities now sometimes view each other as competitors as much as neighbors.[25]

These conflicts suggest that compartmentalizing American residents into ethnoracial territories, while it may have eased the incorporation of newcomers into groups organized to represent their interests, also exacted certain costs. Not only has it hindered possibilities for grassroots political coalition, it has also encouraged what Manuel Castells has called "a remarkable image of the ideal model of free markets," where each group competes against the other for a diminishing share of urban resources.[26] The concomitant decentralization of Los Angeles has reduced the effectiveness of public space demonstration as a tool of publicity and organization and disabled demonstrations that might draw together the disparate ethnic groups of Los Angeles that had become increasingly segregated both geographically and socially.[27] In the aggregate, these developments helped the city's power structure to consolidate control over its immigrant and nonwhite populations. In becoming a "city of quartz," to borrow Mike Davis's evocative phrase, Los Angeles lost a landscape with the flexibility that was more hospitable to bottom-up political and social movements. In its stead emerged a hardened, corporate liberal landscape of monoethnic neighborhoods, an environment that permitted modest amounts of interest group mobilization while preserving the unequal distributions of social, economic, and political power along ethnoracial lines.

The differences between central Los Angeles of the early twentieth century and the central Los Angeles of recent years illuminate some of the changing facets of the immigrant urban experience in the United States. Many scholars have contrasted the economic structure of Progressive-era industrial America with that of the so-called postindustrial late twentieth century in evaluating the experiences and opportunities offered to working-class immigrants. During each era, immigrant and non-Anglo newcomers encountered low wages and limited economic opportunities. Some point to the rise of service industries, the casualization of labor, new obstacles to unionism, and employer leverage against noncitizens during the latter period to contend that opportunities for social mobility have declined for these kinds of urban residents. One might make an equally salient comparison between the ethnoracial diversity of working-class urban neighborhoods in cities like Los Angeles during the same periods. Before World War II central city residents enjoyed many more opportunities for social and political contact with neighbors of different backgrounds than they did in the decades after the war. To be sure, recent patterns of Asian and Latino immigration have reintegrated certain central neighborhoods, but at least some demographers suggest that, should these patterns continue, such areas will become resegregated with new dominant ethnic groups. Regardless, at least one study of Los Angeles's current social geography classifies the city as a "collection of ethnic societies" rather than a "multiethnic society."[28] Moreover, rising ethnic conflict in Los Angeles suggests that nonwhite communities are increasingly likely to view each other as competition for social space and economic resources. The "peaceable mood" that Hampton Hawes recalled in the integrated South Central of his youth has given way to a more contentious urban environment where

Asian, African American, and Latino populations are fractured along ethnoracial lines. Meanwhile, Anglos and the European immigrant communities they absorbed have managed to remain largely above, economically if not morally, the fray via more sophisticated strategies of racial and class exclusion.

During the 1980s and 1990s, Angelenos and other Americans once more began to grapple with the consequences of growing immigrant and nonwhite populations. Reprised versions of Americanizationist and nativist arguments circulated in debates over border and trade policies, bilingual education, affirmative action, and the welfare rights of noncitizens. More than a few opinion makers cited the importance of formal citizenship, English-language skills, patriotism, and other principles dear to middle-class Anglos as prerequisites for a cohesive, "American" community. As this study suggests, however, there have been other ways of approaching the diversity of America's communities, traditions of interaction and coalition building that terms like *multiculturalism* barely begin to describe. Historians need to pay more attention to these traditions, and to the socioeconomic environments that have conditioned them.

The appearance of non-Anglo political leaders, the advent of civil rights legislation, the decline of certain kinds of overt discrimination, and the integration of some middle-class communities in recent decades give cause for celebration. But they should not obscure more troubling trends toward ethnoracial isolation in working-class districts like those of central Los Angeles. Day-to-day life and ethnoracial relations in the central neighborhoods in early-twentieth-century Los Angeles were far from idyllic, but they included possibilities less evident in the central districts of American cities today. For these Angelenos, diversity was not simply a characteristic of their city's population, but an integral part of their experience as urban residents. Exploring the debates, tensions, and relationships that emerged in integrated communities involves more than simply recovering hidden histories of coalition and amalgamation of a bygone era. It may also suggest ways in which Americans, new and old, can begin to resolve the contradictions that race, ethnicity, and class pose for notions of national and civic unity and to suggest alternative means of building a more truly inclusive society where difference does not divide.

Notes

INTRODUCTION

1. I use ethnic descriptions (e.g., Mexican, Chinese) to refer to U.S. citizens of that ancestry as well as to non-U.S. citizens from that country or region. They reflect the terms used at that time and place. "Anglo," which was not used at that time, refers broadly to native-born Americans of western European ancestry who held the preponderance of political power in early-twentieth-century Los Angeles. I use the racial description "white" when sources do not distinguish between Anglos and European immigrants or when the source specifically referred to race. The terms "inter-ethnoracial" and "mixed" refer to relationships that may have been interethnic, interracial, or both. "Immigrant" primarily refers to residents of eastern or southern European, Asian, or Mexican ancestry. While most Angelenos in this group migrated to Southern California in the early twentieth century, certain others, primarily those of Mexican ancestry, had resided in Los Angeles longer than Anglo Angelenos. I employ all of these categories for their salience to certain articulations of ethnoracial identity. I am aware, however, that they mask variations both within and between different groups and that they do not constitute any essentialized framework of identity formation.

2. Beatrice Griffith, *American Me* (Boston: Houghton Mifflin, 1948), 321; *Los Angeles Times*, Aug. 6, 1944, 4.

3. Vivian McGuckin Raineri, *The Red Angel: The Life and Times of Elaine Yoneda, 1906–1988* (New York: International, 1991); Elaine Black Yoneda, interviewed by Betsy Mitson and Arthur Hansen, Mar. 2, 1974, #1377, 53, California State University Fullerton Oral History Program (hereafter CSUFOHP); Karl G. Yoneda, *Ganbatte: Sixty-Year Struggle of a Kibei Worker* (Los Angeles: Resource Development and Publications/Asian-American Studies Center, University of California, Los Angeles, 1983), esp. 96–97.

4. Carey McWilliams, "Moving Out the Japanese Americans," *Harpers Magazine* 185 (Sept. 1942): 363; Michi Weglyn, *Years of Infamy: The Untold Story of America's Concentration Camps* (New York: William Morrow, 1976), 113; Paul R. Spickard, "Injustice Compounded: Americans and Non-Japanese in Relocation Camps," *Journal of American Ethnic History* 5 (spring 1986): 5–22.

5. Michio Kunitani, interview with author, Nov. 27, 1999; Katsuma Mukaeda, interviewed by David Bianiasz, Nov. 28, 1973, #1341, 3, CSUFOHP; Kevin Leonard, "Years of Hope, Days of Fear: The Impact of World War II on Race Relations in Los Angeles" (Ph.D. diss., University of California, Davis, 1992), 66; *Open Forum*, May 27, 1944. See also Valerie Matsumoto, *Farming the Home Place: A Japanese American Community in California, 1919–1982* (Ithaca: Cornell University Press, 1994), esp. 87–118.

6. Ira Katznelson, *City Trenches: Urban Politics and the Patterning of Class in the United States* (New York: Pantheon, 1981), 105–10; Thomas Lee Philpott, *The Slum and the Ghetto: Neighborhood Deterioration and Middle-Class Reform, Chicago, 1880–1930* (Oxford: Oxford University Press, 1978), 137–45; Douglas S. Massey and Nancy Denton, *American Apartheid: Segregation and the Making of the Underclass* (Cambridge, Mass.: Harvard University Press, 1993), 32; Allan H. Spear, *Black Chicago: The Making of a Negro Ghetto, 1890–1920* (Chicago: University of Chicago Press, 1967), esp. 11–29; Howard P. Chudacoff and Judith E. Smith, *The Evolution of American Urban Society* (Englewood Cliffs, N.J.: Prentice Hall, 1994), 111–45; Edward K. Strong, *Japanese in California* (Stanford: Stanford University Press, 1933), 15–17; California Commission of Immigration and Housing, *Report on Fresno's Immigration Problem* (Sacramento: State Printing Office, 1918), 7–12; Douglas Henry Daniels, *Pioneer Urbanites: A Social and Cultural History of Black San Francisco* (Philadelphia: Temple University Press, 1980), 75–82, 144; Quintard Taylor, *The Forging of a Black Community: Seattle's Central District from 1870 through the Civil Rights Era* (Seattle: University of Washington Press, 1994), esp. 86–87, 106–34.

7. See, for example, Gary B. Nash, "The Hidden History of Mestizo America," *Journal of American History* 82 (1995): 941–64; Peter Linebaugh and Marcus Rediker, *The Many Headed Hydra: Sailors, Slaves, Commoners, and the Hidden History of the Revolutionary Atlantic* (Boston: Beacon Press, 2000); Richard White, *The Middle Ground: Indians, Empires, and Republics in the Great Lakes Region, 1650–1815* (Cambridge: Cambridge University Press, 1991); Daniel H. Usner, *Indians, Settlers, and Slaves in a Frontier Exchange Economy: The Lower Mississippi Valley before 1783* (Chapel Hill: University of North Carolina Press, 1992); Tyler Andinder, *Five Points: The Nineteenth-Century New York City Neighborhood That Invented Tap Dance, Stole Elections, and Became World's Most Notorious Slum* (New York: Free Press, 2001).

8. Alexander Saxton, *The Rise and Fall of the White Republic: Class Politics and Mass Culture in Nineteenth-Century America* (London: Verso, 1991).

9. The literature on the broad contours of this period is much too extensive to list in depth here. Studies that have influenced my thinking include Martin J. Sklar, *The Corporate Reconstruction of American Capitalism, 1890–1916: The*

Market, the Law, and Politics (1988; rpt. New York: Cambridge University Press, 1993), esp. 1–40; Robert H. Wiebe, *The Search for Order, 1877–1920* (New York: Hill and Wang, 1967); James T. Kloppenberg, *Uncertain Victory: Social Democracy and Progressivism in European and American Thought, 1870–1920* (New York: Oxford University Press, 1986); Daniel Rodgers, *Atlantic Crossings: Social Politics in a Progressive Age* (Cambridge, Mass.: Belknap Press of Harvard University Press, 1998); T. J. Jackson Lears, *No Place of Grace: Antimodernism and the Transformation of American Culture, 1880–1920* (Chicago: University of Chicago Press, 1994); Alan Trachtenberg, *The Incorporation of America: Culture and Society in the Gilded Age* (New York: Hill and Wang, 1982); Alan Dawley, *Struggles for Justice: Social Responsibility and the Liberal State* (Cambridge, Mass.: Belknap Press of Harvard University Press, 1991).

10. The term, as well as the outline of this argument, comes from Sklar's *Corporate Reconstruction of American Capitalism,* esp. 1–40. See also Michael P. Rogin's discussion of the advent of corporate liberalism in politics in *The Intellectuals and McCarthy: The Radical Specter* (Cambridge, Mass.: MIT Press, 1967), 9–24. For studies that have explored Anglo efforts to order ethnoracial communities during this period, see John Higham, *Strangers in the Land: Patterns of American Nativism, 1860–1925* (New York: Atheneum, 1969); Nayan Shah, *Contagious Divides: Epidemics and Race in San Francisco's Chinatown* (Berkeley: University of California Press, 2001).

11. Some recent surveys of this voluminous literature are Rogers Brubaker, "The Return of Assimilation? Changing Perspectives on Immigration and Its Sequels in France, Germany, and the United States," *Ethnic and Racial Studies* 24 (2001): 531–48; Gary Gerstle, "Liberty, Coercion, and the Making of Americans," *Journal of American History* 84.2 (Sept. 1997): 524–58; Russell A. Kazal, "Revisiting Assimilation: The Rise, Fall, and Reappraisal of a Concept in American Ethnic History," *American Historical Review* 100.2 (April 1995): 437–71; George J. Sanchez, "Race, Nation, and Culture in Recent Immigration Studies," *Journal of American Ethnic History* 18 (summer 1999): 66–84; Jon Gjerde, "New Growth on Old Vines—The State of the Field: The Social History of Immigration to and Ethnicity in the United States," *Journal of American Ethnic History* 18 (summer 1999): 40–65.

12. There are a number of excellent studies on multiethnic labor coalitions during the early twentieth century. See James R. Barrett, "Americanization from the Bottom Up: Immigration and the Remaking of the American Working Class in the United States, 1880–1930," *Journal of American History* 79 (Dec. 1992): 996–1020; Michael Goldfield, "Race and the CIO: The Possibilities for Racial Egalitarianism during the 1930s and 1940s," *International Labor and Working Class History* 44 (fall 1993): 1–32; Gary Gerstle, *Working-Class Americanism: The Politics of Labor in a Textile City, 1914–1960* (Cambridge: Cambridge University Press, 1989); Lisbeth Cohen, *Making a New Deal: Industrial Workers in Chicago, 1919–1939* (Cambridge: Cambridge University Press, 1990). At the same time, some scholars point to a long tradition of discrimination, segregation, and exclusion in mainstream labor unions, even in those that professed a more egalitarian stance. See, for example, David Bruce Nelson, *Divided We*

Stand: American Workers and the Struggle for Black Equality (Princeton: Princeton University Press, 2001).

13. Robert Fogelson, *The Fragmented Metropolis: Los Angeles, 1850–1930* (1967; rpt. Berkeley: University of California Press, 1991).

14. I am generalizing the term coined by Benedict Anderson to refer not just to national communities but also to communities based on any number of other parameters. Benedict Anderson, *Imagined Communities: Reflections on the Origins and Spread of Nationalism* (London: Verso, 1991).

CHAPTER 1

1. California Commission of Immigration and Housing (CCIH), *A Community Survey Made of Los Angeles City* (Sacramento: State Printing Office, 1917), 14; *Los Angeles Times*, Jan. 28, 1923; Greg Hise, "Industry and Imaginative Geographies," in *Metropolis in the Making: Los Angeles in the 1920s*, ed. Tom Sitton and William Deverell (Berkeley: University of California Press, 2001), 13–44.

2. Pauline V. Young, *Pilgrims of Russian-Town: The Community of Spiritual Christian Jumpers in America* (Chicago: University of Chicago Press, 1932), 17.

3. William M. Mason and John A. McKinstry, *The Japanese in Los Angeles* (Los Angeles: County Museum of Natural History, 1969), 5; Rudolfo F. Acuña, *A Community under Siege: A Chronicle of Chicanos East of the Los Angeles River, 1945–1975* (Los Angeles: Chicano Studies Research Center, UCLA), 9; Louis Adamic, *The Truth about Los Angeles* (Girard, Kan.: Haldeman-Julius, 1927), 10.

4. W. W. Robinson, *Tarnished Angels* (Los Angeles: Ward Ritchie Press, 1964), 18–20; *In the Supreme Court of the State of California, People of the State of California vs. Wong Chuey: Appellant's Reply Brief* (Los Angeles: California Voice Print, 1897), 4; Nora Sterry, "The Sociological Basis for the Reorganization of the Macy Street School" (Master's thesis, University of Southern California, 1924), 16.

5. Notes from the June K. Barth Survey of All Nations Parish (no pagination), in "misc. 3," Box 58, G. Bromley Oxnam Papers, Library of Congress, Washington, D.C. (hereafter GBOP); John Vallejo vs. Tulia Arroyo, 1930, Box 40, Department of Industrial Relations, Commission of Immigration and Housing, *Records*, Bancroft Library (hereafter DIR).

6. John Earl Rock, "Twenty Years on Skid Row," n.d., Department of Special Collections, University of California, Los Angeles.

7. Cornelius C. Smith Jr., *Emilio Kosterlitzky: Eagle of Sonora and the Southwest Border* (Glendale, Calif.: Arthur H. Clarke, 1970), 264–68.

8. Roy Taketa, interviewed by Mary McCarthy, July 13, 1973, CSUFOHP, 33; Max Bond, "The Negro in Los Angeles" (Master's thesis, University of Southern California, 1936), 34–49; Statement of J. A. Brigon, c. 1924, in "Segregation Housing" file, Box 2, *Survey of Race Relations*, Hoover Library, Stanford University (hereafter SRR).

9. In Clora Bryant, Buddy Collette, William Green, Steve Isoardi, Jack Kelson, Horace Tapscott, Gerald Wilson, and Marl Young, eds., *Central Avenue*

Sounds: Jazz in Los Angeles (Berkeley: University of California Press, 1999), 179; Patricia Rae Adler, "Watts: From Suburb to Black Ghetto" (Ph.D. diss., University of Southern California, 1977), 243.

10. See Clark Davis, "From Oasis to Metropolis: Southern California and the Changing Context of American Leisure," *Pacific Historical Review* 61 (Aug. 1992): 357–385; Phoebe Kropp, "'All Our Yesterdays': The Spanish Fantasy Past and the Politics of Public Memory in Southern California, 1884–1939" (Ph.D. diss., University of California, San Diego, 1999); William A. McClung, *Landscapes of Desire: Anglo Mythologies of Los Angeles* (Berkeley: University of California Press, 2000).

11. On postwar conceptualizations of "inner city" and "ghetto" neighborhoods, see Carlo Rotola, *October Cities: The Redevelopment of Urban Literature* (Berkeley: University of California Press, 1998), esp. 57, 325–26 n. 2.

12. Becky Nicolaides, "'Where the Working Man Is Welcome': Working-Class Suburbs in Los Angeles, 1900–1940," *Pacific Historical Review* 68 (1999): 517–59.

13. Bond, "The Negro in Los Angeles," 2; Jack D. Forbes, "The Early African Heritage of California," in *Seeking El Dorado: African Americans in California*, ed. Lawrence B. de Graaf, Kevin Mulroy, and Quintard Taylor (Los Angeles and Seattle: Autry Museum of Western History and University of Washington Press, 2001), 79.

14. Douglas Monroy, *Rebirth: Mexican Los Angeles from the Great Migration to the Great Depression* (Berkeley: University of California Press, 1999), 18; Horace Bell, *Reminiscences of a Ranger, or Early Times in Southern California* (Santa Barbara, Calif.: Wallace Hubbard, 1927), 12; Robinson, *Tarnished Angels*, 7–9, 13; Harris Newmark, *Sixty Years in Southern California* (New York: Knickerbocker, 1926), 510.

15. Bell, *Reminiscences of a Ranger*, introd., 12.

16. Richard Griswold del Castillo, *The Los Angeles Barrio, 1850–1890* (Berkeley: University of California Press, 1979), 33–34; Robinson, *The Story of Pershing Square*, 17–9; Newmark, *Sixty Years in Southern California*, 510–18.

17. Louise Colton Appell, "An Historical Folk Survey of Southern California: A Narrative of the Peopling of the Southland" (Master's thesis, University of Southern California, 1927), 37–39; Griswold del Castillo, *Los Angeles Barrio*, 74–77.

18. Bond, "The Negro in Los Angeles," 12.

19. Michael E. Engh, *Frontier Faiths: Church, Temple, and Synagogue in Los Angeles, 1846–1888* (Albuquerque: University of New Mexico Press, 1992); Gregory H. Singleton, *Religion in the City of Angels: American Protestant Culture and Urbanization, Los Angeles 1850–1930* (Ann Arbor, Mich.: UMI Research Press, 1979); Lawrence Guillow, "The Origins of Race Relations in Los Angeles, 1820–1880" (Ph.D. diss., Arizona State University, 1996).

20. Ronald Takaki, *Strangers from a Different Shore: A History of Asian Americans* (New York: Penguin, 1989), 79–131, 239–56; Raymond Lou, "The Chinese American Community of Los Angeles, 1870–1900: A Case of Resistance, Organization, and Participation" (Ph.D. diss., University of California,

Irvine, 1982); Garding Lui, *Inside Los Angeles Chinatown* (Los Angeles: n.p., 1948).

21. The most complete account of the massacre and its aftermath is Paul de Falla's two-part article, "Lantern in the Western Sky," *Southern California Quarterly* 42.1 (Mar. 1960): 57–88 and 42.2 (June 1960): 161–87. See also Guillow, "The Origins of Race Relations," 215–43.

22. For a general discussion of the campaign to restrict Chinese immigration in California, see Alexander Saxton, *The Indispensable Enemy: Labor and the Anti-Chinese Movement in California* (Berkeley: University of California Press, 1971); Lucy Salyer, *Laws as Harsh as Tigers: Chinese Immigrants and the Shaping of Modern Immigration Law* (Chapel Hill: University of North Carolina Press, 1995).

23. Everett G. Hager, George E. Kinney, and Anthony F. Kroll, *An 1886 Chinese Labor Boycott of Los Angeles* (Pasadena, Calif.: Castle Press, 1982); Raymond Lou, "The Chinese American Community of Los Angeles, 1870–1900: A Case of Resistance, Organization, and Participation" (Ph.D. diss., University of California, Irvine, 1982), 165–68.

24. Lou, "Chinese American Community," 17–8.

25. Fogelson, *The Fragmented Metropolis*, 144–45; Carr quoted in Wilson Carey McWilliams, foreword to *Fool's Paradise: A Carey McWilliams Reader*, ed. Dean Stewart and Jeannine Gendar (Berkeley and Santa Clara: Heyday and Santa Clara University, 2001), xv.

26. William Deverell, *Railroad Crossing: Californians and the Railroad, 1850–1910* (Berkeley: University of California Press, 1994), 62–63; Fogelson, *Fragmented Metropolis*, 63–70, 78–84.

27. Gilbert G. Gonzalez, "Factors Relating to Property Ownership of Mexican Americans and Italian Americans in Lincoln Heights, Los Angeles," in *Struggles and Success: An Anthology of the Italian Experience in California*, ed. Paola A. Sensei-Isolani and Phylis Cancilla Martinelli (New York: Center for Migration Studies, 1993), 219–30.

28. Monroy, *Rebirth*; George J. Sanchez, *Becoming Mexican American: Ethnicity, Culture, and Identity in Chicano Los Angeles, 1900–1945* (New York: Oxford University Press, 1993), 38–62.

29. See Dana Bartlett, *The Better City: A Sociological Study of a Modern City* (Los Angeles: Reune, 1907), 73; *Los Angeles Socialist*, Mar. 8, 1902; Monroy, *Rebirth*, 13–14; Bond, "The Negro in Los Angeles," 33.

30. Mikel Hogan Garcia, "Adaptation Strategies of the Los Angeles Black Community, 1883–1919" (Ph.D. diss., University of California, Irvine, 1985), 14; Lonnie G. Bunch, "A Past Not Necessarily Prologue: The Afro-American in Los Angeles," in *Twentieth-Century Los Angeles: Power, Promotion, and Social Conflict*, ed. Norman M. Klein and Martin J. Schiesl (Claremont, Calif.: Regina, 1990), 102–3; Fogelson, *Fragmented Metropolis*, 76.

31. Clara Gertrude Smith, "The Development of the Mexican People in the Community of Watts, California" (Master's thesis, University of Southern California, 1933), 8–10; Mary Ellen Bell Ray, *The City of Watts, California, 1907–1926* (Los Angeles: Rising Publications, 1985), 8–15; Bond, "The Negro in Los Angeles," 44.

32. Arna Bontemps, *God Sends Sunday* (1931; rpt. New York: AMS Press, 1972), 118–19, 148–53. Some accounts identify Mudtown as part of Watts, but Patricia Rae Adler claims Bontemps was referring to the Furlough Tract, north of Watts along Fifty-fifth Street. Adler, "Watts: From Suburb to Black Ghetto," 280.

33. Bell Ray, *City of Watts,* 58, 62; Adler, "Watts: From Suburb to Black Ghetto," 178–205; Kenneth T. Jackson, *The Ku Klux Klan in the City, 1915–1930* (New York: Oxford University Press, 1967), 187–93.

34. Quoted in Adler, "Watts: From Suburb to Black Ghetto," 237–8.

35. Quoted in Bell Ray, *City of Watts,* 34, 44, 16–17.

36. Quoted in Bryant et al., eds., *Central Avenue Sounds,* 103, 115.

37. CCIH, Community Survey of Los Angeles, 15, 23; *Los Angeles Times, A New Survey: 23 Market Areas of Los Angeles County* (Los Angeles: Times-Mirror, 1935), n.p.; Greg Hise, "Industry and the Landscape of Social Reform," in *From Chicago to L.A.: Making Sense of Urban Theory,* ed. Michael J. Dear (Thousand Oaks, Calif.: Sage, 2002), 101.

38. Sanchez, *Becoming Mexican American,* 71–75; Mason and McKinstry, *The Japanese in Los Angeles,* 5; Acuña, *A Community under Siege,* 9.

39. William Wilson McEuen, "A Survey of Mexicans in Los Angeles" (Master's thesis, University of Southern California, 1914), 68.

40. Ricardo Romo, *East Los Angeles: History of a Barrio* (Austin: University of Texas Press, 1983), 148; "Supporting Brief of the Latin American Group in the Los Angeles City Survey, Spanish and Portugese District, Southern California Conference, San Francisco Bay Area" (1920s), and Vernon Coombs to G. Bromley Oxnam, Jan. 17, 1921, in "CAN misc. 3," Box 58, GBOP; Bartlett, *The Better City,* 7–12; David Alexander Bridge, "A Study of the Agencies Which Promote Americanization in the Los Angeles City Recreation Center District" (Master's thesis, University of Southern California, 1920), 8.

41. Don Normark, *Chavez Ravine, 1949: A Los Angeles Story* (San Francisco: Chronicle, 1999), 11, 17, 31, 38, 77, 91; *Community Survey of Los Angeles,* 14.

42. Roberta Greenwood, *Metropolitan Transportation Authority Cultural Resources Impact Mitigation Program: Los Angeles Red Line Segment One (Chinatown)* (Los Angeles: Greenwood and Assoc., 1993), 38–43; Sterry, "Sociological Basis," 14–15, and "Housing Conditions in Chinatown Los Angeles," *Journal of Applied Sociology* (Nov.–Dec. 1922): 70–75; *Linking Our Lives: Chinese American Women of Los Angeles* (Los Angeles: Asian-American Studies Center, University of California, Los Angeles, and Chinese Historical Society of Southern California, 1984), 14.

43. CCIH, *Annual Report,* Jan. 2, 1916 (San Francisco: California State Printing Office), 228; Sterry, "Sociological Basis," 16; Clarence Yip Yeu, interviewed by Suellen Chang, Apr. 24, 1980, #102, Southern California Chinese American Oral History Program, Department of Special Collections, University of California Los Angeles (hereafter SCCA). See also Lillie Mu Lee, interviewed by Suellen Chang, July 24, 30, 1982, #162, SCCA.

44. *Los Angeles Socialist,* Aug. 8, 1903; Ichiro Mike Murase, *Little Tokyo: One Hundred Years in Pictures* (Los Angeles: Visual Communications/Asian-

American Studies Central, 1983), 6; Mason and McKinstry, *Japanese in Los Angeles*, 8.

45. Masao Dodo, "The Japanese Free Methodist Mission," c. 1925, #B-432, Box 37, SRR; *Community Survey of Los Angeles*, 15.

46. Takaki, *Strangers from a Different Shore*, 201–4; Koyoshi Uono, "The Factors Affecting the Geographical Aggregation and Dispersion of the Japanese Resident in the City of Los Angeles" (Master's thesis, University of Southern California, 1927), 31.

47. Mason and McKinstry, *Japanese in Los Angeles*, 4, 24–25, 29; John Modell, *The Economics and Politics of Racial Accommodation: The Japanese of Los Angeles, 1900–1942* (Urbana: University of Illinois Press, 1977), 70–74; Yokota, "From Little Tokyo to Bronzeville," 22. See also Lon Kurashige, *Japanese American Celebration and Conflict: A History of Ethnic Identity and Festival* (Berkeley: University of California Press, 2002); Brian Masaru Hayashi, *"For the Sake of Our Japanese Brethren": Assimilation, Nationalism, and Protestantism among the Japanese of Los Angeles, 1895–1942* (Stanford: Stanford University Press, 1995).

48. Max Vorspan and Lloyd P. Gartner, *History of the Jews of Los Angeles* (San Marino, Calif.: Huntington Library, 1970), 117; "Negro Survey," front section, p. 7, American Design Collection, Huntington Library (hereafter ADC); *Community Survey of Los Angeles City*, 15.

49. Length of residence for whites in the Maple building ranged from one month to eight years, Asians from six months to ten years, Mexicans from one month to five years. The two African Americans had lived there for two years. The survey suggests, however, that residents of integrated apartments tended to stay there short-term rather than long-term. Figures for the East Seventh building show length of residences ranging only from one month to three years. See Box 56, Works Progress Administration, 1938 Survey of Los Angeles, Regional History Center, University of Southern California (hereafter WPA). USC is in the process of uploading these survey cards to the Web as part of its Information System for Los Angeles Project (ISLA). See http://www-rcf.usc.edu/~philipje/MM_PROJECTS/ISLA_99b/default.htm.

50. Bond, "The Negro in Los Angeles," 33; Roy Taketa, interviewed by Mary McCarthy, July 13, 1973, CSUFOHP, 33.

51. George Lee and Elsie Lee, "The Chinese and the Los Angeles Produce Market," *Gum Saan Journal* 9 (Dec. 1986): 5–17; Mason and McKinstry, *Japanese in Los Angeles*, 27; Modell, *Economics and Politics of Japanese Assimilation*, 116–17; *Los Angeles Times*, May 23, 1909. According to Modell, the Terminal Market excluded nonwhites.

52. CCIH, *Community Survey of Los Angeles*, 15; Tasani Plengvidhya, "A Study of Changes of Services of All Nations Foundation as Affected by the Neighborhood's Ecological Changes" (Master's thesis, University of Southern California, 1961), esp. 10, 51–63; Kim Fong Tom, "The Participation of the Chinese in the Community Life of Los Angeles" (Master's thesis, University of Southern California, 1944), 33.

53. *Community Survey of Los Angeles*, 15; Gonzalez, "Factors Relating to Property Ownership," 219–221; Acuña, *A Community under Siege*, 6.

54. Monroy, *Rebirth,* 13–14; Cloyd V. Gustafson, "An Ecological survey of the Hollenbeck Area of Los Angeles" (Master's thesis, University of Southern California, 1940), 19–36.

55. Uono, "Factors Affecting Aggregation," 132–35; Gustafson, "Ecological Survey," 76–81.

56. Gustafson, "Ecological Survey," 38–41, 78–81; Bond, "The Negro in Los Angeles," 24, 34; Charles S. Johnson, *Industrial Survey of the Negro Population in Los Angeles* (Los Angeles: National Urban League, 1926), 13; Los Angeles Times, *A New Market Survey.*

57. "Racial Elements," Box 2, ADC; Lillian Sokoloff, "The Russians in Los Angeles," *Studies in Sociology: Sociological Monograph 11,* 3.3 (Mar. 1918): 1; Young, *The Pilgrims of Russian-Town,* 11–12, 22–23; Aram Serkis Yeretzian, "A History of Armenian Immigration to America with Special Reference to Conditions in Los Angeles" (Master's thesis, University of Southern California, 1923).

58. George M. Day, "Race and Cultural Oases," *Sociology and Social Research,* 18 (March–April 1934): 331; CCIH, *Community Survey of Los Angeles,* 37; Gloria Ricci Lothrup, *Chi Siamo: The Italians of Los Angeles* (Pasadena: Tabula Rasa Press, 1981); Rosalind Giardini Crosby, "The Italians of Los Angeles, 1900," in Sensei-Isolani and Cancilla Martinelli, eds., *Struggles and Success,* 40–41, 51–52.

59. Gonzalez, "Factors Relating to Property Ownership," 219–30; CCIH, *Community Survey of Los Angeles,* 12–15, 37; Lothrup, *Italians of Los Angeles,* 14; Crosby, "Italians of Los Angeles, 1900"; CCIH, *Community Survey of Los Angeles,* 14; Los Angeles Times, *A New Market Survey.*

60. Vorspan and Gartner, *Jews of Los Angeles,* 14, 17, 39, 109–10; Rudolf Glanz, *The Jews of California: From the Discovery of Gold until 1880* (New York: Walden, 1960), 78–93.

61. Vorspan and Gartner, *History of the Jews of Los Angeles,* 109–10; Glanz, *The Jews of California,*78.

62. Wendy Elliot, "The Jews of Boyle Heights, 1900–1950: The Melting Pot of Los Angeles," *Southern California Quarterly* 78 (1996): 1–10; Vorspan and Gartner, *Jews of Los Angeles,* 103–4, 109–10, 117–19, 203; CCIH, *Community Survey of Los Angeles,* 12–15; Gustafson, "Ecological Survey," 44–46.

63. Changing census categories and probable undercounts make it difficult to estimate the Mexican population during this period. For various estimates, see Romo, *East Los Angeles,* 61; Sanchez, *Becoming Mexican American,* 90–91; Fogelson, *Fragmented Metropolis,* 75–84; Albert Camarillo, *Chicanos in a Changing Society: From Mexican Pueblos to American Barrios in Santa Barbara and California,* 1848–1930 (Cambridge, Mass.: Harvard University Press, 1979), 200.

64. James P. Allen and Eugene Turner, *The Ethnic Quilt: Population Diversity in Southern California* (Northridge: Center for Geographic Studies, California State University, Northridge, 1997), 93–95; Sanchez, *Becoming Mexican American,* 72–78; Romo, *East Los Angeles.*

65. Monroy, *Rebirth,* 37; Acuña, *A Community under Siege,* 10; Romo, *East Los Angeles,* 69.

66. Morris Kadish, interview with author, Mar. 19, 1999; Emilia Castañeda de Valenciana, interviewed by Christine Valenciana, Sept. 8, 1971, CSUFOHP, 9–10; also Gustafson, "Ecological Survey," 76.

67. CCIH, *Community Survey of Los Angeles,* 12–15; Gustafson, "Ecological Survey," 19, 87, 91–92; Richard Jackson, "The People: Section II, Volume I," Apr. 15–16, 1936, #1293–4, folder 2, Box 45, Federal Writers Project of California Records, Department of Special Collections, UCLA (hereafter FWP).

68. The survey, recorded on note cards, still requires extensive sorting, making it difficult to ascertain the completeness of the census. After mapping several blocks of data I concluded that most blocks did not receive a full survey or that the data for the neighborhood are scattered among the hundreds of boxes holding the note cards. The sampling cited above includes all the cards in Box 11 of the WPA collection and covers an area running approximately north to Brooklyn Avenue, west to Soto Street, south to Sixth Street, and east to Euclid. Population figures for the area: "Whites, " 1,112; Mexicans, 1,415; "Orientals," 791; African Americans, 196; "other," 6; for a total of 3,520.

69. Bond, "The Negro in Los Angeles," 35–39; Garcia, "Adaptation Strategies," 62–69; Loren Miller, interviewed by Lawrence B. de Graaf, Apr. 29, 1967, CSUFOHP, 18–19; Lloyd H. Fisher, *The Problem of Violence: Observations on Race Conflict in Los Angeles* (San Francisco: American Council on Race Relations, 1946), 8–10.

70. Bond, "The Negro in Los Angeles," 61–65, 72–77.

71. Bryant et al., eds., *Central Avenue Sounds,* 25. See also Bette Yarborough Cox, ed., *Central Avenue: Its Rise and Fall, 1890–c. 1955* (Los Angeles: BEEM, 1993), 112–17.

72. Allen and Turner, *The Ethnic Quilt,* 79; CCIH, *Community Survey of Los Angeles,* 15; Uono, "Factors Affecting Aggregation," 124–25; Modell, *Economics and Politics of Racial Accommodation,* 59–60.

73. Bond's diagrams did not distinguish between native whites and immigrant whites, but whites did remain on those blocks. Bond, "The Negro in Los Angeles," 48–49; Uono, "Factors Affecting Aggregation," map after 111; Kit King Louis, "A Study of American-born and American-reared Chinese in Los Angeles" (Master's thesis, University of Southern California, 1931), 109; Jackson, "The People," FWP.

74. Vorspan and Gartner, *Jews of Los Angeles,* 117–19, 203.

75. Romo, *East Los Angeles,* 85; Vorspan and Gartner, *Jews of Los Angeles,* 117–19.

76. Uono, "Factors Affecting Aggregation," 125–28; Johnson, "Negro Survey," 13; Bond, "The Negro in Los Angeles," 69–72; U.S. Congress, Bureau of Census, *Housing Analytical Maps, Los Angeles California, 1940* (Washington, D.C.: Government Printing Office, 1940), 124–26.

77. Pat Adler, *The Bunker Hill Story* (Glendale, Calif.: La Siesta, 1963).

78. Allen and Turner, *Ethnic Quilt,* 79; Bond, "The Negro in Los Angeles," 65–69; Johnson, "Negro Survey," 13; Los Angeles Times, *A New Market Survey.*

79. Vorspan and Gartner, *Jews of Los Angeles,* 117–19; "Field Agent's Report and Recommendations on Organization of Custer Center," 1920, enclosed in Mary J. Gibson to R. J. Miller, July 21, 1920, in "Los Angeles Com-

munity Service" File, Series 1, Box 4, CIH; "Excerpts from Echo Park Study," Dec. 12, 1950, in "Echo Park" file, Box 42, John Anson Ford Papers, Huntington Library (hereafter Ford Papers).

80. Quoted in Cox, *Central Avenue: Its Rise and Fall*, 114.

81. Hampton Hawes and Don Asher, *Raise Up Off Me* (New York: DeCapo, 1979), 2–3.

82. Bond, "The Negro in Los Angeles," 47.

83. Camarillo, *Chicanos in a Changing Society*, 204–5; *Los Angeles Times*, Feb. 21, 1920.

84. Uono, "Factors Affecting Aggregation," 137; J. Sato, "An American-born Japanese in America (c.1925), #107, Box 25; material in #124, Box 26, and #60, Box 24, SRR.

85. Richard Bigger and James D. Kitchen, *How the Cities Grew: Metropolitan Los Angeles Report Pt. II* (Los Angeles: Haynes Foundation, 1952), 87–88. For a description of the Mexican protest against the proposal see *La Opinión*, June 10, 11, 12, 18, and 22, 1927; Sanchez, *Becoming Mexican American*, 3–4.

86. Bond, "The Negro in Los Angeles," 47.

87. Quoted in Daniels, *Pioneer Urbanites*, 97–100; Sterry, "Sociological Basis," 31. See also Emory Bogardus, "Race Friendliness and Social Distance," *Journal of Applied Sociology* 11 (1926–27): 272–87.

88. Strong, *Japanese in California*, 15.

89. See, for example, Garcia, "Adaptation Strategies," 62–69.

90. Uono, "Factors Affecting Aggregation," 123; Keong Lee, interviewed by Beverly Chan, July 21, 1980, and Feb. 20, 1981, #125, SCCA.

91. 127 N. Savannah census card, Box 11, WPA. See also Everett W. Du Vall, "A Sociological Study of Five Hundred Underprivileged Children in a Selected Area of Los Angeles" (Ph.D. diss., University of Southern California, 1936), 294; Young, *Pilgrims of Russian-Town*, 19–20.

92. "Interview with Mr. Joyce," May 21, 1924, #B-347, Box 36, SRR.

93. See, for example, Uono, "Factors Affecting Aggregation," 122–23; Smith, "Development of the Mexican People," 62–64.

CHAPTER 2

1. See Hise, "Industry and Imaginative Geographies," 13–44; Robert Gottlieb and Irene Wolt, *Thinking Big: The Story of the Los Angeles Times, Its Publishers and their Influence on Southern California* (New York: G. P. Putnam's Sons, 1977), 227; Carey McWilliams, *Southern California Country: An Island on the Land* (New York: Duell, Sloan & Pearce, 1946), 289–94; Gerald Woods, "The Progressives and the Police: Urban Reform and the Professionalization of the Los Angeles Police" (Ph.D. diss., University of California, Los Angeles, 1973), 11.

2. McWilliams, *Southern California Country*, ix; "Life History of Kenichi Kawaguchi," n.d. (c. 1925), 17, #437, Box 37, SRR; *La Opinión*, June 10, 1927.

3. For a general overview, see Woods, "The Progressives and the Police"; Tom Sitton, "Urban Politics and Reform in New Deal Los Angeles: The Recall of Mayor Frank Shaw" (Ph.D. diss., University California, Riverside, 1983).

4. Sklar, *Corporate Reconstruction of American Capitalism,* 1–40. See also Rogin's discussion of the political consequences of this transformation in *The Intellectuals and McCarthy,* 9–24.

5. On the racialized contours of American republicanism, see Saxton, *Rise and Fall of the White Republic.*

6. See, for example, Phil Ethington's discussion of the transformation from a republican-centered "political construction of social identity" to a "social construction of political identity" in late-nineteenth-century San Francisco: *The Public City: The Political Construction of Urban Life in San Francisco, 1850–1900* (Berkeley: University of California Press, 1994).

7. A number of historians have noted that through much of the 1800s African American residents in eastern cities often lived in the same neighborhoods as Anglos, renting rooms or dwellings behind the main house. The end of the century, however, witnessed growing segregation between these two groups and the establishment of black districts. See Howard Rabinowitz, *Race Relations in the Urban South, 1865–1890* (New York: Oxford University Press, 1978); James Borchert, *Alley Life in Washington: Family, Community, Religion, and Folklife in the City, 1850–1970* (Urbana: University of Illinois Press, 1980); Kenneth L. Kusmer, *A Ghetto Takes Shape: Black Cleveland, 1870–1930* (Urbana: University of Illinois Press, 1976).

8. Charles S. Johnson, "Industrial Survey of the Negro Population of Los Angeles," National Urban League, Los Angeles, 1926, esp. 20–55. See also Johnson's summary of findings in Charles S. Johnson, "Negro Workers in Los Angeles Industries," *Opportunity: A Journal of Negro Life* 6 (1928): 233–41.

9. Grace Heilman Stimson, *Rise of the Labor Movement in Los Angeles* (Berkeley: University of California Press, 1955), 267. On the compartmentalization of various ethnic groups in the Los Angeles economy, see Sanchez, *Becoming Mexican American,* 89; Isamu Nodera, "A Survey of the Vocational Activities of the Japanese in the City of Los Angeles" (Master's thesis, University of Southern California, 1936), 72–117; Modell, *Economics and Politics of Racial Accommodation,* 94–126; Sokoloff, "The Russians in Los Angeles," 5–7; Hise, "Industry and the Landscapes of Social Reform."

10. On the troubled career of the "whitening thesis" in twentieth-century Brazil, see George Reid Andrews, *Blacks and Whites in São Paolo, Brazil, 1888–1988* (Madison: University of Wisconsin Press, 1991). Teresa Meade's provocative study of cultural and urban politics in Rio de Janeiro provides an interesting counterpoint to Los Angeles. In Rio, wealthy redevelopers sought to "Europeanize" the city through redevelopment projects (financed by European funds) that effectively displaced working class residents from inner-city districts. The government even instituted a credit program to attract European (mostly Italians) immigrants to settle in Brazil. In an inversion of the Los Angeles context, working-class residents of Rio assumed the mantle of patriotism and charged the elite with drawing "foreign" elements into the city. Teresa Meade, *"Civilizing" Rio: Reform and Resistance in a Modern City, 1889–1930* (University Park: Pennsylvania State University Press, 1997).

11. Articles touting Los Angeles's future housing stock "for the millions" appeared in the *Times* frequently throughout the early twentieth century. For

representative examples, see *Los Angeles Times,* Oct. 9, 1922; Mar. 25, Apr. 29, Aug. 26, Sept. 16, 1923; Oct. 7, 1923; Aug. 1, 1926. The chamber of commerce set up its own "Housing Department" to promote good housing for new settlers. *LACC Minutes,* Oct. 30, 1919,.171; Dec. 18, 1919, 309; Dec. 26, 1919, 312–13; Jan. 2, 1920, 171. The term "good community" is Robert Fogelson's; see *The Fragmented Metropolis,* 144–45.

   12. Fogelson, *Fragmented Metropolis,* esp. 144–45; McClung, *Landscapes of Desire.*

   13. See Paul Boyer, *Urban Masses and Moral Order in America, 1820–1920* (Cambridge, Mass.: Harvard University Press, 1978).

   14. Los Angeles Housing Commission (LAHC), *Report 1908 to 1909* (Los Angeles: LAHC), 17; CCIH, *A Community Survey.*

   15. For descriptions of house courts and the problems reformers identified in them, see Elizabeth Fuller, "The Mexican Housing Problem in Los Angeles," *Studies in Sociology: Sociological Monograph 17,* vol. 1 (Nov. 1920); William H. Matthews, "The House Courts of Los Angeles," *Survey* 30 (July 5, 1913): 461–67; CCIH, "Los Angeles Community Survey"; LAHC, *Reports, 1906–1913,* Los Angeles City Archives; John E. Kienle, "Housing Conditions among the Mexican Population of Los Angeles" (Master's thesis, University of Southern California, 1912); Emory Bogardus, "The House Court Problem," *American Journal of Sociology* 22 (Nov. 1916): 391–99.

   16. CCIH, *A Report on Housing Shortage* (Sacramento: State Printing Office, 1923), 11–13; LAHC, *1910–1913,* 20; *Los Angeles School Journal,* Nov. 14, 1921; Monroy, *Rebirth,* 27–28; *Los Angeles Times,* Mar. 12, 1922; Hope Murchay to Mrs. Frank Gibson, Aug. 6, 1920, in "Applications 1919–1920" file, Box 50, Series 4, California Commission of Immigration and Housing Collection (hereafter CIH), Bancroft Library.

   17. Sterry, "Sociological Basis," 13.

   18. See William Deverell, "Plague in Los Angeles, 1924: Ethnicity and Typicality," in *Over the Edge: Re-mapping the History of the American West,* ed. Valerie J. Matsumoto and Blake Allmendinger (Berkeley: University of California Press, 1999), 172–200; Natalia Molina, "Contested Bodies and Cultures: The Politics of Public Health and Race within Mexican, Japanese, and Chinese Communities in Los Angeles, 1879–1939" (Ph.D. diss., University of Michigan, 2000); Alice Bessie Culp, "A Case Study of the Living Conditions of Thirty-five Mexican Families of Los Angeles with Special Reference to Mexican Children" (Master's thesis, University of Southern California, 1921).

   19. American welfare capitalism of the 1920s focused on housing and the preservation of family life as the key to maintaining a docile and productive workforce. See Stuart D. Brandes, *American Welfare Capitalism, 1880–1940* (Chicago: University of Chicago Press, 1976), esp. 38–51.

   20. "We Must Begin with the Boy: All Nations Boys Club," pamphlet, 1939, in "CAN misc. and Printed Matter" file, Box 58, GBOP; CCIH, *Community Survey of Los Angeles,* 15. See also the convoluted descriptions of ethnic boundaries in Richard Jackson, "The People: Section II, Volume I," April 15 and 16, 1936, #1293–4, folder 2, Box 45, FWP; and the equally intricate maps of Boyle Heights racial groups in Gustafson, "Ecological Survey."

21. William H. Wilson, *The City Beautiful Movement* (Baltimore: Johns Hopkins University Press, 1989).

22. Bartlett, *The Better City,* quotation on 71–72.

23. Marshall Stimson, *Fun, Fights, and Fiestas in Old Los Angeles, An Autobiography* (Los Angeles: n.p., 1966), 58–59; Dana Cuff, *The Provisional City: Los Angeles Stories of Architecture and Urbanism* (Cambridge, Mass.: MIT Press, 2000), 279; *Los Angeles Evening News,* Nov. 29, 1927, in William Mead Ephemera Collection, Huntington Library.

24. Matthews, "House Courts," 461; Walter Wright Alley, "A Brief History of Public Housing Activities in Los Angeles," Los Angeles Municipal Housing Commission, 1936, 1.

25. LAHC, *Report, 1908–1909.*

26. Matthews, "House Courts," 461–67; LAHC, *Report, 1908–1909,* 24, and *Report 1910–1913,* 33–37. In 1913 the Los Angeles Health Department subsumed the activities of the LAHC. In 1925 a new City Charter revived the Municipal Housing Commission as an independent entity but was unable to secure sufficient funding from government officials. See Alley, "Public Housing Activities," 5.

27. LAHC, *Report, 1909–1910,* 12–14; *Report, 1910–1913,* 16–17.

28. LAHC, *Report, 1910–1913,* 20–22. See also Modell, *Economics and Politics of Racial Accomodation,* 56–66.

29. *Los Angeles Times,* Oct. 28, 1913.

30. LAHC, *Report, July 1, 1910 to March 31, 1913,* 40–42. On determining subsistence wages during this period, see Industrial Investigating Committee, *Report,* 1915, in "Reports and Correspondence of Bureaus, Departments, Committees, and Special Committees of the City of Los Angeles, 1890–1915," L.A. City Archives (hereafter LACA).

31. See especially Lubin to Hiram Johnson, Mar. 1, 1913, Box 4; Johnson to Lubin, Oct. 20, 1912, Box 2, Lubin Collection. For general institutional histories of the CCIH, see Anne Marie Woo-Sam, "Domesticating the Immigrant: California's Commission of Immigration and Housing and the Domestic Immigration Policy Movement, 1910–1945" (Ph.D. diss., University of California, Berkeley, 1999); Samuel Edgarton Wood, "The California State Commission of Immigration and Housing: A Study of the Administrative Organization and the Growth of Function" (Ph.D. diss., University of California, Berkeley, 1942).

32. Jacob Riis, *The Making of an American* (New York: Macmillan, 1901), 442–43.

33. S. D. Brooks to CCIH, Dec. 12, 1912, Box 1, Lubin Collection; Simon Lubin to (Frederic) Howe, Mar. 27, 1915, Box 5, Lubin Collection; CCIH, *Annual Report,* 1915, 107–8; *LACC Minutes,* Apr. 1, 1914; Oct. 7, 1914, Box 41; LACC, Apr. 1, 1914, Box 41; CCIH, *Annual Report,* 1923, 19.

34. Los Angeles Chamber of Commerce (LACC), *Minutes,* May 1, 1912, and Jan. 15, 1913, Box 41, Regional History Center, University of Southern California.

35. Max Binham, general manager of the American Colonization League, to Simon Lubin, Oct. 7, 1913, Box 1, Lubin Collection. See also Binham to Lubin, Oct. 25, 1913, and Nov. 4, 1913, Box 1; Walter T. Swingle to R. N. Lynch, Sept.

29, 1913, Box 2; Lubin to Clarence J. Owens, Oct. 17, 1912, Box 4; Martin Madsen to Simon Lubin, Jan. 26, 1914, Box 2, Lubin Collection.

36. CCIH, *Annual Report, 1915*, 104. Booster organizations would resurrect this practice during the Great Depression. See Davis, "From Oasis to Metropolis," esp. 368–69.

37. CCIH, *The Home Teacher* (Sacramento: State Printing Office, 1916), 8; CCIH, *Report of an Experiment Made in Los Angeles on the Americanization of Foreign-born Women* (Sacramento: State Printing Office, 1917). Numerous scholars of Chicano history have examined the Americanization programs, particularly their effects on Mexican American women. See, for example, Mario T. Garcia, "Americanization and the Mexican Immigrant, 1880–1930," *Journal of Ethnic Studies* 6 (1978): 19–34; George J. Sanchez, "'Go After the Women': Americanization and the Mexican Immigrant Woman, 1915–1929," in *Unequal Sisters: A Multicultural Reader in U.S. Women's History*, ed. Ellen Carol DuBois and Vicki L. Ruiz (New York: Routledge, 1990): 250–63; Romo, *East Los Angeles*, 132–35, 140–42.

38. CCIH, *Bulletin of Information for Immigrants*, 53; Edgar Dawson to R. J. Miller, Mar. 23, 1920, in "Citizenship" file, Box 2, Series 1, CIH.

39. Simon Lubin to John H. Bankhead, Feb. 5, 1915, Box 5, Lubin Collection. The CCIH published statistics and reports from its complaint department in its annual reports.

40. Paul Eliel to George Bell, Aug. 19, 1914; George Bell to Paul Eliel, Aug. 29, 1914, in "LA Office 1914" file, Box 43, Series 4, CIH.

41. CCIH, *Annual Report, 1921*, 9.

42. Rev. Dana Bartlett to Robert Newton Lynch, Oct. 28, 1912, Box 1; J. H. McBride to Lubin, June 30, 1915, Box 3, Lubin Collection. During the 1910s, a number of private organizations, including the National Conference of Immigration, Land, and Labor Officials, emerged to promote the same type of rural distribution.

43. Simon Lubin to J. H. McBride, July 2, 1915, Box 5, Lubin Collection.

44. CCIH, *A Report on Large Landholdings in Southern California: With Recommendations* (Sacramento: State Printing Office, 1919); see also CCIH, *A Report on Housing Shortage* (Sacramento: State Printing Office, 1923), 11–13; *LAHC, 1910–1913*, 20; Lubin to M. Wilson, Jan. 17, 1914, Box 4, Lubin Collection. Reformers in other cities also sought to decentralize working-class urban populations. See Zane L. Miller and Bruce Tucker, *Changing Plans for America's Inner Cities: Cincinnati's Over-the-Rhine and Twentieth-Century Urbanism* (Columbus: Ohio State University Press, 1987), 22.

45. CCIH, *A Report on Large Landholdings*, 3–4.

46. CCIH, *Report on Americanization of Foreign-born Women*, 8, 14; CCIH, *Annual Report, 1923*, 129.

47. George E. Melton to Lubin, Jan. 28, 1915, Box 3; John J. Backus (Chief Building Inspector, L.A.) to CCIH, May 17, 1919, Box 1; Simon Lubin to Paul Scharrenberg, May 28, 1919, Box 5; ; George Bell to Simon Lubin, May 15, 1915, Box 1; Simon Lubin to Frederic Howe, Apr. 30, 1915, Box 5, Lubin Collection; CCIH, *State Housing Manual* (Sacramento: State Printing Office, 1919); Simon Lubin to Robert Porter, May 9, 1919, Robert Porter Papers, Bancroft

Library; *LACC Minutes,* May 15, 1919, Box 41; *Los Angeles Times,* Mar. 6, 1915, pt. 2, 2; Feb. 13, 1915, pt. 2, 3

48. Leo Mott to Edward Glass, Apr. 25, 1922, in "Leo Mott-1922 file," Box 43, Series 4, CIH; Morris Siegel to Leo Mott, Apr. 20, 1926, in "L.A. Correspondence, 1926–1928" file, Box 49, Series 4, CIH.

49. Dana W. Bartlett, "Mexican Immigration to California," Apr. 12, 1920, in "Interchurch survey" file, Box 102, GBOP; Joseph Seeworker, *Nuestro Pueblo: Los Angeles, City of Romance* (Boston: Houghton Mifflin, 1940), 178; see also CCIH, *Report on Large Landholdings,* 30.

50. CCIH, *Community Survey of Los Angeles,* 34. See also Molina, "Contested Bodies and Cultures."

51. This generalization did not apply to certain close-knit European communities, such as the Molokan Russians, whom investigators found extremely hard to approach. See, for example, CCIH, *Report on Americanization of Foreign-born Women,* 11–12.

52. CCIH, *Annual Report,* 1927, 10. See also CCIH, *Report on Americanization of Foreign-born Women,* 7.

53. Elizabeth Fuller, "The Mexican Housing Problem in Los Angeles," *Studies in Sociology* 5.1 (Nov. 1920): 8; *Los Angeles Times,* Jan. 24, 1926; LAHC, *Report 1910–1913,* 24–26; CCIH, *Community Survey of Los Angeles,* 63.

54. CCIH, *Annual Report, 1927* (Sacramento: State Printing Office, Jan. 1927), 8.

55. Unsigned to Edward J. Hanna, Mar. 1926, in "Mexican Data" file, Series 1, Box 4, CIH; Louis, "Study of American-born and American-reared Chinese in Los Angeles," 114; Carol Aronovici, "Americanization," *Annals of the American Academy of Political and Social Science* 93 (Jan. 1921): 134–8.

56. Daniel Murphy to Central Labor Councils and Local Unions, May 3, 1923, Carton 1; Simon Lubin to Friend Richardson, Apr. 25 and Nov. 2, 1923, Box 5; H. M. Haldeman to CCIH, Sept. 4 and Oct. 9, 1920, and Feb. 2, 1921, Box 1, Lubin Collection.

57. The publishers created section 5 of the Sunday edition to celebrate the city's economic growth. The section contained lists, descriptions, and pictures of factories and office buildings under construction.

58. CCIH, *ABC of Housing* (Sacramento: State Printing Office, 1915), 5; see also Charles Cheney to Simon Lubin, Jan. 8, 1915, Box 2, Lubin Collection.

59. Camarillo, *Chicanos in a Changing Society,* 204–5; Romo, *East Los Angeles,* 84–86; Modell, *Economics and Politics of Racial Accommodation,* 55–65.

60. On the broad contours of city planning in Los Angeles during this period, see Marc Weiss, *The Rise of the Community Builders: The American Real Estate Industry and Urban Land Planning* (New York: Columbia University Press, 1987); Hise, "Industry and Imaginative Geographies."

61. Los Angeles City Council, "Industrial Limits Committee Report" (typescript, 1911), LACASC.

62. Los Angeles businesses did not universally support spot zoning, for it could also affect property values adversely. See Starr, *Material Dreams,* 109; *LACC Minutes,* July 8, 1926, Box 41.

63. City ordinance #42,666, reprinted in *Los Angeles Municipal Atlas: Official Zoning Maps* (Los Angeles: L.A. City Council), Nov. 19, 1925. Maps 5, 10, 11, 12, 16, 17, and 18 cover the central neighborhoods.

64. *Los Angeles Times*, Feb. 3, 1924; Jan. 28, 1923; Nov. 18, 1923; Apr. 6, 1924; July 5, 1925.

65. *Los Angeles Times*, May 7, 1922; Oct. 8, 1922. See also Hise, "Industry and the Landscape of Social Reform," 115.

66. LACC, "General Industrial Report" (typescript, 1924).

67. LACC, "General Industrial Report" (typescript, 1929, n.p.). This version read, "The labor supply is predominately American, including skilled workers from practically every line of industry." According to the census, only about 70 percent of Angelenos in 1930 were native-born white.

68. Sanchez, *Becoming Mexican American*, 75.

69. Sanchez, *Becoming Mexican American*, 81, 201; *Mexicans in California, Report of C. C. Young's Fact-Finding Committee* (Sacramento: State Printing Office, 1930), 177–78.

70. *Mexicans in California*, 59. For the report's summary of social problems in California's and particularly Los Angeles's communities of ethnic Mexicans, see 205–7.

71. *Mexicans in California*, 89–95.

72. See Mark Reisler, "Always the Laborer, Never the Citizen: Anglo Perceptions of the Mexican Immigrant during the Twenties," in *Between Two Worlds: Mexican Immigrants in the United States*, ed. David G. Gutierrez (Wilmington, Del.: Scholarly Resources, 1996), 23–44.

73. Ygnacio Garcia vs. LAPD, Jan. 20, 1928, Box 38, Series 3; Andres Carranza vs. LAPD, 1928, Box 37, Series 3, CIH.

74. Luisa Naranja vs. County Charities, 1928, Box 38, Series 3, CIH.

75. See Francisco E. Balderrama and Raymond Rodriguez, *Decade of Betrayal: Mexican Repatriation in the 1930s* (Albuquerque: University of New Mexico Press, 1995); Abraham Hoffman, *Unwanted Mexicans during the Great Depression: Repatriation Pressures, 1929–1939* (Tucson: University of Arizona Press, 1974).

76. On Olvera Street and the creation of the "Spanish Fantasy Past," see Phoebe Kropp, "Citizens of the Past? Olvera Street and the Construction of Race and Memory in 1930s Los Angeles," *Radical History Review* 81 (2001): 34–60; Carey McWilliams, *North from Mexico: The Spanish Speaking Peoples of the United States* (New York: Praeger, 1948), 43–53.

77. *Los Angeles Times*, May 9, 1926.

78. The purchase occurred after the Anglo business group sued the Sepulveda family. See Greenwood, *MTA Cultural Resources Impact*, 71–72. On the political battle to build Union Station, see Gottlieb and Wolt, *Thinking Big*, 152–54.

79. See, for example, *Los Angeles Times*, Feb. 22, 1920; Jan. 24, 1926; May 9, 1926.

80. For descriptions of China City and New Chinatown, see Garding Lui, *In Old Chinatown* (Los Angeles: n.p., 1948), 19–36.

81. See Robert E. Park, Ernest W. Burgess, and Roderick McKenzie, *The

City: Suggestions for Investigation of Human Behavior in the Urban Environment (Chicago: University of Chicago Press, [1925] 1967). See also discussions of the Chicago school in John R. Logan and Harvey L. Molotch, *Urban Fortunes: the Political Economy of Place* (Berkeley: University of California Press, 1987), 4–10.

82. E. J. Bumiller, "Housing Conditions of Maravilla Park and Belvedere Gardens," Jan. 6, 1925, Series 4, Box 45; Cuca Rosales vs. McKeon Canning Co., July 28, 1927, A. Ybarra vs. Frank Lopez, 1927, Series 3, Box 37, CIH.

CHAPTER 3

1. Gertrude Ruhnka, "The Church of All Nations: A Study of the Religious and Social Significance of the Church of All Nations as a Social Institution," 1927, no pagination, in "CAN misc.," 1917–27, Box 56, GBOP.

2. The Church of All Nations drew its parish boundaries at Third Street on the north, Washington Boulevard on the south, Main Street on the west, and the Los Angeles River on the east. Robert Moats Miller, *Bishop G. Bromley Oxnam: Paladin of Liberal Protestantism* (Nashville, Tenn.: Abington, 1990), 25–54.

3. D. F. McCarty, "Historical Sketch of Grace M.E. Church," n.d., and newspaper clipping, in "Misc. Notes," Box 56, GBOP.

4. Ruhnka, "The Church of All Nations.

5. "We Must Begin with the Boy: All Nations Boys Club," pamphlet, 1939, in "CAN misc. and Printed Matter" file, Box 58, GBOP; Reuben W. Borough, "Gangs Ousted by Community House," *Los Angeles Record,* Aug. 22, 1927. For a more general argument, see Kienle, "Housing Conditions among the Mexican Population of Los Angeles."

6. *California Christian Advocate,* June 16, 1927; G. Bromley Oxnam, "The Mexican in Los Angeles," Survey Department, Home Mission Division, Interchurch Movement of North America, 1920, 22–23, in "misc. articles 1928–9," Box 71, GBOP.

7. Oxnam, "The Mexican in Los Angeles"; "A Friend by the Side of the Road: The All Nations Foundation," pamphlet, n.d., 12, in "CAN misc. and Printed Matter" file, Box 58, GBOP.

8. Miller, *Bishop G. Bromley Oxnam,* 43; March 10 entry, 1913 Diary, Box 1, GBOP.

9. Walter Rauschenbusch, *Christianity and the Social Crisis* (New York: Macmillan, 1907); Jan. 5, 1925 entry, "Diaries and Notes," Box 32, GBOP.

10. The story of Azusa Street has been told many times. See Harvey Cox, *Fire from Heaven: The Rise of Pentecostal Spirituality and the Reshaping of Religion in the Twenty-first Century* (Reading, Mass.: Addison-Wesley, 1995), 45–66; Ian MacRobert, *The Black Roots and White Racism of Early Pentecostalism in the USA* (London: Macmillan, 1988); Robert Mopes Anderson, *Vision of the Disinherited: The Making of American Pentacostalism* (Peabody, Mass.: Hendrickson, 1992); Robert R. Owens, *Speak to the Rock: The Azusa Street Revival and Its Message* (New York: United Press of America, 1998); L.

Grant McClung, ed., *Azusa Street and Beyond: Pentecostal Missions and Church Growth in the Twentieth Century* (South Plainfield, N.J.: Bridge, 1986).

11. See Carl Douglas Wells, "The Changing City Church," *School of Research Studies 2, Social Science Series*, vol. 5, 1934; E. Burdette Backus, "Los Angeles, 'City of Angels': Its Religion," *Christian Register*, Aug. 10, 1922, 18–19, in "Misc.," Box 57, GBOP; *Los Angeles Times*, Aug. 28, 1927. For two excellent studies of church history in Los Angeles during this period, see Engh, *Frontier Faiths*; Singleton, *Religion in the City of Angels*.

12. Tom Sitton, *John Randolph Haynes: California Progressive* (Stanford: Stanford University Press, 1992), 27–31.

13. May 5 entry, 1913 Diary, Box 1, GBOP; Miller, *Bishop G. Bromley Oxnam*, 39.

14. Notes from Oct. 18, 1912, Baraca-Philanthea Banquet, in "Misc. Notes," Box 56, GBOP.

15. Newspaper clipping, "Me and Manuel's Knights," March 30 entry, 1913 Diary, Box 1, GBOP.

16. Oct. 18, 1912, notes, in "Misc. Notes," Box 56, GBOP.

17. Oxnam to Sherwood Eddy, Nov. 2, 1918, Box 34, GBOP; Miller, *Bishop G. Bromley Oxnam*, 70–72.

18. Engh, *Frontier Faiths*, esp. 26–87; Singleton, *Religion in the City of Angels*, esp. 68–92; May 21, 1918, entry, "Diaries and Notes 3," Box 32, GBOP.

19. Sanchez, "'Go After the Women,'" 254–58; Engh, *Frontier Faiths*, 136–37; see also discussion in Los Angeles Housing Commission, *Annual Report 1908–1909*, Los Angeles City Archives. An extensive literature exists on woman-to-woman contact between Anglo social reformers and immigrants. Notable examples are Kathryn Kish Sklar, "Hull House in the 1890s: A Community of Women Reformers," in DuBois and Ruiz, eds., *Unequal Sisters*, 109–22; Christine Stansell, *City of Women: Sex and Class in New York, 1789–1860* (New York: Alfred A. Knopf, 1986); Sarah Deutch, *No Separate Refuge: Culture, Class, and Gender on the Anglo-Hispanic Frontier in the American Southwest, 1880–1940* (New York: Oxford University Press, 1987); Peggy Pascoe, *Relations of Rescue: The Search for Female Moral Authority in the American West, 1874–1939* (Oxford: Oxford University Press, 1990). All Nations followed the pattern in that Oxnam and other males oversaw the Church, while women, with the exception of the boys clubs leaders, ran many of the day-to-day operations.

20. See Fifth Street Mission, *Minutes, 1910–1918*, in "CAN II," Box 57, GBOP; Esther Magie Thompson, "Classification and Correlation of Certain Traits of Boys in Clubs at the All Nations Boys Club" (Master's thesis, University of Southern California, 1938), quoted in "CAN misc. #3," n.p., Box 58, GBOP.

21. Rock, "Twenty Years on Skid Row," 3, 10.

22. "Minutes," 12–7–06, Epworth League, Chapter 19374, Newman M. E. Church, in "Misc. Notes," Box 56, GBOP; N. J. Elliot, "The Koreans in Southern California," Jan. 15, 1925, #B-416, Box 37, SRR; Samuel P. Ortegon, "The Religious Status of the Mexican Population of Los Angeles" (Master's thesis,

University of Southern California, 1932), 29–47; Sanchez, *Becoming Mexican American*, 151–70. For a list of missions ministering to Asian Angelenos, see "Directory of Oriental Missions" (New York: Home Mission Council and Council of Women for Home Missions, 1920), in Box 4, SRR.

23. "Report of Two Cases of Controversies Between the Buddhist Churches and Christian Churches," 1922, #B-194, Box 35, SRR.

24. See "Beginnings of the Negro Work" (c.1943), file 35, Box 2; "Japanese Branch" files, Box 15, Young Woman's Christian Association Collection, Urban Archives Center, California State University, Northridge (hereafter YWCA).

25. Kango Kunitsugo, interviewed by Sherry Turner and David Biniasz, 1973, #1334, CSUFOHP, 4.

26. Sanchez, *Becoming Mexican American*, 151–70; "Report of Two Cases of Controversy Between the Buddhist Church and Christian Churches," file B-194, Box 35, SRR; Roy Taketa, interview by Mary McCarthy, July 13, 1973, CSUFOHP, 3. Sanchez estimated that only 5 percent of ethnic Mexicans in Los Angeles converted to Protestantism in the 1920s and 1930s.

27. On Americanization programs and settlement houses, see Higham, *Strangers in the Land*, esp. 237–61; Sanchez, "'Go After the Women'"; Judith Rosenberg Raftery, *Land of Fair Promise: Politics and Reform in Los Angeles Schools, 1885–1941* (Stanford: Stanford University Press, 1992); Ruth Hutchinson Crocker, *Social Work and Social Order: The Settlement Movement in Three Industrial Cities, 1889–1930* (Urbana: University of Illinois Press, 1992), 49–66; Allen F. Davis, *Spearheads for Reform: The Social Settlement and the Progressive Movement, 1890–1914* (New York: Oxford University Press, 1967); Mina Carson, *Settlement Folk: Social Thought and the American Settlement Movement, 1885–1930* (Chicago: University of Chicago Press, 1990); Kathryn Kish Sklar, "Hull House in the 1890s"; Crocker, *Social Work and Social Order;* Paul McBride, *Culture Clash: Immigrants and Reformers, 1880–1920* (San Francisco: R & E Associates, 1975); Robert A. Slayton, *Back of the Yards: The Making of a Local Democracy* (Chicago: University of Chicago Press, 1986).

28. While a number of high-profile settlement houses such as Hull House and the College Settlements remained avowedly secular, according to Davis and Crocker, nine out of ten settlements nationally maintained some religious affiliation. Davis, *Spearheads for Reform,* 84–94; Crocker, *Social Work and Social Order,* 41.

29. Raftery, *Land of Fair Promise,* 29. See also Bartlett, *The Better City,* esp. 51–93.

30. See, for instance, the discussion of the College Settlement operations in "The College Settlement," Los Angeles Settlement Association [1905].

31. *Los Angeles Times,* Feb. 10, 1930. See also Raymond A. Mohl, "Cultural Pluralism in Immigrant Education: The YWCA's International Institute, 1910–1940," in *The YMCA and YWCA in the City,* ed. Nina Mjagkii and Margaret Spratt (New York: New York University Press, 1997), 111–37; International Institute Files, Box 15, YWCA. The institute operated under the YWCA until 1935, when it split off to join the National Association for Immigrant Welfare.

32. See George Mowry, *The California Progressives* (Berkeley: University of California Press, 1951); Sitton, *John Randolph Haynes;* William Deverell and Tom Sitton, eds., *California Progressivism Revisited* (Berkeley: University of California Press, 1994).

33. *Los Angeles Express,* Jan. 20, 1925, in folder 5, Box 18, YWCA.

34. See "Dedicatory Services of the Dana W. Bartlett Library," Nov. 7, 1926, in "Misc.," Box 57, GBOP; *Los Angeles Times,* Nov. 5, 1913.

35. Quotation from Dana Bartlett, *The Better Country* (Boston: C. M. Clark, 1911), 364–65.

36. Untitled newspaper clipping in "Misc. Notes," Box 56, GBOP; *Los Angeles Times,* Aug. 27, 1913.

37. This account of the downfall of the Bethlehem Institute is taken from the *Los Angeles Times,* esp. Aug. 27, Sept. 5, 11, 12, 24, Oct. 30, 31, Nov. 5, 26, 1913.

38. See Davis, *Spearheads for Reform,* 220–45; Carson, *Settlement Folk,* 180–85; Rivka Shpak Lissak, *Pluralism and Progressives: Hull House and the New Immigrants* (Chicago: University of Chicago Press, 1989), 79.

39. "Record of Speaking," in "misc #3" file, Box 58; "Pastor's Report," 4th Quarterly Conference, Sept. 7, 1918, and "Report of Pastor," 4th Quarterly Conference, Aug. 7, 1920, in "Misc. Notes," Box 56, GBOP.

40. Stephen R. Miller, "Assignment of Duties," June 15, 1920, and Oxnam, "Report to Board of Trustees of the L.A. Missionary and Church Extension Society," June 22, 1920, in "Misc. Notes," Box 56; "Record of Noon Lunch, June 26, 1918, to July 39, 1919," in "Misc. notes," Box 56; "List of 18 Families Helped at Thanksgiving Time by CAN," n.d., in "CAN II," Box 57, GBOP.

41. See list of theaters in "Report of Recreational Facilities, District 6th to 9th, San Pedro to River, 1920–1921" (no author), in "Parish Records #4," Box 59, GBOP.

42. "Summary Chart—Study of Fifteen Cases Connected with All Nations," n.d. (no author), in "Misc.," Box 57, GBOP; Wells, "The Changing City Church," 8–13. More generally, see Kathy Peiss, *Cheap Amusements: Working Women and Leisure in Turn-of-the-Century New York* (Philadelphia: Temple University Press, 1986); Mary E. Odem, *Delinquent Daughters: Protecting and Policing Adolescent Female Sexuality in the United States, 1885–1925* (Chapel Hill: University of North Carolina Press, 1995).

43. "Minutes of Los Angeles Missionary Church and Extension Society," Nov. 10, 1919, May 11, 1920, "Report of Pastor," 4th Quarterly Conference, Aug. 7, 1920, and Stephen R. Miller, "Assignment of Duties," June 15, 1920, in "Misc. Notes," Box 56, GBOP; Ruhnka, "Church of All Nations"; "Movies for Many without Money," Church of All Nations, Los Angeles, n.d.

44. Esther Thompson, "Classification and Correlation"; Herbert Alexander, "The War on the Slum," *Evening News* (San Jose, Calif.), four-part series beginning Aug. 24, 1922, pt. 2, in "CAN 1917–27," Box 56, GBOP.

45. Ruhnka, "The Church of All Nations"; "Plaza Community Center and Church of All Nations Joint Financial Campaign," pamphlet, n.d., in "Misc.," Box 57, GBOP; "Supporting Brief of the Latin American Group in the Los Angeles City Survey, Spanish and Portuguese District, Southern California Con-

ference, San Francisco Bay Area" (1920s), 1; "Supporting Brief of Latin American Group" and Vernon McCoombs to GBO, Jan. 17, 1921; *California Christian Advocate*, Feb. 18, 1926; April 27, 1925 entry, "Diaries and Notes," Box 32, GBOP.

46. Vivian E. Linden, "Outline of the Clinic Situation," May 4, 1923, in "CAN 1917–27," Box 56, GBOP; Miller, *Bishop G. Bromley Oxnam, 75.*

47. Jan. 1, 1920, entry, "Diaries and Notes," Box 32; G. Bromley Oxnam, "'My House are Fifty-Fifty,'" *International Journal of Religious Education,* July 1928, in "Misc Articles 1928–9" file, Box 71, GBOP.

48. Oxnam, "'My House Are Fifty-Fifty'"; Ruhnka, "Church of All Nations."

49. G. Bromley Oxnam, *Youth and the New America* ([Los Angeles]: Council of Women for Home Mission and Missionary Education Movement, 1928), 35–38; Sam Friedman, "Student Interview with Dr. B. Oxnam in Community House," in "misc. CA clippings" file, Box 112; *In Days to Come,* Sept. 1922, 3–6, Oct. 1922, Box 71; "Report of the Subcommittee on Definition of Religious as Distinguished from Social Welfare Activism," May 25, 1927, in "CAN 1917–1927" file, Box 56, GBOP. Oxnam's political convictions, though not truly radical, were well left of the average reformer, who displayed an aversion to social protest, race mixing, non-Anglo culture, and secularization. See Davis, *Spearheads for Reform;* Lissak, *Pluralism and Progressives;* Crocker, *Social Work and Social Order,* esp. 49–53, 210–21.

50. Jan. 2, 1917, entry, "Diaries and Notes 3," Box 32; "List of Books donated by Woman's Shelley Club to CAN," 1923, in "CAN 1917–27," Box 56, GBOP.

51. See file #10110–564–23, Military Intelligence Files, War Department, National Archives, Washington, D.C.; William F. Deverell, "My America or Yours? Americanization and the Battle for the Youth of Los Angeles," in Deverell and Tom Sitton, eds., *Metropolis in the Making: Los Angeles in the 1920s* (Berkeley: University of California Press, 2001), 277–301; Miller, *Bishop G. Bromley Oxnam, 87.*

52. Miller, *Bishop G. Bromley Oxnam,* 82–83; "Labor Day Sermon at First M. E. Church in Phoenix," Sept. 1 entry, 1916 Diary, Box 1; *Los Angeles Examiner,* Sept. 1, 1924, in "Diaries and Notes," Box 32; Jan. 3, 1918, entry, "Diaries and Notes 3," Box 32; James Jones, "Report of Personal Work among R.R. Workers," 1919, in "Misc. Notes," Box 56; "Pacific Electric Employees," Oct. 20, 1919, lecture, Church of All Nations, in "misc. outline 1" file, Box 82, GBOP.

53. McKibben, *With the Master,* 52; Oxnam, *Youth and the New America,* 103–9; Miller, *Bishop G. Bromley Oxnam,* 83.

54. Untitled paper, author not named, Dec. 1919, in "1914–54 misc. items," Box 31; "Report of Church of All Nations," Oct. 1919, in "Misc. Notes," Box 56, GBOP.

55. "Report of the Church of All Nations," Oct. 1919, Nov. 1919, in "Misc. Notes," Box 56, GBOP.

56. Upton Sinclair, "What Is to Be Done," address at Church of All Nations, Dec. 12, 1919, and "Parish," no date, in "CAN 1917–27," Box 56, GBOP.

57. See pamphlets advertising speeches, in "Misc.," Box 57, and speech transcripts from his publications *The Modern Samaritan, Young Citizen, In Days to Come,* Box 58 and 71, GBOP. Quotation from Oxnam, "The Builders of Tomorrow"; Sept. 1, 1920, entry, "Diaries and Notes," Box 32, GBOP.

58. See, for example, "College Settlement," 21; *Los Angeles Herald,* Nov. 2, 1916; *Los Angeles Times,* Apr. 21, 1930; "The International Institute of the YWCA" (1929), folder 3, Box 3, YWCA.

59. For a summary of Oxnam's views on integration and Americanization, see Oxnam, "'My House Are Fifty-Fifty.'"

60. "Registration Day at All Nations Kindergarten," n.d., in "Misc.," Box 57, GBOP. See Alexander, "War on the Slum," pt. 2; "Knights of King Arthur— Requirements for Page," in "CAN II," Box 57, and "Memo: Nationalities in DVBS," in "CAN misc. 3," Box 58, GBOP.

61. See Oxnam, *Youth and the New America,* 3; Jan. 14, 1920, entry, "Diaries and Notes," Box 32, GBOP. Both newlyweds were longtime members of All Nations boys' and girls' clubs. See "Items from Notebook of Mrs. June K. Barth," 1918, in "Misc.," Box 57, GBOP.

62. Oxnam, "'My House Are Fifty-Fifty'"; Miller, *Bishop G. Bromley Oxnam,* 76.

63. Ruhnka, "Church of All Nations"; Jan 11, 1918, entry, "Diaries and Notes 3," Box 32, GBOP.

64. June 4, 1922, entry, "Diaries and Notes," Box 32; Clara W. Armstrong, "Birthday of the Buddha," *National New Thought Monthly,* n.d., in "Misc.," Box 57, GBOP.

65. Aug. 28, 1922, entry, "Diaries and Notes," Box 32, GBOP.

66. Miller, *Bishop G. Bromley Oxnam,* 34; Oxnam, "Report to Board of Trustees of the L.A. Missionary Society and Church Extension Society," June 6, 1920, in "Misc. Notes," Box 56, GBOP.

67. See "Employee/Applicant Records," and "Centenary Pledges List, Dec. 6, 1920 to Jan. 1, 1922," in "CAN 1917–27," Box 56, GBOP; "A Friend by the Side of the Road."

68. From "The Builders of Tomorrow," sermon, n.d., in "misc. outlines II" file, Box 82, GBOP.

69. Oxnam, "'My House Are Fifty-Fifty.'"

70. See issues of *Young Citizen* and *In Days to Come* in "CAN 1917–27," Box 56, issues of *Modern Samaritan* and *In Day to Come,* Box 71, GBOP. Quotation in Sept. 1922, 5–6, Box 71.

71. Of 119 church members, 87 were "native white" or "native white of native parentage." ISRR, "Intensive Study," 9. See also interview with Mc-Kibben, in Ruhnka, "Church of All Nations."

72. Lydia Glover in collaboration with G. Bromley Oxnam, *These Things Shall Be: A Pageant Play of the Church of All Nations* (New York: Abington Press, 1924), and "The Church of All Nations: Yesterday, Today and Tomorrow or the Transformation of the Doubting One: A Pageant," program presented at Epworth League Institute, Pacific Palisades, 1922, in "CAN 1917–27," Box 56, GBOP.

73. Thompson, "Democracy in Evolution," 11–12; Ruhnka, "Church of All Nations."

74. Ruhnka, "Church of All Nations." On reformers' efforts to restrict the activities of working class girls and women, see Peiss, *Cheap Amusements;* Odem, *Delinquent Daughters;* Stansell, *City of Women.*

75. Thompson, "Democracy in Evolution," 5; Borough, "Gangs Ousted by Community House"; *Five Thousand Children* ([Los Angeles]: Church of All Nations, n.d.), in "Misc.," Box 57, GBOP.

76. "Parish," n.d., in "CAN 1917–27," Box 56, GBOP.

77. "Constitution of Phi Gamma Club," in "CAN II," Box 57, GBOP; Thompson, "Democracy in Evolution," 22–23.

78. See "Members of the Nights [sic] of King Arthur Club," n.d., in "CAN 1917–27," Box 56, GBOP.

79. "Constitution of Phi Gamma Club," in "CAN II," Box 57, GBOP; Thompson, "Democracy in Evolution," 22–23.

80. Newspaper clipping, "Brains, Brawn, and Books Given Boys by Community Chest: L.A. House of All Nations," n.d., in "Misc.," Box 57, GBOP.

81. Newspaper clipping, n.d., in "Misc.," Box 57, GBOP.

82. Alexander, "The War on the Slum," pt. 2 .

83. Thompson, "Democracy in Evolution," 23–26.

84. "Daily Vacation Bible School Report for the Year 1926," and "Memo: Nationalities in DVBS," in "CAN misc. 3," Box 58, GBOP.

85. "Ritual-Sigma Tau Beta Sorority," n.d., in "CAN misc. 3," Box 58, GBOP.

86. "Deaconess Friendly House Program," n.d., in "Misc. Notes," Box 56, GBOP.

87. Thompson, "Democracy in Evolution," 41–48; K. J. Skudder to G. Bromley Oxnam, May 2, 1934, in "CAN letters of commendation" file, Box 59, GBOP.

88. Robert McKibben, *With the Master into the Heart of the City: The First Forty Years of All Nations* (Los Angeles: Robert McKibben, [1977]), 74–77.

89. Thompson, "Democracy in Evolution," 48.

90. Oct. 18, 1923, entry, "Diaries and Notes," Box 32, GBOP; "Parish," n.d., in "CAN 1917–27," Box 56, GBOP; Borough, "Gangs Ousted."

91. Thompson, "Democracy in Evolution," 45–46.

92. Alexander, "War on the Slum," pt. 4; "Workers Education," n.d., in "Misc.," Box 57, GBOP.

93. "Parish," n.d., in "CAN 1917–27," 3, Box 56, GBOP; see also the interview with Oxnam in Ruhnka, "The Church of All Nations."

94. ISRR, "Intensive Study," 23–24; Ruhnka, "Church of All Nations."

95. "Preliminary Report Relating to the Church of All Nations," L.A. Missionary and Church Extension Society, Sept. 21, 1923, in "CAN misc. 3," Box 58, GBOP.

96. Institute of Social and Religious Research (ISRR), "Intensive Study of Representative City Churches: The City Parish, Methodist Episcopal, Los Angeles" (ISRR, New York, 1926), in "CAN 1917–1927," Box 56, GBOP.

97. G. Bromley Oxnam, "Report to the Fourth Quarterly Conference of the City Parish," Sept. 20, 1926, in "CAN misc. 3," Box 58, GBOP; Ruhnka,

"Church of All Nations." The fate of these other churches reflected the problems that All Nations had hoped to solve. The Thirty-eighth Street church closed because of an "influx of Negroes," and the Brooklyn Heights church became a Jewish mission under the auspices of the Presbyterian church. The church that withdrew from the parish was the marginally more prosperous Elysian Heights Church.

98. Notes, in "Misc.," Box 57, GBOP.

99. Jan. 5, 1925, entry, "Diaries and Notes," Box 32, GBOP.

100. Ruhnka, "Church of All Nations." The text of may of his sermons and lectures appear in his publications *The Modern Samaritan, Young Citizen,* and *In Days to Come,* as well as in Box 82, GBOP.

101. Ruhnka, "Church of All Nations"; Miller, *Bishop G. Bromley Oxnam,* 103.

102. Ruhnka, "Church of All Nations"; Plengvidhya, "A Study of Changes in the Services of All Nations Foundation."

103. Catherine Holt, "Interview with K- K-," Dec. 27, 1924, #318, Box 31, SRR.

104. Ruhnka, "Church of All Nations."

CHAPTER 4

1. Kango Kunitsugo, interviewed by Sherry Turner and David Biniasz, Nov. 28, 1973, CSUFOHP, 10.

2. "Life History of Angelita Avila," #B-262, Box 36, SRR. Angelita Avila is a fictitious name.

3. Kazuo Kawai, "Life History of Kazuo Kawai," Mar. 2, 1925, #296, Box 31, SRR.

4. A USC student reported that 99 percent of a sample of All Nations boys' club members went to the movies at least once a week. Spanish-speaking theaters also provided alternatives for some non-English speakers. Paul J. Crawford, "Movie Habits and Attitudes of the Underprivileged Boys of the All Nations Area in Los Angeles" (Master's thesis, University of Southern California, 1934), 17, 41.

5. Emory Bogardus, *The City Boy and His Problems: A Survey of Boys Life in Los Angeles* (Los Angeles: Rotary Club, 1926), 89; William Chew Chan, interviewed by S. Chong and Beverly Chan, Jan. 7 and 12, 1980, #39, Southern California Chinese American Oral History Program, Department of Special Collections, UCLA (hereafter SCCAOHP); Homer K. Watson, "A Study of the Causes of Delinquency among Fifty Negro Boys Assigned to Special Schools in Los Angeles" (Master's thesis, University of Southern California, 1923), 41; Isabel Americanian, "An Educational and Psychological Study of Vagabonds" (Master's thesis, University of Southern California, 1932); Adler, "Watts: From Suburb to Black Ghetto," 241.

6. Bogardus, *City Boy,* 68–70; Archie Green, interview with author, Mar. 18, 1999; Hettie Peary French, "A Study of Juvenile Delinquency in a Selected Area of Los Angeles" (Master's thesis, University of Southern California, 1934).

7. Bogardus, *City Boy*, 30–31; Lillian Sokoloff, "The Russians in Los Angeles," *Studies in Sociology: Sociological Monograph 11*, 3 (Mar. 1918): 5; *Linking Our Lives*, 7, 18; Odem, *Delinquent Daughters*, 170; Alice Mary Fesler, "A Study of the Relationship of Inadequate Parental Control to Truancy among Girls" (Master's thesis, University of Southern California, 1922).

8. Sterry, "Sociological Basis," 90–93; Sokoloff, "Russians in Los Angeles," 11; Ruhnka, "The Church of All Nations," in "CAN miscellaneous, 1917–1927" file, GBOP.

9. William C. Smith, "Interview with Julia Suski," Aug. 13, 1924, #B-64, Box 35, SRR; Kango Kunitsugo interview, 10. Of course, such parental concerns were not limited to central city residents. On the broader issues of daughters' behavior in Los Angeles during this period, see Odem, *Delinquent Daughters*.

10. Edna Fern Gano, "A Study of the Behavior and Ideas of Certain Children of the Church of All Nations in the Light of Their Home Background" (Master's thesis, University of Southern California, 1923); Herbert Asbury, *The Barbary Coast* (New York: Alfred A. Knopf, 1933), 154; "Summaries of Playground Surveys," fall 1918, "Interchurch Movement" file, Box 102, GBOP.

11. Leo Carrillo, *The California I Love* (Englewood Cliffs, N.J.: Prentice-Hall, 1961), 29–31. Carrillo claimed to have developed many of the ethnic-specific characterizations of his successful acting career from people he had encountered in Los Angeles.

12. Emilia Castañeda de Valenciana Oral History, interviewed by Christine Valenciana, Sept. 8, 1971, CSUFOHP, 9–10; Milton Quon, interviewed by Beverly Chan, Oct. 27 and Dec. 1, 1979, #30, SCCAOHP.

13. Woody Strode and Sam Young, *Goal Dust* (Lanham, Md.: Madison, 1990), 7; Bryant et al., eds., *Central Avenue Sounds*, 3–4, 115–16. See also various quotations on 135, 179, 181, 234, 264; and in Cox, *Central Avenue*, 123.

14. See *Los Angeles School Journal*, Jan. 16, 1925, 13–14; Tom Sitton, "The Los Angeles Fender Fight in the Early 1900s," *Southern California Quarterly* 72 (1990): 139–56. Numerous complaints from immigrants involved in accidents appear in the CIH records. See also John Stilgoe, *Metropolitan Corridor: Railroads and the American Scene* (New Haven: Yale University Press, 1983), 167–88.

15. Bogardus, *City Boy*, 31. See also Bartlett, *The Better City*, 142; J. J. Maut, "Causes and Prevention of Crime," in *Law Enforcement in Los Angeles*, ed. August Vollmer (1924; rpt. New York: Arno Press, 1974), 116–17; H. C. Tracy, "The School Boy, His Home," *Los Angeles School Journal*, Nov. 13, 1920, 16–17; H. Loren Mitchell, "Our School Playgrounds," *Los Angeles School Journal*, Jan. 26, 1925, 13–14; Gano, "A Study of the Behavior and Ideas of Certain Children," 4–6; Gertrude Agnes Stephens, "A Study of the Leisure Time Activities of a Group of Fifty Fifth and Sixth Grade Boys of Los Angeles" (Master's thesis, University of Southern California, 1935), 78.

16. James E. Rogers, *The Child at Play* (New York: Century, 1932), 98; Louise Demody, "The Leisure Home of the Child," *Los Angeles School Journal*, April 27, 1923, 19–20. For another study of efforts to curb urban children's street-based activities, see Peter C. Baldwin, *Domesticating the Street: The*

Reform of Public Space in Hartford, 1850–1930 (Columbus: Ohio State University Press, 1999), esp. 147–76.

17. Archie Green, Morris Kadish, Michio Kunitani, interviews with author. African American resident quoted in Bond, "The Negro in Los Angeles," 63. On attitudes of working-class parents toward street play more generally, see Jane Jacobs, *The Death and Life of Great American Cities* (rpt. New York: Vintage, 1989), esp. 74–88.

18. Bogardus, *City Boy,* 89–98, 113. See also José Lopez, "A Gang of Angels: Street Gangs in Los Angeles," in *City of Angels,* ed. Gary Riposa and Carolyn G. Dersh (Dubuque, Iowa: Kendall Hunt, 1992), 32–39.

19. Asbury, *Barbary Coast,* 152–56; Catherine Holt, "Interview with Dr. F. T. Nakaya," Sept. 21 and 28, 1924, Box 29, SRR,

20. Bogardus, *City Boy,* 91–93; Allan Chan, interviewed by George Yee, Feb. 22, 1980, #77, SCCAOHP.

21. Bogardus, *City Boy,* 91–93; Bryant et al., eds., *Central Avenue Sounds,* 95. Griffith, *American Me,* 51; Lopez, "A Gang of Angels," 32–39. More generally, see Joan W. Moore, *Going Down to the Barrio: Homeboys and Homegirls in Change* (Philadelphia: Temple University Press, 1991).

22. Bogardus, *City Boy,* 89–98; Ruhnka, "Church of All Nations"; "Phi Gamma Frat. List," n.d., in "CAN II," Box 57, GBOP.

23. Los Angeles Playground Commission, *Annual Report—Dec. 1, 1908, to June 30, 1910,* 3; W. Ryland Boorman, *Developing Personality in Boys* (New York: Macmillan, 1929), 37; Bogardus, *City Boy,* 34, 140–142. For a study of the Playground Movement in New York, see Cary Goodman, *Choosing Sides: Playgrounds and Street Life on the Lower East Side* (New York: Schocken, 1979).

24. Bessie D. Stoddart, "Recreative Centers of Los Angeles, California," *Annals of the American Academy of Political and Social Science* 35 (Mar. 1910): 210–19, quote on 218.

25. Los Angeles Playground Commission, *Annual Report—Nov. 30, 1907,* 3–21; Stoddart, "Recreative Centers," 210–19.

26. Stoddart, "Recreative Centers," 210–19; Raftery, *Land of Fair Promise,* 30–32; C. L. Glenn, "The Playground—The Kingdom of the Child," *Los Angeles School Journal,* Sept. 29–24, 17–18; Mitchell, "Our School Playgrounds"; Bogardus, *City Boy,* 100, 110; Adelina Bland, "The Girl on the Playground," *Los Angeles School Journal,* Oct. 5, 1925, 13–14; Playground Commission Report, Nov. 30, 1906, 4.

27. On the perpetuation of juvenile delinquency, see Virgil D. Dahl, "Geographical Concentration of Juvenile Delinquency in Los Angeles County" (Master's thesis, University of Southern California, 1932); Lopez, "A Gang of Angels." On Custer street playground, see Wrottenberg, "Field Agent's Report and Recommendations on Organization of Custer Center," 2, in "Los Angeles Community Service" file, Box 4, CIH.

28. Louis, "Study of American-born," 22; Raftery, *Land of Fair Promise,* 106–7; Smith, "The Development of the Mexican People in the Community of Watts," 53.

29. Bogardus, *City Boy*, 100; Strode and Young, *Goal Dust*, 18. See also Stoddart, "Recreative Centers"; Gretchen Tuthill, "Japanese in the City of Los Angeles" (Master's thesis, University of Southern California, 1924), 25.

30. Bruce Wallace, "Recreation for the Japanese in Los Angeles," May 29, 1924, #B-189, Box 35, SRR.

31. See material collected in #315, Box 31, SRR. According to James Chan, a sign at one movie theater read, "No dogs, Orientals, or Blacks Allowed." James Chan interview, SCCAOHP.

32. Walter Chung, interviewed by by George Yee, Jan. 20, 1980, #76, SCCAOHP.

33. The Boyle Heights troop may have been an exception, given that most troops organized around church groups. Bogardus, *City Boy*, 114; Archie Green, interview with author.

Of course, racial tension sometimes flared in these integrated groups. One All Nations boys' club composed mostly of Mexicans, for example, turned down the application of an African American boy. Supervisors at the club protested, and eventually the boy was voted in with only one dissenting vote. See Ruhnka, "Church of All Nations."

34. Louis, "Study of American-born," 19; Uono, "Factors Affecting Aggregation," 91–92; Sokoloff, "Russians in Los Angeles," 10–11; Miriam Johnson, interview with author, June 21, 1999; Manuel Gamio, *The Mexican Immigrant: His Life Story* (Chicago: University of Chicago Press, 1931), 52, 111.

35. See, for example, the discussion of Chinese-language schools in Louis, "Study of American-born," 29–40; Charles Wollenberg, *All Deliberate Speed: Segregation and Exclusion in California Schools, 1855–1975* (Berkeley: University of California Press, 1976), 36–37, 69–72; Him Mark Lai, "Retention of the Chinese Heritage: Chinese Schools in America before World War II," *Chinese America: History and Perspectives* 14 (2000): 10–31; Yoshide Matsubayashi, "The Japanese Language Schools in Hawaii and California from 1892–1941" (Master's thesis, University of San Francisco, 1984). On generational conflict more generally, see Vicki L. Ruiz, "Starstruck: Acculturation, Adolescence, and Mexican American Women, 1920–1950," in *Unequal Sisters: A Multicultural Reader in Women's History*, 3· ed., ed. Vicki L. Ruiz and Ellen Carol Du Bois (New York: Routledge, 2000), 346–61; Emory Bogardus, "Second Generation Mexicans," *Social Science and Research* 13 (1928–29): 276–83; Louis, "Study of American-born"; Young, *Pilgrims of Russian-Town*.

36. J. Gregory Payne and Scott C. Ratzan, *Tom Bradley: The Impossible Dream* (Santa Monica, Calif.: Roundtable Press, 1986), 10–11; Santiago L. Campos, "I Am Only a Foreigner—So This Is America," n.d., #113, Box 26, SRR. See also "And Who Is My Neighbor?" 1924 (reprinted from *Christian Advocate*), Box 4, SRR.

37. Bogardus, *City Boy*, 38; Griffith, *American Me*, 51, 188.

38. Louis, "Study of American-born," 47; William C. Smith, "Interview with Tom Gubbins," August 13, 1924, #B-61, Box 35, SRR.

39. Archie Green, interview with author; Ying Wong Kwon, interviewed by Elaine You, May 16 and 22, 1979, #13, SCCAOHP.

40. Los Angeles Playground Commission, *Annual Report—Nov. 30, 1907,* 21; *Los Angeles Socialist,* Nov. 23, 1901; June 21, 1902.

41. E. J. Lickley, "Child Labor and the Issuance of Work Permits," *Los Angeles School Journal,* Sept. 9, 1918. Helen Watson Pierce, "The Growth of Los Angeles High Schools," *Los Angeles School Journal,* June 8, 1925, 11–12, 42, 44; Raftery, *Land of Fair Promise,* esp. 40–46; Odem, *Delinquent Daughters,* 171–72; U.S. Senate, Immigration Committee, *The Children of Immigrants in Schools,* 61st Cong., 3' sess., vol. 3, 1911, 549; Raftery, *Land of Fair Promise,* 12, 67, 101.

42. Jennings Lavert Snoddy, "A Survey of the Methods Used in Adjusting the Truant Boy in the Los Angeles Schools" (Master's thesis, University of Southern California, 1932), esp. 18–20; Grace M. Turner, "A Study of the Neighborhood Schools of Los Angeles" (Master's thesis, University of Southern California, 1923), 33.

43. "Intensive Study of Representational City Churches: The City Parish," Institute of Social and Religious Research, New York, 1926, in "CAN misc. 1917–1927" file, Box 56, GBOP; Gustafson, "An Ecological Analysis," 66.

44. Michio Kunitani, interview with author, March 22, 1999; Monroy, *Rebirth,* 199. Thomas Weller Donlon, "A Study in Free Reading among Foreignborn Children" (Master's thesis, University of Southern California, 1933), 13; Raftery, *Land of Fair Promise,* 186–91; Irving G. Hendrick, *The Education of Non-Whites in California, 1849–1970* (San Francisco: R&E, 1977), 94; Pierce, "Growth of Los Angeles High Schools." Census figures from Gustafson, "An Ecological Analysis," 58.

45. On California school segregation during this period, see Gilbert G. Gonzalez, *Chicano Education in the Era of Segregation* (Philadelphia: Balch Institute Press, 1990); Wollenberg, *All Deliberate Speed;* Meyer Weinberg, *A Chance to Learn: The History of Race and Education in the United States* (Cambridge: Cambridge University Press, 1977), 140–77, and *Asian-American Education: Historical Background and Current Realities* (Mahway, N.J.: Lawrence Erlbaum Assoc., 1997), 12–73; David George Herman, "Neighbors on the Golden Mountain: The Americanization of Immigrants in California Public Institutions as an Agency of Ethnic Assimilation, 1850–1933" (Ph.D. diss., University of California, Berkeley, 1981), 167–97; Monroy, *Rebirth,* 132–34, 199.

46. Raftery, *Land of Fair Promise,* 110–17; Hendrick, *Education of Non-Whites,* 93.

47. Kango Kunitsugo, interview with Sherry Turner and David Biniasz, Nov. 28, 1973, CSUFOHP, 14–15; Payne and Ratzan, *Tom Bradley,* 17–18; Raftery, *Land of Fair Promise,* 186; Rodney H. Chow, interviewed by Emma Louie, Jan. 24, 1978, #149, SCCAOHP.

48. Nellie Oliver, "Oriental Children in School," n.d., #B-314, Box 36, SRR.

49. William C. Smith, "Oriental vs. Mexican Children in School (int. with Miss James)," n.d., #B-327, Box 36, SRR; Watson, "A Study of the Causes of Delinquency," 13, 20; Louis, "Study of American-born," 68, 104, 119.

50. Rodney H. Chow, interviewed by Emma Louie, Jan. 24, 1978, #149, SCCAOHP; "Life History of K. M.," n.d. #321, Box 31, SRR.

51. Louise Leung Larson, *Sweet Bamboo: A Saga of a Chinese-American Family* (Los Angeles: Chinese Historical Society of Southern California, 1989), 65; Louis, "Study of American-born," 63; Yoshie Marie Tashima, interviewed by Pat Tashima, Feb. 15, 1974, CSUFOHP; Catherine Holt, "Interview with Miss Teru Miyamoto," Jan. 10, 1926, #316, SRR.

52. Claud Sparks interview, Dec. 10, 1924, #B-337, Box 36, SRR; Dorothy Swain, *The Salvage: Japanese American Evacuation and Resettlement,* vol. 2 (Berkeley: University of California Press, 1953), 422–25, 459–60; Larson, *Sweet Bamboo,* 62, 98.

53. Archie Green, interview with author, Mar. 18, 1999; Herbert Leong, interview with Jean Wong, Jan. 22, 1980, and Jan. 14, 1981, #141, SCCAOHP; William C. Smith, "Interview with Julia Suski," Aug. 13, 1924, #B-64, Box 35, SRR; James Chan, interviewed by George Yee, Jan. 12, 1980, #79; William Chew Chan interview, SCCAOHP; Allan Chan interview, SCCAOHP.

54. The 1908 census of Los Angeles schools listed only a single Mexican teacher of 1,147 kindergarten and elementary school teachers. By the mid-1920s officials had hired a handful of black teachers concentrated in the "negro" schools south of downtown, but at most of the other schools faculty members were white. U.S. Congress, Senate, Immigration Commission, *Children of Immigrants in Schools,* vol. 3 (1911), 628–29; Sue Kunitomi Embrey Oral History, interviewed by Arthur Hansen and David A. Hacker, Aug. 24, 1973, CSUFOHP, 6; Katheryn Campbell Graham, "The Negro in Los Angeles," *Los Angeles School Journal,* June 4, 1925, 19–20; Delilah L. Beasley, *Negro Trailblazers of California* (New York: G. K. Hall, [1919] 1998) 236.

55. Sherry Katz, "Socialist Women and Progressive Reform," in Deverell and Sitton, eds., *California Progressivism Revisited,* 117–43; Raftery, *Land of Fair Promise,* esp. 75–80, 93–98, 106–10; Turner, "A Study of the Neighborhood Schools"; Sterry, "Sociological Basis"; *Los Angeles School Journal,* Feb. 15, 1918, 118–19; Nora Sterry, "The Neighborhood School," *California Quarterly of Secondary Education* 2 (Jan. 1927): 117–23.

56. Sue Kunitomi Embrey interview, CSUFOHP, 5.

57. See Emma Reybold, "Brotherization," *Los Angeles School Journal,* Nov. 2, 1924, 18–19; also, in the same journal, Sophie Tucker, "A Pageant in the Third Grade—Hewitt Street School," Feb. 27, 1923, 21–22; Margaret Dooher, "The Junior Citizenship Class—Central Junior High School," Dec. 5, 1920, 3–4.

58. Data showing higher rates of "retardation" in immigrant and nonwhite student appear in *Children of Immigrants in Schools,* 554. See also Gonzalez, *Chicano Education,* 26, 62–76; Alice Young Joe, interviewed by Jean Wong, Dec. 7, 1980, #139, SCCAOHP. See also Stephen Jay Gould, *The Mismeasure of Man* (New York: Norton, 1981).

59. Bogardus, "Second Generation Mexicans"; Rev. K. Unoura, "The Religious Education of the Japanese in California," 1919, Box 3, SRR.

60. H. W. Robinson, "Mrs. Manspeaker's Americanization Class," May 20, 1924, #116, Box 26, SRR; Interview with Mrs. Claude Sparks, Dec. 10, 1924, #B-337, Box 36, SRR.

61. Vocational education began as early as elementary school. See Turner, "Study of the Neighborhood Schools," 23–44; *Los Angeles School Journal*, Oct. 12, 1925 (special issue on vocational training).

62. Raftery, *Land of Fair Promise*, 199.

63. Hope Mendoza Schechter Oral History, interviewed by Malca Chall, 1977–78, University of California Oral History Program, Bancroft Library, 6–10.

64. Clarence Johnson, interviewed by R. Donald Brown, fall 1967, CSU-FOHP, 16; Payne and Ratzan, *Tom Bradley*, 12–13.

65. Bogardus, *City Boy*, 42; Catherine Holt, "Interview with Mr. and Mrs. William S. Yip," Jan. 13, 1925, #315, Box 31, SRR; Griffith, *American Me*, 167, 153.

66. William C. Smith, "Life History of Sophie Yamanaka," June 1, 1924, #234, Box 28, SRR; *Hollywood Daily Citizen*, Nov. 27, 1922, in #266, Box 29, SRR.

67. Raftery, *Land of Fair Promise*, 179; Miriam Johnson, interview with author, June 21, 1999; Smith, "Development of the Mexican People in the Community of Watts," 119.

68. Kango Kunitsugo interview, CSUFOHP, 12; Masao Dodo, "Life History of Masao Dodo," n.d., #345, Box 32, SRR; Enrique Vega, interview with Christine Valenciana, Sept. 3, 1972, CSUFOHP (tape); "Life History of Edward L.C.," c. 1925, #B-437, Box 37, SRR; "Life History of Edward L.C.," c. 1925, #B-437, Box 37, SRR; Sue Kunitomi Embrey interview, CSUFOHP, 6; Payne and Ratzan, *Tom Bradley*, 11.

69. Bogardus, *City Boy*, 107.

70. Archie Green, interview with author.

71. Turner, "Study of Neighborhood Schools," 32.

72. Alfred E. Lee, interviewed by Beverly Chan, Feb. 17, 1979, and Jan. 6, 1980, #46, and Billy W. Lew, interviewed by Beverly Chan, Oct. 19 and Nov. 1, 1979, #20, SCCAOHP; Catherine Holt, "Interview with Mr. and Mrs. William S. Yip," Jan. 13, 1925, #315, Box 31, SSR. See also Louis, "Study of American-born," 68, 104; Kazuo Kawai, "Life History of Kazuo Kawai" (c. 1925), #296, Box 31, SRR, 8.

73. Morris Kadish, interview with author, Mar.19, 1999; Michio Kunitani, interview with author, Mar. 22, 1999. More generally, see Paula S. Fass, *Outside In: Minorities and the Transformation of American Education* (New York: Oxford University Press, 1989), 73–111.

74. Larson, *Sweet Bamboo*, 98; Louis, "Study of American-born," 59. See also Lisa See, *On Gold Mountain: The One-Hundred Year Odyssey of My Chinese-American Family* (New York: Vintage, 1995), 203.

75. "Life History of a Japanese Girl" (no author), n.d., #309, Box 31, SRR; Catherine Holt, "Interview with Chiyoe Sumi," Feb. 21, 1925, #299, Box 31, SRR.

76. See E. J. Lickley, "Child Labor and the Issuance of Work Permits," *Los Angeles School Journal*, Sept. 9, 1918; Snoddy, "Adjusting the Truant Boy," 39; 70–71; William C. Smith, "The Cosmopolitan Population of Los Angeles in

Relation to the Schools," *Los Angeles School Journal,* Apr. 27, 1925, 13–14; Louis B. Perry and Richard S. Perry, *A History of the Los Angeles Labor Movement, 1911–1941* (Berkeley: University of California Press, 1963), 65.

77. The study also revealed that 55.1 percent of Mexican homes were broken, 53.2 percent of "American" homes, 45 percent of African American homes, 23.8 percent of Japanese homes, and 20 percent of European homes. Du Vall, "A Sociological Study of Five Hundred Underprivileged Children," 35. Studies that echo these findings include Clementina de Forest Griffin, "The Mexican and Poverty," Jan. 1920, in "Interchurch Survey" file, Box 102, GBOP, 3–5; 18; Mary Katherine Kelley, "Parental Attitudes Toward the Treatment of Children's Health Problems" (Master's thesis, University of Southern California, 1938), 15–16; Sterry, "Sociological Basis," 48–49.

78. Snoddy, "Adjusting the Truant Boy," 39, 70–71; William C. Smith, "The Cosmopolitan Population of Los Angeles in Relation to the Schools," *Los Angeles School Journal,* Apr. 27, 1925, 13–14; Sokoloff, "Russians in Los Angeles," 5–7; Watson, "Causes of Delinquency," 44; Paul S. Taylor, "Mexican Women in Los Angeles Industry in 1928," *Aztlan* 11 (1980): 99–132; J. Harold Thomas, "Los Angeles Children Who Work," *Los Angeles School Journal,* Jan. 30, 1928, 26.

79. *Children of Immigrants in Schools,* 553–54, 564–68, 626; Bridge, "Study of Agencies Which Promote Americanization," 50; Lanigan, "Second Generation Mexicans in Belvedere," 39–44; Arthur Goud, "Prevocational Courses in the Junior High Schools," *Los Angeles School Journal,* Nov. 27, 1920, 3–6; Ruhnka, "Church of All Nations"; "Phi Gamma Frat. List," n.d., in "CAN II," Box 57, GBOP; Monroy, *Rebirth,* 198–99; Keong Lee, interviewed by Beverly Chan, July 21, 1980, and Feb. 20, 1981, #125, SCCAOHP; William C. Smith, "Interview with Frank Yura" and "Interview with K. Yamamoto," Aug. 25, 1924, #B-56, Box 35, SRR. More generally, see Stephen Lassonde, "Learning and Earning: Schooling, Juvenile Employment, and the Early Life Course in Late Nineteenth Century New Haven," *Journal of Social History* 29 (summer 1996): 839–70, and "Should I Go, or Should I Stay? Adolescence, School Attainment, and Parent-Child Relations in Italian Immigrant Families of New Haven, 1900–1940," *History of Education Quarterly* 38 (spring 1998): 37–60.

80. Kunitani, interview with author; Mary Lanigan, "Second Generation Mexicans in Belvedere" (Master's thesis, University of Southern California, 1932), 39–44; McEuen, "A Survey of Mexicans in Los Angeles," 27; Royal, quoted in Bryant et al., eds., *Central Avenue Sounds,* 26; Keong Lee, interviewed by Beverly Chan, July 21, 1980, and Feb. 20, 1981, #125, SCCAOHP; Monroy, *Rebirth,* 132; Goud, "Prevocational Courses in the Junior High Schools," 3–6.

81. In 1936, for example, Mexicans constituted 24 percent of students at Roosevelt High School 55 percent of fifteen elementary schools and 36 percent of two junior high schools feeding into Roosevelt. Gustafson, "An Ecological Analysis," 57–58, 66–67.

82. In a study of Hartford, Connecticut, Peter Baldwin found several girls selling newspapers, but a Los Angeles study from 1912 found only a single girl and two older women engaged in the trade, among several hundred boys. Ruth Margaret Iliff Nordahl, "A Social Study of the Newsboys' Trade in Los Ange-

les" (Master's thesis, University of Southern California, 1912), 16. Baldwin, *Domesticating the Street*, 93–115. For other accounts and analyses of central city children in "blind alley" jobs, see McEuen, "A Survey of the Mexicans in Los Angeles," 68; *Los Angeles Express*, Oct. 30, 1908; Sydney C. Kendall, *Queen of the Red Lights* (Los Angeles: Wiley Phillips, [1906]), 36; Bogardus, *City Boy*, 101–5; Griffith, *American Me*, 204; Social Service Commission, *Annual Report, July 1, 1920 to July 1, 1921*, 20.

83. Lanigan, "Second Generation Mexicans," 45–50.

84. *Linking Our Lives*, 18; Swain, *The Salvage*, 422–25; Bogardus, *City Boy*, 107; Griffith, *American Me*, 46; Morris Kadish, interview with author.

85. William C. Smith, "Interview with Sun (Peter) Lee," Aug. 13, 1924, #B 62, Box 35, SRR.

86. Sokoloff, "The Russians in Los Angeles."

87. Bogardus, *City Boy*, 38.

88. Kazuo Kawai, "Life History of Kazuo Kawai," Mar. 2, 1925, #296, Box 31, SRR.

CHAPTER 5

1. See, for example, Gail Bederman, *Manliness and Civilization: A Cultural History of Gender and Race in the United States, 1880–1917* (Chicago: University of Chicago Press, 1995); Nancy MacLean, "The Leo Frank Case Reconsidered: Gender and Sexual Politics in the Making of Reactionary Populism," *Journal of American History* 78 (Dec. 1991): 917–48; Nancy MacLean, *Behind the Mask of Chivalry: The Making of the Second Ku Klux Klan* (New York: Oxford University Press, 1994); Odem, *Delinquent Daughters*; Peiss, *Cheap Amusements*.

2. This chapter focuses exclusively on heterosexual relationships, although homosexual relationships certainly existed in central neighborhoods. The Chinatown restaurant run by Lisa See's family, for example, became popular with homosexuals during the Great Depression, and a longtime Skid Row resident recalled that a number of "queers" walked the streets around Fifth and Main. As a child, Michio Kunitani received warnings from friends not to go to Pershing Square because men who solicited young boys frequented the area. See, *On Gold Mountain*, 193–98; Rock, "Twenty Years on Skid Row," 4; Michio Kunitani, interview with author, Mar. 22, 1999. For more on the gay community in early-twentieth-century Los Angeles, see Daniel Lofton Hurewitz, "Made in Edendale: Bohemian Los Angeles and the Politics of Sexual Identity, 1918–1953" (Ph.D. diss., University of California, Los Angeles, 2001).

3. J. McFarline Ervin, "The Participation of the Negro in the Community Life of Los Angeles" (Master's thesis, University of Southern California, 1931), 55–72. See also Bond, "The Negro in Los Angeles," 136.

4. See, for example, Timothy Gilfoyle, *City of Eros: New York City, Prostitution, and the Commercialization of Sex, 1790–1920* (New York: Norton, 1992); Kevin J. Mumford, *Interzones: Black/White Sex Districts in Chicago and New York in the Early Twentieth Century* (New York: Columbia University Press, 1997).

5. I recognize that gender hierarchies render the ethnoracial identity of each participant in a mixed relationship relevant, since different combinations could hold different social meanings for different participants or observers. Male members of a specific ethnic community, for example, may have objected less to inter-ethnoracial relations involving male members of their community than those involving female members. Unfortunately, the sheer number of possible ethnic-racial combinations in central Los Angeles makes it unrealistic to explain the consequences of each. Nevertheless, to the extent that there existed in each ethnoracial group (including Anglos) some desire for ethnic preservation, the impact of mixed relations in the sex trade, regardless of context, affected them equally in some fundamental respect.

6. On prostitution and mixed ethnic districts, see Asbury, *The Barbary Coast;* Barbara Meil Hobson, *Uneasy Virtue: The Politics of Prostitution and the American Reform Tradition* (New York: Basic Books, 1987), 35–36; Fernando Henriques, *Prostitution in Europe and the Americas* (New York: Cathedral Press, 1965), 309–16; Craig Foster, "Tarnished Angels: Prostitution in Storyville and New Orleans, 1900–1910," *Louisiana History* 31 (1990): 387–97; Gilfoyle, *City of Eros;* Mumford, *Interzones.* Also, Immigration and Naturalization Service (INS) records provide primary data and analyses of prostitution in certain early-twentieth-century U.S. cities. See *Records of the Immigration and Naturalization Service—Series A, Part 5: Prostitution and "White Slavery"* (Bethesda, Md.: University Publications of America, 1997).

7. Neil Larry Shumsky, "Tacit Acceptance: Respectable Americans and Segregated Prostitution, 1870–1910," *Journal of Social History* 19 (1986): 665–79.

8. See Robinson, *Tarnished Angels,* 7–9, 13, 18–20; Joseph Gerald Woods, "A Penchant for Probity: California Progressivism and the Disreputable Pleasures," in Deverell and Sitton, eds., *California Progressivism Revisited,* 91–113, esp. pp. 103–5.

9. On the integrated character of vice industries (and certain exceptions to it) in early-twentieth-century central Los Angeles, see Robinson, *Tarnished Angels,* 13–20; *Flash,* July 27, 1929, 12; Woods, "The Progressives and the Police," 109.

10. CCIH, *Annual Report,* 1916, 227–28.

11. CCIH, *Annual Report,* Jan. 2, 1916 (San Francisco: State Printing Office), 228. Stimson, *Fun, Fights, and Fiestas,* 66–67; *Los Angeles Herald,* Dec. 7, 1903.

12. According to the 1880 census, women made up only 4.6 percent of the Chinese population in the United States. George Anthony Peffer, "Forbidden Families: Emigration Experiences of Chinese Women under the Page Law, 1875–1882," *Journal of American Ethnic History* 6 (1986): 29; *Linking Our Lives,* 5; Lou, "Chinese-American Community," 29–31. On the immigration of Chinese women more generally, see George Anthony Peffer, *If They Don't Bring Their Women Here: Chinese Female Immigration Before Exclusion* (Urbana: University of Illinois Press, 1999).

13. Mason and McKinstry, *The Japanese of Los Angeles,* 8; *Los Angeles Times,* Dec. 3, 1903.

14. See, for example, *Los Angeles Times,* Dec. 3 and 14, 1903; *Los Angeles Herald,* Dec. 5, 1903.

15. On the white slavery panic, see Odem, *Delinquent Daughters,* 11–12, 50; Mumford, *Interzones,* 11; M. G. C. Edholm, "Traffic in White Girls," *California Illustrated,* Nov. 1892, 825–38; Frederick Grittner, *White Slavery: Myth, Ideology, and American Law* (New York: Garland, 1990); David J. Langum, *Crossing over the Line: Legislating Morality and the Mann Act* (Chicago: University of Chicago Press, 1994). According to Robert Lee, many Anglos associated immigrants from Asia not only with the sex trade but also with alternative articulations of gender and sexuality. See Robert G. Lee, *Orientals: Asian Americans in Popular Culture* (Philadelphia: Temple University Press, 1999), esp. 82–91.

16. Kendall, *Queen of the Red Lights,* 70. Similarly fantastic stories became common during the white slave panic. See Mary de Young, "Help, I'm Being Held Captive! The White Slave Fairy Tale of the Progressive Era," *Journal of American Culture* 6 (1983): 96–99.

17. See *Los Angeles Herald,* Dec. 15, 1903.

18. "Interview with Wiley J. Phillips," Catherine Holt, Aug. 14, 1924, #298 (8), Box 31, SRR. See also *California Voice,* Dec. 17, 1903; *Los Angeles Times,* Dec. 3 and 14, 1903.

19. Kendall, *Queen of the Red Lights,* 146; *Los Angeles Times,* Dec. 2, 1903.

20. Kendall, *Queen of the Red Lights,* 29, 138; Woods, "The Progressives and the Police," 11, 36.

21. See *Los Angeles Herald,* Dec. 8, 1903. For similar trends in other cities, see Mumford, *Interzones,* 36–49; David C. Humphrey, "Prostitution and Public Policy in Austin, Texas, 1870–1915," *Southwestern Historical Quarterly* 86 (1983): 473–516; Clare V. McKenna, "Prostitutes, Progressives, and Police: The Viability of Vice in San Diego, 1900–1930," *Journal of San Diego History* 35 (1989): 44–65; Neil Larry Shumsky and Larry M. Springer, "San Francisco's Zone of Prostitution, 1880–1934," *Journal of Historical Geography* 7 (1981): 71–89.

22. Daniel J. Johnson, "A Serpent in the Garden: Institutions, Ideology, and Class in Los Angeles Politics, 1901–1911" (Ph.D. diss., University of California, Los Angeles, 1996), 380–90; *Los Angeles Herald,* Jan. 14, 1915; *Los Angeles Tribune,* June 7, 1917; Moral Efficiency Association to Parents Teachers Association of Los Angeles, May 30, 1917, Scrapbook II, Los Angeles Railroad Collection, Huntington Library (hereafter LARR).

23. "Notes from JK Barth Survey," in "misc. 3" file, Box 58, GBOP.

24. A street sweeper working on the block verified the business conducted in the home, which was apparently used by several white prostitutes. See "Notes from Barth Survey," esp. card 2, GBOP. On the LAPD's financial relationships with prostitutes and pimps, see *Los Angeles Herald,* Jan. 14, 1915; *Los Angeles Tribune,* June 7, 1917; Moral Efficiency Association to Parents Teachers Association of Los Angeles, LARR; Johnson, "Serpent in the Garden," pp. 380–90.

25. *Los Angeles Times,* Mar. 22 and 27, 1919. See also Woods, "The Progressives and the Police," 47. I am indebted to Mike Davis for bringing this article to my attention.

26. Catherine Holt, "Interview with R. E. Steckel," July 29, 1924, #298 (11), Box 31, SRR; Sterry, "Sociological Basis," 22.

27.   Du Vall, "A Sociological Study of Five Hundred Underprivileged Children," 315; Bond, "The Negro in Los Angeles," 136. For examples of efforts to curb prostitution in Los Angeles during the 1920s, see *Los Angeles Record*, Dec. 3, 1921; file #1449, 1922, Los Angeles City Council Records, Los Angeles City Archives; Gende E. Carter and Elaine H. Carter, *Police Reform in the United States: The Ear of August Vollmer, 1905–1932* (Berkeley: University of California Press, 1975), 58–62; *Los Angeles Record*, Oct. 5, 1925.

28. Asbury, *Barbary Coast*, 259, 268–69. Craig L. Foster likewise found pricing based on prostitutes' race in New Orleans. Foster, "Tarnished Angels," 398–99.

29.   Linda N. España-Maram, "Brown 'Hordes' in McIntosh Suits: Filipinos, Taxi Dance Halls, and Performing the Immigrant Body in Los Angeles, 1930s–1940s," in *Generations of Youth: Youth Cultures and History in Twentieth-Century America*, ed. Joe Austin and Michael Nevin Willard (New York: New York University Press, 1998): 118–35; Ervin, "Participation of the Negro," 19–20.

30. Ervin, "Participation of the Negro," 55–58. The term is from David Roediger, *The Wages of Whiteness: Race and the Making of the American Working Class* (London: Verso, 1991).

31. Ervin, "Participation of the Negro," 54, 58–63, 72. See also Bond, "The Negro in Los Angeles," 136; Mumford, *Interzones*, 106.

32.   "Life History of a Japanese Girl" (no author), n.d., #309, Box 31, SRR. For a general discussion of the eroticization of African American, Jewish, and Japanese women by white men, see Spickard, *Mixed Blood*, 39–41, 174–76, 257–59.

33. *Los Angeles Herald*, Jan. 14, 1915; "Moral Efficiency Association to Parent-Teachers Association of Los Angeles," LARR; Miriam Van Waters, *Youth in Conflict* (New York: Republic, 1925), 47–50. See also Virginia Scharff, *Taking the Wheel: Women and the Coming of the Motor Age* (New York: Free Press, 1991), 155–56.

34. *Common Sense*, Aug. 26, 1908.

35.   Bond, "The Negro in Los Angeles," 136. According to one scholar, the identification of nonwhite women as prostitutes had a legal tradition in U.S. policy as well. In a study of immigration polices before the 1880s (when most immigration from China was outlawed), Peffer argues that immigration officials treated all female Chinese immigrants of marriageable age as potential prostitutes. See Peffer, "Forbidden Families," 28–46.

36. See "Notes from Barth survey," GPOB; Clara Gilbert and William C. Smith, "Los Angeles Chinatown," June 12, 1924, p. 1, #B-24, Box 35, SRR.

37. *Flash*, Mar. 30, 1929, p. 4; Dec. 31, 1929, 11; Ervin, "Participation of the Negro," 65; Woods, "The Progressives and the Police," 303.

38. "Brothers," unpublished manuscript (not paginated), Box 1, Harold Bruce Forsythe Papers, Huntington Library. See also Forsythe's description of Central Avenue nightclubs in "Mask," unpublished manuscript (not paginated), Box 7, Forsythe Papers, Huntington Library. These manuscripts are not dated but were most likely written in the late 1920s or the 1930s.

39.   Mason and McKinstry, *The Japanese of Los Angeles*, 18–19; Ivan Light, "From Vice District to Tourist Attraction: The Moral Career of American

Chinatowns, 1880–1940," *Pacific Historical Review* 43 (Aug. 1974), 368; *Los Angeles Times*, Jan. 8, 1908. For other descriptions on slumming, see Asbury, *Barbary Coast*, 166, 171; Mumford, *Interzones*, 133–56. See also Lisa See's description of Chinese resentment against Anglos who visited Chinatown in the early twentieth century: *On Gold Mountain*, 180–81.

40. Light, "From Vice District to Tourist Attraction," esp. 377–79, 393; Woods, "The Progressives and the Police," 91. Rev. Allen Chen, a Protestant Chinese minister, worked to eradicate prostitution as well. See May 21, 1918, entry, "Diaries and Notes 3," Box 32, GBOP.

41. See Alec Dubro and David E. Kaplan, "California's Yakuza: Foothold in Little Tokyo," *Californians* 5 (1987): 34–41; Murase, *Little Tokyo*, 13–14; Kariann Akemi Yokota, "From Little Tokyo to Bronzeville and Back: Ethnic Communities in Transition" (Master's thesis, University of California, Los Angeles, 1996), 26.

42. Sevestiana Castro vs. Angela Flores and Josepha Marquez, 1923, Box 26, CIH. For other representative examples, see Adela Delgado vs. Refugio Godoy, 1923, Box 26; Maria Jesus de Chavez vs. Mrs. F. Wise, 1922, Box 23; Monica Gutierrez vs. Antonastacio and Florencio Morales, 1922, Box 23; Refugia Martinez vs. Maria Gonzales de Ponce, 1922, Box 23; Sam Karldisian vs. Jobe Keroman, 1931, Box 40, CIH.

43. *Flash*, Mar. 30, 1929, p. 4.

44. *Los Angeles Times*, Jan. 14, 1923. The story was recounted in the *Times* on July 13, 1998.

45. Peggy Pascoe, "Race, Gender, and the Privilege of Property," in Matsumoto and Allmendinger, eds., *Over the Edge*, 215–30; Peggy Pascoe, "Miscegenation Law, Court Cases, and Ideologies of 'Race' in Twentieth-Century America," *Journal of American History* 83 (June 1996): 44–69.

46. Arleen de Vera, "The Tapia-Saika Incident: Interethnic Conflict and Filipino Responses to the Anti-Filipino Exclusion Movement," in Matsumoto and Allmendinger, eds., *Over the Edge*, 201–14.

47. For a general discussion of resistance to inter-ethnoracial relationships among African Americans, Jews, and Japanese, see Spickard, *Mixed Blood*, 46–50, 168–97, 297, 301.

48. One writer suggests that Kimbrough based this account on an actual incident. See John Thomas, "Defender of the Angels: Jesse Kimbrough and the Los Angeles Police Department, 1916–1939," unpublished manuscript, 1998, Southern California Library for Social Studies and Research, Los Angeles; Jesse Kimbrough, *Defender of the Angels: A Black Policeman in Old Los Angeles* (London: Macmillan, 1969), 44–45.

49. For the writer, the most astonishing part of the story was that the husband had left the wife for black women. This challenged his assumption that men, even African Americans, valued sexual contact with white women more than with nonwhite women. I am grateful to Kate McGinn for bringing this article to my attention. See *Los Angeles Times*, Apr. 18, 1906.

50. See *Los Angeles Times*, June 7, July 15–19, Dec. 12, 1899.

51. Lanigan, "Second Generation Mexicans in Belvedere," 18–25 (quotation on 25); Young, *Pilgrims of Russian-Town*, 140–41.

52. "Case Study of a Boy of Mixed Parentage," n.d., #280, Box 31, SRR.

53. Van Waters, *Youth in Conflict,* 13. Van Waters became noted for emphasizing a more compassionate approach to delinquent youth, but her concerns—the "dangers" of commercial amusements, girls and young women in the workforce—reflected those of many other parents during the Progressive era.

54. Fesler, "Inadequate Parental Control," 9–10.

55. Examples taken from Odem, *Delinquent Daughters,* 172–74. Some Anglo reformers also worried that girls working as domestics were vulnerable to advances from their employers. Van Waters, *Youth in Conflict,* 115.

56. On prosecutions for statutory rape, see Odem, *Delinquent Daughters,* esp. 63–81. The Immigration and Housing Commission also received a number of complaints by immigrant parents against men and boys who had seduced or eloped with teenage girls.

57. Fesler, "Inadequate Parental Control," 23–26, 40–41.

58. Helen Hester Harper, "A Study of Colored Unmarried Mothers in Los Angeles" (Master's thesis, University of Southern California, 1932), 28.

59. See, *On Gold Mountain,* 136.

60. *Linking Our Lives,* 41–42; "Jennie's Story," n.d., #281, Box 31, SRR.

61. Young, *Pilgrims of Russian-Town,* 245.

62. See "Interviews Regarding Millie Yonemura, Mixed Japanese-American High School Girl," (c. 1925), #B-446, Box 37, SRR.

63. "Life History of Edward L.C.," Edward L.C., n.d., #B-443, Box 37, SRR; Gustafson, "Sociological Analysis," 167.

64. Bond, "The Negro in Los Angeles," 2; Miroslava Chavez, "Mexican Women and the American Conquest in Los Angeles: From the Mexican Era to American Ascendancy" (Ph.D. diss., University of California, Los Angeles, 1998); Griswold del Castillo, *Los Angeles Barrio,* 74–77.

65. Louise Colton Appell, "An Historical Folk Survey of Southern California: A Narrative of the Peopling of the Southland" (Master's thesis, University of Southern California, 1927), 37–39; Griswold del Castillo, *Los Angeles Barrio,* 74–77, reported that 25 percent of Mexicans who married between 1856 and 1875 married Anglos.

66. Billy Lew interview, Oct. 19 and Nov. 1, 1979, #20, SCCAOHP; Jackman Hom, n. int., n.d., #156, SCCAOHP; Bond, "The Negro in Los Angeles," 12–19.

67. DeWitt, *The Fragmented Dream,* 149–50; Lou, "The Chinese-American Community," 344.

68. Constantine Panunzio, "Intermarriage in Los Angeles, 1924–1933," *American Journal of Sociology* 47 (Mar. 1942), 695–96. Karen Isaksen Leonard, *Making Ethnic Choices: California's Punjabi Mexican Americans* (Philadelphia: Temple University Press, 1992), 53–68.

69. Taking advantage of the marriage's nonofficial status, See's great-grandfather later married a Chinese woman and brought her to Los Angeles. See *On Gold Mountain;* Notes from June Barth's Survey, GBOP.

70. Vorspan and Gardner, *Jews of Los Angeles,* 95–96.

71. *Los Angeles Times,* Feb. 13, 1897.

72. Panunzio, "Intermarriage in Los Angeles," 695–96. The only other group to have a comparably high rate of intermarriage was the small population

of American Indians. Of 102 marriages involving Indians during the period, 22 were to white "Americans," 16 to Mexicans, 12 to foreign-born whites, and 8 to Filipinos (698).

73. Commonwealth Club of California, "Summary of Filipino Immigration Problems and Recommendations by the Commonwealth Club's Section on Immigration," Sept. 19, 1929, in Box 4, CIH; Vaughan MacCaughey, "The Filipino and Our Cheap Labor Problem," *Commonwealth* 5 (Nov. 5, 1929): 339–41.

74. See, for instance, Ruth Ewald, "A Survey of the Spanish-Speaking Peoples of the Chaffey Union High School District" (Master's thesis, Pomona College, 1922), 13, in "CAN II," Box 57, GBOP; Smith, "Development of the Mexican People in the Community of Watts," 44–45.

75. Young, *Pilgrims of Russian-Town*, 116–17.

76. Nettie Hale, 2619–1/2 e. trinity, vs. Frank Hale, 1012 e. 8th, Box 36, 1927, CIH.

77. Otilla Brown vs. Joseph Brown, 1921, Box 22, CIH.

78. "Jennie's Story," n.d., #281, Box 31, SRR; Young, *Pilgrims of Russian-Town*, 188; Griffith, *American Me*, 194.

79. Smith, "Development of Mexican People in the Community of Watts," 45; Gamio, *The Mexican Immigrant*, 198; Sanchez, *Becoming Mexican American*, 139–40.

80. Young, *Pilgrims of Russian-Town*, 173.

81. "Interview with Mrs. H," n.a., n.d., #235, Box 29, SRR.

82. Young, *Pilgrims of Russian-Town*, 173; Gilbert, "Los Angeles Chinatown," 3. For an account of a Mexican man and an Anglo woman who married in Los Angeles without apparent family or social resistance, see Louis Adamic, *From Many Lands* (New York: Harper Bros., 1940), 237–81.

83. George Weiss interview by ——— Lundy, c. Feb. 16, 1937, "Filipino" file, Box 142, FWP.

84. Panunzio, "Intermarriage in Los Angeles, 1924–1933," 692–99. Panunzio adjusted his figures so as not to include ethnic Mexicans who described themselves as "native-born whites" in the marriage application. Ricardo Romo conducted a statistical analysis of marriages involving Mexicans between 1917 and 1918. He found that 147 of 660 such marriages, or 22 percent, were mixed. Romo, *East Los Angeles*, 161.

85. Panunzio, "Intermarriage in Los Angeles," 692–98. Panunzio speculated that clerks ignorant of the antimiscegenation laws may have permitted intermarriages involving whites or may have assumed that "foreign" whites did not fall under the law's designation. The four black-white marriages involved black men. In each case, the husband was born outside the United States, which Panunzio believes explains why the marriages "got past the clerks." All of the other interracial marriages involved black women, a fact that Panunzio attributes to the large proportion of women (only 84 men to 100 women) in the city's black population at the time.

86. Gustafson, "Sociological Analysis," 151.

87. See, for example, "The Communist Situation in California," Report of Sub-Committee on Subversive Activities of the Crime Prevention Committee, Peace Officers Association of California, Oakland, Sept. 16–18, 1937.

88. See, for example, one sociologist's account of a Japanese-Mexican boy. William C. Smith, "Life History of Peter," n.d., #251, Box 29, SRR.

89. Chloe Holt, "Account of a Visit with a White Woman Married to a Japanese Man," Aug. 14, 1924, #104, Box 25, SRR.

90. Clara Gilbert and William C. Smith, "Los Angeles Chinatown," June 12, 1924, #B-24, Box 35, SRR. Masao Dodo also claimed that a Japanese home received a young Japanese girl from a Mexican family that had been caring for her. See Masao Dodo, "Miss C—," 1920, #B-422, Box 37, SRR.

91. William C. Smith, "Life History of Peter," n.d., #251, Box 29, SRR. The interviewer also noted that the boy's sister had no tendency toward delinquency.

92. Dorothy Siu interview, Jan. 12, 1979, and Nov. 6, 1980, #56, SCCAOHP; Interview with Hida Watanabe, from "Interviews regarding Melba Yonamura, Mixed Japanese-American High School Girl," Catherine Holt, #B-446, Box 37, SRR.

93. "Case Study of a Boy of Mixed Parentage" (no author), c. 1925, #280, Box 31, SRR.

94. Ramona Martin vs. Mr. Martin, 1921, Box 22, CIH. The outcome of the dispute was not recorded in the file; Pulguseria Mora de Matsusaka vs. Maria de Long, 1923, Box 26, CIH.

95. Gustafson, "Sociological Analysis," 167. Two other examples involving custody disputes for the offspring in Italian-Mexican families are described in Francisco Cardenas vs. Carolina Cardenas, 1927, Box 36; Romeo Rossy vs. Estanislau Guerrero, 1931, Box 40, CIH.

CHAPTER 6

1. On soapbox speakers and national reactions to them, see James W. Collins, "When Soap Box Meets Soap Box," *Saturday Evening Post*, Nov. 20, 1920.

2. For a summary of this movement, see Johnson, "A Serpent in the Garden."

3. Adler, "Watts: From Suburb to Black Ghetto," 197–98.

4. Douglas Flamming, "African-Americans and the Politics of Race in Progressive-Era Los Angeles," in Deverell and Sitton, eds., *California Progressivism Revisited*, 203–28; Sanchez, *Becoming Mexican American*, 250. More generally, see Katznelson, *City Trenches*, 110–15. Quote from George Weiss, interviewed by Lundy, Feb. 16, 1937, in "Filipino" File, Box 142, FWP.

5. Stimson, *Rise of the Labor Movement*, 227.

6. W. W. Robinson, *The Story of Pershing Square* (Los Angeles: Title Guarantee and Trust Co., 1931); Sanchez, *Becoming Mexican American*, 135–36.

7. McEuen, "Survey of the Mexicans," 68.

8. Timothy G. Turner, "Free Speech Ends at the Plaza," *Los Angeles Times Sunday Magazine*, July 14, 1935.

9. *Los Angeles Socialist*, July 15, 1905.

10. *Los Angeles Record*, Jan. 20, 1931; Rock, "Twenty Years on Skid Row," 6.

11. On the centrality of downtown during this period, see Robert Fogelson, *Downtown: Its Rise and Fall, 1880–1950* (New Haven: Yale University Press, 2001).

12. Ernest Jerome Hopkins, *Our Lawless Police: A Study of the Unlawful Enforcement of the Law* (New York: Viking, 1931), 152, 154.

13. For general histories of the Socialist Party in Los Angeles, see Paul Greenstein, *Bread and Hyacinths: The Rise and Fall of Utopian Los Angeles* (Los Angeles: Los Angeles Classics, 1992); Johnson, "A Serpent in the Garden"; Stimson, *Rise of the Labor Movement.*

14. On nineteenth-century strains of Socialist activity in Los Angeles, see Stimson, *Rise of the Labor Movement,* 218–25. More generally, see Francis Robert Shor, *Utopianism and Radicalism in Reforming America* (Westport, Conn.: Greenwood Press, 1997); Nick Salvatore, *Eugene V. Debs: Citizen and Socialist* (Urbana: University of Illinois Press, 1982).

15. Ralph E. Shaffer, "Radicalism in California, 1869–1929" (Ph.D. diss., University of California, Berkeley, 1962), 154. Advertisements for street meetings and larger lectures appeared in most issues of the *Los Angeles Socialist* and *Common Sense.* For a typical example, see *Common Sense,* July 14, 1906.

16. Johnson, "A Serpent in the Garden," 360–62; *Los Angeles Socialist,* July 22, 1905; *Common Sense,* Feb. 8, 1908.

17. Stimson, *Rise of the Labor Movement,* 243, 343–44; *Los Angeles Socialist,* July 15, 1905.

18. *Common Sense,* Mar. 7, 1908; Stimson, *Rise of Labor Movement,* 274.

19. *Common Sense,* May 27, 1907; *Los Angeles Herald,* June 23, 1908.

20. *Common Sense,* Apr. 27, 1907, June 28, July 11, 1908; *Los Angeles Times,* Feb. 5, Mar. 4, 1908; *Los Angeles Herald,* Feb. 27, 1908.

21. *Common Sense,* Mar. 7, 1908; July 25, 1908; *Los Angeles Herald,* Feb. 23, 1908, July 19, 1908.

22. *Arena* 40.266 (Oct. 1908): 350–51; *Common Sense,* Aug. 8, 1908; Shaffer, "Radicalism in California," 245; *Los Angeles Herald,* Aug. 10, 1908.

23. See, for example, Greenstein, *Bread and Hyacinths.* At least one historian has disputed the argument that Harriman's victory in the primary indicated he was the true front-runner for the office. The 50,000 votes Harriman received in the primary represented only a fraction of what he needed to win in the general election. Harriman actually received 85,000 votes in the general election but still lost badly to Alexander. James P. Kraft, "The Fall of Job Harriman's Socialist Party: Violence, Gender, and the Politics of Los Angeles, 1911," *Southern California Quarterly* 70 (spring 1988): 43–68.

24. This face mirrored the national membership of the Party, which in 1908 was 71 percent native-born white, with another 17 percent consisting of northern European immigrants. Charles Leinenweber, "The American Socialist Party and the New Immigrants," *Science and Society* 32 (winter 1968): 1–25.

25. *Common Sense,* Oct. 19, 1905; *Los Angeles Herald,* Feb. 24 and 27, 1908.

26. Women first achieved the right to vote in municipal elections in Los Angeles for the 1911 mayoral race. They remained excluded from national elections, however, until 1920. Kraft, "Fall of Job Harriman," 55–56, 64–68. For a description of Party women's home meetings, see *Common Sense,* Sept. 29, 1903.

27. *Common Sense,* Mar. 28, July 18, 1908; *Los Angeles Herald,* Feb. 24 and 26, 1908.

28. See Sherry Katz, "Socialist Women and Progressive Reform," and Judith Raftery, "Los Angeles Clubwomen and Progressive Reform," in Deverell and Sitton, eds., *California Progressivism Revisited*, 117–74; and Sherry Katz, "Dual Commitments: Feminism, Socialism, and Women's Political Activism in California, 1890–1920" (Ph.D. diss., University of California, Los Angeles, 1992).

29. See *Los Angeles Times*, Jan. 29, 1908; Los Angeles County Central Labor Council, *Executive Board and Council Meeting Minutes*, Mar. 26, 1909, Mar. 14 and June 10, 1910, Urban Archives Collection, California State University, Northridge (hereafter CLC).

30. For general histories of Magón and the PLM in the United States, see Juan Gómez-Quiñones, *Sembradores: Ricardo Flores Magón y el Partido Liberal Mexicano* (Los Angeles: UCLA Chicano Studies Center, 1973); W. Dirk Raat, *Revoltosos: Mexico's Rebels in the United States, 1903–1923* (College Station: Texas A&M Press, 1981).

31. See Raat, *Revoltosos*, 40–61; Gómez-Quiñones, *Sembradores*, 33–35.

32. See *Common Sense*, Sept. 21, Nov. 16, 1907, Mar. 14, 1908; Raat, *Revoltosos*, 49–51.

33. Escobar, "Chicano Protest," 145–66.

34. Raat, *Revoltosos*, 59–60.

35. Shaffer, "Radicalism in California," 162–63; *Los Angeles Socialist*, Jan. 11, Mar. 15, Oct. 25, 1902.

36. *Los Angeles Socialist*, July 12, 1902; *Common Sense*, Apr. 27, 1907. On the San Diego Free Speech fight, see Grace L. Miller, "The I.W.W. Free Speech Fight: San Diego, 1911–12," *Southern California Quarterly* 54 (1972): 211–38; Rosalie Shanks, "The I.W.W. Free Speech Movement: San Diego, 1912," *Journal of San Diego History* 19 (1973): 25–33.

37. Philip Foner, ed., *Black Socialist Preacher* (San Francisco: Synthesis Publications, 1983), 22–23.

38. Shaffer, "Radicalism in California," 209; Mar. 24 and 31, Apr. l 7, June 2, 1911, CLC; "Socialism and the Negro—Position of the Socialist Party Set Forth—Not Race Equality, but Economic Equality Demanded," *Los Angeles Socialist*, Nov. 21, 1903, 1; Johnson, "A Serpent in the Garden," 477; Kraft, "Fall of Job Harriman," 63. Adler paints a somewhat kinder picture of Socialist organizing among African American Angelenos in Watts: Adler, "Watts: From Suburb to Black Ghetto," 139–41.

39. Shor, *Utopianism and Radicalism in Reforming America*; Foner, *Black Socialist Preacher*, 28–30.

40. Gómez-Quiñones, *Sembradores*, 47. For an account of an ethnic Mexican who migrated to Los Angeles and became involved in the IWW, see Manuel Gamio's interview of "Guillermo Salorio" in *The Mexican Immigrant*, 128–30.

41. Hyman Weintraub, "The I.W.W. in California, 1905–1931" (Master's thesis, University of California, Los Angeles, 1947), 9–14, 297. Weintraub found publications in French, Italian, Spanish, Portuguese, Russian, Polish, "Slavish," Lithuanian, Hungarian, Swedish, and "Jewish." He did not find any in Asian langues, which may have accounted for their paltry success with those workers. On national IWW attempts to recruit Asians in America, see Daniel

Rosenberg, "The IWW and Organization of Asian Workers in Early Twentieth Century America," *Labor History* 36 (1995): 77–87.

42. The classic study of the IWW is Melvyn Dubovsky's *We Shall Be All: A History of the Industrial Workers of the World* (Urbana: University of Illinois Press, 1969).

43. Jimmie Hicks, *W. W. Robinson: A Biography and Bibliography* (Los Angeles: Ward Ritchie Press, 1970); Kimbrough, *Defender of the Angels,* 9.

44. Weintraub, "I.W.W. in California," 292.

45. Shaffer, "Radicalism in California," 209, 221, 355–58; *Los Angeles Examiner,* Feb. 3, 1919; *Los Angeles Times,* Feb. 17, 1919; B. M. Crogan to G. P. Reiman, Feb. 2, 1919, "IWW Activities File," Box 4, Military Intelligence Division, Plant Protection Files (Record Group 165), National Archives—Pacific Southwest Region, Laguna Niguel, California (hereafter Plant Protection). On masculinity and the IWW, see Francis Robert Shor, "'Virile Syndicalism' in Comparative Perspective: A Gender Analysis of the IWW in the United States and Australia," *International Labor and Working-Class History* 1999 (56): 65–77.

46. *Los Angeles Times,* Jan. 6, 1913. I am grateful to Mike Davis for bringing this citation to my attention. For accounts of IWW free speech fights in other parts of the United States during the same period, see Philip S. Foner, ed., *Fellow Workers and Friends: I.W.W. Free Speech Fights as Told by Participants*r (Westport, Conn.: Greenwood Press, 1981).

47. The account of this incident and following events is taken from December 26, 1913, to January 5, 1914, issues of the *Los Angeles Record* and the *Los Angeles Times;* also testimony of Job Harriman, Sept. 14–15, 1914, in U.S. Congress, Senate, Commission on Industrial Relations, *Industrial Relations* (64th Cong., 1st sess., 1916), vol. 6, 5803–4; Edward J. Escobar, *Race, Police, and the Making of a Political Identity: Mexican Americans and the Los Angeles Police Department, 1900–1945* (Berkeley: University of California Press, 1999), 42–49.

48. See especially *Los Angeles Times,* Dec. 30, 1913; Jan. 23, 1914; Escobar, *Race, Police, and the Making of a Political Identity,* 46–49.

49. *Los Angeles Times,* Jan. 5, 1914; Los Angeles Municipal Charities Commission, *First Annual Report* (July 1, 1913–July 1, 1914), 66–68.

50. *Los Angeles Times,* Apr. 1, 1917; Raat, *Revoltosos,* 276–77. For a more thorough discussion of this phenomenon, see Eric I. Boime, "Fluid Boundaries: Southern California, Baja California, and the Conflict over the Colorado River, 1848–1944" (Ph.D. diss., University of California, San Diego, 2002), 129–272; Eugene Keith Chamberlain, "The Magdalena Incident" (Master's thesis, University of California, Berkeley, 1939).

51. Quotations from *Los Angeles Times,* Apr. 1, 1917.

52. Cornelius C. Smith Jr., *Emilio Kosterlitsky: Eagle of Sonora and the Southwest Border* (Glendale, Calif.: Arthur H. Clark, 1970), 264–68. See also reports collected in rolls 871 and 873, Box 2776, War Department, Military Intelligence Division, National Archives, Washington, D.C. (hereafter MID).

53. On the strategy of the program, see, for example, G. W. Burk to Edmund Leigh, Ap. 12, 1918, Box 2, Plant Protection Records. The collection consists in large part of inspections and "officer" lists of workers enrolled in the program.

54. *Los Angeles Times,* Sept. 20, 1917; Weintraub, "I.W.W. in California," 140; see also Edmund Leigh to MID, Mar. 12, 1918, roll 875, Box 2776, MID.

55. See Raoul Palma to Librado Rivera, Aug. 5, 1921, Mexican Files, roll 875, Box 2776, MID.

56. Kate Crane Gartz, *The Parlor Provocateur: From Salon to Soapbox* (Pasadena, Calif.: Mary Craig Sinclair, 1923), 34–35.

57. *Los Angeles Times,* May 7 and 15, 1917; Laborers of San Salvador to L.A. Chief of Police, Apr. 22, 1918, roll 875, Box 2776, MID; Sylvia Lubow, "The Espionage Act in Southern California" (Master's thesis, University of California, Los Angeles, 1968), 137.

58. *Los Angeles Times,* May 28, 1917; Escobar, "Chicano Protest," 179–81; Howard A. DeWitt, *Images and Racial Volence in California Politics, 1917–1930* (San Francisco: R&E, 1975), 11.

59. *Los Angeles Express,* July 9 and 15, 1918; *Los Angeles Examiner,* Sept. 9, 1918; DeWitt, *Images of Ethnic and Racial Violence,* 13–14, 38. See also materials in Scrapbook III-A, Marshall Stimson Collection, Huntington Library; Guy M. Bishop, "Strong Voices and 100 Percent Patriotism: The Four Minute Men of Los Angeles County," *Southern California Quarterly* 77 (1995): 199–214. For a contemporary account of national trends in countersubversive soapbox speaking during and after World War I, see Collins, "When Soap Box Meets Soap Box."

60. Vernon Monroe McCombs, "Stopping the Reds," *El Mexicano* 7 (Jan.–Mar. 1919): 2–3.

61. William Deverell, "My America or Yours? The Los Angeles School Board Fight of 1923," in Deverell and Sitton, eds., *Metropolis in the Making,* 277–301. For a general history of the BAF, see Edward Layton, "The Better America Federation: A Case Study of Super-Patriotism," *Pacific Historical Review* 30.2 (1961): 137–47.

62. Better America Federation, *Weekly Bulletin,* Nov. 24, 1920; George T. Atchley to BAF, Oct. 28, 1920, BAF Pamphlets, California Room, California State Library; "Better America Federation," Box 1, Margaret A. Kerr Papers, Hoover Library, Stanford University; *Los Angeles Times,* Nov. 17, 1920.

63. Woodworth Clum to Elek Markowitz, Mar. 14, 1921, folder 46, Box 5; Schedule of speeches, n.d., in file 9, Box 6, John Randolph Haynes Papers, Department of Special Collections, UCLA.

64. Woodworth Clum to "Miss Smith," Dec. 3, 1920, file 44, Box 5; *Weekly News Letter* (BAF), Feb. 29, 1920, file 1, Box 6, Haynes Papers.

65. See Woodrow C. Whitten, "Criminal Syndicalism and the Law in California: 1919–1927," *Transactions of the American Philosophical Society* 59 (1969): pt. 2.

66. *Los Angeles Times,* Nov. 15, 17, and 19, 1919; Whitten, "Criminal Syndicalism," 33, 38.

67. Leone Esmond to Mortimer Downing, June 4, 1921, roll 875, MID; "Summary of Prosecutions under California Criminal Syndicalism Law" (no author), 1926, Box 107, GBOP.

68. Stewart Bird, Dan Georgakas, and Deborah Shaffer, eds., *Solidarity Forever: An Oral History of the IWW* (Chicago: Lake View Press, 1985), 152–54;

Clinton J. Taft, "Fifteen Years on Freedom's Front," American Civil Liberties Union, Los Angeles, 1939, 13–14; "Mob Violence on the Rampage in San Pedro" and "Mob Scalds Children," IWW pamphlets (no dates), Southern California Library for Social Studies and Research (hereafter SCL).

69. Kate Crane Gartz, *Letters of Protest* (Pasadena: Mary Craig Sinclair, c. 1936), 32–33.

70. See material in folder 29, Box 1, Leo Gallagher Papers, SCL.

71. Files #1567 (1912), #601 (1913), LACCF. On the general problems of urban congestion during this period, particularly with respect to automobile use, see Scott Bottles, *Los Angeles and the Automobile: The Making of the Modern City* (Berkeley: University of California Press, 1987).

72. Files #327 (1914), #14 (Jan. 4, 1915), #1022 (Apr. 10, 1915), #1032 (Apr. 12, 1915), #887 and #1064 (Mar. 29, 1915), LACCF; Taft, "Fifteen Years," 21–22. Seewerker, *Nuestro Pueblo,* 58; Shaffer, "Radicalism in California," 239–40.

73. "Report of Committee to Investigate Soap Box Orators on Los Angeles Street," Dec. 15, 1922, file #147 (Jan. 9, 1923), LACCF; Charlotta A. Bass, *Forty Years: Memories from the Pages of a Newspaper* (Los Angeles: Charlotta Bass, 1960), 37.

74. File #4395 (Aug. 9, 1923) and #4579 (Aug. 22, 1923), LACCF.

75. See text of Ordinance No. 20,534, sec. 4, copy in folder 5, Box 3, Southern California American Civil Liberties Union Collection, Department of Special Collections, UCLA (hereafter SCACLU).

76. *Meet Me at Brooklyn and Soto,* video, Jewish Historical Society of Southern California, c. 1996.

77. A. W. Griewe, "A Study of the Habitues of the Downtown Parks of Los Angeles, with a View to Ascertaining Their Constituency, Their Social Process, and Their Relation to the Larger Community Life" (Master's thesis, University of Southern California, 1926), 32.

78. "Seldom is the police department called upon to administer forcible means to preserve order. The average habitue is law abiding, whether he speaks from the soap box, or listens from the sidewalk." Griewe, "Habitues of the Downtown Parks," 106.

79. Adamic, *The Truth about Los Angeles,* 10–16.

CHAPTER 7

1. Turner's story appears in a collection of his writings. See Timothy G. Turner, *Turn off the Sunshine: Tales of Los Angeles on the Wrong Side of the Tracks* (Caldwell, Ind.: Claxton, 1942).

2. Paul Buhle, "Jews and American Communism: The Cultural Question," *Radical History Review* 23 (spring 1980): 9–33; John J. Ballam, "Report of the California Situation," 1929, Delo 1796, Reel 126, Communist Party of the United States of America Records, Library of Congree, Washington, D.C. (hereafter CPUSA).

3. "Two Decades of Progress," 13; Lil Carlson, interview with author; Miriam Johnson, interview with author, June 21, 1999; Ralph E. Shaffer, "The

Formative Years of Communism in the West: The California Phase, 1919–1924," unpublished manuscript, n.d., in Dorothy Healey Collection, Department of Special Collections, California State University, Long Beach; Peggy Dennis, "Memories from the '20s," in *Red Diapers: Growing Up in the Communist Left,* ed. Judy Kaplan and Linn Shapiro (Urbana: University of Illinois Press, 1998), 17–19.

4. Peggy Dennis (Carson), *The Autobiography of an American Communist* (Westport and Berkeley: Lawrence Hill and Creative Arts Book Co., 1977), esp. 24; Shaffer, "The Formative Years of Communism."

5. For an overview of the CPUSA, see Paul Buhle, *Marxism in the United States: Remapping the History of the American Left* (London: Verso, 1987).

6. See *Conditions in Los Angeles,* Film and Photo League, 1934, Southern California Library for Social Studies and Research, Los Angeles, California. For a general history of Los Angeles during the 1930s, see Leonard Leader, *Los Angeles and the Great Depression* (New York: Garland, 1991).

7. Davis, "From Oasis to Metropolis"; Mark Wild, "'If You Ain't Got That Do-Re-Mi': The Los Angeles Border Patrol and White Migration in Depression-Era California," *Southern California Quarterly* 83 (fall 2001) : 317–34. For a general account of the depression's impact on the state, see Kevin Starr, *Endangered Dreams: The Great Depression in California* (New York: Oxford University Press, 1996).

8. Francisco E. Balderrama and Raymond Rodriquez, *Decade of Betrayal: Mexican Repatriation in the Thirties* (Albuquerque: University of New Mexico Press, 1995); Hoffman, *Unwanted Mexican Americans.*

9. Karl Yoneda, "The Heritage of Sen Katayama," *Political Affairs* (Mar. 1975): 38–57; Scott Tadao Kurashige, "Transforming Los Angeles: Black and Japanese American Struggles for Racial Equality in the 20th Century" (Ph.D. diss., University of California, Los Angeles, 2000).

10. On the connection between Mexican activism in California and the Mexican Revolution, see Devra Weber, *Dark Sweat, White Gold: California Farm Workers, Cotton, and the New Deal* (Berkeley: University of California Press, 1994); Douglas Monroy, "Anarquismo y Comunismo: Mexican Radicalism and the Communist Party in Los Angeles during the 1930s," *Labor History* 24 (1983): 34–59; Dorothy Healey, interview with author.

11. Flamming, "African Americans and the Politics of Race," 203–28; Josh Sides, "Working Away: African American Migration and Community in Los Angeles from the Great Depression to 1954" (Ph.D. diss., University of California, Los Angeles, 1999).

12. The classic top-down study is Theodore Draper's *The Roots of American Communism* (New York: Viking, 1957). This argument, with all of its shortcomings, has recently reappeared in "postrevisionist" histories based on sources recovered in post–Soviet Russia. See, for example, John Earl Haynes, Harvey Klehr, and Kyrill M. Anderson, *The Soviet World of American Communism* (New Haven: Yale University Press, 1998). Both generations of scholarship overestimate the influence of party bureaucracy on the everyday activities of rank-and-file Communists.

13. Dorothy Healey, interview with author, Oct. 22, 1998. See also Memo from CPUSA Central Office, New York, Oct. 1934, 1934 folder, Communist Party Chronological File, SCL; testimony of Meyer Beylin, "HUAC–aka McCormack Committee," 8–4, pt. 1, Box 5, n. 3, CRC. Other local studies of the CPUSA that corroborate this argument are Mark Naison, *Communists in Harlem during the Depression* (New York: Grove Press, 1984); Robin D. G. Kelley, *Hammer and Hoe: Alabama Communists during the Great Depression* (Chapel Hill: University of North Carolina Press, 1990).

14. Alice McGrath, interview, 61–68; Lil Carlson, interview with author. See also Al Bryan, "Los Angeles County Communist Party: A Manual for Organization," Los Angeles: Communist Party Education, Department, 1938, 1938 file, Communist Party Chronological File, SCL.

15. On the uneven relationships between Communists and African Americans, for example, see Kelley, *Hammer and Hoe;* and *Race Rebels: Culture, Politics and the Black Working Class* (New York: Free Press, 1994), 103–58; Earl Ofari Hutchinson, *Blacks and Reds: Race and Class in Conflict* (East Lansing: Michigan State University Press, 1995); Mark I. Solomon, *Red and Black: Communism and African Americans, 1929–1935* (New York: Garland, 1988).

16. Ben Dobbs, UCLA Oral History, 49; U.S. Congress, House, Special Committee on Un-American Activities, *Hearings,* no. 73-D.C.-5 (report 7), 73d Cong., 2d sess., 263 (hereafter HUAC Hearings); *Western Worker,* July 1, 1932; "To All Communist Party Unite in California, Arizona, and Nevada," San Francisco, June 29, 1933, Delo 296, Reel 255, CPUSA; Memo from John Leach to "Central Committee," July 12, 1935, Delo 3875, Reel 297, CPUSA.

17. Rose Pesotta, *Bread upon the Waters* (rpt. Ithaca: Cornell University Press, 1987), 333–42. See also Luis Leobardo Arroyo, "Industrial Unionism and the Los Angeles Furniture Industry, 1918–1954" (Ph.D. diss., University of California, Los Angeles, 1979); Perry and Perry, *History of the Los Angeles Labor Movement,* esp. 194.

18. See Box 5, file 10, "McCormack Committee: Reports, 1934," Community Relations Council of Jewish Federation Council of Los Angeles Collection (CRC), California State University, Northridge; testimony of William F. Hynes, HUAC Hearings, 242; "How to Organize Mass Meetings," Workers Library, New York, 1939, 41; Dorothy Healey, interview with author; Lil Carlson, interview with author.

19. The CPLA's practice of purging its records makes it difficult to get accurate figures of party membership. Fragmentary recruiting reports appear throughout the CPUSA records. See, for example, "Analysis of Membership, Los Angeles, District 13," June 14, 1931, Delo 2499, Reel 189; "Analysis of New Members Recruited During Month of April, 1934," Delo 3613, Reel 280; "Chart from January First to September First, 1935," Delo 3876, Reel 297, CPUSA.

20. "Two Decades of Progress: Communist Party, Los Angeles County 1919–1939," Los Angeles, 1939, 11; Richard O. Boyer, "Pettis Perry: The Story of a Working Class Leader," Self-Defense Committee of the 17 Smith Act Victims, New York, 1952.

21. Material on these and other CPLA activities located in Reel 125, National Republic Collection (NPC), Hoover Library, Stanford University; "Two Decades of Progress."

22. *Los Angeles Times,* June 6, 20, 1934; Elaine Black Yoneda Oral History, interviewed by Betsy Mitson and Arthur Hansen, California State University Fullerton Oral History Archives, 1974,.18–19; Karl Yoneda, *Ganbatte,* 15; Lil Carlson, interview with author.

23. See, for example, Dorothy Healey's account of Party work in the Imperial Valley strikes. Dorothy Healey Oral History, 91–107; Devra Weber, "The Organization of Mexican Agricultural Workers: Imperial Valley and Los Angeles: An Oral History Approach," *Aztlan* 3.2 (1973): 324; Howard DeWitt, *Violence in the Fields: California Farm Labor Unionization during the Great Depression* (Saratoga, Calif.: Century 21, 1980), 57–63.

24. On the councils, see *Hunger Fighter,* no. 2 (April–May 1932); Daniel J. Leab, "'United We Eat': The Creation and Organization of the Unemployed Councils in 1930," *Labor History* 8.2 (fall 1967): 300–315; Leader, *Los Angeles and the Great Depression,* 183; *Los Angeles Times,* Feb. 5, 1932; *Western Worker,* Sept. 1, Oct. 1, 1932; Clark Kerr, "Productive Enterprises of the Unemployed, 1931–1938" (Ph.D. diss., University of California, Berkeley, 1939), 114–22. The Communist parentage of the councils apparently remained concealed enough to escape the notice of a few scholars. Kerr, for instance, mistakenly suggests that the Party infiltrated preexisting Unemployed Councils, when in fact they created them.

25. Letter to Joseph Kramer, May 3, 1934 (no author), pt. 1, Box 13, "Communism" file, and June 25 and Aug. 4, 1934, reports, "F. D. Shreve, Investigative Reports," Box 5, CRC; *Los Angeles Times,* Jan. 4, 1930.

26. See, for example, Dorothy Healey's account of her street-speaking experiences in California. Dorothy Healey Oral History Transcript, interviewed by Joel Gardner, UCLA Oral History program, 1982, 48–50; *Los Angeles Herald Express,* Feb. 11, 1931.

27. "LAPD—Intelligence Division (aka the Red Squad)," Sept. 15, 1933, pt. 1, Box 30, n. 21, CRC; Steve Nelson, James R. Barrett, and Rob Buck, *Steve Nelson, American Radical* (Pittsburgh: University of Pittsburgh Press, 1981), 242–46.

28. U.S. Congress, Senate, Committee on Education and Labor, *Violations of Free Speech and the Rights of Labor* (78th Cong., 1st sess., 1943) vol. 1, 129–47, vol. 2, 1001–3; letter to Joseph Kramer, May 2, 1934, pt. 1, Box 13, n. 21, CRC; see also memoranda in pt. 1, Box 30, n. 21, CRC.

29. See, for example, accounts in the *Los Angeles Record,* May 2, 1930; Sept. 2, 1930; *Los Angeles Times,* Sept. 2, 1930; Jan. 19, 1933.

30. Dorothy Healey, UCLA Oral History, 61; Dennis, *Autobiography of an American Communist,* 49. See also accounts and photographs in *Los Angeles Times,* Mar. 7, 1930: *Los Angeles Record,* Sept. 2, 1930.

31. Dennis, *Autobiography of an American Communist,* 46–48; Lil Carlson, "A California Girlhood," in Kaplan and Shapiro, eds., *Red Diapers,* 25.

32. See the discussion in "The Chief Shortcomings and Lessons of our 3-month Work, Jan. 24 to May 1, 1931," Delo 2497, Reel 189, CPUSA.

33. *Los Angeles Times,* Feb. 27, 1930; *Los Angeles Record,* Feb. 27, 1930. I thank Phoebe Kropp for bringing these events to my attention.

34. Miriam Johnson, interview with author.

35. *Los Angeles Times,* Mar. 7, 1930; *Los Angeles Record,* Mar. 7, 1930.

36. *Los Angeles Times,* May 2, 1930; "Two Decades of Progress," 14; Dobbs, UCLA Oral History, 32–33.

37. Taft, "Fifteen Years," 21–22; *Los Angeles Times,* Feb. 19, 1931; *Western Worker,* Oct. 1, 1932.

38. Lil Carlson, interview with author; *Los Angeles Times,* Mar. 20, 1931; material in "LAPD 1935–1936" folder, CRC; "The Communist Situation in California," Report of Sub-Committee on Subversive Activities of the Crime Prevention Committee, Peace Officers Association of California, Sept. 16–18, 1937, 5.

39. See materials in Box 1, file 30, Leo Gallagher Papers, SCL; Taft, "Fifteen Years," 25; file #5912 (Dec. 5, 1933), LACCF.

40. Yoneda, *Ganbatte,* 17.

41. Letter to Joseph Kramer, May 3, 1934 (no author), CRC; *Los Angeles Times,* May 2, 1934; see also Sept. 7, 1929.

42. *Los Angeles Times,* Jan. 20, 1931. See also *Western Worker,* Nov. 20, Dec. 25, 1933.

43. "The Communist Situation in California" (Sept. 16–18, 1937) and "The Crime Prevention Committee's Report on Subversive Activities" (Oct. 17–19, 1940), Sub-Committee on Subversive Activities, Crime Prevention Committee, Peace Officers Association of California.

44. Robert A. Hill, ed., *The FBI's RACON: Racial Conditions in the United States during World War II* (Boston: Northeastern University Press, 1995), 373; *Los Angeles Herald Examiner,* Sept. 21, 1932; *Los Angeles Times,* June 2, Aug. 8, 1934, June 4, 1932; *Western Worker,* Apr. 1, 1932; Apr. 24, Aug. 7, 1933; "Two Decades of Progress," 14; Earle Tinney testimony, folder 7, Box 2, Leo Gallagher Papers, SCL; Ben Dobbs, Oral History, 91–92; Elaine Black Yoneda, Oral History, 22; Alice McGrath, Oral History, 89–91.

45. A *Times* photographer captured the beating on film. See *Los Angeles Times,* Feb. 11, 1931; Yoneda, *Ganbatte,* 41.

46. "LA County: Manual for Organization," SCL, and "Japanese Reds— May, 1934," sec. 1, Box 13, file 21, "Communism" file, CRC. Investigators, probably working from subscription lists purloined from radical publications, counted more than 350 ethnic Japanese "Communists" in Los Angeles.

47. *Rafu Shimpo,* May 2, 1934; *Los Angeles Times,* Aug. 2, 1930; Yoneda, *Ganbatte,* 37.

48. Dorothy Healey, UCLA Oral History, 47–48; *Los Angeles Record,* Sept. 2, 1930. Steve Nelson noted that California had an unusually large number of Communist women in leadership positions. Nelson, Barrett, and Buck, *Steve Nelson,* 256.

49. Dorothy Healey, interview with author; Lil Carlson, interview with author; Dennis, *Autobiography of an American Communist,* 41–42, 56–57.

50. Some scholars have argued that masculine imagery excluded women's participation in the Communist Party. See, for example, Elizabeth Faue, *Com-*

munity of Suffering and Struggle: Women, Men, and the Labor Movement in Minneapolis, 1915–1945 (Chapel Hill: University of North Carolina Press, 1991); Kelley, *Race Rebels,* 112–14; Robert Shaffer, "Women and the Communist Party USA: 1930–1940" (n.d.), Department of Special Collections, California State University, Long Beach. In Los Angeles, at least, this was clearly not the case.

51. *Los Angeles Times,* Mar. 7, 1930; "California's Brown Book," Los Angeles Committee, American League Against War and Fascism, c. 1935.

52. Karl Yoneda mentions several other Japanese women who played prominent roles in Japanese Communist circles. Yoneda, *Ganbatte,* 21–23; "Two Decades of Progress," 22.

53. See, for example, *Los Angeles Times,* Nov. 1, 1933.

54. E. B. Yoneda Oral History, 4–12, 21–31; *Los Angeles Times,* Dec. 5, 1931. See also Raineri, *The Red Angel.*

55. Boyer, "Pettis Perry"; testimony of Pettis Perry, HUAC-McCormack Hearings, 1934; "Twenty Years of Progress," 11.

56. Articles in the short-lived Japanese CP newspaper *Doho* provide some excellent illustrations of the ideological basis of this principle of interethnic cooperation based on commonalities within distinct ethnic histories. See, e.g., Apr. 5 and 25, Sept. 5, Oct. 5, and Nov. 1, 1939.

57. One other major political movement of the period, Upton Sinclair's End Poverty in California (EPIC) program, proved extremely popular among white residents of the central city. But its focus on electoral politics, which appeared most dramatically during Sinclair's 1934 campaign for California governor, left little room for the participation of noncitizens, especially Asians and Mexicans. Many African Americans also distrusted Sinclair because of his connections to Southern white politicians (his father-in-law was Mississippi senator John Sharp Williams). See Loren Miller, interviewed by Lawrence B. de Graaf, Apr. 29, 1967, CSUFOHP, 14. Moreover, EPIC's refusal to address noneconomic issues also turned off some Angelenos, according to *Los Angeles Record* columnist Reuben Boroughs. Reuben Boroughs, interviewed by Elizabeth I. Dixon, 1968, University of California Oral History Program, Department of Special Collections, UCLA.

58. Ben Dobbs, UCLA Oral History, 45–46; Hutchinson, *Blacks and Reds,* 227–36.

59. Mario T. Garcia, *Memoirs of Chicano History: The Life and Narrative of Bert Corona* (Berkeley: University of California Press, 1994), 127–28; Monroy, "Anarquismo y Comunismo"; Carlos Bulosan, *America Is In the Heart* (New York: Harcourt, Brace, 1946), 266–70; Sides, "Working Away," 210; Loren Miller, Oral History, 15. According to Adler, "Watts: From Suburb to Black Ghetto," 221, Pettis Perry received only 3 percent of the black vote in Watts in his 1934 race for lieutenant governor.

60. Healey, interview with author. See also Healey, UCLA Oral History, 55–56; Yoneda, *Ganbatte,* 34–5.

61. See *Hunger Fighter,* Sept. 8, 1934; Pesotta, *Bread upon the Waters,* 34–35; Arroyo, "Industrial Unionism and the Los Angeles Furniture Industry."

62. Miriam Johnson, interview with author. See also Carlson, "California Girlhood," 20–26.

63. Notable examples are Michael Denning, *The Cultural Front: The Laboring of American Culture in the Twentieth Century* (London: Verso, 1996); Buhle, *Marxism in the United States.*

64. "When and How to Recruit," CPUSA, c. 1938, 1939 folder, and "Resolution and Proposals for Los Angeles County Convention, March 27–28, 1937," 1937 folder, Communist Party Chronological File, SCL; Peace Officers Association, "Communist Situation in California" (1937), 45; "Local Civil Liberties Committee: Report 1937–8," ACLU, 1938.

65. Leon L. Lewis to Charles Kramer, May 3, 1934, pt. 1, Box 5, CRC; *Los Angeles Times,* May 2, 1936; May 2, 1937; May 2, 1938; May 2, 1939.

66. For a similar argument in a different context, see Kelley, *Hammer and Hoe.*

67. Dorothy Healey, interview with author; Ben Dobbs, UCLA Oral History, 86.

68. Timothy G. Turner, "Free Speech Ends at the Plaza," *Los Angeles Sunday Times Magazine,* July 14, 1935, 16–18; Los Angeles Municipal Code—Ord. 77,000, sec. 14.20, copy in Box 3, folder 5, SCACLU.

CONCLUSION

1. Kariann Akemi Yokota, "From Little Tokyo to Bronzeville and Back: Ethnic Communities in Transition" (Master's thesis, University of California, Los Angeles, 1996); Kim Fong Tom, "The Participation of the Chinese in the Community Life of Los Angeles" (Master's thesis, University of Southern California, 1944), 37.

2. Josh A. Sides, "Battle on the Home Front: African American Shipyard Workers in World War II Los Angeles," *California History* 75 (1996): 250–63.

3. Pascoe, "Miscegenation Law," 61–63; Loren Miller, *The Petitioners: The Story of the Supreme Court of the United States and the Negro* (New York: Pantheon, 1966), 321–29.

4. On the labor movement, see Josh Sides, "Battle on the Home Front," 250–63; Kevin Allen Leonard, " 'In the Interest of All Races': African Americans and Interracial Cooperation in Los Angeles during and after World War II," in de Graaf, Mulroy, and Taylor, eds., *Seeking El Dorado,* 309–40, and " 'Brothers under the Skin?': African Americans, Mexican Americans, and World War II in California," in *The Way We Really Were: The Golden State during the Second World War,* ed. Roger Lotchin (Urbana: University of Illinois Press, 2000): 187–214; Modell, *Economics and Politics of Racial Accommodation,* 124–26, 140–53. On race relations organizations, see Shana Beth Bernstein, "Building Bridges at Home in a Time of Global Conflict: Inter-racial Cooperation and the Fight for Civil Rights in Los Angeles, 1933–54" (Ph.D. diss., Stanford University, 2003); Allison Varzally, "Ethnic Crossings: The Making of a Non-White Identity in the Second Quarter of Twentieth Century California" (Ph.D. diss., University of California, Los Angeles, 2002); Kevin Leonard, "Years of Hope,

Days of Fear: The Impact of World War II on Race Relations in Los Angeles" (Ph.D. diss., University of California, Davis, 1992).

5. Eduardo Obregón Pagán, *Murder at the Sleepy Lagoon: Zoot Suits, Race, and Riot in Wartime L.A.* (Chapel Hill: University of North Carolina Press, 2003); Mauricio Mazon, *The Zoot Suit Riots: The Psychology of Annihilation* (Austin: University of Texas Press, 1984); Escobar, *Race, Police, and the Making of a Political Identity,* 155–253; Bryant et al., eds., *Central Avenue Sounds,* esp. 177, 272–73, 299–300, 404. More generally, see Kyle Julien, "Sounding the City : Jazz, African American Nightlife, and the Articulation of Race in 1940s Los Angeles" (Ph.D. diss., University of California Irvine, 2000).

6. Sides, "Battle on the Home Front"; Collins, *Black Los Angeles,* 48–68; Tom, "Participation of the Chinese," 21–32. See also Marilynn Johnson, *The Second Gold Rush: Oakland and the East Bay in World War II* (Berkeley: University of California Press, 1993).

7. Hill, *The FBI's RACON,* 373–82.

8. Kenneth T. Jackson, *Crabgrass Frontier: The Suburbanization of the United States* (New York: Oxford University Press, 1985), 196–218; Dana Cuff, *The Provisional City: Los Angeles Stories of Architecture and Urbanism* (Cambridge, Mass.: MIT Press, 2000), 150–51.

9. Gustafson, "Ecological Survey," 87–88; Vorspan and Gartner, *History of the Jews of Los Angeles,* 242–44; Neil C. Sandberg, *Jewish Life in Los Angeles: A Window to Tomorrow* (New York: University Press of America, 1986), 43–46.

10. "Negro Survey," c. 1935, front section, 6, American Design Collection, Huntington Library; Collins, *Black Los Angeles,* esp. 26–28; Adler, "Watts: From Suburb to Black Ghetto," 236–37, 262, 265; Irving C. Hendrick, *The Education of Non-Whites in California, 1849–1970* (San Francisco: R&E), 105; "Statement of the Los Angeles Communist Party on the Proposed Budget of the Board of Education," Aug. 1, 1946, in "1940s file," Communist Party vertical file, SCL; Lloyd H. Fisher, *The Problem of Violence: Observations on Race Conflict in Los Angeles* (Los Angeles: Haynes Foundation, 1946), 10–11.

11. According to Robert Fogelson, American urban planners and politicians had already developed the rationale and rhetoric for redevelopment by the 1930s. *Downtown: Its Rise and Fall,* 317–80. On proposed redevelopment programs in Los Angeles during the 1930s, see material collected in "Housing 1935–9" file, John Anson Ford papers, Huntington Library (hereafter Ford Papers).

12. On the transformation of downtown districts during this period and its impact on central city populations, see Eric R. Avila, *Popular Culture in the Age of White Flight: Fear and Fantasy in Los Angeles* (Berkeley: University of California Press, 2004); Cuff, *Provisional City,* 272–309; Don Parson, "The Search for a Centre: The Recomposition of Race, Class and Space in Los Angeles," *International Journal of Urban and Regional Research* 17 (1993): 232–40; Parson, "'This Modern Marvel': Bunker Hill, Chavez Ravine, and the Politics of Modernism in Los Angeles," *Southern California Quarterly* 75 (1993): 333–50; Parson, "Los Angeles' 'Headline-Happy Public Housing War,'" *Southern California Quarterly* 65 (1983): 251–85.

13. Eric R. Avila, "The Folklore of the Freeway: Space, Culture, and Identity in Postwar Los Angeles," *Aztlán* 23 (1998): 14–31; Plengvidhya, "Study of Changes in the Services of All Nations Foundation."

14. Collins, *Black Los Angeles,* 14; Bernard Marchand, *The Emergence of Los Angeles: Population and Housing in the City of Dreams, 1940–70* (London: Pion, 1986), 92–4; Jo{at}o H. Costa Vargas, "Blacks in the City of Angels' Dust" (Ph.D. diss., University of California, San Diego, 1999), 77–92.

15. Sides, "Working Away"; Gustafson, "Ecological Survey," 87–88; Griswold del Castillo, *The Los Angeles Barrio,* 146; Rudolfo Acuña, *Anything But Mexican: Chicanos in Contemporary Los Angeles* (London: Verso, 1996); Sanchez, *Becoming Mexican American,* 77.

16. Japanese American Citizens League to John Anson Ford, Oct. 3, 1949, "Japanese" file, Box 74; Arthur F. Miley to John Anson Ford, July 12 ,1943, "Negro" file, Box 76; "Statistical Appendix, City Housing Authority," 1945, "Housing 1940–4" file, Box 65; City Housing Authority, "Comparative Summary—Group Occupation, December 1948," in "Housing 1940–44" file, Box 65, Ford papers; Cuff, *Provisional City,* esp. 120–227; Parson, "Los Angeles' 'Headline Happy Public Housing War,'" 251–54.

17. See Greg Hise, *Magnetic Los Angeles: Planning the Twentieth Century Metropolis* (Baltimore: Johns Hopkins University Press, 1997); Becky Nicolaides, "'Where the Working Man Is Welcomed': Working-Class Suburbs in Los Angeles, 1900–40," *Pacific Historical Review* 68 (1999): 517–59; Mike Davis, "Sunshine and the Open Shop: Ford and Darwin in 1920s Los Angeles," in Sitton and Deverell, eds., *Metropolis in the Making,* 96–122. More generally, see Allen Pred, "The Intrametropolitan Location of American Manufacturing," in *Internal Structure of the City: Reading on Space and the Environment,* ed. Larry S. Bourne (New York: 1971), 384–85; Fogelson, *Downtown: Its Rise and Fall,* 194–95.

18. Edward W. Soja, *Postmodern Geographies: The Reassertion of Space in Critical Social Theory* (London: Verso, 1989); Allen Scott, "Industrial Urbanism in Southern California: Post-Fordist Civic Dilemmas and Opportunities," *Contention* 5 (1995): 39–65.

19. McWilliams, *Southern California Country,* 326. On the postwar segregation of urban populations in Los Angeles, see Allen and Turner, *The Ethnic Quilt,* 45–52; Eshref Shevky and Marylin Williams, *The Social Areas of Los Angeles: Analysis and Typology* (Berkeley: University of California Press, 1949), 47–74; Mike Davis, *City of Quartz: Excavating the Future in Los Angeles* (London: Verso, 1990).

20. Katherine Underwood, "Promoting Minority Representation: Edward Roybal and the Los Angeles City Council, 1949–1962," *Pacific Historical Review* 66 (1997): 399–425; Rafael J. Sonenshein, *Politics in Black and White: Race and Power in Los Angeles* (Princeton: Princeton University Press, 1993).

21. Avila, "The Folklore of the Freeway"; Gerald Horne, *Fire This Time: The Watts Uprising and the 1960s* (Charlottesville: University Press of Virginia, 1995); Vargas, "Blacks in the City of Angels Dust," esp. 108–36.

22. John H. Burma, "Interethnic Marriage in Los Angeles, 1948–59," *Social Forces* 42 (Dec. 1963): 156–65; Frank G. Mittelbach, Joan W. Moore, and

Ronald McDaniel, "Intermarriage of Mexicans," Advance Report #6, Mexican-American Study Project, Division of Research, Graduate School of Business Administration, UCLA, 1966.

23. Anthony Macias, "From Pachuco Boogie to Latin Jazz: Mexican Americans, Popular Music, and Urban Culture in Los Angeles, 1940–1965" (Ph.D. diss., University of Michigan, 2001); Matt Garcia, *A World of Its Own: Race, Labor, and Citrus in the Making of Greater Los Angeles, 1900–1970* (Berkeley: University of California Press, 2001), 189–214.

24. Collins, *Black Los Angeles,* 29; *Common Ground,* Sept. 10, 1945, "Japanese" file, Box 74, Ford Papers; *Los Angeles Daily News,* Mar. 4, 1947; Horne, *Fire This Time,* 35; Lloyd H. Fisher, *The Problem of Violence: Observations on Race Conflict in Los Angeles* (Chicago: American Council on Race Relations, 1947).

25. Recent scholarship on ethnoracial relations in Los Angeles tends to place discussions in a context of potential conflict. See, for example, Eui-Young Yu and Edward T. Chang, eds., *Multiethnic Coalition Building in Los Angeles* (Claremont, Calif.: Regina Books/Institute for Asian American and Pacific Asian Studies, 1995); Edward T. Chang and Russell C. Leong, eds., *Los Angeles— Struggles toward Multiethnic Community: Asian American, African American, and Latino Perspectives* (Seattle: University of Washington Press, 1994); Paul Ong, Kye Young Park, and Yasmine Tong, "The Korea-Black Conflict and the State," in *The New Asian Immigration in Los Angeles and Global Restructuring,* ed. Paul Ong, Edna Bonacich, and Lucie Cheng (Philadelphia: Temple University Press, 1994), 264–94.

26. Manuel Castells, *The City and the Grassroots: A Cross-Cultural Theory of Urban Social Movements* (London: Edward Arnold, 1983), 171.

27. My argument here parallels that by Néstor García Canclini, who claims that in recent decades the use of the city for "political theatricalization" has been reduced, leading to the city's "loss of meaning" and failing prospects for "all-encompassing social movements." Néstor García Canclini, *Hybrid Cultures: Strategies for Entering and Leaving Modernity,* trans. Christopher L. Chiappaus and Silvia L. Lopez (Minneapolis: University of Minnesota Press, 1995), 205–8.

28. Allen and Turner, *The Ethnic Quilt,* 252–53.

Bibliography

ARCHIVES AND COLLECTIONS

American Design Collection. Huntington Library.
Communist Party Chronological File. Southern California Library for Social
    Studies and Research.
Communist Party of the United States of America Records. Library of Congress,
    Washington, D.C.
Federal Writers Project of California Records. Department of Special Collec-
    tions, University of California, Los Angeles.
Harold Bruce Forsythe Papers. Huntington Library.
Leo Gallagher Papers. Southern California Library for Social Studies and
    Research.
John Randolph Haynes Papers. Department of Special Collections, University of
    California, Los Angeles.
Dorothy Healey Papers. Department of Special Collections, California State
    University, Long Beach.
Jewish Federation and Council of Greater Los Angeles Community Relations
    Committee Collection. Urban Archives Center, California State University,
    Northridge.
Margaret A. Kerr Papers. Hoover Institution Archives, Stanford University.
Los Angeles Chamber of Commerce Records. Regional History Center, Univer-
    sity of Southern California.
Los Angeles Railroad Collection. Huntington Library.
Simon Lubin Papers. Bancroft Library.
William Mead Ephemera Collection. Huntington Library.
National Republic Collection. Hoover Library, Stanford University
G. Bromley Oxnam Papers. Library of Congress, Washington, D.C.

Southern California American Civil Liberties Union Collection. Department of Special Collections, University of California, Los Angeles.

Marshall Stimson Papers. Huntington Library.

Survey of Race Relations Collection. Hoover Institution Archives, Stanford University.

Karl Yoneda Collection. Department of Special Collections, University of California, Los Angeles.

YWCA Records. Urban Archives Center, California State University, Northridge.

GOVERNMENT RECORDS AND REPORTS

California. Commission of Immigration and Housing. *ABC of Housing.* Sacramento: State Printing Office, 1915.

——. *Annual Reports.*

——. *Bulletin of Information for Immigrants.*

——. *A Community Survey Made of Los Angeles City.* 1917.

——. Department of Industrial Relations. Commission of Immigration and Housing Records. Bancroft Library, University of California, Berkeley.

——. *The Home Teacher.* 1916.

——. *Report on an Experiment made in Los Angeles on the Americanization of Foreign-born Women.* 1917.

——. *Report on Fresno's Immigration Problem.* 1918.

——. *Report on Housing Shortage.* 1923.

——. *Report on Large Landholdings in Southern California.* 1919.

——. *State Housing Manual.* 1919.

California. Supreme Court. *In the Supreme Court of Caifornia, People of the State of California vs. Chuey Wong: Appellants Reply Brief.* Los Angeles: California Voice Print, 1897.

Los Angeles. City Council. *Industrial Limits Committee Report.* 1911.

——. *Los Angeles Municipal Atlas: Official Zoning Maps.* November 19, 1925.

——. *Minutes.* Los Angeles City Archives.

Los Angeles. Housing Commission. *Reports.* Los Angeles City Archives.

Los Angeles. Industrial Investigating Committee. *Report,* 1915, in "Reports and Correspondence of Bureaus, Departments, Committees, and Special Committees of the City of Los Angeles, 1890–1915." Los Angeles City Archives.

Los Angeles. Parks Commission. *Annual Reports.* 1906–15. Los Angeles City Archives.

Los Angeles. Social Service Commission. *Annual Reports.* 1916–25. Los Angeles City Archives.

Mexicans in California, Report of C. C. Young's Fact-Finding Committee. Sacramento: State Printing Office, 1930.

United States Congress. House. Special Committee on Un-American Activities, *Hearings,* 73d Cong., 2d sess., 1934.

United States Congress. Senate. Commission on Industrial Relations. *Industrial Relations.* 64th Cong., 1st sess., 1916.

————. Immigration Commission. *The Children of Immigrants in Schools, Volume III.* 61st Cong., 3d sess., 1911.

————. Select Committee on Education and Labor. *Violations of Free Speech and the Rights of Labor.* 78th Cong., 1st sess., 1943.

United States. Department of War. Military Intelligence Division. *Records.* National Archives, Washington, D.C.

United States. Works Progress Administration. *American-born Mexican Survey.* 1935.

————. *Household Survey of Los Angeles, 1939.* Regional History Center, University of Southern California.

INTERVIEWS AND ORAL HISTORIES

Abramson, Manya. Interviewed by Sylvia Frank, March 25 and 28, 1977. Urban Archives Center, California State University, Northridge.

Carlson, Lil. Interview with author, Laguna Beach, California, November 15, 1998.

Castañeda de Valenciana, Emilia. Interviewed by Christine Valenciana, September 8, 1971, #700, California State University, Fullerton, Oral History Program.

Dobbs, Ben. Interviewed by Michael Furmanovsky. University of California, Los Angeles, Oral History Project, 1990.

Embrey, Sue Kunitomi. Interviewed by Arthur Hansen and David A. Hacker, August 24, 1973, #1366, California State University, Fullerton, Oral History Program.

Green, Archie. Interview with author, San Francisco, March 18, 1999.

Healey, Dorothy. Interview with author, Washington D.C., October 22, 1998.

Healey, Dorothy. Interviewed by Joel Gardner. University of California, Los Angeles, Oral History Program, 1982.

Hunter, Allan A. Interviewed by Christine Valenciana, August 22, 1971, #744, California State University, Fullerton, Oral History Program.

Johnson, Clarence. Interviewed by R. Donald Brown, 1967, #139, California State University, Fullerton, Oral History Program.

Johnson, Miriam. Interview with author, San Francisco, June 21, 1999.

Kadish, Morris. Interview with author, San Francisco, March 19, 1999.

Kunitani, Michio. Interview with author, Berkeley, March 22, 1999.

Kunitsugo, Kango. Interviewed by Sherry Turner and David Biniasz, 1973, #1334, California State University, Fullerton, Oral History Program.

McCormick, LaRue. Interview with author, by telephone, March 14, 1999.

McGrath, Alice. Interviewed by Michael Butler, University of California, Los Angeles, Oral History Project, 1987.

Miller, Loren. Interviewed by Lawrence B. de Graaf, April 29, 1967, #174, California State University, Fullerton, Oral History Program.

Robinson, W. W. Interviewed by Winston Wutkee, 1982, University of California, Los Angeles, Oral History Program.

Schechter, Hope Mendoza. Interviewed by Malce Chall, 1977–78, Oral History Program, Bancroft Library, Berkeley.

Southern California Chinese American Oral History Program, Department of Special Collections, University of California, Los Angeles. Selected interviews.

Taketa, Roy. Interviewed by Mary McCarthy, July 13, 1973, #1330, California State University, Fullerton, Oral History Program.

Vega, Enrique. Interviewed by Christine Valenciana, September 3, 1972, #1295, California State University, Fullerton, Oral History Program.

Yoneda, Elaine Black. Interviewed by Betty Mitson and Arthur Hansen, March 2, 1974, #1377, California State University, Fullerton, Oral History Program.

SELECTED SECONDARY SOURCES

Adamic, Louis. *The Truth about Los Angeles.* Girard, Kan.: Haldeman-Julius, 1927.

Adler, Pat. *The Bunker Hill Story.* Glendale, Calif.: La Siesta, 1963.

Allen, James P., and Eugene Turner. *The Ethnic Quilt: Population Diversity in Southern California.* Northridge: Center for Geographical Studies, California State University, Northridge, 1997.

Alley, Walter Wright. "A Brief History of Public Housing Activities in Los Angeles." Municipal Housing Commission, Los Angeles, 1936.

Americanian, Isabel. "An Education and Psychological Study of Vagabonds." Master's thesis, University of Southern California, 1932.

Anderson, Benedict. *Imagined Communities: Reflections on the Origins and Spread of Nationalism.* London: Verso, 1991.

Andrews, George Reid. *Blacks and Whites in São Paolo, Brazil, 1888–1988.* Madison: University of Wisconsin Press, 1991.

Aronovici, Carol. "Americanization." *Annals of the American Academy of Political and Social Science* 93 (January 1921): 134–38.

Asbury, Herbert. *The Barbary Coast.* New York: Alfred A. Knopf, 1933.

Arroyo, Luis Leobardo. "Industrial Unionism in the Los Angeles Furniture Industry, 1918–1954." Ph.D. diss., University of California, Los Angeles, 1979.

Austin, Joe, and Michael Nevin Willard. *Generations of Youth: Youth Cultures and History in Twentieth-Century America.* New York: New York University Press, 1998.

Avila, Eric R. "Reinventing Los Angeles: Popular Culture in the Age of White Flight, 1940–65." Ph.D. diss., University of California, Berkeley, 1997.

Bagwell, Asbury A. "The Los Angeles Plan of Naturalizing the Alien." Master's thesis, University of Southern California, 1929.

Baldwin, Peter C. *Domesticating the Street: The Reform of Public Space in Hartford, 1880–1930.* Columbus: Ohio State University Press, 1999.

Bartlett, Dana. *The Better City: A Sociological Study of a Modern City.* Los Angeles: Reune, 1907.

———. *The Better Country.* Boston: C. M. Clark, 1911.

Barrett, James R. "Americanization from the Bottom Up: Immigration and the Remaking of the American Working Class in the United States, 1880–1930." *Journal of American History* 79 (December 1992): 996–1020.

Barrett, James R., and David Roediger. "Inbetween Peoples: Race, Nationality, and the 'New Immigrant' Working Class." *Journal of American Ethnic History* 16 (spring 1997): 3–44.

Bass, Charlotta. *Forty Years: Memories from the Pages of a Newspaper.* Los Angeles: Charlotta Bass, 1960.

Bederman, Gail. *Manliness and Civilization: A Cultural History of Gender and Race in the United States, 1880–1917.* Chicago: University of Chicago Press, 1995.

Bernstein, Shana Beth. "Building Bridges at Home in a Time of Global Conflict: Inter-racial Cooperation and the Fight for Civil Rights in Los Angeles, 1933–54." Ph.D. diss., Stanford University, 2003.

Bird, Stewart, Dan Georgakas, and Deborah Shaffer, eds. *Solidarity Forever: An Oral History of the IWW.* Chicago: Lake View Press, 1985.

Bodnar, John. *Remaking America: Public Memory, Commemoration, and Patriotism in the Twentieth Century.* Princeton: Princeton University Press, 1992.

———. *The Transplanted: A History of Immigrants in Urban America.* Bloomington: Indiana University Press, 1985.

Bogardus, Emory. *The City Boy and His Problems: A Survey of Boys Life in Los Angeles.* Los Angeles: Los Angeles Rotary Club, 1926.

———. "The House Court Problem." *American Journal of Sociology* 22 (November 1916): 391–99.

———. "Second Generation Mexicans." *Social Science and Research* 13 (1928–29): 276–83.

Bond, Max. "The Negro in Los Angeles." Ph.D. diss., University of Southern California, 1936.

Bontemps, Arna. *God Sends Sunday.* 1931. Reprint, New York, AMS Press, 1972.

Boorman, W. Ryland. *Developing Personality in Boys.* New York: Macmillan, 1929.

Boyer, Paul. *Urban Masses and Moral Order in America, 1820–1920.* Cambridge, Mass.: Harvard University Press, 1978.

Boyer, Richard O. "Pettis Perry: The Story of a Working Class Leader." Self-Defense Committee of the 17 Smith Act Victims, New York, 1952.

Boyte, Harry C. *The Backyard Revolution: Understanding the New Citizen Movement.* Philadelphia: Temple University Press, 1980.

Brandes, Stuart D. *American Welfare Capitalism, 1880–1940.* Chicago: University of Chicago Press, 1976.

Bridge, David Alexander. "A Study of the Agencies Which Promote Americanization in the Los Angeles City Recreation Center District." Master's thesis, University of Southern California, 1920.

Bryant, Clora, Buddy Collette, William Green, Steve Isoardi, Jack Kelson, Horace Tapscott, Gerald Wilson, and Marl Young, eds. *Central Avenue Sounds: Jazz in Los Angeles.* Berkeley: University of California Press, 1998.

Buhle, Paul. *Marxism in the United States: Remapping the History of the American Left.* London: Verso, 1991.

Bulosan, Carlos. *America Is in the Heart.* New York: Harcourt, Brace, 1946.

Burma, H. J. "Interethnic Marriages in Los Angeles, 1948–1959." *Social Forces* 62 (1963): 156–65.

"California's Brown Book." Los Angeles Committee, American League Against War and Fascism, c. 1935.

Camarillo, Albert. *Chicanos in a Changing Society: From Mexican Pueblos to American Barrios in Santa Barbara and Southern California, 1848–1930.* Cambridge, Mass.: Harvard University Press, 1979.

Canclini, Néstor García. *Hybrid Cultures: Strategies for Entering and Leaving Modernity.* Trans. Christopher L. Chiappaus and Silvia L. Lopez. Minneapolis: University of Minnesota Press, 1995.

Carrillo, Leo. *The California I Love.* Englewood Cliffs, N.J.: Prentice-Hall, 1965.

Carson, Mina. *Settlement Folk: Social Thought and the American Settlement Movement, 1885–1930.* Chicago: University of Chicago Press, 1990.

Castells, Manuel. *The City and the Grassroots: A Cross-Cultural Theory of Urban Social Movements.* London: Edward Arnold, 1983.

Castillo, Pedro. "The Making of a Mexican Barrio: Los Angeles, 1890–1920." Ph.D. diss., University of California, Santa Barbara, 1979.

Chamberlain, Eugene Keith. "The Magdalena Incident." Master's thesis, University of California Berkeley, 1939.

Cohen, Lisbeth. *Making a New Deal: Industrial Workers in Chicago, 1919–1939.* Cambridge: Cambridge University Press, 1990.

Collins, James. W. "When Soap Box Meets Soap Box." *Saturday Evening Post,* November 20, 1920.

Conzen, Kathleen Neils, David A. Gerber, Eva Marawska, George E. Pozzetta, and Rudolph J. Vecoli. "The Invention of Ethnicity: A Perspective from the USA." *Journal of American Ethnic History* 39 (March 1992): 3–41.

Cox, Betty Yarborough. *Central Avenue: Its Rise and Fall, 1890–c. 1955.* Los Angeles: BEEM, 1996.

Crawford, Paul J. "Movie Habits and Attitudes of the Underprivileged Boys of the All Nations Area in Los Angeles." Master's thesis, University of Southern California, 1934.

Crocker, Ruth Hutchinson. *Social Work and Social Order: The Settlement Movement in Three Industrial Cities, 1889–1930.* Urbana: University of Illinois Press, 1992.

Crosby, Rosalind Giardina. "The Italians of Los Angeles, 1900." In *Struggles and Success: An Anthology of the Italian Immigrant Experience in California,* ed. Paola A. Sensei-Isolani and Phylis Cancilla Martinelli, 38–57. New York: Center for Migration Studies, 1993.

Dahl, Vergil D. "Geographical Concentration of Juvenile Delinquency in Los Angeles County." Master's thesis, University of Southern California, 1932.

Daniels, Douglas Henry. *Pioneer Urbanites: A Social and Cultural History of Black San Francisco.* Philadelphia: Temple University Press, 1980.

Davis, Allen F. *Spearheads for Reform: The Social Settlements and the Progressive Movement, 1890–1914.* New York: Oxford University Press, 1967.

Davis, Clark. "From Oasis to Metropolis: Southern California and the Changing Context of American Leisure." *Pacific Historical Review* 61 (August 1992): 357–85.

Davis, Diane. *Urban Leviathan: Mexico City in the Twentieth Century.* Philadelphia: Temple University Press, 1994.

Davis, Mike. *City of Quartz: Excavating the Future in Los Angeles*. London: Verso, 1990.

Davis, Susan E. *Parades and Power: Street Theatre in Nineteenth-Century Philadelphia*. Philadelphia: Temple University Press, 1986.

de Falla, Paul M. "Lantern in the Western Sky." *Historical Society of Southern California Quarterly* 42.1 (March 1960): 57–88; 42.2 (June 1960): 161–87.

Dennis, Peggy. *The Autobiography of an American Communist: A Personal View of a Political Life.* Westport and Berkeley: Lawrence Hill and Creative Arts Book Co., 1977.

Deverell, William, and Tom Sitton, eds. *California Progressivism Revisited*. Berkeley: University of California Press, 1994.

DeWitt, Howard. *Violence in the Fields: California Farm Labor Unionization during the Great Depression*. Saratoga, Calif.: Century 21, 1980.

Donlon, Thomas Weller. "A Study in Free Reading among Foreign-born Children." Master's thesis, University of Southern California, 1933.

Du Vall, Everett W. "A Sociological Study of Five Hundred Underprivileged Children in a Selected Area of Los Angeles." Ph.D. diss., University of Southern California, 1936.

Engh, Michael E. *Frontier Faiths: Church, Temple, and Synagogue in Los Angeles, 1846–1888*. Albuquerque: University of New Mexico Press, 1992.

Ervin, J. McFarline. "The Participation of the Negro in the Community Life of Los Angeles." Master's thesis, University of Southern California, 1931.

Escobar, Edward J. *Race, Police, and the Making of a Political Identity: Mexican Americans and the Los Angeles Police Department, 1900–45*. Berkeley: University of California Press, 1999.

España-Maram, Linda N. "Brown 'Hordes' in McIntosh Suits: Filipinos, Taxi Dance Halls, and Performing the Immigrant Body in Los Angeles, 1930s–1940s." In *Generations of Youth: Youth Cultures and History in Twentieth-Century America*, ed. Joe Austin and Michael Nevin Willard, 118–35. New York: New York University Press, 1998.

Ethington, Phil. *The Public City: The Political Construction of Urban Life in San Francisco, 1850–1900*. Berkeley: University of California Press, 1994.

Ewald, Ruth. "A Survey of the Spanish-speaking Peoples of the Chaffey Union High Schoool District." Master's thesis, Pomona College, 1922.

Fesler, Alice May. "A Study of the Relation of Inadequate Parental Control to Truancy among Girls." Master's thesis, University of Southern California, 1922.

Fogelson, Robert. *The Fragmented Metropolis: Los Angeles, 1850–1930*. 1967. Reprint, Berkeley: University of California Press, 1991.

Foley, Neil. *The White Scourge: Mexicans, Blacks, and Poor Whites in Texas Cotton Culture*. Berkeley: University of California Press, 1997.

Foner, Philip, ed. *Black Socialist Preacher*. San Francisco: Synthesis Publications, 1983.

French, Hettie Peary. "A Study of Juvenile Delinquency in a Selected Area of Los Angeles." Master's thesis, University of Southern California, 1934.

Friedrichs, William B. *Henry E. Huntington and the Creation of Southern California*. Columbus: Ohio State University Press, 1992.

Fuchs, Lawrence H. *The American Kaleidoscope: Race, Ethnicity, and the Civic Culture.* Hanover, N.H.: Wesleyan University Press, 1990.

Fuller, Elizabeth. "The Mexican Housing Problem in Los Angeles." *Studies in Sociology* 5.1 (November 1920).

Gabaccia, Donna R. "Is Everywhere Nowhere? Nomads, Nations, and the Immigrant Paradigm in United States History." *Journal of American History* 86 (December 1999): 1115–34.

Gaines, Kevin K. *Uplifting the Race: Black Leadership, Politics, and Culture in the Twentieth Century.* Chapel Hill: University of North Carolina Press, 1996.

Gamio, Manuel. *The Mexican Immigrant: His Life Story.* Chicago: University of Chicago Press, 1931.

Gano, Edna Fern. "A Study of the Behavior and Ideas of Certain Children of the Church of All Nations in the Light of Their Home Background." Master's thesis, University of Southern California, 1923.

Garcia, Mario T. "Americanization and the Mexican Immigrant, 1880–1930." *Journal of Ethnic Studies* 6 (1978): 19–34.

———. *Memories of Chicano History: The Life and Narrative of Bert Corona.* Berkeley: University of California Press, 1994.

Garcia, Matt. *A World of Its Own: Race, Labor, and Citrus in the Making of Greater Los Angeles, 1900–1970.* Berkeley: University of California Press, 2001.

Garcia, Mikel Hogan. "Adaptation Strategies of the Los Angeles Black Community, 1883–1919." Ph.D. diss., University of California, Irvine, 1985.

Garreau, Joel. *Edge City: Life on the New Frontier.* New York: Anchor, 1992.

Gartz, Kate Crane. *Letters of Protest.* Pasadena: Mary Craig Sinclair, c. 1936.

———. *The Parlor Provocateur: From Salon to Soapbox.* Pasadena: Mary Craig Sinclair, 1923.

Gerber, David A. *The Making of an American Pluralism: Buffalo, New York, 1825–1860.* Urbana: University of Illinois Press, 1989.

Gerstle, Gary, "Liberty, Coercion, and the Making of Americans." *Journal of American History* 84 (September 1997): 524–58.

———. *Working-Class Americanism: The Politics of Labor in a Textile City, 1914–1960.* Cambridge: Cambridge University Press, 1989.

Gjerde, John. "New Growth on Old Vines—The State of the Field: The Social History of Immigration to and Ethnicity in the United States." *Journal of American Ethnic History* 18 (summer 1999): 40–65.

Glanz, Rudolph. *The Jews of California: From the Discovery of Gold until 1880.* New York: Walden, 1960.

Glassberg, David. *American Historical Pageantry: The Uses of Tradition in the Early Twentieth Century.* Chapel Hill: University of North Carolina Press, 1990.

Glazer, Nathan, and Daniel Patrick Moynihan. *Beyond the Melting Pot: The Negroes, Puerto Ricans, Jews, Italians, and Irish of New York City.* Cambridge, Mass.: MIT Press, 1963.

Goldfield, Michael. "Race and the CIO: The Possibilities for Racial Egalitarianism during the 1930s and 1940s." *International Labor and Working Class History* 44 (fall 1993): 1–32.

Gómez-Quiñones, Juan. *Sembradores: Ricardo Flores Magón y el Partido Liberal Mexicano.* Los Angeles: Chicano Studies Center, University of California, Los Angeles, 1973.

Gonzalez, Gilbert G. *Chicano Education in the Era of Segregation.* Philadelphia: Baleh Institute Press, 1990.

———. "Factors Relating to Property Ownership of Mexican Americans and Italian Americans in Lincoln Heights, Los Angeles." In *Struggles and Success: An Anthology of the Italian Immigrant Experience in California,* ed. Paola A. Sensei-Isolani and Phylis Cancilla Martinelli, 219–30. New York: Center for Migration Studies, 1993.

Gottlieb, Robert, and Irene Wolt. *Thinking Big: The Story of the Los Angeles Times, Its Publishers, and Its Influence on Southern California.* New York: G. P. Putnam's Sons, 1977.

Greenstein, Paul. *Bread and Hyacinths: The Rise and Fall of Utopian Los Angeles.* Los Angeles: Los Angeles Classics, 1992.

Greenwood, Roberta. *Metropolitan Transportation Authority–Cultural Resources Impact Mitigation Program: Los Angeles Red Line Segment One (Chinatown).* Los Angeles: Greenwood and Assoc., 1993.

Griewe, A. W. "A Study of the Habitues of the Downtown Parks of Los Angeles, with a View to Ascertaining Their Constituency, Their Social Process, and Their Relation to the Larger Community Life." Master's thesis, University of Southern California, 1926.

Griffith, Beatrice. *American Me.* Boston: Houghton Mifflin, 1948.

Guillow, Lawrence. "The Origins of Race Relations in Los Angeles, 1820–1880." Ph.D. diss., Arizona State University, 1996.

Gustafson, Cloyd. "An Ecological Survey of the Hollenbeck Area." Master's thesis, University of Southern California, 1940.

Gutierrez, David G. "Migration, Emergent Ethnicity, and the 'Third Space': The Shifting Politics of Nationalism in Greater Mexico." *Journal of American History* 86.2 (1999): 481–517.

Hager, Everett G., George E. Kinney, and Anthony F. Kroll. *An 1886 Chinese Labor Boycott in Los Angeles.* Pasadena: Castle Press, 1982.

Handlin, Oscar. *The Uprooted.* Boston: Atlantic Monthly Press, 1953.

Harper, Evelyn S. Adams. "A Survey of the Eugene Street Development Center in Los Angeles." Master's thesis, University of Southern California, 1934.

Harper, Helena Hester. "A Study of Colored Unmarried Mothers in Los Angeles." Master's thesis, University of Southern California, 1932.

Hawes, Hampton, and Don Asher. *Raise Up Off Me.* New York: DeCapo, 1979.

Hayashi, Brian Masaru. *"For the Sake of Our Japanese Brethren": Assimilation, Nationalism, and Protestantism among the Japanese of Los Angeles, 1895–1942.* Stanford: Stanford University Press, 1995.

Hendrick, Irving C. *The Education of Non-Whites in California, 1849–1970.* San Francisco, R&E, 1977.

Hicks, Jimmie. *W. W. Robinson: A Biography and Bibliography.* Los Angeles: Ward Ritchie Press, 1970.

Higham, John. *Strangers in the Land: Patterns of American Nativism, 1860–1915.* New York: Atheneum, 1966.

Hise, Greg. "Industry and Imaginative Geographies." In *Metropolis in the Making: Los Angeles in the 1920s,* ed. Tom Sitton and William Deverell, 13–44. Berkeley: University of California Press, 2001.

———. *Magnetic Los Angeles: Planning the Twentieth-Century Metropolis.* Baltimore: Johns Hopkins University Press, 1997.

Hoffman, Abraham. *Unwanted Mexican Americans during the Great Depression: Repatriation Pressures, 1929–1939.* Tucson: University of Arizona Press, 1974.

Holston, James, and Arjun Appadurai. "Cities and Citizenship." *Public Culture* 8 (1996): 187–204.

Institute of Social and Religious Research (ISRR). "Intensive Study of Representative City Churches: The City Parish, Methodist Episcopal, Los Angeles." ISRR, New York, 1926.

Issel, William. "Citizens Outside the Government: Business and Urban Policy in San Francisco and Los Angeles, 1890–1932." *Pacific Historical Review* 57.2 (1988): 117–45.

Jackson, Kenneth T. *Crabgrass Frontier: The Suburbanization of the United States.* New York: Oxford University Press, 1985.

Jacobs, Jane. *The Death and Life of Great American Cities.* 1961. Reprint, New York: Vintage, 1989.

Jacobson, Matthew Frye. *Special Sorrows: The Diasporic Imagination of Irish, Polish, and Jewish Immigrants in the United States.* Cambridge, Mass.: Harvard University Press, 1995.

Johnson, Charles S. *Industrial Survey of the Negro Population in Los Angeles.* Los Angeles: National Urban League, 1926.

Johnson, Daniel J. "A Serpent in the Garden: Institutions, Ideology, and Class in Los Angeles Politics, 1901–1911." Ph.D. diss., University of California, Los Angeles, 1996.

Jones, Gareth Steadman. *Outcast London: A Study in the Relationship between Classes in Victorian Society.* Oxford: Clarendon Press, 1971.

Kaplan, Temma. *Red City, Blue Period: Social Movements in Picasso's Barcelona.* Berkeley: University of California Press, 1992.

Katznelson, Ira. *City Trenches: Urban Politics and the Patterning of Class in the United States.* New York: Pantheon, 1981.

———. *Marxism in the City.* Oxford: Clarendon Press, 1996.

Kazal, Russell A. "Revisiting Assimilation: The Rise, Fall, and Reappraisal of a Concept in American Ethnic History." *American Historical Review* 100 (April 1995): 437–71.

Kelley, Mary Katherine. "Parental Attitudes toward the Treatment of Children's Health Problems." Master's thesis, University of Southern California, 1938.

Kelley, Robin D. G. *Hammer and Hoe: Alabama Communists during the Great Depression.* Chapel Hill: University of North Carolina Press, 1990.

———. *Race Rebels: Culture, Politics and the Black Working Class.* New York: Free Press, 1994.

Kendall, Sydney C. *Queen of the Red Lights.* Los Angeles: Wiley Phillips, [1906].

Kerr, Clark. "Productive Enterprises of the Unemployed, 1931–1938." Ph.D. diss., University of California, Berkeley, 1939.

Kienle, John E. "Housing Conditions among the Mexican Population of Los Angeles." Master's thesis, University of Southern California, 1912.

Kimbrough, Jesse. *Defender of the Angels: A Black Policeman in Old Los Angeles.* London: Macmillan, 1969.

Klein, Norman. "The Sunshine Strategy: Buying and Selling the Fantasy of Los Angeles." In *Twentieth-Century Los Angeles: Power, Promotion, and Social Conflict,* ed. Norman Klein and Martin J. Schiesl, 1–38. Claremont, Calif.: Regina, 1990.

Kloppenberg, James T. *Uncertain Victory: Social Democracy and Progressivism in European and American Thought, 1870–1920.* New York: Oxford University Press, 1986.

Kropp, Phoebe. "'All Our Yesterdays': The Spanish Fantasy Past and the Politics of Cultural Memory in Southern California, 1884–1939." Ph.D. diss., University of California, San Diego, 1999.

———. "Citizens of the Past? Olvera Street and the Construction of Race and Memory in 1930s Los Angeles." *Radical History Review* 81 (2001): 34–60.

Kurashige, Scott Tadao. "Transforming Los Angeles: Black and Japanese American Struggles for Racial Equality in the 20th Century." Ph.D. diss., University of California, Los Angeles, 2000.

Lanigan, Mary. "Second Generation Mexicans in Belvedere." Master's thesis, University of Southern California, 1932.

Larson, Louise Leung. *Sweet Bamboo: A Saga of a Chinese-American Family.* Los Angeles: Chinese Historical Society of Southern California, 1989.

Layton, Edwin. "The Better America Federation: A Case Study of Superpatriotism." *Pacific Historical Review* 30.2 (1961): 137–48.

Leab, Daniel J. "'United We Eat': The Creation and Organization of the Unemployed Councils in 1930." *Labor History* 8.2 (fall 1967): 300–315.

Lee, George, and Elsie Lee. "The Chinese and the Los Angeles Produce Market." *Gum Saan Journal* 9 (December 1986): 5–17.

Leonard, Karen Isaksen. *Making Ethnic Choices: California's Punjabi Mexican Americans.* Philadelphia: Temple University Press, 1992.

Leonard, Kevin. "Years of Hope, Days of Fear: The Impact of World War II on Race Relations in Los Angeles." Ph.D. diss., University of California, Davis, 1992.

Light, Ivan. "From Vice District to Tourist Attraction: The Moral Career of American Chinatowns, 1880–1940." *Pacific Historical Review* 43 (August 1974): 367–94.

Lipsitz, George. *The Possessive Investment in Whiteness: How White People Profit from Identity Politics.* Philadelphia: Temple University Press, 1998.

Lissak, Rivka Shpak. *Pluralism and Progressives: Hull House and the New Immigrants.* Chicago: University of Chicago Press, 1989.

Linking Our Lives: Chinese American Women of Los Angeles. Los Angeles: Asian-American Studies Center, University of California, Los Angeles and Chinese Historical Society of Southern California, 1984.

Logan, John R., and Harvey L. Molotch. *Urban Fortunes: The Political Economy of Place.* Berkeley: University of California Press, 1987.

Lopez, José. "A Gang of Angels: Street Gangs in Los Angeles." In *City of Angels,* ed. Gary Riposa and Carolyn G. Dersh, 32–39. Dubuque, Iowa: Kendall Hunt, 1992.

Los Angeles Settlement Association. "The College Settlement." Los Angeles, c. 1905.

Lothrup, Gloria Ricci. *Chi Siamo: The Italians of Los Angeles.* Pasadena, Calif.: Tabula Rasa, 1981.

Lou, Raymond. "The Chinese-American Community of Los Angeles, 1870–1900: A Case of Resistance, Organization, and Participation." Ph.D. diss., University of California, Irvine, 1982.

Louis, Kit King. "A Study of American-born and American-reared Chinese in Los Angeles." Master's thesis, University of Southern California, 1931.

Lowe, Lisa. *Immigrant Acts: On Asian American Cultural Politics.* Durham: Duke University Press, 1996.

Lubow, Sylvia. "The Espionage Act in Southern California." Master's thesis, University of California, Los Angeles, 1968.

Lui, Garding. *Inside Los Angeles Chinatown.* Los Angeles: n.p., 1948.

MacCaughey, Vaughan. "The Filipino and Our Cheap Labor Problem." *Commonwealth* 45 (November 5, 1929): 339–41.

Macias, Anthony. "From Pachuco Boogie to Latin Jazz: Mexican Americans, Popular Music, and Urban Culture in Los Angeles, 1940–1965." Ph.D. diss., University of Michigan, 2001.

McCombs, Vernon Monroe. *From over the Border: A Study of the Mexicans of the United States.* New York: Council of Women for Home Missions/ Missionary Education Movement, 1927.

McEuen, William Wilson. "A Survey of Mexicans in Los Angeles." Master's thesis, University of Southern California, 1914.

MacRobert, Ian. *The Black Roots and White Racism of Early Pentecostalism in the USA.* London: Macmillan, 1988.

McWilliams, Carey. "Moving Out the Japanese Americans." *Harpers Magazine* 185 (September 1942): 363.

McWilliams, Carey. *North from Mexico: The Spanish Speaking Peoples of the United States.* New York: Praeger, 1948.

Mason, William H., and John A. McKinstry. *The Japanese of Los Angeles.* Los Angeles: Los Angeles County Museum of Natural History, 1969.

Massey, Douglas S., and Nancy Denton. *American Apartheid: Segregation and the Making of the Underclass.* Cambridge, Mass.: Harvard University Press, 1993.

Matthews, William H. "The House Courts of Los Angeles." *Survey* 30 (July 5, 1913): 461–67.

Meade, Teresa. *"Civilizing" Rio: Reform and Resistance in a Modern City, 1889–1930.* University Park: Pennsylvania State University Press, 1997.

Miller, Robert Moats. *Bishop G. Bromley Oxnam: Paladin of Liberal Protestantism.* Nashville, Tenn.: Abingdon Press, 1990.

Miller, Zane L. "Pluralism, Chicago Style." *Journal of Urban History* (May 1992): 251–62.

Miller, Zane L., and Bruce Tucker. *Changing Plans for America's Inner Cities: Cincinnati's Over-the-Rhine and Twentieth-Century Urbanism.* Columbus: Ohio State University Press, 1987.

Mitchell, Don. "Fixing in Place: Progressive Science and Landscapes of Repression in California." *Historical Geography* 23 (1993): 44–61.

Modell, John. *The Economics and Politics of Racial Accommodation: The Japanese of Los Angeles, 1900–1942.* Urbana: University of Illinois Press, 1977.

Monroy, Douglas. "Anarquismo y Comunismo: Mexican Radicalism and the Communist Party in Los Angeles during the 1930s." *Labor History* 24 (winter 1983): 34–59.

———. *Rebirth: Mexican Los Angeles from the Great Migration to the Great Depression.* Berkeley: University of California Press, 1999.

Mumford, Kevin J. *Interzones: Black/White Sex Districts in Chicago and New York in the Early Twentieth Century.* New York: Columbia University Press, 1997.

Murase, Ichiro Mike. *Little Tokyo: One Hundred Years in Pictures.* Los Angeles: Visual Communications/Asian American Studies Central, 1983.

Nelson, Steve, James R. Barrett, and Rob Buck. *Steve Nelson, American Radical.* Pittsburgh: University of Pittsburgh Press, 1981.

Nordahl, Ruth Margaret Iliff. "A Social Study of the Newsboys' Trade in Los Angeles." Masters thesis, University of Southern California, 1912.

Normark, Don. *Chavez Ravine, 1949: A Los Angeles Story.* San Francisco: Chronicle Books, 1999.

Odem, Mary E. *Delinquent Daughters: Protecting and Policing Adolescent Female Sexuality in the United States, 1885–1925.* Chapel Hill: University of North Carolina Press, 1995.

Omi, Michael, and Howard Winant. *Racial Formations in the United States, from the 1960s to the 1990s.* New York: Routledge, 1994.

Oxnam, G. Bromley. "The Mexican in Los Angeles from the Standpoint of the Religious Forces in the City," *Annals of the American Academy of Political and Social Science* 93 (January 1921): 130–33.

———. *Youth and the New America.* [Los Angeles]: Council of Women for Home Mission and Missionary Education Movement, 1928.

Panunzio, Constantine. "Intermarriage in Los Angeles, 1924–1933." *American Journal of Sociology* 47 (March 1942): 690–701.

Pascoe, Peggy. "Miscegenation Law, Court Cases, and Ideolgoies of 'Race' in Twentieth Century America." *Journal of American History* 83 (June 1996): 44–69.

Park, Robert E., and Edmund W. Burgess. *Introduction to the Science of Society.* Chicago: University of Chicago Press, 1921.

Payne, J. Gregory, and Scott C. Ratzan. *Tom Bradley: The Impossible Dream.* Santa Monica, Calif.: Rountable Press, 1986.

Peiss, Kathy. *Cheap Amusements: Working Women and Leisure in Turn-of-the-Century New York.* Philadelphia: Temple University Press, 1986.

Perry, Louis B., and Richard S. Perry. *A History of the Los Angeles Labor Movement, 1911–1941*. Berkeley: University of California Press, 1963.

Pesotta, Rose. *Bread Upon the Waters*. 1944. Reprint, Ithaca: Cornell University Press, 1987.

Plengvidhya, Tasani. "A Study of Changes in the Services of All Nations Foundation as Affected by the Neighborhoods Ecological Changes." Master's thesis, University of Southern California, 1961.

Pittman, Riley Herman. "Building an Interracial Church." *Sociology and Social Research* 29 (March–April 1945): 297–303.

Raat, W. Dirk. *Revoltosos: Mexico's Rebels in the United States, 1903–1923*. College Station: Texas A&M Press, 1981.

Raftery, Judith Rosenberg. *Land of Fair Promise: Politics and Reform in Los Angeles Schools, 1885–1941*. Stanford: Stanford University Press, 1992.

Raineri, Vivian McGuckin. *The Red Angel: The Life and Times of Elaine Yoneda, 1906–1988*. New York: International, 1991.

Ray, Mary Ellen Bell. *The City of Watts, California, 1907–1926*. Los Angeles: Rising Publications, 1985.

Reisler, Mark. "Always the Laborer, Never the Citizen: Anglo Perceptions of the Mexican Immigrant during the Twenties." In *Between Two Worlds: Mexican Immigrants in the United States*, ed. David G. Gutierrez, 23–44. Wilmington, Del.: Scholarly Resources, 1996.

Robinson, W. W. *Tarnished Angels*. Los Angeles: Ward Ritchie Press, 1964.

Rock, John Earl. "Twenty Years on Skid Row." Los Angeles, n.d. Department of Special Collections, University of California, Los Angeles.

Rodgers, Daniel T. "In Search of Progressivism." *Reviews in American History* 10 (1982): 113–32.

Roediger, David. *The Wages of Whiteness: Race and the Making of the American Working Class*. London: Verso, 1991.

Rogers, James E. *The Child at Play*. New York: Century, 1932.

Rogin, Michael P. *The Intellectuals and McCarthy: The Radical Specter*. Cambridge, Mass.: MIT Press, 1967.

Romo, Ricardo. *East Los Angeles: History of a Barrio*. Austin: University of Texas Press, 1983.

Salgado de Snyder, V. Nelly, and Amando M. Padilla. *Interethnic Marriages of Mexican Americans after Nearly Two Decades*. Spanish-Speaking Mental Health Research Center, Occasional Paper no. 15, 1985.

Salvatore, Nick. *Eugene V. Debs: Citizen and Socialist*. Urbana: University of Illinois Press, 1982.

Sanchez, George J. *Becoming Mexican American: Ethnicity, Culture, and Identity in Chicano Los Angeles, 1900–1945*. New York: Oxford University Press, 1993.

———. "'Go After the Women': Americanization and the Mexican Immigrant Woman, 1915–1929." In *Unequal Sisters: A Multi-Cultural Reader in U.S. Women's History*, ed. Ellen Carol DuBois and Vicki L. Ruiz, 250–63. New York: Routledge, 1990.

———. "Race, Nation, and Culture in Recent Immigration Studies." *Journal of American Ethnic History* 18.4 (summer 1999): 66–84.

Saxton, Alexander. *The Rise and Fall of the White Republic: Class Politics and Mass Culture in Nineteenth-Century America.* London: Verso, 1990.

Schlesinger, Arthur M. *The Disuniting of America.* New York: W. W. Norton, 1992.

See, Lisa. *On Gold Mountain: The One-Hundred-Year Odyssey of My Chinese-American Family.* New York: Vintage, 1995.

Seeworker, Joseph. *Nuestro Pueblo: Los Angeles, City of Romance.* Boston: Houghton Mifflin, 1940.

Sennett, Richard, and Jonathan Cobb. *The Hidden Injuries of Class.* New York: Alfred A. Knopf, 1972.

Shaffer, Robert E. "The Formative Years of Communism in the West: The California Phase, 1919–1924." Department of Special Collections, California State University, Long Beach.

———. "Radicalism in California, 1869–1929." Ph.D. diss., University of California, Berkeley, 1962.

———. "Women and the Communist Party USA: 1930–1940. Department of Special Collections, California State University, Long Beach.

Shor, Francis Robert. *Utopianism and Radicalism in Reforming America.* Westport, Conn.: Greenwood Press, 1997.

Sides, Josh. "Working Away: African-American Migration and Community in Los Angeles from the Great Depression to 1954." Ph.D. diss., University of California, Los Angeles, 1999.

Singleton, Gregory H. *Religion in the City of Angels: American Protestant Culture and Urbanization in Los Angeles, 1850–1930.* Ann Arbor, Mich.: UMI Research Press, 1979.

Sitton, Tom. *John Randolph Haynes: California Progressive.* Stanford: Stanford University Press, 1992.

Sklar, Martin J. *The Corporate Reconstruction of American Capitalism, 1890–1916: The Market, the Law, and Politics.* 1988. Reprint, New York: Cambridge University Press, 1993.

Slayton, Robert A. *Back of the Yards: The Making of a Local Democracy.* Chicago: University of Chicago Press, 1986.

Smith, Clara Gertrude. "The Development of the Mexican People in the Community of Watts, California." Master's thesis, University of Southern California, 1933.

Smith, Cornelius C. *Emilio Kosterlitsky: Eagle of Sonora and the Southwest Border.* Glendale, Calif.: Arthur H. Clarke, 1970.

Snoddy, Jennings Lavert. "A Survey of the Methods Used in Adjusting the Truant Boy in the Los Angeles Schools." Master's thesis, University of Southern California, 1932.

Soja, Edward W. *Postmodern Geographies: The Reassertion of Space in Critical Social Theory.* London: Verso, 1989.

Sokoloff, Lillian. "The Russians in Los Angeles." *Studies in Sociology: Sociological Monograph 11,* 3.3 (March 1918).

Spickard, Paul R. "Injustice Compounded: Americans and Non-Japanese in Relocation Camps." *Journal of American Ethnic History* 5 (spring 1986): 5–22.

————. *Mixed Blood: Intermarriage and Ethnic Identity in Twentieth-Century America*. Madison: University of Wisconsin Press, 1989.

Sterry, Nora. "Housing Conditions in Chinatown Los Angeles." *Journal of Applied Sociology* 7 (November–December 1922): 70–75.

————. "The Sociological Basis for the Reorganization of the Macy Street School." Master's thesis, University of Southern California, 1924.

Stilgoe, John. *Metropolitan Corridor: Railraods and the American Scene*. New Haven: Yale University Press, 1983.

Stimson, Grace Heilman. *Rise of the Labor Movement in Los Angeles*. Berkeley: University of California Press, 1955.

Stimson, Marshall. *Fun, Fights, and Fiestas in Old Los Angeles*. Los Angeles: n.p., 1966.

Stoddart, Bessie D. "Recreative Centers of Los Angeles, California" *Annals of the American Academy of Political and Social Science* 35 (March 1910): 210–19.

Strode, Woody, and Sam Young. *Goal Dust*. Lanham, Md.: Madison, 1990.

Strong, Edward K. *Japanese in California*. Stanford: Stanford University Press, 1933.

Sub-Committee on Subversive Activities of the Crime Prevention Committee. "The Communist Situation in California." Peace Officers Association of California, Oakland, September 16–18, 1937.

————. "The Crime Prevention Committee's Report on Subversive Activities." Peace Officers Association of California, Oakland, October 17–19, 1940.

Sugrue, Thomas J. *The Origins of the Urban Crisis: Race and Inequality in Post-War Detroit*. Princeton: Princeton University Press, 1996.

Taft, Clinton J. "Fifteen Years on Freedom's Front." American Civil Liberties Union, Los Angeles, 1939.

Takaki, Ronald. *Strangers from a Different Shore: A History of Asian Americans*. New York: Penguin Books, 1989.

Taylor, Quintard. *The Forging of a Black Community: Seattle's Central District from 1870 through the Civil Rights Era*. Seattle: University of Washington Press, 1994.

————. *In Search of the Racial Frontier: African-Americans in the American West, 1528–1990*. New York: W. W. Norton, 1998.

Thomas, John. "Defender of the Angels: Jesse Kimbrough and the Los Angeles Police Department, 1916–1939." Southern California Library for Social Studies and Research, Los Angeles, 1998.

Trachtenberg, Alan. *The Incorporation of America: Culture and Society in the Gilded Age*. 1982. New York: Hill and Wang.

Turner, Grace M. "A Study of the Neighborhood Schools of Los Angeles." Master's thesis, University of Southern California, 1923.

Turner, Timothy G. *Turn Off the Sunshine: Tales of Los Angeles on the Wrong Side of the Tracks*. Caldwell, Ind.: Claxton Press, 1942.

"Two Decades of Progress: Communist Party, Los Angeles County 1919–1939." Communist Party of America, Los Angeles, 1939.

Uono, Koyoshi. "The Factors Affecting the Geographical Aggregation and Dispersion of Japanese Residents of the City of Los Angeles." Master's thesis, University of Southern California, 1927.

Van Waters, Miriam. *Parents on Probation*. New York: New Republic, 1927.
———. *Youth in Conflict*. New York: Republic, 1925.
Varzally, Allison. "Ethnic Crossings: The Making of a Non-White Identity in the Second Quarter of Twentieth-Century California." Ph.D. diss., University of California, Los Angeles, 2002.
Vorspan, Max, and Lloyd P. Gartner. *History of the Jews of Los Angeles*. San Marino, Calif.: Huntington Library, 1970.
Watson, Homer K. "A Study of the Causes of Delinquency among Fifty Negro Boys Assigned to Special Schools in Los Angeles." Master's thesis, University of Southern California, 1923.
Weglyn, Michi. *Years of Infamy: The Untold Story of America's Concentration Camps*. New York: William Morrow, 1976.
Weibe, Robert. *The Search for Order, 1877–1920*. New York: Hill and Wang, 1967.
Weintraub, Herman. "The I.W.W. in California, 1905–1931." Master's thesis, University of California, Los Angeles, 1947.
Weiss, Marc. *The Rise of the Community Builders: The American Real Estate Industry and Urban Land Planning*. New York: Columbia University Press, 1987.
Wells, Carl Douglas. "The Changing City Church." *School of Research Studies no. 2, Social Science Series* 5, 1926.
West, George P. "Good News from California." *Nation*, June 22, 1921, 867–69.
Whisnant, David E. *All That Is Native and Fine: The Politics of Culture in an American Region*. Chapel Hill: University of North Carolina Press, 1983.
Whitten, Woodrow C. "Criminal Syndicalism and the Law in California: 1919–1927." *Transactions of the American Philosophical Society* 59 (1969): pt. 2.
Wilson, William H. *The City Beautiful Movement*. Baltimore: Johns Hopkins University Press, 1989.
Woods, Gerald. "The Progressives and the Police: Urban Reform and the Professionalization of the Los Angeles Police." Ph.D. diss., University of California, Los Angeles, 1973.
Yokota, Kariann Akemi. "From Little Tokyo to Bronzville and Back: Ethnic Communities in Transition." Master's thesis, University of California, Los Angeles, 1996.
Yoneda, Karl. "The Heritage of Sen Katayama." *Political Affairs* 54.3 (March 1975): 38–57.
Yoneda, Karl G. *Ganbatte: Sixty-Year Struggle of a Kibei Worker*. Los Angeles: Resource Development and Publications/Asian-American Studies Center, University of California, Los Angeles, 1983.
Young, Pauline V. *The Pilgrims of Russian-Town: The Community of Spiritual Christian Jumpers in America*. Chicago: University of Chicago Press, 1932.
Ziskind, David. "A Sociological Study of Public Opinion Concerning Certain Police Practices in Los Angeles." Master's thesis, University of Southern California, 1933.
Zunz, Olivier. *The Changing Face of Inequality: Urbanization, Industrial Development, and Immigrants in Detroit, 1880–1920*. Chicago: University of Chicago Press, 1982.

FILMS

Conditions in Los Angeles. Southern California Library for Social Studies and
   Research, Los Angeles, 1934.
Meet Me at Brooklyn and Soto. Jewish Historical Society of Southern Califor-
   nia, Los Angeles, 1996.

Index

Page numbers in italics indicate photos, maps, or tables.

Indexer: Victoria Baker
Text: 10/13 Sabon
Display: Sabon
Compositor, printer, and binder: Sheridan Books, Inc.